Truly

LIONEL RICHIE

WILLIAM
COLLINS

TRULY

William Collins
An imprint of HarperCollins*Publishers*
1 London Bridge Street
London SE1 9GF

WilliamCollinsBooks.com

HarperCollins*Publishers*
Macken House, 39/40 Mayor Street Upper
Dublin 1, D01 C9W8, Ireland

First published in Great Britain in 2025 by William Collins
First published in the US in 2025 by HarperOne

1

Set in Fournier MT Std
Printed and bound in the UK using 100%
renewable electricity at CPI Group (UK) Ltd

MIX
Paper | Supporting
responsible forestry
FSC
www.fsc.org   FSC™ C007454

This book contains FSC™ certified paper and other controlled
sources to ensure responsible forest management.

For more information visit: www.harpercollins.co.uk/green

To my hometown of Tuskegee, Alabama, for teaching me what it means to serve a higher purpose.

To the Commodores, because without the Commodores, there would be no Lionel Richie.

And to my fans, for letting me and my songs be a part of your lives for all of these years.

Contents

Flying Solo (1982–1999)

Reinvention (1999 to present)

Author's Note

BERRY GORDY, FOUNDER AND LONG-TIME chairman of Motown Records, used to ask a question every time he got up to speak—even in informal settings. He would say, "Is anyone taping this? I might say something brilliant."

I'd laugh every time, but only in writing this book has it occurred to me that I should have done a better job over the years at recording or jotting down highlights of the stories that form the atomic structure of my journey so far.

Even so, I want to emphasize that the events and experiences recalled herein are faithfully rendered. Although I have a good ear for recalling what was said, and how it was expressed, the conversations I've included are not written to represent word-for-word reenactments. My job has been to evoke the real feeling of the words spoken, in keeping with the true essence of the mood and spirit in which they were conveyed.

Zoom

"What the *hell* is goin' on?!"

That's *all* I can say as I step onto the edge of Glastonbury's Pyramid Stage, mid-show, and stop, right there, to look out at the sea of what has been estimated to be anywhere between 175,000 and 200,000 folks. They're spread before me like a rolling wave—in every direction as far as the eye can see.

Unbelievable.

For weeks I'd been plagued by doubt. The story of my life.

You would have thought that at the grown-up age of sixty-six, after a career spanning almost fifty years, that would no longer be the case. And yet, somehow, just when I thought I'd finally banished the old fears, they came back full force as soon as this gig was proposed—*You haven't played a massive venue like this in a while! Do these festival fans even know you or your songs?*

But wait. Fear of missing out—also the story of my life— kept me from saying no to the offer. C'mon, y'all, this was Glastonbury! *The* mecca for die-hard music fans who brave the elements and trek out to the English countryside where they expect to hear the hottest artists alive.

"You haven't lived until you've played Glastonbury!" I'd been hearing from fellow entertainers for years.

So I said yes.

Hours before showtime, I flew down from London by helicopter, a mess of nerves. As we began to descend through a misty cloud cover, I caught my first sight of the festival grounds. What I saw below, even under gray skies, looked like something out of a storybook—with folks already streaming in through the gates.

Yet nothing prepared me for what happened in the minutes before I hit the stage.

Standing there in the wings, already sweating, I took a breath to calm myself and was instantly jolted by a *roar*, a distant rumble—*What the hell is THAT?* Thunder? No, it was some kind of chant and it grew louder by the second. That's when I looked out, saw the magnitude of the crowd, and realized that it was my name being sung in greeting.

Lawd, have mercy, as we say back in Tuskegee, Alabama, where I was born and bred.

The concert is a true lovefest.

That's why, midway through the show, I ask, a second time, "What the *hell* is going on?"

My arms are open wide, hands extended and palms up.

In response comes thunderous laughter.

These beautiful people think I'm joking. Oh, no, I am *serious*. I swing my arms, march down to the other end of the stage, and look out again.

Am I really seeing thousands of kids with seventies-era Afro wigs?

I am.

And are they also wearing stick-on mustaches?

They are.

Some have climbed up onto the shoulders of others, creating

a double-decker crowd. One line of fans has painted faces spelling out ENDLESS LOVE.

Multicolored peace signs are held high. Flags of many nations ruffle in the wind like ships' sails, alongside banners that read: PARTY ALL NIGHT LONG and EASY LIKE SUNDAY MORNING and LIONEL, WILL YOU MARRY . . . *MY MOTHER?* A huge likeness of me resembling the cartoon guy from *Where's Waldo?* is captioned: HELLO . . . IS IT ME YOU'RE LOOKING FOR?

Did I dream all of this up?

If not, I mean—*How in the world did this even happen?*

That, my friends, is a million-dollar question. It's one that I've been asking myself since I was nineteen years old, in a similar state of disbelief, on the precipice of the most unlikely future that has blessedly led me to the Pyramid Stage at Glastonbury. And beyond.

X MARKS THE spot—Harlem in the summer of 1968.

The moment I caught my first glimpse of the legendary building on West 135th Street—between Seventh and Lenox—I knew that my bandmates and I had arrived. We were on the verge of becoming household names.

The instant we parked the 1967 white Chevy van that had carried us here all the way from Tuskegee, I threw open the front passenger door and hopped out.

The rest of the guys followed.

"C'mon, Skeet, let's go," I heard someone say, using the childhood nickname that I wanted badly to outgrow.

I didn't answer. I just stood on the sidewalk trying to capture every detail, to take in the thrill of the moment. Lifting my eyes to the top of the fourteen-story tower that crowned the landmark brick building, I basked in the sight of the red neon sign and its four proud block letters: Y M C A.

The Promised Land.

The fact that I'd overcome my parents' objections to this escapade was an honest-to-God miracle. None of it would have happened if not for an unexpected occurrence the previous fall, in my freshman year of college.

Before this time, I had rarely been among "the Chosen" for anything. Not in Tuskegee, where I grew up until the tenth grade, nor in Joliet, Illinois, where I spent my last two years of high school. But then, shortly after I'd moved back to Alabama to attend Tuskegee Institute (as the university was then known), as I was standing in line to sign up for classes, along came fate.

A fellow freshman, just behind me, tapped on my shoulder and introduced himself as Thomas McClary from Florida—business major and guitar player. "Hey, Richie," he added, "heard you brought your horn to school."

Huh?

Not sure how Thomas knew this information, I nodded—without confessing that I'd only brought my saxophone to learn how to play the thing. Well, now, I could sort of play by ear and had begun to have a feel for it, following along with records of Jazz greats John Coltrane and Sonny Stitt.

That was it. Because I owned a saxophone, I was invited to join the Mystics, a ragtag little band that Thomas McClary put together for the sole purpose of performing in the upcoming Freshman Talent Show. That's how I came to be "chosen" for the first of only two bands I was ever in—something I never would have pursued on my own.

FROM THE TIME I was young, I accepted as gospel that I was not trustworthy enough to travel far from the safety of home by myself. The dangers lurking in our small town of about fifteen square miles, population approximately 7,500 (3,000 students), weren't the main concern.

The issue was *me*.

Why? Evidently, I was too hyper, too easily distracted to return home at the appointed hour—which would worry the family to no end. If I went to the market to pick up eggs and ice cream, six hours later I'd return with dairy products gone bad. If I got lost, I'd rarely ask for directions because I was so painfully, awkwardly, *horribly* shy.

Whenever I wanted to leave the house, for any reason, the first question I heard was—"Well, now, Skeet, who's goin' with you?"

Thankfully, I had friends, slightly more responsible than me, and if I was in their company, I was free to leave. Harold would come by, and we'd go traipse around, past the stately campus buildings—famous for their red bricks hand-formed by the first classes of students in the early 1880s.

Howard would come by, or Shorty. Somebody would come by, and, like magic, being part of a group became my ticket to freedom.

These rules created a push and pull inside of me. On the one hand, I could never wait to get outside the Tuskegee "Bubble," as we all called it; on the other hand, I panicked whenever heading onto unfamiliar ground alone.

Even as a college student! Go to a movie by myself? Nope. Never. To this day, I've never been to the movies alone. What about, at the appropriate age, going out to a club on my own, maybe meeting some special someone?

Are you kidding me?

When it came to introducing myself to members of the

opposite sex, I was *the worst*. Tongue-tied and awkward, I was self-conscious to the point of nausea. Imagine—I was a hopeless romantic, yet even as a college freshman, if I got it together to approach a young lady, before I said a word, I'd panic.

Was I a late bloomer? Not exactly. Let's clear this up. I was a *tragically* late bloomer. Without friends who helped make introductions, God only knows where I'd be today.

We've all heard the success stories of people who always knew they had a calling. Not me.

Aside from a love for music—*all* kinds—nothing about me hinted that one day I'd make it as an entertainer, a showman!

I liked to play sports, but I was never the athlete who ran onto the playing field shouting, "Gimme the ball!" No . . . I'd run the other way. I was traumatized changing into gym clothes for PE. Somebody would say, "Y'all, can you believe how skinny Skeet is?" Like it was news to me. Gym shorts only came in small, medium, and large. There was no slim fit, no size for a kid like me who was built like a pencil. If I slid my two legs into one of the legs of the smallest shorts, it draped like a skirt.

Whenever sides were picked for teams, whatever the sport, I'd be one of the last to get chosen—with a begrudging, "Okay, we'll take Lionel."

My inability to focus was the problem. *I* was the problem. There was something wrong with me. There were too many distractions. And, in all that noise, there was this Other Side calling to me. Like a radio signal from a distant planet that I wanted to hear better but couldn't quite tune in to.

At school, I could never sit still. I'd have to tap my foot or drum my hands to a beat only I could hear, and then try somehow to process multiple soundtracks of sensory overload.

In those days, nobody talked about ADD or ADHD. Aside

from murmurs about "poor Lionel" being "too hyper" and "too sensitive," I never heard the more clinical terms. Ever. What I heard was, "Lionel, would you care to join us?" and "Mr. Richie, you have something more important to do?" or, "Skeet, would you respond to the question?"

What *was* the question?

I heard grown folks saying to my parents and grandparents, "You know, that Lionel . . . he's a slow learner." "He's not a strong reader." "He has trouble in school."

Those statements would be hard for any young person to hear, especially for an uncertain kid like me growing up, basically, on the Tuskegee campus—where the energy, brilliance, and heroism of the likes of Booker T. Washington and the Tuskegee Airmen loomed large. We were expected to be next-level.

True success, we were told, would not be defined by money. No. The measure of your worth was your level of education, your scholastic achievement—a reality that hit me one afternoon when I was eleven years old.

Out on my bike, riding around campus, I took a break from the heat to sit, head in hands, on the steps of one of our great halls of learning, near the overhang of an old oak tree. That's when it dawned on me—*Wow, if you're a PhD, you've reached the top.*

Proof was in front of me—professors walking around in tweed jackets, smoking their pipes, and talking in big words.

Right there, I faced a hard truth—*It's all Greek to me.* Actually, it *was* Greek! And Latin! The smart students took Latin and Greek and the other classical languages.

The revelation—*Oh man, that ain't me!*—sent a message to my brain that something was fundamentally broken in me. My driving question became, *How can I cope with my brokenness?*

The solution was to become an escape artist.

Instead of fighting the Other Side, I gave in, and by age twelve began to escape to it all the time, and to live in the creative laboratory of my imagination. On the Other Side, there was no self-doubt, no boredom, no fear of being alone, no limits on my freedom to be whatever I chose.

More than a decade later, in my mid-twenties—early in my songwriting efforts—I summoned my twelve-year-old escape artist self to help write what became a theme song for my life:

I may be just a foolish dreamer
But I don't care
Cause I know my happiness
Is waiting out there, somewhere . . .

Whoa, zoom, I'd like to fly far away from here
Where my mind, oh Lord, is fresh and clear
And I'll find the love that I long to see
Where everybody can be what they wanna be . . .

Whoa, I wish the world were truly happy
Living as one
I wish the world they call freedom
Someday would come

"Zoom" was a wish, a vision, a dream by a foolish, unrealistic dreamer.

That was me for most of my youth, this imaginary person. And then, the most unlikely thing happened. What happened, through the strangest twists of fate, was that the imaginary person became the real person.

Everything happened on purpose. By divine intervention.

IN GLASTONBURY AND in Harlem—separated by decades—the message was clear: When opportunity knocks, it may come in disguise.

I am thinking of a very cold Monday evening at my grandmother's house in Tuskegee—where I grew up with my parents and sister, and where I had returned to live with Grandma during my college years. This was January 1968, after the holiday break in the middle of freshman year. This was the night when I heard the Big Knock.

The gregarious young man on the front porch said he wanted to holler at me about something he promised might be of interest. He was a third-year engineering student from Arkansas by the name of Michael Gilbert.

We sat down in the living room as he informed me, "I'm with the Jays."

Holy shit!

Right then, sure enough, I recognized him as the bass player and lead singer of the Jays, a group of upperclassmen who did covers of Top 40 hits and some standards. Mostly juniors and seniors, they were the *biggest* thing in music on campus. They were good. I mean, *really* good.

The Jays paired up with a Tuskegee girl group called the Joyettes to perform a variety of paying jobs—including a show at Harlem's hoppin' Smalls Paradise. They were pros!

Michael had a problem though. "The Jays are breaking up." All but three of the band members were about to graduate, and fly off to be pilots, or take posts as commissioned officers, or pursue the professional careers they'd studied hard for.

"Really?"

Michael spat it out. "Richie, I've been looking at you and think you might be perfect for the new band we're putting together."

Did he say he was "looking" at *me*? That was a surprise.

At the Freshman Talent Show I had suffered such crippling stage fright, I tried to walk off with the curtain when it opened to reveal the Mystics to the entire auditorium. It was the annual tradition for unwitting freshmen to sign up only to have older students laugh and throw stuff at us. But that didn't happen in our case. Somehow—once I made it back onstage—we got going on our rendition of James Brown's "Cold Sweat" and we were tight, man. The show put us on the map, at least for the first semester.

Maybe Michael Gilbert had seen us and was impressed. But why had he singled me out? No clue. I wasn't a real saxophone player. More like a sax holder or blower.

The real story is that Michael had a concept for what a hot new band might look and sound like, and he wanted players willing to be coached.

I would love to report that I was the first new member recruited by Michael Gilbert. He made it seem that he was, secretly, only talking to me. And that was the same conversation he secretly had with Thomas McClary and two other members of the Mystics—which I discovered after I went to "audition," basically our first rehearsal. Within two weeks we had our first paying job. The only thing missing was the band's name.

There are differing versions of how the naming went down. The version I recall is that it was the middle of the night and there was a dictionary, and Michael Gilbert, eyes closed, opened it up randomly and pointed to the first word that jumped out at him. That word came right after *commode*. It was *commodore*—the term for a high-ranking naval officer, just below admiral. Perfect for adding a "the" and making it plural. Thus, the name Michael gets credit for choosing was—you guessed it—the Commodores.

The joke, for years, was—*Thank the Lawd we didn't have to go with "the Commodes."*

The months that followed were magic. The band spent every weekend on the road—*outside* the Bubble! Being a Commodore was about belonging, about being part of a group *and* getting to do something I actually, *truly* loved.

The end of freshman year came much too soon. Time to return to Joliet—where Dad had wrangled a summer job for me in the munitions division of Uniroyal, his employer, so I could help pay for ongoing college expenses. In effect, I was now out of the Commodores. And miserable.

But *wait*. After a few weeks, here came fate again.

Michael Gilbert called and announced, "We're going to New York to take the town by storm. We'd love for you to be with us, Richie."

After all the times I'd heard, "Okay, we'll take Lionel," this was a whole other kind of being chosen, as in—*We gotta have you!*

This was my golden ticket to adventure. Nothing like this had *ever* been presented to me. And nothing had *ever* given me a reason to defy my dad—who would never approve of me quitting the job he pulled strings for me to have.

Michael urged me to hold my ground, because, as he said, "You don't wanna be a wimp." He added, "But be respectful."

Predictably, my mother, oh so proper, yet prone to worry, would say little. Not my father. He'd have a lot to say, I knew.

With his hard-ass army readiness, he'd give me a flat-out "No!"—which would kill me because 1) for the first time in my life I was not gonna back down; and 2) there was nobody in the world I admired more than my dad—complicated and stubborn as he was.

Lyonel Richie Sr. had been forced to change the spelling of his first name at officer training school because there was a white officer also named Lionel, and the change stayed on Dad's papers from then on. Yet he bestowed upon me, his only son and the firstborn of his two kids, his given name in its original spelling. He wanted me to have every advantage he did not.

And I understood. Still, I had to take a stand—and go into the lion's den. Or, rather, the *Lyon's* den.

At dinner I announced politely that I had to quit the summer job because "the Commodores were asked to play at a famous Harlem nightclub." There was an audible gasp from Mom and my sister, Deborah, two years my junior. Dad cussed, folded his arms, and fumed.

The family had to assume this was only a phase. How many times had I gotten on a kick only to lose focus? How about my plan to design go-carts for a living? Or my short-lived interest in taxidermy? Dad predicted I'd be over the music thing in weeks.

I pleaded, "Could you just *think* about it?"

"Absolutely not, boy. I am not gonna do that."

End of discussion.

It would have been the end of this story, forever, except for the intervention of our neighbor, the father of my close friend Butch Jefferson. Mr. Jefferson was the glass man in Joliet, and he also had the most unforgettable operatic voice that brought down the house each Sunday when he sang with his church choir.

Mr. Jefferson overheard me telling Butch about my predicament—working my ass off at the bomb factory that supplied the Vietnam War (which I opposed!) *or* running off with the band to break into the big time. Mr. Jefferson jumped in with, "Lionel, I think you oughta go." When he heard how my dad felt, he offered to help move a mountain that refused to move.

Mr. Jefferson stopped by our house a couple hours later and told a story we never knew. "Rich," he said to my father, "I had an opportunity many years ago to join the Metropolitan Opera. And I was talked out of it."

His fiancée at the time (eventually his wife) wanted him to

get married, stay home, and make a steady income. He loved his family, he liked being the glass man, but he had to admit, still, "Every time I get a standing ovation in church, every time, I have to ask myself—*Could that have been the standing ovation at the Metropolitan Opera?*" He sounded broken up about it, all these years later.

There was a tense silence.

Mr. Jefferson said, "Don't do that to Lionel. Let the boy have a shot. Don't have him wonder for the rest of his life could this have been his big break? I know exactly how that feels. It's just an adventure. He'll be back in school in September."

And my dad, Lyonel Brockman Richie Sr., muttered a half-hearted "Okay."

Are you hearing that? He said *okay*!!! The mountain moved—but not without insisting, "From now on I'm not gonna pay a dime."

In other words, if I quit the job that was supposed to help pay for college, he was not gonna pick up the slack. From then on, I would pay the annual tuition—five hundred dollars.

With my newly found freedom I reminded him, "I got a check." My one paycheck convinced me I had earning power. Dad gave me the gift of a challenge—to soon discover one paycheck ain't *nuth'n*! Yet, at that moment, for the first time in my acutely sheltered life, *I didn't need his money.* Lucky for Dad too, because he didn't have it to give to me.

So it was settled. More or less. *Except* for one more unexpected hurdle.

At the last minute—after I had already gone to the airport to fly back to Tuskegee so that I could make it to rehearsal—my parents decided to get into their car, drive the twelve hours all the way to Alabama, check out the band, and interrogate Michael Gilbert about his means for supervising their nineteen-year-old son.

When my parents stepped quietly into the practice hall, we were in the middle of a horn section of a song we had just learned. I can't remember what it was, but I do recall that I was killing it! And that Alberta and Lyonel Sr. were stunned.

They had never heard me play the saxophone given to me by my uncle Bertram Richie, my father's brother. They knew I had a pleasant singing voice but had never heard me on a mic, doing backup, in harmony, on Top 40 hits. They had never seen me do freestyle dance moves while playing a horn. And my parents appeared to be just as wowed by the rest of the band.

On a break, Michael huddled with Mom and Dad, answered their questions about safety, and soon had them laughing. He insisted, "This is a wonderful opportunity for your son."

Finally, I heard Mom note that my uncle Bertram lived in New York and that he could be contacted if need be. Michael then mentioned how we were set to stay at the YMCA.

That was the clincher. I mean, c'mon, what could be safer than the Young Men's Christian Association—the original epicenter of the Harlem Renaissance?

The next day, on a Saturday morning, all the Commodores (seven of us that summer) loaded up into the white Chevy van packed full of our instruments, amps, and uniforms. Squeezed like proverbial sardines in a tin can, we took turns sleeping and driving. We got to Harlem on Sunday afternoon, went to check out the club, and then, at long last, turned onto 135th Street.

We parked not far from the YMCA entrance—the spot marked *X* where I stood gazing up, pinching myself.

Some of the guys went to stretch their legs as the rest of us dashed inside to get our room keys and arrange to put our equipment into storage.

Everyone hurried back to meet where we had parked. And

what do you think happened next? At the sight of our white Chevy van, we stopped dead in our tracks.

The van's two back doors were hanging wide open. And we all knew what we would find as we slowly went around to look inside. It was completely empty. Everything was gone. The suitcases, horns, organ, guitars, amps, mics, uniforms, the whole kit and caboodle.

Gone, gone, gone.

Oh, that's not the end of that story, though I could only conclude it was a career-ending disaster. But, of course, there was so much more to come, all of it hilarious, terrifying, and more thrilling than I could have ever dreamt.

YOU COULD SAY that this book was born in that split second of a flashback that came to me as I looked out at the crowd from my perch on the Pyramid Stage at Glastonbury in 2015— asking myself how the little rocket ship I boarded in the summer of 1968 arrived in this stratosphere.

Incredible. I had survived my own self—my brokenness—to become who I was supposed to be all along. That's when it hit me: *Wow, I have always been the reluctant hero of my own story.* Yet, somewhere along the way I discovered *me* and, in the process, the joy of flight.

For a long time, whenever anyone asked not just *what* happened at the different stages of my career but *how* it was even possible, I struggled to answer. Imagine you're in a race car going one hundred miles an hour and you stick your head out the window and you're asked what do you see. The answer is, "It's a blur."

Most of my twists and turns are so unbelievable, in fact, that I toyed with calling my book *Lies, Lies, and Mo' Lies: The True Life Story of Lionel Richie.*

That's a joke. Or how about—*You Can't Make This Shit Up: The Lionel Richie Story?* I'm kidding again. Seriously, I'm just glad to have lived to tell the story.

And now, here I am, a judge on *American Idol*, with kids looking to me as the guru on the mountain to offer wisdom about how they, too, can have the career of a lifetime. Most of the contestants remind me of myself when I was starting out. By sharing my unlikely journey, I hope to reassure these amazingly talented, brave kids—and readers of all ages— that those things you may think are broken inside of you can turn out to be your true gifts. You may start out your life in freefall, and yet, by some stretch of God's imagination, you land solidly on your own two feet.

I'm also writing to acknowledge the unsung heroes— mentors and friends and family who pushed me to keep at the grindstone, even when the rest of the world told me what I was doing would ruin me.

There are a couple of truths of my life that I hold to be self-evident. One of them is that without the Commodores there would be no Lionel Richie, and I say that on a daily basis. Being part of a band was all I ever wanted, and, in fact, had it been entirely up to me, I would never have *not* been a Commodore.

The second truth is that I didn't begin to heal my brokenness until I became a songwriter. The golden ticket was figuring out that all the distraction from the Other Side was what enabled me to be a storyteller—to give voice to the love and the pain that we all feel. And that were also hits. How 'bout that?

I am aware that I'm writing in a time in which we are more divided than we have ever been—or so it feels. My hope is to bridge some of those divisions. This is not to downplay the celebration of our roots and the pride we each have in our own community, our own culture. I'm talking about the power of song to bring us together. We have a lot in common.

As human beings, we have mothers and fathers and sisters and brothers and kids and grandkids, families and weddings and anniversaries, tragedies and pain, and agony and frustration. Nothing connects us more than love. We all can relate to wanting love, giving love, despairing for love, soaring for love. We all can relate to the common bonds of the human experience. Too often I hear this phrase some use to marginalize others as "*those* people." What does that mean? Who the hell are "*those* people" if not fellow members of our human family?

No matter where I am in the world, I never tire of the questions and the anecdotes that prove our connections and make me feel instantly at home. The statement I hear the most, wherever I am, from folks of every background is, "You know, I grew up with your music"—to which I always have to say, "Funny thing, so did I."

Origin Story

(1949—1970)

Success is to be measured not so much by
the position that one has reached in life as by
the obstacles which he has overcome.

—BOOKER T. WASHINGTON

1

Tuskegee

WHEN I CLOSE MY EYES and think back to the long-ago past, I surprise myself by landing on a super-vivid early memory. I'm in preschool, and believe it or not, I'm paying attention to all the details of playing in a sandbox.

I'm looking at all my soon-to-be friends—who are truly destined to be my friends for the rest of my life.

Everything is serene, safe, and fun, but then it shifts and I'm not as secure. The vibe is not terrible because I don't know to be afraid that any minute my mother, like other mothers, will depart, leaving me to suffer from my life's first bout of separation anxiety.

Yet I survived. Soon enough my vibe shifted as I bonded with the other kids.

A pattern emerged. The sandbox became my new cocoon. It was my first foray into creativity. And it was soothing as hell to be able to play, even to be crazy and mess around. Nothing ever felt that fun to me until I wound up in a recording studio and never wanted to leave. The sandbox was where I first caught a glimpse of the Other Side—a place in my imagination where I could go to escape.

Most of my early years are much less vivid. They are more like sense memories, the stuff of daily life—the sights and sounds and smells that transport me instantly to Tuskegee, Alabama, my forever home.

Simple impressions arise—the weight of the air, how thick and wet it was, year-round. Extreme humidity was a given in that subtropical climate of Macon County, over in the eastern-central part of the state—forty miles east of Montgomery, and about 150 miles north of the Gulf of Mexico. As a kid, I thought that Alabama, one of the most humid states in the country, had originated the phrase "Lawd, have mercy, *it's hot!*" I am telling you, skinny as I was, it's a wonder how much sweat could pour from me.

The lesson was to roll with it and accept that life had a rhythm. The changes of the seasons always stood out—how just when you couldn't take one more steamy day of summer, not one more flying roach, not one more mosquito bite, *finally* everything would tumble into the cool of autumn. Then, in no time the leaves would turn into all the yellows, browns, and oranges, and drift to the ground. Soon the winter clouds would hover, and the winds would bite until most of the trees were left naked to stand guard, shivering, across the landscape.

I remember cold walks through the woods with friends, frost on the ground, and discovering that if you didn't cut some trails for later, the rains of spring would come, and by June you could get lost in the overgrowth.

Summertime in Tuskegee. That's Memory Central. Nothing puts me there faster than the smell of newly cut grass. In a flash, I'm a kid again, outside with Dad, who is standing with authority, all six foot three of him, surveying the terrain we are soon to conquer. In other words, we are about to cut the grass and trim the hedges. I can tell you what the mower looked like, how it worked, and about the oily smell of gas it burned that hung in the air for hours. Then there's the unmistakable smell of car wax that, no matter where I am, has me back in my youth, again outdoors with my father—always determined, as he was, to instill a few life skills in me.

I can hear his voice and feel the weight of his hand on my shoulder. "You hear me, Skeet?" Dad would ask, emphasizing my nickname—which he had made up when I was very small. It was just his silly, playful scat song that went from Skeebo and Skeeboo to Skeeter until Skeet stuck.

My father used every opportunity to send me the message— *Pay attention!*

I got the double whammy: I'm a Gemini—born June 20, 1949. If you know anything about astrology, you know that with the twins of the zodiac, there's never a dull moment . . . because—yes, *ha*—we have no attention span. (No problem for me because I had a couple of people inside of me to talk to.)

Dad had his work cut out for him.

My father's voice provided the dominant chord in the soundtrack of my childhood and teen years. Every single morning, without fail, like the crowing of the rooster at the break of dawn, Dad would begin his day with the same song.

"Oh, Danny boy, the pipes, the pipes are calling . . ." he sang in a booming tenor, letting his voice echo from the bathroom throughout the house. He sang the song from beginning to end and then over again as he shaved, as if loud vocalizing was the only way to get a good clean shave.

Why that song, I never knew. Dad's favorite artist was Count Basie, bandleader and piano player, the King of Swing. My parents listened to Duke Ellington, Ella Fitzgerald, Louis Armstrong, Harry Belafonte, Johnny Mathis, and the *unforgettable* Nat King Cole.

Mom and Dad loved Sammy Davis Jr., Dean Martin, and especially Frank Sinatra. What made those guys, the Rat Pack, so great was clear to me even as a kid: They had *style*. They were the coolest of the cool.

There's not a square inch I've forgotten of the gray house with the white trim where I grew up—right across from the home of the president of Tuskegee Institute, close to the college's main gates. I can still smell the honeysuckle that grew in a vine along the backyard fence. In a snap I can summon the fragrance of fresh mint that was planted back there too. Mom often sent me out to pick some for her, and before long she'd have the leaves brewed into a pitcher of iced mint tea.

The kitchen, my mother's domain, commanded some of the greatest smells ever. Start with homemade peach cobbler or blackberry pie, fresh out of the oven, cooling on the windowsill. Then add to that the mix of aromas from what is still my favorite meal: chicken (however you can make it—roasted, smothered, or fried—Mom had it down), a batch of corn bread, a pot of greens, and a casserole of candied yams. And don't let me leave out the macaroni and cheese.

My mother, Alberta Foster Richie, was about the best cook I've ever known. She made a smothered steak for special occasions that would drive you to distraction. Any night of the week—and we had dinner at 5:30 p.m. every evening—Mom would prepare and present meals, each different from the night before, that were wonders to behold. She was so meticulous that if anything was slightly wrong, it was a crisis.

Eventually, I'd have to laugh and say, "Mom, I don't think we're suffering."

We were not affluent by any stretch—my father was an insurance man for many years and my mother a seventh and eighth grade English teacher, later a principal. That's workin' folks, middle class, but there was enough to put food on the table.

To my mother, upholding standards, according to the rules of etiquette, was everything. Those social graces, to her, were indicative of your stature, your character. Dad disagreed, making it plain—at least to me—that there was more to life than some bourgeois ways. He'd call that trying to keep up with "hifalutin, educated Negroes." In other words—if you wanted some real talk, Dad, who came from across the tracks, was the one you'd go to.

In spite of their differences, Mom and Dad were the perfect yin and yang of parents. My mother taught me to be polite, even with the curse of my shyness, whenever I was in unfamiliar settings. And my father, who was street, taught me how to walk into those settings in the first place.

Dad would say, "Son, I'm gonna tell you about the real world and how to survive in it." Mom and Grandma Foster portrayed the world as it should be (but was nowhere near), or rather, the way they wanted me and Deborah to see it. After Grandpa Foster passed away when I was six, I was the only other male in the house. Dad saw me as the sole recruit for his philosophies.

Lyonel Richie Sr. was outnumbered from the day I was born. First off, he'd just returned from serving in World War II, and shortly afterward began married life by moving in with his wife and her mother, in the Foster family home in Tuskegee. Then, in no time, along came me and, two years later, Deborah.

That was a lot of responsibility right away, all under the glare of his mother-in-law, Adelaide Foster. The pressure! *Yikes.*

My grandmother was among our town's "who's who" and was highly regarded.

Adelaide, a child prodigy at the piano, had received her degree in music from Fisk University in Nashville, where she was raised. Her plan had been to pursue a career as a concert pianist. Her daring to dream that high, in 1910, was amazing to me—how she chose a calling far above the grade then offered to young women of color.

Once in Tuskegee, Adelaide joined with other members of the music department who traveled, performed, or attended concerts at other prestigious Black colleges. It was a refined Chitlin' Circuit, so to speak. She went on to play with the Tuskegee Choir under the direction of William L. Dawson, the renowned composer and arranger whose composition the *Negro Folk Symphony* merged Spirituals with classical orchestral music.

Before long, Grandma began teaching music at the Institute and became the organist at St. Andrew's Episcopal Church, and this was all while raising three daughters.

From their earliest days in Tuskegee, my grandparents were like family to Booker T. Washington—who, in 1881, was first hired to guide Tuskegee Normal and Industrial Institute into the fully fledged university it became. In fact, the gray house with the white trim where I grew up had been the faculty house for the Institute and was originally owned by Dr. Washington, before his heirs deeded it to my grandparents.

Grandma and Grandpa were also longtime friends with Tuskegee's other leading light, George Washington Carver, one of the most influential Black scientists of the twentieth century. Ingrained in my DNA was the history of Dr. Carver and his contributions to science, agriculture, and the environment. He had left his mark on everything from peanuts and sweet potatoes to medicine, philosophy, and Civil Rights.

My grandmother used to speak about Booker and George like they were coming for dinner that night.

Grandpa, from what I recall, was not a talkative man. He had once prospered in the retail grocery business but lost most of it in the 1929 crash. Grandma didn't talk much about the hardship of those years. Let's be clear—Adelaide avoided any topic that hinted at unpleasantness.

We eventually learned that Adelaide Brown was born in 1893, in Nashville, and was an only child, raised by our great-grandmother, Volenderver—a free spirit who was Black and came from money on her paternal side, and was Cherokee on the side of her mother. If you ever saw a photo of Volenderver—glamorous to the hilt—you would have concluded that the word *slavery* was nowhere in her vocabulary.

My big question for the longest time was *Who was Adelaide's daddy?* Decades passed before we would find answers to the mystery, thanks to some genealogy sleuths who led me to the discovery that Grandma couldn't or wouldn't tell us.

Make a note on this one, we'll come back to it.

MY PARENTS HELD class every evening at the dinner table. The main topic was current events. One half of the conversation was about us kids, which began with the usual, "And how was your day?" The other half of the discussion consisted of the adults exchanging the latest gossip in Tuskegee, far more interesting than anything my sister and I could volunteer.

If they asked about school, the answer from me would be, "Terrible." I couldn't report, "I'm having trouble reading out loud in front of the class because I am dyslexic" (nobody had explained that). So, as fast as possible, I'd turn it around and ask, "Dad, what did *you* do today?"

Whatever he said usually involved someone who had been difficult on the job and he always began—"Lemme tell you about that *sonuvabitch* . . ."

"Lyonel, Lyonel!" Mom and Grandma, appalled, would interrupt.

Deborah and I, a captive audience, got used to the nightly banter. Not being old enough to know many details of Dad's story, I could still tell the brother had to put a campaign together to get anything through Congress—i.e., the womenfolk in the household. I felt for him, the clear underdog, and I admired him for how he survived nightly and negotiated his way through— especially because he also ran into another problem . . . the superstar academics on that campus.

And this was how it was in Tuskegee, the Garden of Eden of my origin story. In a Black middle-class town of leaders and achievers, you had to be outstanding. We were a town of Black success stories: educators, professionals, tradespeople, small business owners, PhDs, doctors, lawyers, engineers, pilots, veterinarians, inventors, and orators. Egos like you've never witnessed before.

For Dad, it had to be difficult to find his own footing.

Lyonel Brockman Richie, who later on became an army systems analyst in the private sector, did not have a PhD. He was an insurance man, not exactly the highest on the hill of hometown dignitaries. Again, in the Bubble, your degree, not your income, defined the altitude of your status.

Imagine having your legitimacy measured in a town full of superior-ass smart people with no money, who, because of their academic titles, carried themselves like the richest folks of the land.

At the dinner table, Dad usually began almost every commentary by saying, "Back in the War . . ." when he was a World War II Army officer—first lieutenant no less. Nothing happened in real time. Everything was "over there" and "during the War."

As kids, we didn't understand the tragedy of what had happened to Dad and to the more than 1.2 million African Americans who served and sacrificed in uniform during World War II.

Years passed before I'd read of the valor of the all-Black Ninety-Second Division, in which my father had been an officer. We didn't even know much about the Tuskegee Airmen—trained in a program at our own airfield. They were dubbed the Red Tail Angels because of the red vertical markings on the planes and their incredible performance protecting the bombers they escorted. They rarely lost a plane.

Whenever I saw Tuskegee Airmen walking across campus, I looked up to them, of course, but it was no big deal. I didn't know that they were heroes. That's not how the news portrayed them. Every Sunday we'd watch Walter Cronkite on his TV show *Twentieth Century*, and we'd see pictures of World War II veterans—all of them white. They never showed us a Black soldier running up off the beach at Omaha or in any of the coverage of D-Day.

Imagine, if you'd served with honor, how it would feel to be treated as a nobody after you came home from the War.

Think how it felt for my dad and his fellow Black officers after returning in the wake of the victorious defeat of Nazi Germany when they were refused the right to be a full-class citizen. Black soldiers in uniform were attacked by violent white mobs. Many Black GIs who served in the War were denied GI Bill benefits.

You can't vote, you can't get tuition, you can't get a loan from a bank? You think—*Wait, I just fought for America.* The answer you hear back is, *In Jim Crow's America, you're nobody. If you think you're somebody, be warned. In some places you could be hung . . . in your uniform.*

The only way that Lyonel Brockman Richie Sr. survived the degradation was with the superpower of his scathing wit. With a poker face, he pushed his sarcasm and sometimes silliness right up to the edge, to where you thought, *Oh, no, he won't pull it off!* But he knew how to take the mickey out of a disaster, how to seize the moment and find the irony, and make you laugh so hard you'd forget that he was being absolutely murderous.

Once, at a funeral for his friend Larry—with everybody in the church crying their eyes out—I'll never forget holding my breath, after the pastor said, "We'd like to hear some parting words from Brother Richie." This was after a moving eulogy and words of praise for Larry as "a fine member of our community," and now my father, standing in the pulpit, was expected to wrap-up the service. Others chimed in, "C'mon now, Rich, tell us . . ."

Dad nodded thoughtfully, took a beat, and said, "Well, I don't know about you all, but Larry owed me some money."

Everyone in the church fell out, because that was the real Larry. And then Dad told the most inappropriate stories of Larry being the character that he was. Soon everyone was doubled over in laughter. A healing.

My father didn't shy away from the pain. He mixed the tragic with the absurd and made his life joyous.

One time, at the barbershop, we had just arrived, father and son, only to hear a man in one of the chairs being all pitiful 'cause his woman ran out on him. My dad had never met this man before, but somebody had to ask, "Lyonel, what do you think?" And to my embarrassment Dad looked at the poor guy and said, "Well, I don't know why she was with your ugly ass in the first place."

The whole barbershop exploded with laughter, including that same brokenhearted man.

Lyonel's irreverence wasn't always appreciated. Grandma Foster, so proper and sophisticated, would bristle whenever Dad, so loud and wrong, said something inappropriate. My mother, pristine as she was, would do her best to restore calm and order but, clearly, Lyonel Sr. was out of control and never gonna change.

How my parents ended up together baffled me for years. Alberta Foster, born in Nashville, Tennessee, raised in Tuskegee from the time she was young, was a prize, as they say, an intellect, a teacher no less, and beautiful—having been crowned Miss Tuskegee. We knew Alberta had enjoyed her share of suitors. But at some point, while she was starting her teaching career—in Anderson, South Carolina—she met Dad. And that was that.

Finally, one day, I blurted out, "Mom, *why?* What was it about Dad that you liked?"

Without hesitation, she answered, "He made me laugh."

I never had to ask again.

The harder question to answer, knowing the traumas he had lived through, was *why* he was funny.

When you study history, you find a similar question being asked by slave owners when they heard laughter coming from the slave houses at night. After long tortured days in the fields, laughter may have been the only reprieve you could control. The slave owners didn't get it. They were just as confused by the music. *What kind of people endure the whip and the chain, and then gather to laugh and clap their hands, play makeshift instruments, and sing songs?* The question that drove the enslavers crazy was, *What do they have to be happy about?*

Dad didn't talk about how he felt that his mother, our grandmother Frances, worked for years as a domestic to support her four children. Dad didn't talk about being a widower when he met Mom—after his first wife died from influenza on Christmas Day 1938, only months after they had married. He suffered from depression in later years but never had therapy. He drank and smoked to take the edge off—self-medication, if you will.

Maybe irony pulled him out of the jaws of despair.

Dad told me numerous times, "You can lose everything but

your sense of humor." He could see that I didn't really get it. That's when he warned me, "If you lose your sense of humor, they got you."

"LIONEL," MY MOTHER began one afternoon, in the elegant way she said my name, and, smiling, told me, "We have arranged for you to have a tutor."

I'd been going to elementary school for a few years and the ballad of my poor progress had begun to be sung far and wide. Mom was now opting for a fresh approach—and I was to pay attention. "Make me proud, son."

"I will!" was my promise, because I was a natural-born people pleaser, but I felt miserable waiting for the tutor, a student from Tuskegee Institute. I pictured one of those future PhDs in a tweed jacket with a pipe. What could he manage to teach me?

Wrong question. What could *she* teach me?

The minute *she* walked in the front door, I was smitten. She was kind, beautiful, and patient. After thirty minutes of reviewing for the next day's test at school, my tutor reassured me, "You just need to calm down, so your emotions do not get the best of you."

I nodded, unable to lift my eyes to hers, not wanting to break the spell.

Had I fallen inappropriately in love . . . in the second grade? All I wanted was to deliver on her concern and her tenderness. And, sure enough, I did improve—slightly. Now I had to face a harsh reality that I was doomed to be a secret hopeless romantic.

Maybe these were the seeds for becoming a songwriter one day—from the turmoil of being precocious as hell in my romantic fantasy but a total late bloomer in reality. Falling in love felt like a literal fall—a loss of control, a pounding of my heart whenever the *one* (whoever *she* was) walked by. The girls never knew. I couldn't tell them!

All I could do was swallow the feelings—blissful and painful. Who knew that one day I'd find an outlet? You didn't have to have a PhD to write if you stayed with how you felt—*I love you, I want you, I need you, I miss you forever, you hurt me when you left me,* and so on. I had the paints and the brushes. All that was missing was the canvas.

Again, for the record, I had no inkling in the second grade that I would have a calling in music. My immediate goal was less lofty—just to survive my terror of a little sister.

"LIONEL JUNIOR IS in charge," was the last thing Mom said, looking right at me and at five-year-old Deborah, just before leaving with my dad and grandma for a church function one Sunday afternoon.

To my parents my little sis was an angel. To me she was a hellion, determined to get on my last nerve. She could break my things, pinch me, and try to trip me all she wanted, but I could not retaliate. The law was clear: *No hitting girls. Never, ever.*

This day I turn the TV on and it's a Western. Deborah changes it to a science show.

"Boring!" I say. She thinks so too. She then tries to test my limits—with a kick, a push, and taking my snack. After an hour and a half, I decide to avoid her killing me by running outside to blow off steam.

There's a baseball bat that I pick up in case she follows me. Not to hit her, but to swing as a warning.

Deborah appears outside and starts walking toward me. I swing, telling her, "Stay away!"

She ignores me. She's just walking, not running, like she knows better. Right before I realize she ain't stopping, she walks into the bat!

Bonk!!

You know that cry where you start off with your mouth open and the sound comes later? Deborah does that. Then I look to see a knot on her head and the real crying starts.

It gets worse. Just as she hits the bat, or the bat hits her, who do you think returns home?

Mr. and Mrs. Richie!

They jump out of the car and come running, I drop the bat, and Deborah goes over the top with a *scream*.

Now, I'm here to tell you, ladies and gentlemen, I was framed! The Universe showed me grace that day, because there was no blood and, other than a bump, Deborah was fine. I don't remember my punishment. Most likely I fell out in the grass with amnesia.

Mom and Dad chose not to leave me in charge again anytime soon. Deborah gloated, refusing to admit that it was her fault. She had scored a win in our contest as to who would be seen as the more loving one and who was more of a troublemaker. My rep from then on was, *Well, Skeet's just uncontrollable.*

Our sibling rivalry kept things lively. We were similar, both hyper kids who were not traditional academic learners. Deborah was also creative, which would later take her into fashion design.

Within a few years I realized that any competition between the two of us ended at the door to our school. Which was proven one day when Deborah found out that a bully in my fifth-grade class was picking on me—meaning *she* needed to handle the situation.

No joke. My eight-year-old sister had some Jedi moves. She walked onto the playground during recess and beat the hell out of that bully!

I got mocked for having my kid sis come to my defense. I didn't mind. We have had each other's backs 100 percent ever since.

[TIT|TIT]

"FEEL LIKE GOIN' for a ride?" my dad asked me one weekend morning, in early summer 1957, just before my eighth birthday. He proceeded to tell me he was going to make the forty-minute drive over to Montgomery to run an errand.

Thrilled, all I could do was say, "Yesssss!" and hustle out to the car.

Now, up until this point, I could count on one hand how many times I'd ever left the Bubble. There was a whole unknown world that lay outside our city limits.

Occasionally we traveled as a family to Nashville and to Detroit, where we'd visit relatives. On these longer trips, I didn't realize that there were only certain places where a Black family could safely stop.

Most of us who grew up in Tuskegee took for granted how charmed our lives were and how uniquely self-sufficient we were in our little hub.

This was possible, in part, because of segregation. We were also not immune to its ills, as I now know. Yet for a long time, our parents shielded us from the fear of being a target—a tiny, educated, Black enclave, smack-dab in the middle of the rural Jim Crow South.

If word got around that the Klan planned to drive through town on a given night, the adults quietly conferred. No one said anything to me and Deborah. All we knew was that they put us to bed early.

Generally, we didn't go out much after dark. Those were just the rules for young people in our controlled environment. Although Black folks outnumbered whites four to one in Tuskegee, there was a clear dividing line between the Black neighborhood around the campus and the area near downtown where white people lived, worked, and went to school and church.

The unspoken rule among adults was that you could be killed for being at the wrong place at the wrong time. Nobody spelled it out, but kids were raised to stay on the straight and narrow. Wherever we went, we could expect to be checked—by our own elders or our friends' elders.

The whole village was on your ass.

These were survival lessons in how to stay safe and alert—that is, to be attuned to real danger. We would all eventually hear about what happened in Mississippi in 1955 to Emmett Till, a well-mannered fourteen-year-old boy visiting from Chicago who was brutally lynched. His crime was allegedly being too familiar with a store owner, a young white woman. Some said he was "thinking under her dress."

Around this time, I first heard about Rosa Parks, originally from Tuskegee, who refused to give up her seat on the bus to a white passenger, and about the Montgomery bus boycott. We started to hear about Martin Luther King Jr., a young Baptist minister, one of the leaders who helped organize local activists, spurring the lawsuit that went all the way to the Supreme Court—which later declared that bus segregation violated the constitution.

The Civil Rights Movement—its epicenter in Alabama—was on the march. This wasn't being taught. History was happening in real time.

Most of this was still above my grade level on the day Dad and I set off for the general store in Montgomery to purchase some household goods. A simple errand. Just me and Dad, getting out of the Bubble and going to the Big City, me up in front on the passenger side, looking out the window, my head on a swivel.

Finally, we arrived at the store and parked curbside. Dad kept his hand on my shoulder, guiding me toward the entrance. It took all of ten minutes to find the items we needed and pay for them. Then we headed out the door.

In one arm, my father had the bag of goods we'd just bought, leaving his other hand free to take my hand. On the way back to our car, I spotted a public drinking fountain. Thirsty and hot, I did what any eight-year-old would do—let go of Dad's hand and ran right up to the fountain. There was a box that I could step up onto to be able to reach my mouth to the water, but I wasn't tall enough to see above it—where there was a sign that read: WHITES ONLY.

My focus was only on getting up to where I could get a big drink of water.

As soon as I finished gulping from the fountain, I heard men's voices—white guys talking down to my dad—and I heard the word *nigger* for the first time in my life directed toward someone I knew. They all said it over and over to Dad. When I turned around, I could see the men's faces looked red and real angry, but almost glad—like they had an excuse to be loud and threatening. Nothing told me that I was the culprit.

They were saying words to the effect of, "Get your nigger boy away from the fountain. Can't you read?" And they kept it up, egging each other on, closing in on Dad.

My father didn't respond, but came over to me in a hurry, and the men continued, talking louder and saying bad things. I kept thinking, *Dad? Do you hear what they're saying? Dad?*

Naive to the danger we were in, I had a comforting thought. *Yeah*, I told myself, *they don't know Lyonel Richie Sr., cause he's gonna open up a can of you-know-what and kick some ass!* Instead, Dad leaned in and said in a low but direct voice, "Get in the car, son."

He didn't say a word on the drive home. Like *nuth'n* happened. The subject was closed. I was crushed. My hero of a father had fallen from grace. The shock haunted me. The question *How come my dad let those men put him down?* ate at me. I couldn't let it go.

Nearly five years passed before I referenced the incident. And then I did—at the dinner table. The subject of desegregation of the schools had come up and my dad didn't want to say too much. "That's a cop-out," I said, and then added, "You don't want to be an Uncle Tom, Dad." Without thinking, I mentioned that day in Montgomery at the drinking fountain.

I will never forget how fast he came back. "Let me tell you something, boy," Dad said. "I had two choices that day— whether to be your father or be a man. I chose to be your father because I wanted to be here to see you grow up."

That was all he said, and I let it go—even though, more and more, I had questions. In Tuskegee, Black leaders organized a boycott of white businesses after state lawmakers redrew our voting district. To intimidate us, Alabama's attorney general ordered raids on the offices of the organizers. Later, when there was an effort to integrate the high school downtown, Governor George Wallace sent in the Alabama National Guard.

Not long after that, when Black community leaders attempted to integrate the Episcopal church downtown, I heard from friends that there were armed men in uniform, probably state troopers, lined up outside the church—guarding the entrance.

What did it mean? Our all-Black Episcopal church on campus never needed guarding but the white Episcopal church apparently looked like it was about to be attacked.

At dinner that night, I asked my parents one of the most important questions of my youth: "Mom, Dad . . . whose side is God on?"

My mother asked me to clarify.

I explained, "The Episcopal church downtown has an army. And the Episcopal church uptown doesn't. So, God has an army downtown."

Nobody attempted an explanation.

I thought about the God I knew from attending St. Andrew's Episcopal Church almost every Sunday. He and I were cool. From the first time I sensed that there was an order in the Universe, a loving Supreme Being, I was all in.

My point was that Black and white churches had the same God, so why would one church have an army and the others not? Why couldn't we go to any Episcopal church? The God I believed in, as far as I knew, wouldn't be on a side. Was I now supposed to think there was a Black God for us and a white God for everybody who was not Black? I didn't want that to be the case.

So, from then on, I stuck with my version of how I thought the world should be.

2

Escape Artist

AT AGE TWELVE, AFTER YEARS of hearing, "Who's going with you?" every time I left the house, I accepted one of life's great truths: *Yes, hallelujah, there is strength in numbers.*

Bottom line, I needed a posse.

Being part of a troop was a concept I embraced in the Cub Scouts. By the time I earned all my badges as a Boy Scout, I concluded that without some kind of backup, I would not survive my fatal flaw. And what was that? I discovered it from reciting the Boy Scout Law, while pledging to be all these things: *trustworthy, loyal, helpful, friendly, courteous, kind, obedient, cheerful, thrifty, brave, clean, and reverent.* Most of those traits fit me to a degree, with one exception—I was *not* brave.

The proof came just before high school when I heard, "You only need one last badge to make Eagle Scout." All I had to do was spend the night alone in the woods.

By myself. Not even a flashlight.

I told the Scout leader, "I know you *want* me to get Eagle

Scout, but you gotta find something else besides a night in the woods. That ain't gonna happen."

"Oh, c'mon now, Richie, this is *it*. One last merit badge."

All I would say was—"I ain't doin' it." So much for convincing my friends and family that I could stick with a goal.

There are certain things in life that will reveal your character up front. Scouting taught me that I was not a rugged individualist. If there was a risk, I needed somebody close by in case some shit was about to go down. Without apology, I'd always be *that* brother.

By junior high school, luckily, I had my first real posse. If I was nervous about something—you know, checking out a cave, say—I could tell one of my guys, "Do me a favor, you try it first and then let me see how you come out."

I just didn't have the ego needed to even pretend I was brave. But—let me confess—I was also an instigator, a daredevil in my imagination, while goading others to come with me and test the waters on my behalf.

For instance, one hot summer day in between sixth and seventh grades, circa 1961, my friends Harold Boone, Howard Kenney, and Shorty Miller came by, and as soon as we left the house, I quietly announced, "We gotta go to Deadman's Peak today."

The three of them nodded. We trekked off on foot to this massive, deep gully, off the beaten path, where the two sides were connected by a big fallen tree. At our age, when you looked down into the gully, it resembled the Grand Canyon. And our dangerous mission—attempted by me only after everyone else did it—was to bravely walk across the fallen tree and *live*.

Of course, as we got older, we realized it wasn't that deep, but back then, nothing got our blood pumping more than making it across. We lived and breathed coming up with these exciting adventures to nowhere.

In the company of my friends, walking along with time to kill, I remember the freedom and joy of looking into the future and imagining what lay ahead, far down the tracks beyond our view.

We talked like eleven- and twelve-year-olds do, as if we could choose to never grow up and be boring. "Aw, you know," one of the guys said, "we can't be in Tuskegee, Alabama, forever." Somebody else suggested that we should start a club, so that no matter where our lives took us, we'd stay connected.

And that's how the Home-Boy Association was born.

We were a band of brothers who had so much in common we were practically the same person. We were right in between the misfits on one side and the popular posse on the other. We were not the jocks or the nerds. We were just a bunch of high-energy goofballs who couldn't articulate our futures, but we believed we had something that could maybe set us apart one day.

We made everything the most exciting shit you ever heard in your life, even if we did nothing but go up to Deadman's Peak to hold meetings or ride our bikes to each other's houses. We made each other laugh to the point of passing out.

Harold L. Boone (alias "Cookie Man") became our duly assigned, self-proclaimed president for life because, conveniently, his dad ran the print department at Tuskegee Institute and gave us access to the printing press. Harold surprised us with certificates of membership he designed that looked like fancy diplomas. Mine is framed and hangs, to this day, in my home library.

Like Harold, who became Major Boone in the air force and a well-respected community and business leader in Alabama, all the Home-Boys went on to great success, including fellow founding member Tom "Fungus" Joyner (or the more digni-fied nickname "Blue") who would go on to be the first Black

DJ inducted into the Radio Hall of Fame—after becoming known as the Fly Jock because all in a day he was on in the morning on KKDA-FM in Dallas and then flew to Chicago to host the drive time show on WGCI-FM.

We had a couple smart Home-Boys. John "Sonnyboy" Hines was our true brain, and today he is a biomedical nuclear engineer and served as the chief technology officer for NASA. He was so smart, hanging out with him made us feel smart too. Kenneth "Shorty" Miller became renowned as a community leader in San Francisco, and William Smith (a.k.a. "Smitty") rose to be a highly successful corporate manager. The only one of us who refused to have a nickname was Milton Carver Davis—which was how he always introduced himself, with emphasis on "Carver" (his grandmother named him after George Washington Carver, who else?). He'd drag it out like an aristocratic Southerner—*Cahhhhhvahhhh*. Milton said a nickname would be bad for his image when he became a high-ranking officer or a famous lawyer. In fact, he did become a major in the air force and from there went on to be the first Black assistant attorney general of the state of Alabama.

The Home-Boy Association still holds meetings to this day—otherwise known as birthday celebrations via Zoom. If I'm performing in somebody's current city, everyone in the Home-Boy Association flies in for the show. And if someone else hits a milestone, I'm there if I can make it.

Thanks to my posse, as I came out of my shell, somewhat, I found out that I apparently could make people laugh.

You know that saying "They aren't laughing at me but they're laughing with me"? Yeah, they were laughing at me alright—which meant I could laugh at myself too, a secret for neutralizing the room whenever I was feeling less than brave.

Richard Pryor had a bit about going to a state prison to shoot a movie. He said he realized that if you go to jail you've got to be one of three things. You've got to be the baddest guy in the world, the craziest guy, or failing those two options, the funniest. And that's what I landed on, in trying to figure out my angle—being funny was a coping mechanism for being uncomfortable.

Plus, I wasn't a half-bad mimic.

In my imaginary world—that place I inhabited more and more by junior high—I'd invent lines to dazzle cute girls with my humor. In real life, my crushes were more excruciating than ever. I couldn't speak to a girl without hyperventilating. My dead giveaway was that I could not stop sweating.

Starting in elementary school, I'd been a member of the Jack and Jill organization of Tuskegee—part of a national fraternity/sorority for college-bound Black kids to mingle.

The whole organization seemed a little hifalutin, like Dad would say. Then again, the lure of Jack and Jill was getting to meet girls from out of town. When I was nine or ten, I had fallen in love with Cynthia Diane Wesley, a member of Jack and Jill from Birmingham, who would come often to Tuskegee with her family. Cynthia had a grace and a smile that were breathtaking.

In the weeks leading up to functions, I counted the days, rehearsing what funny thing to say, or better yet, working up the courage to raise a topic to show I could be deep too. But in the presence of Cynthia—who was so smart, loved to read, played in the band, and was good in math—I froze every time.

The hope of improving my odds with the opposite sex made me *try* to improve as a student. Mostly in vain.

Being dyslexic doesn't mean you are illiterate. Think of Leonardo da Vinci, George Washington, and Albert Einstein, not to mention Mozart, Beethoven, and John Lennon.

Granted, I was no Albert Einstein. My best hope was to listen closely and memorize, because I was an auditory learner and could retain what I heard.

As for reading, if I took my time, zeroing in on each letter, I could get it. The problem was that my eyes didn't track the words in their intended order—resulting in a word jumble. If the book had a story, I could slowly read to myself and come away with the gist. But reading was exhausting.

Whenever I was asked a question or had to read aloud in class, it was a horror show. A faucet of sweat would pour down my whole body. I learned in time that this wasn't so unusual. Louis Armstrong, a classic sweater, would be drenched in perspiration just getting out of the car. That's why he carried a handkerchief everywhere—a signature of sophistication.

Why couldn't I do that too? That self-critical voice taunted, *You ain't no Louis Armstrong,* one of the greatest trumpet players who ever lived, and one of the most influential Jazz musicians in history.

True. But who was to say that someone like me couldn't grow up to be a famous musician or a comedian or a public speaker? In a small but important act of rebellion, my answer to that question was *No one.*

"STOP THAT BANGING," was a familiar refrain from my grandmother, Adelaide Foster, who would always pop up whenever I thought the house was empty and I'd found a stolen moment to sit down at her piano to try to plunk out a melody.

It was no secret that I loved music. The secret was that in the imaginary workshop in my brain, I wasn't just making up songs, I was singing my ass off. In front of cheering audiences! In my mixed-up state of ADD/ADHD, I could hear made-up music. At the piano, I'd play minor and major chords, close my eyes, and imagine myself singing like the last Sam Cooke out of Tuskegee. If I was absolutely sure that nobody could hear me, I'd actually sing "You Send Me" by Sam Cooke and sound something like him. My voice wasn't terrible.

There were countless musical influences coming at me in my teens—from showmen like Jackie Wilson, James Brown, and Little Richard, to Marvin Gaye and Smokey Robinson and all the Motown artists. When it's make-believe, you're free to try on other voices. Why not Elvis? Or, later on, why not one of the Beatles, the Rolling Stones, Jimi Hendrix, or Elton John?

Much later, when I began to try my hand at songwriting, the shocker was that thanks to my mother, junior high English teacher, I already knew song structure. Mom had drilled into me what a topic sentence was—your thesis. Same as the song's hook. Your composition had to have a beginning, a middle, and an end. Or, in songwriting, you've got verses, a bridge, and a chorus.

None of this was wasted. Somehow, after learning the basics of how to write an essay, I knew how to adapt them later on. As Dad would remind me, *You can't break the rules if you don't know the rules*. By my early twenties, all of this clicked, and as a lyricist, I could change up the phrasing to where it pleased my ear, and it became poetry. It started with banging and imagining.

Nobody in the household knew how far out in the boondocks my escapism ran. Finally, my parents suggested, "If you are serious about music, the best place to start is with piano lessons."

At first, I was sent to Carnegie Hall—the Tuskegee Institute's music department building, built by the Carnegies, who were among the school's leading benefactors. My teacher, Mrs. Weeks, taught me piano fundamentals. We did finger exercises, and I learned to play scales. Everything went smoothly until it was time to learn to read music.

The issue was that I had the same problem tracking notes on

the page as I did written words. If I followed a few notes in a phrase, *da-dah, da-dah* . . . I'd rush to the end and start to hear a new melody. Or two or three.

Spotlight on the classical concert pianist in the family, Adelaide Foster—who saw that I was eager to learn and agreed to give me lessons. Grandma had a plan to get me past my impatience.

After a few lessons to review the basics, I recall the day when she opened a well-worn book of music to a very simple, short piano piece. It was still hieroglyphics to me. Grandma smiled with reassurance and played it for me, demonstrating as she played the piano with one hand while pointing out the notes on the page with the other.

"You see?"

I nodded vigorously.

Then she played with both hands, showing me how it all came together. Grandma finished and said, "Now you play it."

After composing myself on the piano bench, as she had, and placing my hands on the keys, as she had, I played the same short passage, as she had. Grandma was impressed. "Correct," she said, pleased with my effort. She must not have noticed that when she played for me, my eyes were glued to her hands, not to the page of music.

My assignment was to practice. Then, at the next lesson, I demonstrated my ease with the short piece. Progress! Grandma then selected another simple piece. She played it for me and I paid very close attention. "Now it's your turn."

After a stumble or two, I played it well. I was catching on.

We had a few more lessons. Instead of listening to me "banging" on the piano—her bedroom was right next to the living room—she could hear me playing the piece I'd learned. The household breathed a sigh of relief.

At about our fourth lesson, Grandma, looking proud,

opened the book to a longer piece. Well, *two* pages long. She played it for me first. We went over it together, and she corrected me here and there. Then she announced, "Now, I'm going to leave, and you practice it, and then when I return, we'll see what you learned."

Grandma returned before dinner to check my progress. With poise and confidence, I placed my hands on the keys and played the piece from start to finish without a mistake.

Smiling, I turned to her and waited for her praise. To my surprise, she folded her arms and said, "I am not going to go further, because you're not reading the music." Adelaide M. Foster had spoken.

"Why on earth would you say I am not reading the music, Grandma?"

"Because you played it from beginning to end and you didn't turn the page."

My chest deflated. It was true—I'd forgotten to turn the damn page.

That was the end of my formal music education. Grandma was somewhat startled that I'd managed to memorize so easily. Frankly, I was surprised myself. Ironically, though I didn't learn to read music, memorization became key to my playing by ear. This didn't bode well for a future songwriter—but we'll get to that later.

In the meantime, I continued to play the bluesy "Skeet" chords on the piano every painful day of my teenage angst, making up scenarios of me romancing the world. Nobody came into the room to say, "Oh, my, that's great." Instead, the family just ignored me, except for Grandma who would hear me at night and call out, "Okay, Lionel, that's enough of that noise."

Maybe, I decided, the piano wasn't for me anyway. What I really wanted to play was the saxophone. A lot of my friends who were taking music lessons were starting off with the trumpet. That seemed cool and I was a huge Miles Davis fan, but my lips were too big to get the sound right, and it was frickin' painful. So I asked for saxophone lessons.

My parents conferred. The concern was, *Skeet tends to lose interest and a saxophone is expensive.* They proposed I work my way up to the sax, starting with the clarinet.

They tried to make the clarinet sound like a great choice. "Look at Benny Goodman!" That was their generation.

My inner monologue buzzed, *Ain't nothin' sexy about a clarinet.* My friends were now moving on from the trumpet to the drums, and I was going to walk in with the clarinet— not what I was hearing in any hot horn sections. But I gave it a shot. Though I made no progress in reading music, as an upside, I did learn to play the clarinet by ear.

Like Mom said, maybe I was working myself up to the saxophone.

FATHER VERNON A. JONES, the minister at St. Andrew's Episcopal Church—where I was an altar boy—was one of the most inspirational public speakers I have ever witnessed. Through his words, his demeanor, and his warmth, he made even the most timid parishioner feel courageous.

Remember, I was not brave. Worse, I was the disastrously shy altar boy who couldn't walk down the center aisle for fear that all the two-hundred-some congregants in the small chapel would stare at me. Early in my acolyte training—while in grade school—I would help before the service with lighting the incense and the candles. Afterward, I stood off to the side unnoticed, where I could hear the Sunday sermon.

I loved how Father Jones could cite chapter and verse of

Scripture but make it relevant, like somebody had said it to him that day. *Wow,* I'd think, *how amazing it would feel to touch and uplift people's lives with my words.* A new career path opened up—public speaking!

Sure, I wasn't the obvious choice for that job. Still, I had cultivated my sense of humor, and in the right setting, a slight gift of gab—even if I was often self-conscious and afraid of my own shadow.

However, I could study Father Jones, how his delivery connected to people. His storytelling structure was the same as an English composition, like Mom showed me, and had the same elements of a song, as I'd later learn. A sermon has a topic (a hook), and three arguments (verses) for the main message, and a chorus—the refrain you wanted everyone to remember.

Father Jones had the most inventive approach to religious instruction. In answer to the question *How do you get a group of ten- to fifteen-year-olds to want to show up and learn?*, his stroke of genius was Ping-Pong.

He not only put a Ping-Pong table in the undercroft of the church where we met before our Saturday rehearsals, but Father Jones was also one of the greatest Ping-Pong players ever. We all showed up early to improve our skills. In between games, Father Jones taught us the fundamentals of how to be an acolyte, citing Biblical passages and parables here and there. For a hyperactive Gemini who couldn't stay focused long, this was revolutionary. We exhausted ourselves playing to the point that all we could do afterward was go upstairs to practice as altar boys.

Ping-Pong turned out to be a game I could win on occasion. *Hallelujah.* Yes, I was too short for basketball, too small for football, too slow to run track, and too scared of getting hit by the baseball in the outfield, and wrestling meant I'd have to smell someone's armpit. But I was quick enough for Ping-

Pong, and I could survive it without getting my ass killed with a projectile.

Bam!

With that boost in confidence, the fourteen-year-old escape artist tiptoed into reality when I asked Father Jones to assess my potential as a public speaker.

"You know, Lionel, I believe you have leadership abilities."

I do?

"Yes." He felt I was being called to a mission.

Called?

A light switch in the dark of my low self-esteem flipped on. Maybe the way I could uplift others was with some humor as I spread the message of the Gospel—the message of love.

Father Jones told me, "I would encourage you to join the EYC." Otherwise known as the Episcopal Young Churchmen, the group offered a setting for studying the Bible and talking about how we could relate the lessons to our own lives. Later I even ran for president of EYC. And won! As president, I was handed the opportunity to make my public speaking debut with remarks in front of the church on Easter. Wait. Nobody told me I'd have to talk in front of the church! Before walking up to the pulpit, I came close to collapsing from my first real bout of stage fright. My heartbeat was so loud it sounded like it was coming from the back of the pews. Three church ladies said to me, in unison, "You can do it!" Somehow, I survived.

Rough start and all, I actually had the makings of a life plan—to be of service by becoming ordained as a priest in the Episcopal faith. That meant graduating high school, and after two or three years of college, going on to study at a seminary. For several years to come, the passion to have a ministry of my own one day was never far from my heart.

Certainly, my desire to serve was inspired by the Civil Rights Movement, a dominant chord in these years. And in Tuskegee, again, we were expected to attain a life of consequence. At a pivotal moment in history, the Reverend Dr. Martin Luther King Jr. was leading a mission for equality with the power of his words.

Whenever I'm asked, "Tell me the soundtrack of your youth," I start the list by recalling the music of the voice of Dr. King. I grew up during his rise to prominence, watching him on television, in interviews, and as time went on, hearing his speeches.

Dr. King was extremely eloquent but he used simple language. If you were Black, you could relate. If you were poor and white, if you were an immigrant or a Native American, you could relate. If you were Jewish, or Muslim, or an atheist, you could relate.

And when Dr. King decided to use a big word, it wasn't that people were screaming because they already knew what it meant. No, it was because of the pride they felt in him and how he walked everyone into that big word, so that they could use it too.

The moment that grabbed not just me but the whole country, of course, was the August 1963 "I Have a Dream" speech on the steps of the Lincoln Memorial in front of a crowd of 250,000. The music of that dream was a soundtrack for the world. I was in awe of the spectacle and, most of all, in awe that a change was gonna come.

"HAVE YOU MET the new boarder?" my sister asked me, right before the beginning of my ninth-grade year.

The Foster/Richie household had turned our basement into a student apartment and had begun to take in Tuskegee Institute students who couldn't afford the dorms. Everybody so far was easygoing, but they mostly kept to themselves. This new boarder, Ed Menifee, from Opelika, Alabama—near Auburn—was different. He fit in like a family member, like a big brother to me and Deborah. He was gregarious with a smile that lit up the room.

Whenever I asked him how he was doing, he'd always say, "This is the best day of my life." Every day.

Once I laughed and said, "Aw, man, you said that yesterday."

Ed made a powerful point: *Every day should be better than the day before.*

Eighteen years old, Ed was a business management major and an ardent activist. He traveled regularly, taking part in marches and rallies. Ed explained that economic equality—opportunities to create and run businesses, to be successful—was crucial to ending inequality in America.

I was sold. So much so, I later chose economics and business as my majors in college.

Ed always reported details the news didn't cover—who the speakers were, how many people showed up, what kind of threats and dangers they faced. It was all very real. He reminded me of that guy who comes along and right before Christmas says, "Okay, listen, let me tell you about Santa Claus."

Ed became my Civil Rights instructor, educating me about everything that was happening in our own backyard—starting a mile and a half out of Tuskegee, which is called rural Alabama.

Thirty-eight miles from our city was our capital of Montgomery, where Governor George Wallace promised in his 1963 inaugural address, "Segregation now, segregation tomorrow, segregation forever."

In May 1963, two hours north, in Birmingham—the most racist, segregated city in America—what was known as the Children's Crusade took place when more than a thousand students marched to protest segregation. Many were arrested and put in makeshift jails.

On Walter Cronkite we watched the high-pressure hoses turned on the students, knocking them down. We saw police dogs going after kids, and a city of angry white folks shaking their fists, demanding a stop to the marchers. But they didn't stop. We witnessed the courage of young people breathing new life into the movement.

Ed gave me his eye-witness accounts of these historic events. Because I was too young to travel to the marches on my own, he became my connection to what the stakes really were. Whenever he had time, I'd go down to the basement and sit there with him, soaking up knowledge of the real world that my parents were protecting us from. Ed told me about efforts to register Black voters being organized by SNCC (Student Nonviolent Coordinating Committee) and CORE (Congress of Racial Equality)—and about new voices entering the movement. I welcomed and bathed in the knowledge. Ignorance wasn't an option, Ed said, because it took away your power.

Oppressed people often don't know our own histories. Oppressors prefer it that way. Today, in the twenty-first century, I find it shameful there are efforts to ban the teaching of Black history. You can't separate out Black history from American history. You're denying the whole story. If you refuse to tell the terrible parts, you miss out on the glorious passages too—which belong to all of us.

Ed Menifee believed that the struggle for freedom was not something you could sit out on the sidelines. Everyone had a role to play, even if you were an escape artist like me, dreaming about the right thing to say to Cynthia Diane Wesley who lived in Birmingham, and you were hoping to see her the next time there was a Jack and Jill function.

That opportunity never came, sadly. For many years I

thought that was because my family moved away during my last two years of high school. The image of passing trains on opposite tracks occurred to me, but after a while I stopped wondering what had become of her.

Then, one day in 1977, I was out of college, on the road most of the time, and I caught a piece on the news that solved the mystery. A long-overdue murder conviction had come down for one of the four men, members of the KKK, who were responsible for the bomb that had exploded in Birmingham at the Sixteenth Street Baptist Church, killing four girls and injuring twenty or more people, many of them young. The church basement was a well-known Civil Rights meeting place, but that Sunday in September 1963 it was set up with tables for the young people to finish their morning prayers. The bomb was cheap, made of nineteen sticks of dynamite, and had been left in the stairwell with a timer, set to detonate when everyone would be filing in.

When I first heard about the bombing, shock and horror had hung over everything. I heard that one of the girls was eleven and the three others were fourteen—my age that September.

Over a decade later, the news reported on the man who had been convicted (two of the others would later be as well, while the fourth man died before being charged). The footage showed pictures that included the names of the four murdered girls.

There was a picture, filling the screen of the TV, of Cynthia Diane Wesley. Her face was exactly as I remembered her. She looked directly at me from out of the past, and I sat frozen, for I don't know how long, shaken to my core.

I couldn't make any sense of it. Not then. Not now.

The church bombing marked a turning point for everyone in the Civil Rights Movement. For me it came as the end of innocence, the bursting of the once all-protective Bubble.

By the end of tenth grade, just as things started to quiet down, Dad announced that the Richie family was moving. *Brutal!* My small consolation was that my uncle Bertram had offered to give me his gently used saxophone—if I could figure out a way to get to New York to pick it up.

3

Saxophone Holder

IF I WERE TO DO a movie of my high school years in Joliet, Illinois, the opening would be:

> *I'm lying on the ground, looking up at the sky, but my view is blocked by the grinning face of a big kid with a gold tooth and a black cashmere coat. The breath has been knocked out of me and now I'm trying to inhale and get back on my feet.*
>
> *Besides the ringing in my ears, the only thing I can make out is him saying, "Stay DOWN, until I walk away. If you stand up, I'm gonna knock you down again. Is that CLEAR?"*
>
> *And with the half breath of air I have left in my body, I manage to squeeze out a very weak, "Uh-huh."*

In my memory, I just stayed down there for the rest of the afternoon, too afraid to get up. (Okay, it was only fifteen minutes, though I did look around before I got up. I ain't stupid.) The point is, at sixteen I gave in to the belief that if I tried to take on a bully, I was going to die. They didn't box in Joliet. You either got shot or stabbed.

This was a bad-ass brother from Joliet with an attitude, just looking for a glasses-wearing country boy dumb enough to use the word "Hi" as a way of saying hello.

"And where are your glasses?" my dad asked after I got home with my humiliating story. When I told him the guy took them or I left them on the ground, Dad said, "Skeet, go back, and get your glasses." If the guy had taken them, he went on, "Go kick his ass." If I didn't get the glasses back, Dad warned, "Or I'll kick your ass."

"Are you nuts? The guy's gonna kill me."

My father had no clue. This was not the Bubble. These guys in Joliet were not EYC church kids.

This was in that same period when I was becoming more vocal and giving my father a hard time for being too much a part of the status quo.

Hey, I'm coming into my own, man, feeling my oats, and expressing myself more. An awareness of Civil Rights is educating me, and I'm putting the pieces together.

As many as twenty-five thousand people had taken part in the three marches over fifty miles from Selma to Montgomery earlier in 1965. Without everyone getting involved, I reminded my father, voting rights would never have passed.

When we'd get into heated arguments, Mom worried aloud the whole time—*You two, now that's enough.* We, in truth, enjoyed ourselves in what became bonding sessions. Sometimes we'd save our comebacks for later, like when I accused him of being a "cop-out" for working for "the Man." One time I blurted out, "You sure are kissing a lot of ass," and he waited years before he gave me his comeback. Of course, on occasion I'd be feeling my oats too much, and I'd go too far—like the time I called Dad an Uncle Tom for not standing up to the men who threatened him at the water fountain in Montgomery.

I had to tell him he was out of line for asking me to risk getting shot over some glasses. My choice was—*Do I go without glasses and embarrass myself by walking around nearsighted? Or be dead?* Clearly, I had to live. And you'll never believe what happened. A miracle. God gave me back my sight.

Joliet forced me to get my survival shit together.

Overnight, I had to learn about gangs with names like the Blackstone Rangers, the Pyramids, and the Vice Roys, and what neighborhoods they were in.

The silver lining was that after two years in Joliet, I learned to adapt. I conquered the basics of improv. If I had gone straight from Tuskegee into life on the road without learning survival in Joliet, I would have been clueless.

Joliet was a blue-collar town, forty minutes southwest of Chicago, with a population of about sixty-five thousand people—93 percent white. About 10 percent were in the prison. The downtown was an old-timey Midwestern suburban town with new modern buildings and clusters of industrial plants like Uniroyal, where my father worked in his specialty as a systems analyst. I had no idea what that entailed—by design. He had top security clearance and responsibilities that were on a need-to-know basis.

In this period, fall of 1965, after the first US ground troops had been sent into combat in Vietnam in March, the commitment had already risen to 125,000 soldiers. Nobody around me was talking about the threat of being drafted, but that fear was percolating.

Joliet was *nuth'n* like Tuskegee. We lived in a tiny subdivision, mostly Black, stuck in the middle of cornfields. These were the flatlands, where some of the deadliest twisters on the map came through each year. We had close calls but managed to get through unscathed. Nothing prepared me for wintertime in Joliet—when all you could see for miles were snowbanks and you'd have to dig yourself out. You went into training for winter, for shoveling the snow and ice.

Missing the school bus at the end of the street could kill you. The bitter, freezing wind sliced through your clothes. All I had was a flimsy maroon car coat with bone buttons that was high style in Tuskegee and useless in Joliet.

Our days were much more up-tempo than back home. With one car, nowhere in walking distance, adults going to work and kids going to school, we had to coordinate, like a team. Or, if you follow me, more like a band.

The day still began with Lyonel Richie Sr. singing "Oh, Danny Boy" while shaving. After that, we moved in and out of the bathroom as fast as we each could, then hit the breakfast table, and made sure our schedules were in sync.

We ended up referring to this period as the greatest time of bonding the Richie family ever had.

WE HAD LEFT Tuskegee in the wake of a dramatic effort to desegregate our schools, a couple of years after Black families in Macon County sued to force the issue. In the fall of 1963, thirteen Black students (including friends of mine) had bravely volunteered to attend the white high school downtown. On the first day, the white minority population caused enough of an uproar that Governor Wallace shut down Tuskegee High School for a week.

The next week, as Black students arrived at school, out-raged white students refused to show up—out of fear, they said. Soon, all 275 white students dropped out and transferred to an all-white private school in the area, with tuition paid for by the state. Without sufficient enrollment, Tuskegee High didn't survive.

The story could have ended there. Instead, the disaster in Tuskegee fueled a lawsuit that resulted in an order for the nationwide desegregation of schools, upheld by the Supreme Court in 1967. States now had a blueprint for integrating schools.

Away from all of that, I was having a first experience of attending an integrated high school. The contrast was stark. In our poorly funded segregated Black school back home, we had used books, older desks, cramped classrooms, secondhand athletic equipment and uniforms. Now, at East Joliet High School, where enrollment was about 80 to 85 percent white, everything was brand spanking new—class supplies, teaching equipment, the weight room, the football field and track, the tennis courts.

I have a vivid memory of being in the locker room for the first time with a group of the most muscular, powerhouse athletes— all brothers in prime condition. *I'm still built like a #2 pencil! Ain't a muscle bulging anywhere near me.* Most of the star athletes in Joliet had short Afros, while I had no Afro to back me up. My head was almost shaved. Clean-cut as you can get.

Slowly, all eyes were on me. Imagine a group of just the most intimidating badass brothers looking me up and down.

One of the guys asked, "What are you doing in here? You play football?"

"No, no, no," I assured him.

"Baseball?"

"No."

The other guys piped up. "Basketball?"

"Wrestling?"

"No."

"Then what the fuck you doin' in this varsity locker room?" the first guy asked.

That's when I confessed, "I play tennis."

"*Tennis!?*" one of them asked. Others echoed him. It was true. Thanks to Ping-Pong and watching the pros, I'd gained skills on the tennis court and had made the team.

Nobody in the locker room high-fived me. They sat there glancing at each other like *Is tennis even a real sport?*

A group of the guys came by and watched me practice. One of them said, "Hey, give me the racket. You ain't even that good." He tried returning a serve but swung the racket like a baseball bat. No control. None of the guys caught on.

Then came my first match. Oh my God. For the first time in the history of Joliet, the tennis court was surrounded by a crowd intent on seeing how this skinny Black kid from Alabama would fare against a ranked player, white, from our rival high school.

Who was in this crowd?

Let me tell you. They weren't parents or tennis fans. The crowd was the top tough varsity stars of the baseball, basketball, track, and football teams, many from the South Side. They looked ready to go pro. The seas would part in the hallways whenever they arrived in their black cashmere coats and Stacy Adams shoes. And there I'd be in my maroon car coat.

Do you think these athletes had gathered at the tennis court to cheer me on? Hell no. As I nervously made my way onto the court, I realized they were there to give me a warning: "You better kick that white boy's ass." The unspoken part was—*Or else.*

If I had to put a subtitle to my entire life, the theme emerged that day—*I sure as hell better achieve something meaningful or I'm gonna die.*

Those superior athletes—who knew nothing about tennis— threatened me into excellence.

At no time did they say, "Lionel, we're pulling for you, babes," like cool fellows talked.

Fighting off terror, once I got to my side of the court and took out my racket, I pulled out an improv move. If I let my opponent think he'd have an easy time of it, I could psyche him out, he'd get lazy, and that's when I could edge ahead.

Every now and then, I glanced at the fence and saw all those varsity athletes trying to follow the scoring. If I was ahead, they didn't say much, but if my opponent did well, I'd hear them say, "Why'd you let him get away with that point, man?"

Well, the good news was that I won the match and didn't have to go down in infamy. From there, tennis became the thing I could do that I liked and was good at, and my academics were not as disastrous as in the past. The bummer was that I picked one of the few sports where there were no cheerleaders or girls in the stands screaming my name.

MY HIGH SCHOOL tennis coach taught me basic principles for winning not just at tennis but in life. He'd say, "Stop thinking about the point you lost." At first, I didn't get it. Then I realized, of course, you should focus on winning the point that's in front of you. But if you lose the point, thinking about the loss distracts you. He warned, "Don't let the lost point cause you to lose the game, and don't let the lost game cause you to lose the set."

This principle came from a book my coach recommended— *Tennis* by Pancho Gonzales, who had one of the greatest serves ever. Later, in college, I attended a tennis clinic where I met a protégé of Gonzales—none other than a young Arthur Ashe, fresh off becoming the first African American player to win the US Open.

For a brief phase, I decided that maybe tennis was my calling. So much so, when I met Mr. Ashe, I confidently told him, "I'm ready to be a pro, sir."

He smiled and gave me the hard truth: "You're too old." I was only nineteen. The problem, he said, was that most tennis pros begin professional instruction at least by twelve or thirteen and are ready to go pro by high school. Well, there went tennis as a career option.

In high school, I'd been way too preoccupied trying to get over my painful shyness to think about my future. Same old story. Each time I fell for *her* (whoever the latest was) *she* didn't know I was alive. But how could *she?* Every time I saw *her* walking in my direction, I'd hide.

As hard as I tried to have a better self-image, I was convinced that the whole school knew about my lying on the ground after the brother with the gold tooth took my glasses. Worse, I was convinced that it was going to happen again.

But then, in what could have been one of the most awkward times in my new-kid-on-the-block experience, the greatest thing happened. Miraculously, I got to know Butch Jefferson—the son of the glass man, the same Mr. Jefferson who sang in his church choir and regretted never having pursued his opera career. Butch and another friend, David Mead, were the two stars of the wrestling team. They walked like conquerors, chest up, shoulders back, biceps flexed. Everybody knew—*Don't fuck with these two guys. They will crack your face.*

Butch and David took me on as a project. As my spokespeople, their message was clear: "Leave Lionel alone. If you touch him, we'll kick your ass."

Why they decided to stand up for me was never stated. Sometimes people do the right thing. Whatever the reason, Butch and David helped me gain a level of popularity that transformed my entire experience during those two years into something fantastic. I promised myself to pay it forward one day, however I could.

Later on, whenever people asked where I grew up, I'd respond in a way to show that I had a dash of street, a certain worldliness. "Yeah, you know, mostly Tuskegee and then I went to Joliet."

"Wow," they'd say, not expecting that answer. "How long were you in Joliet for?" They seemed impressed that I'd served in the prison that was the local claim to fame.

"Nah," I'd confess, "I was not in jail. I was in high school."

THE FAMILY (INCLUDING ME) breathed a massive sigh of relief with the news that I'd earned admission to Tuskegee Institute, commencing in the fall of 1967. Grandma, going strong at seventy-four years old, was delighted that I'd be taking over the student apartment in her basement.

Everything felt different. Then again, I was different. The world was different, a tornado of cultural, racial, and political crosscurrents.

The once safe and secure Bubble had not been the same after state efforts to prevent our majority Black population from voting. The Tuskegee boycott helped raise national awareness—playing a part in the landmark Voting Rights Act—only to face the blowback of having the local economy fall apart.

I started to pay attention to what I call the American two-step. Every time we leap the mighty hurdles of injustice, we are thrown back to where we were before. We had legally secured the right to vote—glory, hallelujah—but it was becoming harder to exercise that right. While in high school in Joliet, I heard devasting news of the death of Sammy Younge. Born and raised in Tuskegee, Sammy had been a college student at the Institute, had served in the navy, and returned to become a huge voting rights activist.

In early 1966 he helped register forty Black voters on the one day in Tuskegee when the registrar's office was open locally. He attended a victory party that night, and on the way home, according to one report, he stopped to get gas at a station where he asked to use the restroom. The older white attendant told him to go out to the back hole "where Negroes go." Younge cited the law—that segregation of bathrooms was illegal. The attendant pulled a gun, fired but missed, at which point Younge drove off to seek police protection, to no avail. He apparently went back to argue for his right to use the actual bathroom. Hours later, Sammy's body was found behind the gas station with a single bullet wound to the head.

The man who killed Sammy moved his trial to a nearby county, claimed self-defense, and was acquitted by an all-white jury.

For me, the murder of Sammy Younge was a wake-up call to the reality of America. When the news reached us in Joliet, deathly quiet filled our household. My parents didn't need to say anything, but I knew what they were thinking—*Sammy was twenty-one years old, a kid, not so different from our son*. The Tuskegee myth of "It can't happen here" crumbled.

A new truth of my origin story revealed itself. Yes, I'd been given a front-row seat to the reality of Black achievement. We all understood that if you were Black, you had to be *twice* as good as the standard. And you had to withstand doubt and overcome obstacles that were *twice* as tough.

Yet the great achievers didn't pass that pain on. They passed on proof not only that victory was possible but that failure was not an option.

Over time, I was to discover the lie of how victory, and everything else we thought protected us from hurt, in fact did not. No matter how successful or how high your status—from Colin Powell to Michael Jordan—what you endured for that recognition became a burden. Imagine Sidney Poitier—the first Black actor to win the Oscar for leading man—and the death threats and disrespect and everything he withstood to get that "sumbitch" of an award. And as I would see firsthand, when you make it big and everyone wants to know, "Oh, did you enjoy the journey?" you have to respond with two answers: 1) "Yes, I enjoyed it, because I won." But 2) "Damn, I got shot at a lot."

In short, you may forget how bad it was, but you never forget who shot at you.

My reaction after Sammy Younge's death was not sorrow so much as it was anger. Outrage. And I was not alone. Our campus had become a hub of Civil Rights activism—a lesser-known fact about Tuskegee—and I joined right in. Dad was skeptical. He didn't disagree with nonviolent protest, but he warned against being too visible. His position was, *Stay away from the militant ones. I'm warning you.*

I'd call him on it—*Copping out again? You gotta be more involved!* That's how I felt. Malcolm X—who had been killed in 1965—had said everything I needed to hear. "A man who stands for nothing, will fall for anything."

There was an explosion of campus activism by fall 1967 with Black Power gathering steam and anti-war efforts escalating rapidly. The death toll from Vietnam was already 12,316 Americans, with almost 74,000 wounded and several hundred MIA or captured.

This was the era when Muhammad Ali, heavyweight champion of the world, was convicted for refusing to be drafted, after being denied conscientious objector status. When asked why he refused to go, he said, "No Viet Cong ever called me a nigger." He was willing to face the consequences—having his title stripped and not being allowed to box. Ali famously said, "Why should they ask me to put on a uniform and go ten thousand miles from home and drop bombs and bullets on Brown people in Vietnam while so-called Negro people in Louisville are treated like dogs?" He was sentenced to five years in prison but appealed his sentence, which was later overturned.

There was now talk of a lottery draft that would go into effect in 1969. For the time being, if you were enrolled in college, you were exempt. Or you could qualify for a medical exemption. It had always been a given that, with money and connections, you could get out of the draft—as long as you weren't Black or brown or poor.

Tuskegee had a tradition that valued service to your country. I knew some of our upperclassmen who trained as pilots and who were being recruited for commissioned positions. Every male student admitted to the Institute was required to join ROTC and attend training activities. I didn't mind the drills but dreaded the thought of going to war. At one time I dreamt of being a fighter pilot, although, frankly, I was no longer so enthused.

The country was going mad. We had the Summer of Love and hippies and people getting high and dropping acid and burning bras and dropping out. Talk about sensory overload. Everything was fresh. Dear Lawd, there were girls in miniskirts on campus that could stop traffic. May Pearl Clark caused more rear end collisions than anybody on campus. Forget about studying and planning for the future.

Somehow, I managed to apply myself and make academic choices that could give me practical skills too—classes in business management and economics. My plan was still in force to enter the seminary and one day minister to a flock of my own. Father Jones was happy I had not lost my resolve to serve in the pulpit.

That said, I kept thinking about the path chosen by my

uncle Bertram—which I observed when I visited him in New York the summer before I started college.

A Jazz musician, conservatory trained, and big band arranger, my uncle—who had made good on his promise to give me his saxophone—seemed to be living his dream.

"So, you want to be a preacher?" Uncle Bert asked, in so many words.

"A preacher or . . ." I went down the list of other options for helping humanity. Did I want to be a doctor and heal the sick? No, too much blood. An astrophysicist? Nah, too much math and science. Veterinarian? Well, I loved animals but what if I got bit?

Uncle Bert then asked, "Is it your dream to become a pastor?"

That gave me pause. Practically speaking, yes, I could see myself working with Dr. King or carrying on the Episcopalian tradition with my own congregation.

But was that the dream of the kid in the sandbox? There was this creative, imaginative power source—like a flame—that I didn't know how to protect or how to use.

All I knew was: *Now I have this horn, the ticket to life.*

|||||||

THE MYSTICS, THAT first college band I joined after being tapped by guitarist Thomas McClary, were only planning to play that one night of the Freshman Talent Show.

Turned out, the other members were mostly self-taught like me and we all played primarily by ear. We were all Jazz enthusiasts but fairly eclectic as far as other genres. Andre Callahan, our drummer, seemed pro to me, but didn't even own a drum set when he was recruited. William "WAK" King, the trumpet player, had studied music before coming to Tuskegee. WAK and

I hit it off right from the start. Originally from Birmingham, Alabama, he also lived with his grandmother and, later, became a serious tennis player.

Grandma was not happy about this newly formed band using my basement living quarters as a rehearsal space, but she didn't make a big deal out of it. After all, Grandma knew Lionel Junior couldn't hold an interest longer than fifteen minutes. She probably told my parents, "Well, he made some new friends."

The other Mystics and I met right away, and all began suggesting songs for the talent show. On the saxophone, I played a riff from "Cold Sweat"—James Brown's red-hot hit that had come out a couple months earlier—and everybody joined in.

That was the one. We killed the Funk and got *into it*.

Thomas took the lead vocal, but we discovered that everybody could sing, including me, so I was promoted to sharing in backup vocals. I calmed myself by imagining that I'd be in the back holding the sax and chiming in on my parts, unnoticeably.

To my shock and horror, upon arriving at the auditorium, I realized there was no "in the back." Waiting in the wings for our slot, I broke into a bona fide, straight-up, scared-to-death sweat. None of the other Mystics looked a bit nervous, so— peer pressure—I calmed myself down. Before I could sneak away, I heard our group name being called and followed the other guys onto the stage, behind the closed curtain.

William "WAK" King, standing next to me, shrugged, lifted his trumpet, and said, "This will be fun."

"Yeah," I echoed him, raising my sax. "Fun."

Then, *Lawd, save me.* The curtain began to open slowly and I looked out and saw a packed-to-the-rafters auditorium of Tuskegee students ready to laugh us off the stage. That was the rite of passage, for upperclassmen to mock the unwitting freshmen.

I started to lean into the mic with my saxophone, but I could hear my heart pounding so loud I was sure everyone in the audience could hear.

What happened next changed my life forever.

Picture it: As the curtains opened, I leaned into the mic, the girls screamed, and I quickly followed the curtains off the stage. The sensory overload made me hyperventilate—and you can't blow into the horn if you can't breathe.

The other Mystics called to me in loud stage whispers, "Richie! Get your ass back out here!" For a beat, I couldn't do it. But I summoned the nerve to go back onstage and play my part.

"Cold Sweat" was an apt song for a moment when I almost didn't make it. What James Brown and his band did on the record, that we followed, was to make every instrument part of the beat, not just the horns (which are dominant) but the drums, the keyboards, and the guitar. Playing in sync, the rhythm had a *pop* you couldn't miss if you tried. I forgot about being scared. The Funk was in the house and the Mystics were on fire.

I had a feeling of flying, like, *Oh, I'm in a band and we're good, really good.* Then I'd remember, *I don't know how to do this and I'm just a horn holder and I have no control.*

Somehow, I found my footing. As I leaned into the mic to sing the background part, the girls screamed even louder and one girl called out, "Sing it, baby!"

Right there and then, when the Mystics became one of very few acts in the Freshman Talent Show not to be totally laughed off the stage by the seniors, I couldn't shake the realization that this was everything I had dreamt of doing and being.

I was hooked.

TO UNDERSTAND THE origin story of the Commodores, it's worth noting that we were different from a lot of bands, in part, because we were born out of the dreams and schemes of one Michael Gilbert, lead singer and bass player of the Jays.

In the fall of 1967, with most of the other Jays set to graduate, the younger members—only midway through college—were eager to form a new band. So, during the same couple of months when the Mystics began picking up a few local gigs, Michael and Jimmy Johnson, the Jays' sax player, came up with a written plan for this new band.

They didn't want undependable types who smoked or drank. They didn't want a clash of egos or musicologists. Michael's view was, "I am sick and tired of those goddamn musicians who argue about an augmented seventh with a raised ninth and all of that. Can we play a hit record or not? Is the crowd screaming or not?"

Michael and Jimmy started scouting for talent in area venues. Most musicians in local bars were in any old clothes, playing the same kind of drinkin' rotgut Blues, ignoring the crowd. There was a void in the market, a ripe opportunity to fill with this new dream band—clean-cut, Top 40, college-student showmen.

Hello. Sound like the members of any band you might know?

Somebody mentioned Andre Callahan as a possible drummer, and then Michael remembered hearing the Mystics play "Cold Sweat" at the talent show—which was how he ended up recruiting three more of us.

There we were that cold night in late January 1968, at our first meeting. Upstairs in the building on campus was a rehearsal hall filled with instruments, amps, mics. Downstairs in the basement was a bunker-like room, which was where the three remaining Jays lived—Michael, Jimmy Johnson, and keyboardist Milan Williams, an industrial engineering student from Mississippi. This was like I'd entered a scene from a spy movie, a secret campout for real band members who were also college students.

When I arrived, I spotted my fellow Mystics—Andre Callahan, Thomas McClary, and William King. That made four Mystics, all of us freshmen, and the three remaining Jays—Michael, Jimmy, and Milan—all midway through five-year programs. We were about to merge into a seven-person band.

Michael Gilbert's priority was to assemble a group that could compete at the highest levels.

"I figure you all could make anywhere from thirty-five to fifty dollars a night working in this band."

What did he just say?

Moments before, I was excited to play for free. He had our attention, alright.

"Any questions?"

The six of us sat there like we were in the presence of rare genius. Nobody said a word.

"Alright. Let's go upstairs and see if we can make some music."

We went upstairs, in a hush, and "plugged in." Michael wanted to hear us on "Cleo's Back" by Junior Walker and the All Stars, mainly an instrumental with a few ad-libbed vocals. He taught us each our parts from the record. Note by note.

Everything clicked. In fifteen minutes, we were all playing "Cleo's Back" like we were Junior Walker and the All Stars.

It was magic. From the get-go.

Michael Gilbert said, "Not too bad. Let's learn another song." He didn't want to compliment us too much because, in his role as Mr. Pull Everybody Together, we had to be on our toes to get ready for our first paying gig ($150 split seven ways) in two weeks.

Months earlier Michael had booked the date of Saturday, February 17, 1968, as a special post-Valentine's appearance. The manager of the Tri-County Country Club on Route 29 in Union Springs, Alabama—also known as Club 29 because of the location—had said, "If you can get a band together, that date is yours."

Just before the gig, we realized we didn't have a name—which led to the desperate measure of taking out a dictionary and hitting on the Commodores, in time for our debut at Club 29.

This may sound like a country club for Black folks, just across the county line from Tuskegee. Nah, ain't no country club like that in the rural Alabama back roads. This was a *club* in the *country*, and the only Black establishment offering live entertainment for miles around.

Never once in my eighteen and a half years had I stepped foot in a bar or club. Nobody prepared me for performing to a crowd at tables right up against the stage. Nobody explained that there was no backstage for breaks.

Michael didn't warn us that we were the ear and eye candy for the female clientele—grown women winking and licking their lips, as they moved to the music and made these kind of "*Unnnhhhh* yeah" sounds. And then, on the breaks, when we had no choice but to try to get to the kitchen, they'd undulate and summon you to their side, saying—"Baby, mmmmmmmmmm, *unnnhhhh*, you come over here, Momma wanna talk to you." By the third and fourth breaks those dragon sounds led right into, "You come over here, baby, I'm gonna corrupt me a young boy tonight."

Oh, no! And I was from the school of "Yes, ma'am," and "No, ma'am." How was I gonna get out of there?

Our success that night meant we were soon playing Club 29 on a regular basis. I got used to the dragon sounds. But every time we left the club, honestly, I was scared. Those ladies were not kidding.

THE BLACK-AND-WHITE MOVIE of my life just burst into technicolor. We played every weekend and holiday for the rest of my freshman second semester. Michael had a strategy that if he couldn't get us booked as part of a larger show, he'd volunteer us to play for a modest fee during intermission—in exchange for a mention in the program. Then we'd get a slew of gigs.

The hardest city to crack was Montgomery—because of the so-called Music Mafia. They wanted name acts. The kingpin was a local Black DJ named Al Dixon, who had a talent show that he recorded and then played clips on his radio program on WAPX AM 1600. Even though we were a cover band, we got a slot at the talent show, murdered the competition, and then split. Al Dixon and his people were like, "Who are these guys?" Next thing we knew he had us on the radio and Montgomery gave us jobs out the wazoo.

That was the goal, to have people wondering, *Who are these guys?* We were three months old and we acted as if we were legendary. We had uniforms for stage and travel—these cool, lightweight coveralls in light blue and avocado green. You just stepped into the legs, put your arms in the sleeves, zipped up the front. We were cool, man. People would see us and ask if we were an act. "We're the Commodores. Y'all should come see us."

Bands in these days were booked for dancing or background music. We decided we were there to put on an unforgettable show. But to get the crowd to listen, we needed a dramatic intro. Let's say we were coming on after another band finished, most of them in jeans or in a hodgepodge of 1960s casual wear. We'd show up like a top nightclub act in our dark blue ROTC slacks, our light blue ROTC shirts, and then we got some white satin cloth and all wore ascots.

We'd line up onstage in the dark, our backs to the crowd, and we'd wait until the audience began to notice us and there was a lull in the noise. And then, over a mic, Jimmy Johnson would say, "Ladies and gentlemen, your attention please."

A hush of suspense followed.

"You are about to be exposed to something that will blow your mind. We're going to change the way you look at music."

Now we could hear little *oooohs* and *ahhhs*.

"You are about to be exposed to the supersensitive soulful sounds of the Commodores. And once you have been exposed, you will never again be the same." The drumroll came next as each of us was introduced and we'd turn around, one by one. Then the lights went up and we'd launch right into the unmistakable intro of "Tighten Up" by Archie Bell and the Drells.

We used to preface our act by saying, "Stand up and dance or sit down and watch . . . Showtime!"

We sounded like we'd played together for years. The love vibe we had for the music was infectious.

Michael insisted that he wasn't the leader. All seven of us could bring ideas and suggestions for improvement. Our big assignment was to listen to the radio and especially the weekly Top 10. All up and down the dial, AM and FM, R&B, Pop, Country, you name it. If you suggested a popular enough song, the next question was, "Do you have the instrumentation to do this song?" If yes, that song was a go. None of us knew how effective this process was going to be in the long run.

Quickly, I'd gone from never having a girl scream at me to

being embarrassingly swamped with attention. Michael built on our appeal to females in the audience. Like an engineer, he mapped the room.

"Now look here," he explained, "women travel in packs."

We'd go to the tables in twos—one of us for the girl everyone wants to talk to, and another for her friend, the sidekick who's not used to getting the attention. Every now and then when some of the ladies were getting too aggressive, one of the guys would help me sneak out a back door.

Before our shows, I still had tremendous stage fright—even at the high school proms we played in every corner of Alabama. My adversary was the mic. Whenever we began to play, the guys called in stage whispers, "Richie, blow the horn in the microphone." "Richie, lay the horn on the mic and play." I got so tired of hearing, "Richie!" all the time, I told everyone, "Call me George." That became one of my nicknames. "George, put the horn *in* the mic!"

Michael kept me focused. "You could be a good choreographer," he suggested. "You and WAK oughta come up with some dance steps."

Could I do that?

I loved to dance. Or should I say that I loved to move to music—as an escape artist in the privacy of my pretending to be James Brown. Getting any of his moves down was never going to happen. The only move I had in common with him was the lake of sweat under my feet. Then I started paying attention to Mick Jagger. The first time I saw the Rolling Stones on *Ed Sullivan* the heavens parted. *Wait a minute, I can do that!*

That was a pivotal moment—when I fell in love with the concept of nondancing dancers. Jagger, for one, and Tina Turner, for another.

William King, WAK, could really dance. Between the two

of us, we came up with simple hip moves that became part of how we "Commodorized" our presentation. The weirdest thing was that if I acted as a character dancing sexy, I forgot to be self-conscious.

Just when I was having this minor growth spurt of confidence, Michael Gilbert decided I should sing lead on a Wilson Pickett song. The whole song.

"I don't know . . ." My self-doubt spoke for me.

Michael's wheelhouse was Pickett—he killed on hits like "Mustang Sally."

He argued that he could use a vocal rest, and I'd do great with the more mellow, emotional ballad, "I'm in Love." He added, "You already know the song. The band knows the song."

I promised to think about it. We left it there . . . *until* a few nights later when I heard Jimmy announce me singing the next song.

I froze.

Michael leaned over, telling me, under his breath, "Just open your mouth and sing."

And I did. The world did not collapse. The crowd roared. I survived. After that, nerves and all, I grew to love singing my one song.

Michael, a born mentor, got me. A true mentor is someone who has a vision of who you can be before you do. I think he was that way with each of us.

It was like someone had waved a wand. Girls where we played weren't just screaming. They were talking to me. Some were waving and pointing at me. How was I supposed to handle that?

"Find one you like and kiss her," one of the guys said.

What? No! I had kissed a few girls. I wasn't a monk. But I wasn't gonna just try to kiss a stranger.

Without mercy, the other guys joined in and egged me on. "C'mon, Richie, kiss the girl in the front row."

"I can't kiss the girl in the front row! I don't know the girl in the front row!"

"Richie," one Commodore told me, "when she's waving at you, you reach out and touch the girl's hand and bend over . . . and kiss the girl."

Reluctantly, I gave it a try one night when I saw a beautiful girl in the front row with three friends. She held out her hand. So I touched that hand, leaned over and . . . I . . . kissed her. A full-on kiss. It was fireworks. The music I heard in my mind was the theme from the movie *2001: A Space Odyssey*—which had been released that same month. *What just happened?!*

From then on, every time I kissed a girl, the whole place would erupt in screams. I got so tired of hearing, "Richie! Kiss the girl in the front row!" But the next thing I heard from my fellow Commodores was "Richie! Stop kissing the girl in the front row!"

That first time, though, was a revelation.

Not many days later, I went to St. Andrew's and asked to speak to Father Jones and to Father Carson. I confessed, "I'm having second thoughts on my plan. I don't think I'm going to be priest material."

They gave me wise words of encouragement and told me that if things changed the door was always open. In fact, in the coming years, whenever I worried that the music thing was to be short-lived, I'd talk about returning to my earlier plans.

I even picked out a seminary in Wyoming. Never went. The moment of truth probably arrived when I began to write songs—and realized they were my real sermons.

4

1968

IN A VERY SHORT AMOUNT of time the Commodores claimed our turf, city by city, and became the hottest thing in Central Alabama. We soon branched out across the state, dipping occasionally into Mississippi, Louisiana, and Georgia.

In the beginning, most of the audiences—at about 95 percent of the venues where we played—were Black. As our reputation grew, we started to book more gigs at venues that catered to white audiences. We fit the bill for the in-style band that could put on a show, played Top 40, and everybody could dance. Our weekends were packed with proms and frat parties, white and Black.

Rarely did we play in front of mixed crowds. We never changed our repertoire or how we performed based on who was in the audience or the color of their skin.

Music doesn't have a color, does it?

Before joining the Commodores, other than the time in Montgomery with my dad when I drank from the "Whites Only" water fountain, I don't remember being called the N-word *personally.* I'd heard it used before by public figures, like it was a form of pronunciation that most thought was acceptable. It was a slippery slope, the way some would say *Negro* carefully, but with a country twang it could turn easily into *nigra* and then, with others, the casual racist might just have a slip into *nigger.* When spoken to instill fear in a person of color, it is a brutal, violent word that feels like a form of being whipped.

As a musician, I had not heard those variations directed at me or my bandmates. That is, until one gig when the Commodores got booked to play a prom at a white high school in a small town in rural Georgia.

We gave ourselves enough time, we thought, to navigate the 240 miles of back roads and still arrive early. We were not always on-the-dot punctual loading up the van to leave but we'd make up time on the road. Usually. Yes, we were college students majoring in economics and business, but with scheduling, sometimes we could be a little off.

Thinking big and fancy, like pros, we sent the equipment ahead to have it set up and ready for us in the high school gym. And then we got goin' in the van, timed to make an entrance and dazzle everybody at the start time of 8 p.m.

One minor oversight. When we made our plan, we forgot that Alabama and Georgia are in two different time zones. Tuskegee is Central Time and Georgia is Eastern Time.

We don't even remember the time difference when we get there, forty-five minutes late, and we see three teenage girls in their prom dresses, crying outside the high school.

As we jump out and prepare to run inside, we are met by three grown men, looking mad as hell.

One says, "Now, git yer ass back in the goddamn van, 'cause y'all have ruined my little girl's prom."

"Wait, wait, wait," I begin, and step forward, as the hour difference is now apparent. But I can explain everything.

"Listen up, nigger," says a second man to me, and then he points to the guys. "And you niggers . . ." And he just makes sure we get that he is deliberate. "You niggers hear me? What you niggers need to know . . ."

And then the first man echoes him and it's a call and response of "Nigger, nigger, nigger . . ."

Some of the guys are still in the van, but three of my bandmates—Milan, Thomas, and William—are beside me, carefully moving backward, whispering, "Get back in the van." Milan's from Mississippi and Thomas is from Florida, and they've heard all this before. So has WAK, who is from Birmingham, Alabama—the belly of the beast.

Not me. For all the dumb things that scare me, at this very instant when I should be afraid, I feel strangely confident I can get us beyond our issues—like I'm the Jacques Cousteau of racism, and here I have uncovered my opportunity to solve race relations because I have found me three racists. And I have heard the N-word said . . . to me.

"Sir," I volunteer, with my sudden dose of non–Eagle Scout bravery, "I assure you that we can clear this up right away. It's just a matter of letting us go in and we'll play longer. Whatever it takes."

Everyone's in the van already and Milan leans out and calls, "Richie, Richie, get your ass back in the van. Let's get outta here."

"No, no, guys, we can make this work." Can't they see I'm having a discussion with my newfound racists? I've never encountered (that's a word only a campus person would use right there) three straight-up, dyed-in-the-wool bigots who don't want to use reason rather than prejudice. There is a discovery at hand.

Even after hearing "nigger" this and "nigger" that, I know we can resolve the situation and work something out, in spite of the ignorance being sent our way.

While trying to reassure my bandmates, I'm in a standoff against the three men until I notice that one of them has pulled out a bowie knife. Let me say that louder. A BOWIE KNIFE! It's got a long sharp blade on one side and jagged edges on the other—used for deer hunting and carving up the kill.

He's *wiping* the blade on his pant leg.

In a delayed reaction, I finally get it. Negotiations are over. My interview has ended.

Gingerly, I step back to the van, get in, and we drive off.

Two problems: 1) We had to leave our equipment inside the high school gym. It took us a week to get it all back. 2) The drive home on the two-lane back road was a nightmare. Every ten miles we got pulled over. We were out in the boonies in complete darkness, on a moonless night—*terrifying*. No streetlights or road signs. All we saw were flashing red lights that came out of nowhere, and then we heard police with good ole boy accents. Had any of them decided to kill us, for no reason, nobody would have known.

Every time they pulled us over, Milan, or whoever was driving, gave me a look that said, *Do not open your mouth.* And I didn't. Frankly, I was over it.

None of it was funny at the time. The truth I learned was that not everyone's gonna love you and judge you by the content of your character, regardless of the color of your skin.

My tendency was to push back, "No, no, no, we're the Commodores, man. Y'all like us." Or—"All this will clear up if you just let us play some music."

Looking back, I realize that part of our appeal as a band that played to both Black and white folks had to do with how Michael Gilbert leaned musically. We didn't consider ourselves a "crossover" band, a term we didn't even know. In the course of our travels, I started to pay attention to how racism could show up in obvious and subtle ways. In Savannah, Georgia, we played a white country club for a week where we became local stars. We felt right at home—except for the reality that we could never be admitted to the membership there.

We were going to find out that racism in the South versus the Northeast was not a one-size-fits-all form of prejudice. Some folks didn't go so far as to use the N-word, but they sometimes still said things like "Oh, you're too Black" or "Your music is too Black." The flip side was not being Black enough to your own folk.

Every now and then, I'd hear something like—*Y'all high yella niggaz think you better than everyone.*

That stigma was hard to shake, sadly, and it only added to all the feelings of not being "enough." My recourse was to become *more* Black, another reason to grow the biggest Afro you ever saw.

There is an old code that's woven into being shamed by the label of "high yella." It's from the plantation days when darker-skinned slaves who worked the fields were put on the low end, and the lighter-skinned slaves who worked more as servants inside the house were higher up—often given more privileges, but resented more.

If it wasn't for the Commodores, these contradictions would have been harder to handle. We didn't have all the answers but at least we were going through everything together, things that couldn't be dreamt up in my wildest hopes or most awful fears.

WE WERE PLAYING the Elks Club in Montgomery on April 4, 1968, when we got the news. At first, we just heard screams in the crowd. Someone rushed up to us and, sobbing, said that Dr. King had been killed and we needed to get out of the building and back to Tuskegee safely. Our hope, our guide, our protector, our father and brother, had been taken from us—shot dead in cold blood.

It remains a moment in our collective memories of "What were you doing when you heard?" The world felt irreparable.

Two days later, three hundred students, including me, in grief and outrage, organized a protest that involved taking the members of the Tuskegee Institute's board of trustees hostage and presenting demands in writing that included the initiation of a Black studies program, along with better financial aid for student athletes and no longer requiring participation in the Reserve Officers' Training Corps (ROTC) program. We needed some kind of action that honored the beliefs Dr. King expressed in his last days—that we have an opportunity to make America a better place. And we had to do it starting on our campus, in our town.

Tuskegee had a minority presence of white students, about 15 percent, as well as white professors, administrators, and several white members of the board of trustees. We didn't do our homework that well because one trustee taken hostage was a congressperson. That triggered the calling up of the Alabama National Guard to end the protest before shutting down campus. During the shutdown, the board of trustees and administrators met and agreed to adopt many of the policies the students wanted.

Still, we were beyond shell-shocked. The Commodores opted to leave town early and get to a gig we had that weekend. We didn't feel like playing. Thomas McClary said he couldn't get his fingers to work when he picked up the guitar, like he had lost the music.

Over the rest of that year and the following one, whenever there was a threat of campus being closed—which happened a handful of times—we'd go, "Yeah, shut the school down!" and get on the road for one of our shows.

In the aftermath of Dr. King's assassination, I remember a darkness that set in. A heaviness hung over everything. Relief came from going out to play music and from activism.

In solidarity, I followed the Black Panthers, who I thought were the greatest. If Stokely Carmichael had something to say, I wanted to hear it. And if there was a rally to protest Vietnam and shout for revolution, I was going to be there.

The random draft notices were coming in greater numbers. Nobody wanted to get kicked out of school or lose their exemption status. And for those who were drafted, there was nothing hopeful to say. We started hearing reports from upperclassmen, many of them commissioned officers who trained at Tuskegee as fighter pilots and who left at the end of our freshman year. One of them, Richard Trent, had been our hero. On campus, Richard, a.k.a. "Papersuit," who was tall and skinny, was the happiest, funniest joke-cracking character of life—with the wild, fearless, jive-talking-but-intense personality you need for flying a bomber into the line of fire.

When he came back from Vietnam, Richard was not the same person. He was a textbook example of PTSD. He warned us, *This ain't a war that can be won*. That was the first I heard of a new thing called surface-to-air missiles. You had to fly in low to outmaneuver them but you only had fifteen seconds to hit your target or the missiles would blow you out of the sky. The words I never forgot him say were: "You are flying in your casket." Then he added, "Whatever you do, at all costs stay in school."

That was it for the dreamer named Lionel Richie who'd been thinking if I had to go to war, the best job would be fighter pilot. *Nope, that ain't me*, I decided then and there.

In all the noise swirling around us about the war and about the struggle for full racial equality in these here United States, there was also a glorious cultural, musical explosion.

In 1986, with Grandma, Adelaide Foster— concert pianist, music professor, church organist— my earliest inspiration.

My family home, where I grew up—originally deeded to my grandparents by Booker T. Washington.

Alberta (my mom), Lyonel Sr. (my dad), and my sister, Deborah, around 1983.

Picture of little seven-year-old me.

I received my degree and an honorary doctorate from Tuskegee on the same day. What an incredible moment for me and my family.

An altar boy, age fourteen, painfully shy but serious about being a minister one day.

USKEGEE INSTITUT

FOUNDED 1881

ALABAMA

Benny Ashburn—manager of the Commodores. Our #1 fan, champion, and surrogate father.

This is where it all started for the Commodores in New York City— Smalls Paradise.

The early days. The first promo shoot for the Commodores for Motown.

Backstage at Madison Square Garden with Bob Marley (center back) when he and the Wailers opened for the Commodores in 1980.

The Commodores on tour opening for the Jackson 5 in 1971.

On tour with the Commodores.

The soundtrack of 1968 was insane—Jimi Hendrix, Aretha Franklin, Simon and Garfunkel, Otis Redding, the Rolling Stones, Marvin Gaye, and of course, the Beatles.

The Commodores not only took to saying we were gonna be the Black Beatles, but we studied them. In fact, William King went on to write a research paper for extra credit about the phenomenon of the Beatles' success. Musically, I was in awe of their evolution—going into experimentation, totally going against the grain with *Sgt. Pepper's Lonely Hearts Club Band*, and ending up with one of the top-selling albums ever.

The year 1968 was a collision of choices. Everybody had some form of ADHD, frankly. It was an uncomfortable, painful time of change, a "Ball of Confusion"—as the great Motown songwriter and producer Norman Whitfield would soon write in a classic hit record for the Temptations.

IT'S GETTING CLOSE to the end of freshman year. I'm at Grandma's house in the kitchen in the morning, before classes, and I look out as a rented car pulls into the driveway. It's a rented car with dad in it. *Holy shit.*

There are reasons to worry: 1) He didn't tell me he was coming. 2) He must have flown down from Joliet and rented a car at the airport. And 3) He has no luggage. Not good signs.

I meet him at the door, and Dad says, "I want to talk to you for a minute, Mister." When he says that, I know this is Lyonel Brockman Richie Sr.—Mr. Frickin' Military.

We go into the dining room, not talking, and I sit down. He sits, placing his briefcase on the table. His face is unreadable.

Ladies and gentlemen, this is a bad sign.

Dad begins, "Lionel, what did I tell you *not* to do?"

"What do you mean, Dad?"

"Didn't I tell you, *Don't get involved in any militant groups?*"

Several thoughts crash into each other. As a systems analyst, whatever that was, he would leave for a couple days or a week at a time. Mom would say, "Dad had to go to DC." He occasionally mentioned he was going to a military base to discuss a new weapon. The term ammunition procurement would be thrown in. None of it added up. To this day, I don't know what exactly he did, other than it was top secret.

So, now, here comes a major real-world awakening. Dad's fired up, ready with questions. "Didn't I tell you not to get involved because I have clearance, and you can't do this?"

"What are you talking about?" I pretend that I have no idea.

Dad opens his briefcase and a folder filled with photographs. He takes the photo on top, slides it over, and I look down to see a picture of me about to descend the steps of the front porch. Dad asks, "Is this you, leaving the house at eight thirty in the morning?"

Hiding my shock that this photo exists, I mutter, "Yeah."

He shows me a second photo. "Is this you up on the campus at a rally at nine thirty, ten?"

I can't believe someone was taking pictures of me and that my dad has them. Glumly, I say, "Yeah."

"Is this you at noon at another rally?"

I nod.

Another photo comes out. He points to a recognizable Black Panther and to the young man next to him. "Is this you standing right there?" Again, I nod yes. Dad has more photos. "Is this you in the evening at the Stokely Carmichael thing?" I look down. He leans in. "Were you at the rally?"

I got nothing, but with a whiff of defiance I say, "No, Dad." He sternly repeats his question, and I admit, "Yeah."

"Son, I'm gonna tell you something and I want you to listen to me."

I listen, still looking down at the photographs, not at him.

"Every Black organization has been infiltrated." He pauses, then gathers steam. "Everybody who calls you *Brother* is not your brother. Everybody with a camera is not working for the campus newspaper." Dad makes it even clearer, telling me, "They are informants, you idiot. And they're working for the government."

At that exact moment, my activist days were done. No question, I was freaked out. To think this could even happen in the world shook me to my core.

Going forward my focus—my priority—had to be the Commodores.

Right before the summer break, Dad brought up the issue of how I planned to earn money for the next year's tuition during my time off. I told him, "Well, I think I'm gonna hang with the band in Tuskegee and play some gigs."

My dad muttered something along the lines of *Forget that nonsense*. The time had come to grow up. And he had just the job for me.

My heart sank. Dad was forcing me to quit the band. William King calmed me down. He too had plans to take a break and go make steady money with a lifeguard job for the summer.

Michael Gilbert was sorry to see us both go. He left the door open for when WAK and I returned in the fall, but couldn't guarantee our spots.

Bummed as hell, I pulled it together, packed my bags, and headed back to Joliet.

MY SUSPICIONS ABOUT Dad's work were confirmed my first day on the job at Uniroyal. This was no goddamn tire place, this was a bomb factory. The plant had two areas—one for manufacturing the TNT and the other for filling the shell casings with the liquid "melt" TNT.

Tracks outside connected the areas. A trolley carried the materials into the plant. My first job was pulling railroad ties that needed replacing regularly. Straight-up manual labor. Yes, I had worked outdoors mowing acres of grass in Alabama and had once painted a whole house—and once was enough. Pulling railroad ties was a job for big, strong guys starting at 200 pounds, while I might have weighed in at 125 pounds— *soaking wet.*

My father said the job was easy. "Just join the crew. It's fun."

Pulling ties required two groups of guys—one group to push down the tie with a bar and the other to pull it through the tracks. When it was my turn to reach up and grab the bar, I just hung there, dangling in the air. Under the hot sun, this was not fun in the least. I was clear—*I ain't got no shot at workin' on the railroad.*

When Dad heard my concerns, he lined up another job he described as "very fun." Well, I begged to differ, but it was better than pulling railroad ties. My job was to push a rack of sixty empty cylinders into a large bay, pull down a lever for the pouring of the liquid TNT into the cylinders, and then roll the rack back out into the hallway, where it would cool before being taken away to the next stop for bomb assembly. Of course, the detonators were nowhere near our facility, but in our training, all of us summer job kids had to watch a film to instruct us in the seriousness of where we were.

This was just black-and-white footage of an incident in 1942—no sound—that showed workers reacting to an alarm, running frantically out of the open bay to bunkers made from mounds of dirt, and the most terrifying flash of light you can imagine before the whole plant blew up. The biggest fear we had was causing any metal friction that might light a spark and ignite everything—which was why our shoes and the wheels on the racks had to be made of rubber. Talk about walking on eggshells.

My only consolation, thanks to my new-found capitalist mindset, was getting paid. Other than that, the first three weeks of summer proved to be painfully slow and uneventful. *Nuth'n* like the excitement of being in the band. Being a Commodore was all I cared about in the world, and I was going to rejoin the band in September come hell or high water.

Well, thank God, again—as you may remember—because I received that phone call from Michael Gilbert about the plan to go to New York.

You may also recall the part about my father saying he wouldn't pay a dime if I went against his objections, and how I stood up to him by saying, "I have a check."

And that, my friends, is what you call an extended backstory. Cue us now to the ransacked empty white van parked outside the YMCA in Harlem on West 135th Street. Now get a close-up of the shocked faces of me and my six bandmates. Nobody said a word about how bad we'd been robbed, but we could read one another's thoughts. We were all thinking the same thing—*Oh, shit!*

5

Smalls Paradise

WHERE WE CAME FROM, if you'd been robbed, the first thing you did was call the police. So, in the summer of 1968, on our first night in Harlem, after discovering our empty van in front of the YMCA, we ran to find the nearest policeman to say, "We've been robbed!"

"Oh, yeah?" he said. Meaning, *What else is new?*

My man did not have a sense of urgency. In that moment, I realized something that I'd missed when I visited my uncle a few years earlier. Very simply, Tuskegee is not New York. And New York is not Tuskegee.

He had a little smirk on his face as we went over our inventory of loss—our suitcases, the horns, guitars, the red Farfisa organ, drums, mics, amps, wiring, our personalized jackets, and the rest of our stage uniforms. "Aren't you gonna write up a report?" we asked.

A report? No, he gave us advice. "You need cash. Put some fives and tens in your pockets. And get some twenty-dollar bills. You got any money?"

"A little."

"Stake yourself on the corner. All your equipment is here in this one block."

We were skeptical. How did he know our stuff was that close by?

"Try it." He shrugged. "See what happens."

We positioned ourselves on the four corners of the block. Within ten minutes, this guy walks up and says, "Hey, uh, wanna buy an organ?"

And I go, "Yeah."

"Gimme . . . gimme $200."

I say, "I got ten."

"That's good."

I bought the Farfisa back. This went on for hours. We got everything back, every piece of equipment, every suitcase, every mic, and all the uniforms. That is, with one exception. The one item we didn't get back was my white jacket with RICHIE emblazoned on the back.

Disaster was averted, but after all that, and paying for the YMCA rooms, we were now *broke!* This would have freaked me out even more, if not for Michael Gilbert's confidence that this big opportunity of ours was about to pay off.

This once-in-a-lifetime shot had been arranged before we left Tuskegee, with help from a mover and shaker Michael knew from when the Jays had been to New York and had played one night at Harlem's Smalls Paradise. Benny Ashburn was the guy—a wheeler-dealer of Harlem, forty years old, heavyset, whom Michael described as "connected." Benny, a liquor sales rep, worked for a leading distributor, making sure their top labels were poured at all the right places. He lived in Harlem and knew the managers and owners of almost every club and bar in the city.

Benny was the one who finagled the audition for us on the

night of Monday, July 8. He made it sound much bigger—"We're gonna launch you guys at Smalls!"

This was *Big Wilt's* Smalls Paradise—the iconic night-spot bought in the early sixties by basketball superstar Wilt Chamberlain and businessman Pete McDougal. Just around the corner from the YMCA at 135th and Seventh Avenue, Smalls attracted the crème de la crème of Harlem nightlife.

Some nights, cars would park three deep in front. That Sunday evening when we drove by to check out the club, we couldn't believe the colorful mix of people we saw coming and going—drop-dead gorgeous sisters dressed to kill, superfly-looking dudes, and Afros and Dashikis galore. There were athletes, high rollers, couples on dates, just all the shades of Harlem in the summer of 1968. Everybody walking in looked famous. I caught a flash of someone who looked just like Muhammad Ali. The other guys confirmed: "That is *Ali*!"

We were now officially scared as hell.

WORDS ARE POWERFUL.

We could have said to our friends and family, "We have a big audition at a club in Harlem and nobody has ever heard of us so please come give us moral support." We did not. We said, "The Commodores are having our opening at 9 p.m. Monday night." We also called it "our New York premiere." We added, "The show is free."

We had the audacity to tell our people that this was an exclusive offer.

All seven of us called anybody and everybody we knew in or around New York and New Jersey, urging them not to miss out. We called our people back home and had them call everyone on the lists of Tuskegee Institute's alumni chapters, every member of any associated fraternal organization, everyone who knew anyone in the history of the university or had family who did.

The grapevine buzzed. "Y'all come see the Alabama boys in their debut! Free!"

Smalls Paradise was open on Mondays—unlike many New York establishments—but was notoriously dead that night of the week. They didn't even bring in the house band—Don Gardner, an established R&B group with a recent hit record. When we came over midday to set up our equipment and do a sound check, the only people there were the cleaning crew.

The layout was weird, I gotta say. When you walked in, the main room had a round bar with seating off to the left, and then the floor had the usual tables and booths facing the stage, which was in the back. All told, this room could seat about 250. There was another, larger showroom with a dance floor that sat up to 800 people, which was behind the stage and off to the right—and was kept closed off by a curtain.

We were told the showroom was only fully used for the biggest-name stars. If it got really crowded in the main room, they'd open up the showroom for overflow and the band could turn to play for both rooms. It was daunting.

Even Michael was rattled. But he told us no matter how many people came out for us or how few, we had to score a knockout because, "Our entire musical life depends on it."

Or, as Michael put it, we could die for lack of effort to "theoretically orient ourselves" (adjust our attitude) and perform as though we were playing to thousands or more screaming fans. We had never bombed anywhere. Never, never, never. Never been booed or ignored. We had to play like we'd been in Smalls Paradise forever.

Pumped, we held on to that mindset as we left our sound check. When we returned to Smalls that night, well before our 9 p.m. first show, our hearts sank. The place looked only slightly less dead. The only staff were the manager, two bartenders, and a waiter.

We went over the schedule—six forty-minute shows, with a twenty-minute break in between each: 9 p.m. to 3 a.m. Grueling. We were used to playing two hours at a time with longer breaks in between. If this was an audition to see how the audience responded, I was worried about just getting on a roll and then taking a break. And how do you warm up a room if nobody shows?

When we took the stage at 9 p.m., there were thirty customers in the main room with the bar who weren't our people. We opted to start slow, do some crowd-pleasers, but save our showstoppers for later. In knots, I'd been sweating my ass off in the dressing room but made it onto the stage, and once we began to play, I relaxed. Strange.

Right away, I felt a shift in the energy. I looked at Michael on his bass, over at WAK on the trumpet, Andre on the drums, Jimmy on the sax next to me, Thomas on the guitar, and Milan on the keyboards, and we were all nodding to one another. It was a moment of *What do we have to lose?* We looked up and saw another twenty or so people had trickled in. Still, our hometown contingency was nowhere to be seen.

As we left the bandstand, so as not to lose the momentum, Jimmy announced, "Ladies and gentlemen, we'll be right back . . . so don't go anywhere. Wait till you hear what we've got in store for you next." Instead of taking a break, we worked the room, going table to table, introducing ourselves, chatting with the customers. Typically, during breaks, people decide to move on for the night, but our vibe was *Hey, we're just getting to know each other, why not stick around?*

At the end of the second show, at 10:40 p.m., we look up and see we're close to capacity, with two hundred people in the main room and, in case more come, they're opening up tables in the showroom for the overflow. The manager's over in the corner on a phone, calling in extra waiters and bartenders— "We got a situation! You need to come in right now!"

Everybody is blown away, like, *Who are these kids?*

Then things get better. On our break, we realize the cavalry has arrived, bringing all the Tuskegee folks into the club for the third show. The accents are all coming out. Alabama is in the house. This thing is getting real. We take to the stage in darkness and *now* let go the Commodore whammy that never has failed us back home.

Jimmy's on the mic acting like everything they've heard so far has been only a tease: "Ladies and gentlemen, your attention please. You are about to be exposed to the supersensitive soulful sounds of the Commodores . . ." And he goes through it, wrapping up with, "And once you have been exposed, you will never, ever, *ever* again be the same."

He introduces each one of us and then we launch right into "Tighten Up" by Archie Bell and the Drells, because if anybody in the house is thinking of finishing up their drink and calling it a night, the intro to that song will grab you and set you back down again. Or stand you up and get you dancing. Everyone's listening, watching, calling out, like none of them have ever been exposed to a band like ours, and yeah, they are never going to be the same again.

Unbeknownst to us, the manager calls the co-owner Pete and says, "You need to get down here and listen to these college kids."

Tuskegee is here, along with another batch from off the streets. We are *killing* it. By the time Pete arrives they've opened up more tables and rows in the showroom, and we are performing to both rooms, taking turns working the two sides of the stage.

We blew the roof off.

By the end of the night, Don Gardner and his combo were no longer the house band and were gone for the summer. And we were offered the spot, starting the very next night, playing for the next three weeks. Benny brought the news to Michael Gilbert—$1,750 per week.

Michael turned it down.

What the hell? Michael told Benny to go back and say we wanted $1,800 because you never want to take the first offer. And Mike insisted we only accept an offer for one week, so we could renegotiate as our popularity grew. His belief was, "Never give anybody a long-term contract on you. Never give up your ownership."

Michael Gilbert had that quality called *sight*. And he knew how to hustle.

Our one-night stand at Smalls put those lessons into action. We renegotiated each week and we stayed the whole rest of the summer. We had used our words to speak our dream of an opening—a premiere—into being. It was *on*.

IF I HAD to pick any time or any place to fully come of age, tragically late bloomer though I was, hands down I would choose the summers of going from nineteen years old to twenty-one—1968, 1969, and 1970—in Harlem.

It was epic. The costuming of the era alone was outrageous. Never before had I seen grown men in mink coats. And everybody in mink hats. Maybe that was pimp couture, but nobody told me. In the midst of social ills, Vietnam, and the Civil Rights Movement, it was a hifalutin party in Harlem. The Isley Brothers released "It's Your Thing" in these years and it was our anthem song. They played Yankee Stadium and the city bowed to them. If you were there then, you would never forget it.

Every night at Big Wilt's Smalls Paradise was a new adventure. Before long that very first summer, the house occasionally reached full capacity—almost a thousand people or close to it. Soon it was commonplace that we'd be doing a Wilson Pickett song and look out and see none other than Wilson Pickett in the house.

We always used to say that Michael could out-sing Wilson Pickett on Wilson Pickett's own songs. And don't you know that Wilson paid Michael the greatest praise by saying, "I should've had you in the recording studio."

Then there was one Saturday night when who do we see—being led to a booth with his entourage—and the whole place going crazy? James Brown, the Godfather of Soul, the originator of Funk, the one and only. Mr. *Please, Please, Please* himself.

Whatever we were playing, we stopped and launched into "Cold Sweat." I couldn't help myself from gawking at James to watch his reaction. He looked mildly entertained. Michael was goin' to town on the vocal and the rest of us were playing our hearts out. Next thing we knew, the *unthinkable* happened. James Brown, the Godfather of Soul, got up and walked to the stage and said, "Can I have the mic?" Right away, Michael handed it to James, who then added, "I want my drummer to join me onstage," and up came his drummer, Nate, as Andre Callahan gladly got up from behind his drums.

You know that saying "And the crowd went wild"? Everybody went wild. The place was on fire.

At the break, Benny popped his head into our dressing room with a huge smile. Right behind him was James with a bartender carrying in a magnum of champagne. We were speechless. James Brown gave us the supreme compliment, saying, "You all make the biggest sound."

He put his finger on something that we didn't even appreciate—how the seven of us together could create a sound you'd associate with much bigger bands. We were just staring at each other in disbelief. Was this really happening? If all I ever did was be a horn holder, my life would have been fulfilling.

Because we were always adding new songs and building our repertoire, we could do it on the fly. About a week after James Brown was in, we looked up to see the Isley Brothers walking into Smalls, and, of course, we knew their songs—and started playing on cue. Everybody in the house jumped to their feet and we made room on the stage for as many Isleys as we could fit up there.

YOU NEVER KNEW who was gonna walk in next. For example, we'd been at Smalls Paradise for about two weeks when from the stage, out of the corner of my eye, I saw a white jacket pass by me that looked like the one that went missing from my suitcase when the van was robbed.

My suspicion was confirmed as soon as the guy wearing it came closer to the bandstand. Three clues made it clear: 1) Yes, it was my Commodores uniform with RICHIE on the back; 2) the guy wearing it was built like a linebacker at 6'4"; so 3) I knew it wasn't his because the cuffs were barely past his elbows.

The minute we took a break, I went over to the main bouncer. The security personnel would haul people out of there for looking at someone the wrong way. I said, "Hey, see that guy over there?" as I pointed. "He's wearing my jacket."

The bouncer checked out the size of the guy and told me,

"Well, go over there and kick his ass and get your jacket." My hesitation prompted him to add, "Don't worry, I got your back."

"Nah," I said, "I'm not gonna go tell that man to give me my jacket back." I wasn't stupid.

We started playing again. The guy hung around for a set and then left with my jacket. This ate at me.

The bouncer took me aside later and said, if I really wanted my jacket, I needed to understand the streets. This was Harlem in the summer of 1968, when war in 'Nam was raging, sending kids home in body bags or badly maimed, many drug addicted, many getting spat on because they had fought in a war that was becoming less and less popular, even if it wasn't of their choosing. Given the economics, the bouncer suggested, why not offer the guy some money?

This was after everything we'd spent getting our stuff back after the robbery. For that reason—and because going broke was not an option—I had held on tight to the cash we'd been making so far. After all, this was going to be my tuition. The guys gave me a hard time about being so frugal, but I didn't care. We'd been told by New Yorkers, "You never want to put all your money in one place." If you got mugged, it was better to stick your hand in your pocket and pull out a couple of dollars and show that was all you had. Not all the guys listened and were frequently having their cash taken. Not me. My secret? I hid money in my socks. Not only that, but I kept a ledger for tracking earnings and expenses.

Can you believe it? Two nights after I first spotted the guy with my white jacket, he came back into the club again with my jacket on. No longer scared, I thought, *Let me reunite with my long-lost jacket*. The Universe had brought it back to me. But just as I walked toward the guy, ready to go make an offer he couldn't refuse, I took a closer look. *Fuck, it was dirty!* He must have slept in it. Outside. On the ground. It was no longer possible to even think of putting it on. My pride and joy was no longer mine. It was not *my* jacket anymore. It was *his* jacket.

I never saw it or the guy walking around with RICHIE on his back ever again. And I never wanted to see it again either.

DAILY LIFE IN Harlem brought lessons by the dozens. I'd see things that would conjure the classic feeling of, *Well, Toto, we are not in Kansas anymore.* Or, *Well, Skeet, you ain't in Alabama no more.*

Whenever I checked in with my folks, they let it slip that they were expecting me to come home early, tail between my legs, after going broke.

"Everything's great!" was all I'd say and then give them a highlight or two, like to save money eight of us were staying at Benny Ashburn's apartment, between Lenox and Seventh Avenues on 135th Street, close to Smalls. Did I mention that my spot for sleeping at Benny's was under the dining room table? Nah, but with pillows and blankets, I made it cool.

Nearby was 22 West, a famous Harlem restaurant, where we'd see politicians and business leaders like community activist Percy Sutton coming and going, along with the best-dressed actors and athletes of the era. Across from Benny's building was the hottest basketball court in Harlem, where top NBA names would show up for pickup games with local badass players.

This was a world unto itself. We had the best of Harlem royalty on one block and the grittiest of the street Harlem on the next.

Of course, whenever I called home, I avoided saying anything that might suggest I didn't have my shit together. I had to prove I could be my own man. So, no, I didn't mention that we got robbed our first night in town. And I skipped the story of how one evening at Smalls we were on the bandstand when three shots rang out at the front entrance of the club.

Unaware of what was happening, I didn't realize how serious it was until I heard, "Somebody got shot!" But what I did notice was that all of these dressed-to-kill, powerful Harlem guys—the hippest of the hip, the strongest of the strong—were not who I thought they were. You know what gave it away? As soon as the shots rang out, all those macho men rushed to hide in the ladies' room next to the bandstand. Clearly, under the pressure of gunfire nobody's macho.

Once the drama was over, everybody went back to where we'd been and the party continued inside the club, as if it was just another night like any other. Somehow, we felt safe, maybe because we didn't know any better.

The biggest lesson I had to learn was the difference between being book wise and streetwise. Yes, in college, there was an education to be acquired as far as what could be studied in books, but in the summer of 1968 in New York I got the education of my life—from the streets.

Every day taught me the basics of how to navigate the hustle, which came in many forms.

One afternoon, for example, I stopped on the sidewalk to admire this sharp-looking jacket in the window of an expensive men's clothing store.

Out of nowhere, a guy walks up and asks, "You like that jacket?"

"Yeah, but . . . it's too much money."

"I can get that jacket for you," he says, "You got twenty dollars?"

Was he kidding? It was a one-hundred-and-seventy-dollar jacket! "How you gonna get it for twenty dollars?"

"I can get you the jacket," he says, all matter-of-fact. "Give me the twenty." He sees the money in my hands and takes it from me, saying as he goes, "Be right back."

Forty minutes later, he hadn't come back out. Oldest trick in the book. He went through the store and out the back door, and took off down the alley with my twenty.

How naive could I be?

Back home, there was no street life. Most of it was new to all of us. We were college kids. Church boys. We didn't know about pimps, prostitutes, or gangsters. It was hard not to meet them at Smalls Paradise, especially because they were fans.

Take, L. R. Madison (not his real name). L.R. was one of the biggest players in the street. He always had a group of guys around him. If they sold drugs, that was hard to believe, because none of them were drug users, whatsoever.

L.R. himself had a tennis club membership. And he was a vegetarian. We kept thinking, *Okay, he's a big-time dealer, but where does he do it? And where are the drugs?*

We got around to asking him, and he gave the best lesson ever about drug use. L.R. began, "Let me tell you guys something, schoolboys . . ." He called us that.

We were all ears.

He said, "I have judges, doctors, lawyers, politicians, all calling me, you know?"

We were surprised.

"Yeah, with their education." He went on, explaining, "And my job is to make 'em feel hip." He let that sink in before adding, "I don't do drugs, I sell 'em to the suckers."

Bam! I never forgot that statement.

L.R. said, "I like you schoolboys. I don't want anybody to fuck you guys up. I don't want to see you caught in any of this shit out here."

That was his form of protection.

There were others who had our backs who we didn't even know about. At some point, a blanket memorandum had gone out, that said, in effect, *Anybody fuck with the schoolboys, and get your ass killed.*

As we learned, the part of Harlem that ran from 135th Street between Lenox and Seventh down to 125th—where we were local stars—turned out to be a small world.

I could safely walk down the street day or night with my horn and all the money I had to my name—hidden in my socks and underwear and a pouch around my neck. Anybody else would be a walking billboard for mugging. But nobody touched me.

Everybody was lookin' out. Like Big Ann and Cookie. They were older, attractive women who seemed to know every beautiful young girl in all Harlem. Big Ann and Cookie were madams. We didn't get that memo. Why? Because the girls had their orders: *No doing business with the schoolboys.*

Our biggest protector—Benny later told us—was a semi-regular at Smalls, a charismatic man by the name of Frank Lucas. Many years later he was portrayed by Denzel Washington in the movie *American Gangster,* and it was only then that I realized the extent of his life story. We did not know that in 1968 Lucas had just taken over one of the biggest crime and drug syndicates, beating the Italian Mafia at their game of going direct to Southeast Asia for heroin.

The Frank Lucas we observed from the bandstand was the most charismatic guy I'd ever seen. Smoother than smooth, he was always dressed to the nines, with a two-toned fur coat and hat. He was from North Carolina, we heard, and had a down-home charm. People did say, under their breath, that he was someone you didn't want to cross.

We never spoke directly, but I was fascinated by how he paid attention to every movement in the club. Ultra aware.

When Big Frank Lucas put the word out not to mess with

the Commodores, he also let it be known he was a fan who believed we were going places.

Yep, we were. Benny twisted some arms and got us booked downtown at the Cheetah Club, one of the hottest nightclubs in the city.

Our slot was after the house band—Johnny Maestro and the Brooklyn Bridge, who had a recent hit—and before the head-liners, none other than Sam and Dave of "Soul Man" fame. Nobody at the Cheetah had heard of us and kept talking when we took the stage.

We had seen this movie before. What do we do? We give our "Showtime!" intro, cast a spell over the room, and get everyone on their feet. We brought the Funk downtown. Same thing that happened to Don Gardner at Smalls happened to the Brooklyn Bridge at the Cheetah Club. We impressed the management so much, they hired us to take over the house band slot for the next week.

WHENEVER ANY OF the Commodores happened to meet a girl, we couldn't just invite her back to our place. We were seven guys living in a two-room apartment that wasn't ours. My bed was under the dining room table. No privacy.

The only option was to be invited to her place. Lucky for me, I befriended two dancers, roommates, who danced at Smalls Paradise and who had no problem with me hanging out at their place. Lola and Denice—we'll call them—had bodies so perfect they didn't look real. More than that, they were hip, funny, bright, and so, so cool. Lola and I hit it off, and before long, I started staying over and enjoying every minute.

We were on the same work schedules, so everybody would

come home around the same time. The weeks flew by. Everything was an education.

In early August, it strikes me that the summer is winding down and it's time to get back to Tuskegee, gear up for sophomore year, all that. And I'm over at Lola's, it's the afternoon, sun is shining, we're getting ready to go to work at Smalls, having a bite to eat, and we're talking.

I ask, "So when are you supposed to report back to school?"

Lola reacts like this is a weird question. She says, "Lionel, I'm not going back to school."

"Everybody's going back to school," I say.

Lola stops and looks right at me. "Lionel, I'm not in school." And then she asks, "What do you think it means when I say I work as a call girl?"

I pause and say, "Well, you work for the phone company, right?"

So much for being worldly.

Lola said, "Sit down, Lionel, we have to talk."

Over the next three weeks, I was shockingly brought up to speed. Think of it as Lionel Richie going from preschool to PhD in the reality of the street by the end of summer.

Somehow, I shook off the blinders of my youth and lived through the education. At any moment I could have been swept under, but I avoided that fate, mainly by divine guidance.

The other saving grace was that the folks we met in Harlem became our family. We were included in the local grapevine to tell us who got shot, why they got shot, and why it's best not to hang for too long with people in the fast life.

This lesson could save many lives: *Do not hang with people who are living fast because you don't know whether on any given day it's their time to go. There is no long lifetime at street level.*

Others accept street rules with the motto, *It's not how long you live, it's how well you live while you're living.*

Thankfully, I didn't agree with that philosophy.

Before we left New York, Big Wilt's Smalls Paradise held a farewell party for the Commodores. There were toasts and speeches. Management wanted us back during the school year and for the following summer again.

I'd been talking to WAK about how far we'd come so quickly. We were now known as the inseparable duo of the band, always in sync, and we'd been asking ourselves if maybe our summer in Harlem was the limit to how far we could go. But at our going-away party, all of us got the message: "Schoolboys, this is just the beginning."

That's when I looked at WAK and he nodded back. He had to be thinking what I was—*Holy crap, this could be serious business.*

6

On the Road

IN MY BLURRY MEMORY, I believe the fall of 1968 was when "taking a vacation" officially left my vocabulary. Why? Because we were on constant tour with time off from gigs only so we could go to college and not flunk out.

What happens for us on Christmas? You play. What happens at New Year's? You play. What happens on Easter? You play.

When you join a band at eighteen and keep going, that's years and years of missed pep rallies and bonfires, family reunions, birthdays, and all the major and minor holidays.

You convince yourself that if you take a pause, opportunities will go away. In the back of my mind was the paranoia instilled in me by my folks: *What are you gonna do when the thing you love to do doesn't pan out?*

When doubts distracted me—for instance, while driving the van—I'd get lost or take a wrong exit. We were now playing as far away as Boston and Montreal, and that was a problem. After I missed a turn one night, Michael decreed, "Richie's not driving anymore."

Tiny fears, if not addressed, can grow like weeds. *What if I get kicked out because I'm not good enough?* That worry made me even more conscious about saving what I could from the gigs we played. The others spent what they earned. Not me. The guys didn't get my concern about going broke. They assumed I'd grown up with a damn silver spoon. Not true. They'd say, "Skeet, you wouldn't know what it's like to be poor."

Tuskegee had taught me how the appearance of wealth doesn't ward off poverty. And the more I learned about folks who made it big in entertainment, the more I saw the danger of living beyond one's means. Being thrifty, as every Boy Scout should be, was simply a defense against losing everything, if I ever made some real money.

I wasn't much of a pot smoker, but I could make a nickel bag last a whole semester. The joke was that I could roll a joint so tight it had no marijuana—just smoking paper. Seemed practical. Downright cheap.

I was hardcore—to where the other Commodores referred to me as "Jack Benny."

In Hollywood Jack Benny had the rep of being the cheapest (and wealthiest) comic in town because he could choke a dollar. Jack Benny was *funny*. He played the violin and told stories with a killer deadpan. He made fun of himself for being a tightwad. As a kid, I realized, *That man is smart to get a rep for being cheap, so nobody asks him for money.*

Later I learned he was a very generous man, but he played the role of being tight. Sounded smart either way. Well, a rumor went around Tuskegee, "Don't ask Lionel Richie for money. He's the tightest man on campus."

Funny thing, you know who started that rumor? *Me.* So nobody would ask me for money.

At the same time, I'd bend over backward for any of the guys who didn't have the stability of the homelife I enjoyed living with

Grandma. If we were cooking, they were always invited to join us for dinner—one way they could save money on their meal plan. Everybody did laundry at our house too. That basically put me in charge of laundry and uniforms for the band.

Michael Gilbert came to me one day in the middle of sophomore year to suggest there was something more I could do as a Commodore. What did he have in mind?

"Sing," he said, reminding me that my one song was a crowd-pleaser. "You know, Skeet, I've always seen you as a crooner." My thought was, *He can't be talkin' to me.*

We went down a list of the latest radio hits. One that I chose was "Little Green Apples." Written by Bobby Russell for Roger Miller in 1968, it went Top 40 (Pop) and #6 on *Billboard*'s Country chart. O. C. Smith's version, the same year, hit #2 on *Billboard*'s Hot 100 and R&B. The story got me—a guy noticing the little things that show how his woman loves him. It broke the rules, merging Pop, Soul, and Country. No Funk at all.

Michael then selected "Wichita Lineman," written by Jimmy Webb for Glen Campbell. Another 1968 release, it had gone to #3 on the Hot 100, and #1 on the Country chart. Could I do it? I loved it. I didn't know it yet, but "Wichita Lineman" set the bar for me as to what a beautifully written song really is. The lyrics painted a picture, and I could relate to the story— not because I knew how to be a lineman for the county but because I knew loneliness. By singing "I need you more than want you" in character, I freed myself every time.

Could a song do that? The question got me to tinker in my head with scraps of melody leftover from my years of banging on the piano. Ideas started to come from somewhere during the second summer in New York at Smalls Paradise.

Everything picked up where we'd left off, as if we hadn't been gone at all.

A couple of the characters who took an active interest in

our future were Andy and Charlie, master instructors of everything—how to work a club, how to deal with girls, how to understand the street, and how to get over your ego. They loved to dole out advice.

Andy stuck his head in the greenroom one day after over-hearing a few of us arguing over stuff that wasn't important. "Guys, I've been listening to you all talking . . ."

We got quiet.

"Let me tell you what you all are suffering from—you all have a case of po' folks' tension."

Andy explained that being po' gave you the luxury to fuss about minor shit. But that tension would pass. The tension to avoid was when we had money and fame. He said, "Let me tell you a funny thing about winning. When you're trying to make it, you can't break a group up with dynamite." He let that sink in. "When you make it, you can separate the group with a butter knife."

I thought about the Temptations, killing themselves over who sang lead. Even the Beatles could break up, rumors said. Some blamed Yoko Ono for pulling John Lennon away. Others put the blame on Paul McCartney for wanting to go solo.

"That's the dumbest shit in the world," was what I felt about the Beatles breakup. "They're making millions and they're upset? They should just be quiet and get their money."

Andy sighed. "Yeah, seems simple like that . . . till you really make it."

Nah, said my twenty-year-old self, *that ain't never gonna happen to the Commodores.*

THE FIRST INKLING of a song that's trying to form starts with a *hum*. Sometimes it's a *hmmmm-hmmmm*. Other times it's a *lalala* or a *duhduhduh*.

Outside that hum, we're smack-dab in the summer of 1969 and every sound and sensation is coming at us in the news and on the streets. There's the disaster of the Vietnam War and the horrific Manson murders out in LA—it freaks me out to hear Manson wanted revenge against a record producer who refused to sign him. Meanwhile, there are half a million fans converging for four thrilling days at Woodstock—ringing in the era of massive music festivals and artists redefining Rock—capped by Jimi Hendrix playing "The Star-Spangled Banner" like it's never been heard. All of this coincides with the "Summer of Soul"—the Harlem Cultural Festival, starring the most beloved Black artists of the day, including Nina Simone, whose "To Be Young, Gifted, and Black" became an anthem for the times.

Watching the Apollo moon landing on TV, I thought of that saying that you could kill the dreamers—like John F. Kennedy, who was responsible for this moon shot, and Dr. King, who told us to keep going without him—but you could not kill the dream.

The summer marked a turning point because of the hum.

It wasn't like I was inventing it on my own. This melody was being sent over on a transmitter from the Universe, the radio station on the Other Side. The connection wasn't clear, but it was enough that I would try to plunk it out whenever I was near a piano and could get a minute alone.

This was the case during a visit to Martha's Vineyard, where Benny Ashburn's family had a house. The Commodores had never experienced anything like Martha's Vineyard of 1969.

The island was a tale of two places. The better-known side had the quaint fishing village appeal, along with vast estates owned by multiple generations of wealthy white Americans. The other, lesser-known section of the island was where we stayed—in the vibrant Black community of Oak Bluffs. Lots of

Harlem muckety-mucks owned homes or visited often, as did many Black celebrities who congregated at the Inn at Shearer Cottage—in the Highlands section of Oak Bluffs known as East Chop.

Benny and his sister, Miriam Walker, were members of the Shearer family who owned and ran the inn—the center of Black cultural life on the Vineyard, along with the nearby Shearer Theatre.

The only person who saw me at the piano in East Chop was Michael Gilbert.

None of us were writing original material yet, but we'd started to talk about the importance of having hits of our own. Earlier in the year, we were signed to a demo deal (a glorified audition for a full album deal) on a subsidiary of Atlantic Records. We recorded several songs selected for us by a producer. "Keep On Dancing" was released as a single that went nowhere. The good news was that it got us thinking—*What would a song written for the Commodores by the Commodores sound like?*

Michael Gilbert came over to listen to my first effort on the piano. "Whatcha got?"

I liked the title, "House of Clay." I played and sang a few bars. He liked it. A little tentative, not sure of myself, I mostly liked the *feeling*—full of hope and longing. It was a preview of a song I'd later write called "This Is Your Life."

Over the summer, I fine-tuned "House of Clay," which made me feel just a little bit closer to being a songwriter but not there yet. The concept was of a couple trying to mold a life together. It had come to me, out of my imagination. My reaction was, *Huh, I wrote a song.* Nothing came of it. Still, wheels were turning creatively.

DURING MY SECOND summer in Harlem, I started seeing Sharon Williams, someone I'd met the year before. She was a schoolteacher, sweet, pretty, and a deep thinker. Her passion was her students—"You should see my kids. All my kids, they have so much to give."

Sharon wasn't a girl who was all "I got a guy in a band." She wasn't a "Baby, baby, baby, baby, come on, come on, come on" kind of girl. Sharon was not that. She had me on my toes, like there was a voice telling me, *Don't fool with that lady, boy.*

When we met, I saw how appealing it was to be with a woman that cerebral, that smart. We talked about how to find our footing with so much going on.

When we reconnected, Sharon had changed. When I'd last seen her, she looked like a schoolteacher. Now she was sporting an Afro bigger than mine. The summer before she had questions. At this stage she seemed to have more an-swers. Revolution, Eldridge Cleaver, Huey Newton . . . We sat outside on a great park bench on Lenox Avenue, just hangin' in the cool of a summer night. And I understood a truth about growth—that people change, always, and that's part of the human experience.

We talked about how we needed to have purpose. She was catching the fire of the Black Panthers. I had caught the fire of the Commodores.

One of the last times I saw her, Sharon announced, "You know I'm moving to the West Coast?" I didn't know. This was drastic. She had quit her teaching job and was off to California, to become more involved with the Panthers.

We never saw each other again. I would think of her fondly. And then, well into the 1970s, I heard her name in the news. My reaction was, *Sharon Williams! I know her from Harlem.* There had been a shoot-out at a house in Los Angeles involving the

Panthers and the police, and as I recall, she most likely died when the house she was in burned down.

Our paths had crossed only briefly. Still, I wanted to remember her, how she got me closer to understanding the struggle of my people. I wanted to let her live a little longer—if only in my memory.

BY THE START of junior year in the fall of 1969, the threat of being drafted loomed over the campus.

The year before, around Thanksgiving, I'll never forget hearing from my Home-Boy, Harold Boone, who lived three doors up from us, that his brother William was going to Vietnam.

William Boone was a Rhodes scholar. He was brilliant. He should have been given a draft deferment for going to medical school, his plan, but he wasn't given that option. He decided, "I'll go to the navy as a medic."

I was about to take a train to Joliet for the holiday when Harold called. William had come back from boot camp and was shipping out to Vietnam. Harold said, "You can say goodbye if you come over now."

William looked resolved. He was handsome in his navy uniform. The family gathered around him, clearly emotional because nobody sends off their loved one to war without fear. But you pray and have faith, because that's the sacrifice military families make.

Harold and I, and other longtime friends, sat with William. Right before he left he said, "Listen, guys, I'm gonna do this, it's for my country, and I'll be back. It's something I just have to take care of."

Did he believe in this war? No. Did he want to go? No. Did he want to make a big huff out of it? No. In Tuskegee, the tradition was to serve. But we all knew this war was not the same kind of war our parents fought before.

William left the house and I rushed off to catch my train.

Two weeks later, Mr. and Mrs. Boone are coming back from church, and there, sitting on the front porch of their house, is a navy recruiter. You see the recruiter and you want to break down and collapse in the street. The recruiter is there to inform them that William has been killed in Vietnam.

That changed everything. I was not engaged until that moment. Not really. But everything shifted. Adding to the shock, it took forever for William's body to come home. A month and a half. At the funeral, I walked up to the navy recruiter who was there, and I said, "Sir, I just want to ask you one question. What did he die for?"

And he said, "He died for his country, for democracy, for all the things that we stand for. Freedom and justice, the American way." I heard these as empty words. Here we were, fighting for our Civil Rights in America, and William died in a civil war that we had nothing to do with. Maybe the recruiter could have said that William died saving the lives of others and that would have given me something.

My response was, "I'm awfully sorry you said that." And I turned around and went to stand next to Harold.

The following week, on that Monday, I turned in my ROTC uniform. Membership was no longer required of every male student, but I'd stuck with it out of a sense of duty. No more. The war could no longer be ignored as being "over there."

That was my Wake-Up Call.

THE LOTTERY DRAFT—set for December 1, 1969—was to replace the random selection draft notices. The goal was to escalate the number of soldiers for the Vietnam War but, supposedly, in a way that was fairer—for all those born between 1944 and 1950.

Everything would depend on your birthday and the number assigned to that day. If it was a low number, you could be hauled off immediately, sent to basic training, and then into combat, no turning back.

Again, if you were enrolled in college and in good standing, you could get an educational deferment. You could avoid being sent to the front, the recruiters reminded us all the time, by enlisting in an officer training position.

Instead of waiting for the chips to fall, drummer Andre Callahan shocked the rest of us earlier in the summer by announcing that he was going to join the navy. Andre had started with the Mystics to play in the talent show freshman year. He had not planned on an open-ended commitment.

We didn't have to wait long before finding Walter "Clyde" Orange, a sensational drummer with a powerful, dynamic voice, who had headed up his own band, the J-Notes. We had no idea that a few months later we would need a lead vocalist to replace, of all people, Michael Gilbert—who, on September 23, 1969, seemingly vanished.

Right before school started, the Commodores had wrapped a two-week stint performing in Québec City, Canada. We did not know that, every September for the past few years, Michael—a fifth-year engineering student in good standing—had to jump through many hoops to submit paperwork for his student deferment. This year the Arkansas draft board denied deferment; the FBI then put out a warrant to arrest him for draft evasion.

Michael didn't tell us because he didn't want to cause alarm. Instead, he immediately set a "show proof" hearing with a judge in Little Rock on that September 23 date. The warrant was supposed to be on hold. The only two people who knew any of this were Jimmy Johnson, the other sax player in the band, and Benny Ashburn.

The only thing that seemed unusual to me was that Mike, just before we drove home, said, "Y'all get on the road. See you back at campus in a few weeks."

For months, we didn't know of the nightmare that followed. In court in Little Rock, Mike listened as the judge approved his deferment paperwork and dismissed the federal charges. But just before the gavel banged, in walked someone from Selective Service showing draft papers he never received—making him late for his induction. The judge couldn't stop them. They marched Mike out in handcuffs and took him straight to the army. In boot camp in Louisiana he wrote his mother a short letter and six weeks later was given one five-minute phone call. That was to Benny. The message was that he wanted us to carry on and stay focused.

Mike's sudden departure was one of the biggest heartbreaks of my early career. We all knew Michael Gilbert had poured his life and brilliance into opening the door to something in-credible for us. Yet it was a door he could not walk through himself.

We saw him once before he went to Vietnam. He showed up during a Christmas show at Smalls Paradise as a surprise. He didn't perform, just sat and watched us—proud and, I'm sure, devastated. On the breaks we sat together and cried and laughed and cried. Over the next two years or more, we com-municated sporadically, but it might have been too painful for him to hear our news and he didn't want to share much of his.

During that first week when we learned he wasn't coming back, I had called everyone to a meeting. My grandmother's basement, my student apartment, which had become our Commodore headquarters, had its own entrance. And as everyone filed in, I found myself trying to lift everyone's spirits. "We have to fight to keep what we've built together. I know that's what I'm gonna do!"

Everyone started to chime in, agreeing. Everyone except Jimmy Johnson.

Being the antagonist, he waved his hand, saying that none of us knew what was involved in running a band. Except for *him*.

"Now wait a minute," I said, and reminded him that nobody ran the band. The rest of the guys added in their opinions.

Jimmy was cocky, a very musicians' musician who did not have the nurturing skills of Michael Gilbert. Jimmy said words to suggest we were a waste of time.

And we all said, in effect, "Hey, you don't wanna be here, and so it's best if you leave."

After Jimmy left, I had a delayed reaction, realizing that we had lost our founder and we had just parted ways with his sidekick.

Doubt surfaced. Could we keep going without a leader?

We sat in silence for minutes, until, one by one, we came to the same conclusion. We were not done. We were not giving up.

Out of sheer love for our creation, we summoned the defiance to push ahead.

We not only had found Clyde as our new drummer and lead vocalist, but we quickly found Ronald LaPread, who would become our killer bass player. Now we were six.

You have it right, ladies and gentlemen. We had just put together *the* Commodores.

WE WERE MORE than a band. I believe God formed us as a brotherhood—to experience real life together. Everything that I learned outside the protective Bubble of Tuskegee, I learned alongside other Commodores.

We joked and teased each other mercilessly, but we never had one serious argument or rift. And even when problems arose later, none of it took away from the reverence I would always feel for what we sparked in one another.

Musically, we spoke the same language. If the band were a melody, there was no single dominant chord.

Individually, we each had quirks and strengths and different personalities, but the glue that held us together is what we had in common. We were a band of fun-loving, knuckleheaded, naturally talented, mostly self-educated musicians. Whenever a group features a single virtuoso, the other players may feel more like "backup"; or when everybody's a virtuoso, the musical opinions are bound to clash.

We were not in either category. Yet we were good. Really good.

Playing together never got old, never felt boring. People later asked me how I chose music over getting my degree and that's not exactly what happened. As a junior (1969/1970), I was still an economics and business major (going on to seminary was very iffy) who played the saxophone by ear and sang three songs. Milan Williams, a wiz engineering student, gave new meaning to keyboard-driven Funk, and his improvised instrumental solos were always riveting—and Milan would eventually give us our first hit record. Thomas McClary, another business major, played the ukulele before he picked up every kind of guitar—including a five-string Mosrite that today is iconic. Was he Eric Clapton? No, but he played the guitar like a percussionist, adding to what was unmistakably the Commodores sound.

Likewise, William Atwell King, a.k.a. WAK—who had training as a trumpet player before choosing his major in business management—added his own flavor on every song we played that made us sound like us. The same went for the bass playing of Ronald LaPread.

We found him at a show he was playing at the American Legion and asked him before he went on: "You play the bass? We have a spot in the Commodores, travel required."

Ronald confidently replied, "I play bass." In fact, he lied. He didn't play bass, he played keyboards. But he wanted a spot.

Ronald later confessed, "I went home and picked up a bass and told myself, 'Lemme practice this real fast.'" He proved to be phenomenal. If I could choose my bass player for life, that would be Ronald LaPread.

Walter "Clyde" Orange—our drummer and lead singer— was the only Commodore who had been a music major, not at Tuskegee but at Alabama State.

Vocally, Clyde could give you a dead-on James Brown— doing justice to the Godfather of Soul—and then swing from R&B to Rock to Jazz to Country, with nuance. And he had great musicality harmonizing with me.

What I loved most was how we all knew just enough to complement each other. I'd hear Thomas play a guitar lick and listen to Ron, on bass, kick it back. Thomas understood how his style of guitar playing fit perfectly with the unorthodox way that LaPread played bass—a mash-up of melody and Funk, probably from his orientation as a keyboardist. And if you add lead guitar and bass to the foot and consistency of Clyde and his drums, you have altogether what I call "the engine." Then what Milan did on keyboards set the sonic direction. With WAK and me on our horns, all we had to do was ride the wave.

WHEREVER WE PLAYED, we'd get invited back. Benny Ashburn, making it big in the liquor distribution business, kept new, good-paying opportunities coming our way. "Hey, the Bottle and Cork Convention wants to book you guys and Kool and the Gang."

This trade show for the liquor business was one of the biggest in New York City.

Kool and the Gang had just released their first album and were better known. We still didn't record, but we thought we were every bit as hot as Kool and the Gang.

We shuffled some classes—now, in my third year, our instructors were losing patience with the members of the band who were still in school. Was that gonna stop us from taking off to New York to the Bottle and Cork Convention? Hell, no. And, oh by the way, we killed.

Usually, I'd be the first to know what Benny had lined up for us. I mean, the phone at Grandma's was basically our business line.

And this explains how it happens that in the spring of 1970, late one evening, about 11 p.m., I hear the phone ring downstairs in my room (where it won't wake up Grandma).

For most of us music folks, late at night is more like four or five in the morning. That started for me our first summer in Harlem and just became a way of life. It is 1 a.m. in New York and Benny is also wide awake.

Benny begins, "I really hope you guys want to be famous."

"Yeah, Benny, we're gonna be famous, we're gonna take over the world. We're the baddest that ever was . . ." talking some shit like we always do.

"I hope you're really gonna be the Black Beatles 'cause I just quit my job to be your manager full-time."

Holy shit.

I hang up and bolt into action. The first person I reach is Thomas McClary.

Almost out of breath, holding the phone on a long cord as I pace, I tell him, "Get over here right away. It's an emergency. Help me get the rest of the guys. Benny just quit his job to manage us." We split up the calls.

Within the hour, everyone comes walking down the side of the house to the basement entrance, and they crowd in, all of us wearing the same expression of *What now?*

We quickly went from our egotistical "We're gonna kill!" to a desperate "We really gotta make it!" to finding the steel of "We gotta win because we can't let Benny down!"

And to his everlasting credit, Benny Ashburn got his hustle *on*.

WE WERE BACK in Harlem in late May 1970, in residence at Smalls for a third summer, when Benny met a young French music promoter who was an associate of Barrie Marshall, a heavyweight European promoter based in England. In the blink of an eye, arrangements were underway for us to make our European debut.

Europe? Unbelievable.

Benny, grinning like the new Harlem baller that he was becoming, rattled off our itinerary—we were going to fly first-class from New York to London before flying down to Nice. For the next three weeks we'd be performing at the three most happening, star-studded nightclubs along the French Riviera.

I called my folks to give them the exciting news.

Both were still in major denial. I had been a Commodore for two and a half years, but they hadn't stopped believing that it was only a phase. Their main concern was: "You'll be back in the fall in time for the start of classes?" It was only three weeks, I promised, and I'd check in often.

The timing of our stop in London meant that I'd be turning twenty-one in jolly old England, launchpad of the Beatles and the Rolling Stones. This was a dream come true.

Over the next month in New York, we maintained our usual

schedule at Smalls—playing until 4 a.m., then heading out to after-hours clubs until sunrise. We'd crawl back to crash until midday in our rooms at the Paris Hotel on Ninety-Seventh and West End, where we were staying. The art deco–style residential hotel, twenty-three stories high, was past its glory days, though it was a step up from Benny's apartment.

About ten days before we were set to leave for Europe, I ran into Greg, a friendly guy, as I passed through the sprawling lobby. He invited me to someone's party that night upstairs at the hotel.

Greg wouldn't take no for an answer.

Being a people pleaser, I said, "Sure!"

After work, around 4:30 a.m., I returned to the hotel exhausted. Why did I tell Greg I'd come? There would be drugs and I didn't do any of that, other than smoking pot now and then.

WAK—my roommate as usual—couldn't be talked into going. Only place he was going was to sleep.

I wavered, hating the idea of going by myself, but no, I promised. And besides, I was trying to get past my shyness.

As expected, at the party upstairs everybody's doing various drugs. I'm not partaking. Just to be social, yet safe, I go over to a little bar that's been set up with a few barstools, pour myself a glass of punch, and have a seat.

Goddamn punch.

Assuming it's alcohol, I sip on it. After a bit, I'm talking to the guy behind the bar and notice out of the corner of my eye that there's a brother at the end of the bar, two seats down from me, who's about to fall off his barstool. I turn back around to the guy behind the bar to continue the conversation. Moments later, to my horror, when I glance down again, I see the brother hasn't fallen completely off the barstool. He's still slo-mo falling.

Holy shit. I'm tripping on something.

Fuck, the punch must have been spiked. Later I'll think how ironic it is that I only drank it to be cordial. My immediate thought, as I bolt from my barstool, is, *Man, I gotta leave and get back to my room downstairs to be safe!*

I reach the hallway and make a beeline for the elevator. After running for it and pushing the call button, I forget pressing it and start to walk the other way. "Okay, Lionel," I say out loud, "calm down."

The sound of the elevator door opening freaks me out. I turn around to see that the wall has opened up and there are people trapped behind the open wall.

The wall has eaten them!

And very slowly, a guy in there says, "Come . . . on . . . in . . . fella," and motions with his hand like he's gonna grab my arm and pull me in.

Terrified, I turn and see the exit door and decide to take the steps. Next thing I know, I'm running down all the nine or so flights of stairs to the lobby. Out of breath—but I don't know why—my heart is beating out of my chest, pounding loud like a drum. I throw the door open. The lobby, more massive than I remember, is full of bright light and lots of colors. It's a maze. *Get me OUT!*

Nothing in my almost twenty-one years of life has ever made me feel like I've lost my mind or my control like this.

And it gets worse. I throw open the front doors of the lobby, now leaving the safety of the hotel, and run onto the streets of New York City. After running for what feels like a few blocks but is probably only to the next corner, I pause to hold on to a lamp post, and all of a sudden, I hear the most terrible sound— *BAMMMMMMM!* A taxicab has just missed hitting me and has crashed into . . . the phone booth. *Fuck!*

Okay, somehow, I need to calm myself.

Just then, you known what I see? Right across the street, I see a church. Hallelujah, there's a church. I run into the empty church and sit down in the nearest pew. And I'm talkin' to God for I don't know how long. Maybe for an hour.

God, you gotta get me out of this. I don't know what's goin' on, but I'm losing my mind. Cover me . . .

Eventually, I made my way back to the hotel and tried to wake up WAK, saying softly, "I gotta tell you something."

"Just go to bed, Richie."

The problem was that when I closed my eyes, all I'd see was a speedometer moving faster and faster. And there was a soundtrack. What song do I remember most of all? "The Long and Winding Road." The Beatles had just put that out.

This was the soundtrack to my nightmare that played over and over that disastrous day.

NOBODY KNEW WHAT happened to me. I didn't know that I had experienced an acute panic attack in reaction to a hallucinatory drug. The worst part was that I was having flashbacks all night that got worse the next day.

WAK thought I might be exaggerating. To prove to him how close I came to near catastrophe, I dragged him out to retrace my steps and show him. There was no sign of the wreckage of a taxicab. There was no phone booth. There was no church. "Richie," he said, "shake it off."

Easy for him to say. One minute I'd be normal, and then the next, walls would bend and people would move in slow motion and the floor would open up.

Months passed before I could shake the flashbacks.

There was no time to go home to recuperate, and New York City was not a prime location for recovery. The cars, the crowded sidewalks, the sounds of radios, conversations coming at you.

My inner monologue wouldn't shut up. *Am I crazy? I'm crazy! I have finally lost my damn mind in New York City.*

Very quickly I gave myself PTSD. The only positive was that in losing control, I felt freer to get to the Other Side, like my imagination was being supercharged. The imagery was wild. It was scary but darkly fascinating.

For years I have laughed that I have no recollection of my twenty-first birthday in London. That damn punch—I was still high.

Then we all had to laugh that, as the saying goes, everything that could go wrong did go wrong. Benny had made us promise that under no circumstance would we give our passports and our tickets to anyone who asked for them. We listened, we heard.

In our separation of duties in the band, WAK, the practical, organized guy, kept our passports and plane tickets when we traveled. As the banker, my job was to oversee the money—because who should keep track of cash, the guy who holds on to it or the guy who spends too much?

Immediately upon our arrival, the promoter who met us in the South of France said, "I need to have your passports and plane tickets to check your visas," and WAK, Mr. By-the-Book, did so promptly. Somehow our papers ended up missing for the whole summer, as I recall.

Then I fell down on my budgeting duties when we all ended up paying $300 each for hamburgers. I could never figure out the French currency, and I would hold up the money and the waiters would just grab bills and say, "Merci, Monsieur."

But the best part of that long summer was soaking up a totally new way of life. In Nice, where we played at Acu-Acu, a trendy club, we lived in a comfortable flat above a bakery. I was in love with the countryside, the rolling hills, not many cars, people out walking and riding bikes—everything beautiful and peaceful.

We used to go to a great place to eat, run by a very charming, bohemian-style Frenchwoman, a fantastic cook and hostess. Everything tasted delicious, as close to home cooking as we could have asked for. When she didn't serve coq au vin, we would be treated to rabbit. Or so we thought. We were later told that if rabbit is served and there is no rabbit's foot on the plate, then you, my friend, are eating cat. As in kitty cat.

Every day was a new experience.

It became clear to me why France had attracted so many African American artists, musicians, and writers—Josephine Baker, Charlie Parker, James Baldwin, Quincy Jones. In those decades, the hang-ups about racial differences seemed to have no place in civil society.

We could not have gone at a more mind-altering time. *Hair* was the hottest musical in Europe, and everyone on the French Riviera was talking about the new *it* couple—Mick and Bianca. This was the cusp of the seventies, ground zero for the explosion of free love in popular culture. Someone walking nude down the street was just—*Okay, so what?* For beach attire, topless was fully dressed.

At twenty-one I had never experienced walking on the beach and passing girls—ladies, really—and having one lady hold up her bottle of suntan oil at Hotel Byblos Saint-Tropez and say, in an accent, "Pardon me. Can you rub oil on Mommy's back?" *Oh. My. God. What would a gentleman say?*

"Yes, ma'am," was my well-mannered, Southern answer.

Did I rub oil on her back? Yes! Was she older than me? Yes! And so were many of the patrons in the clubs where we were performing. Who cared?

We'd be in the middle of playing, say, at Acu-Acu, and I'd look into the audience and see a couple relaxing on cushions, making love right there, almost like in a painting. I'd blink to make sure I was seeing this correctly. And I was.

Mon Dieu, this was crazy.

"When in Rome . . ." as the old saying goes.

Back in the States, I was familiar with how it worked. We have a thing in Alabama where you meet a girl and you take her home after the show. Over here in France, the clubs are set with low-to-the-ground futons and everyone can lounge. The club-goers are the show. They're massaging scented oil on people's toes, and they're disrobing and kissing and making love. Meanwhile, I'm trying to play, and what the frick am I looking at?

And the girls we're meeting are so welcoming and it's free love, and nobody seems to be jealous. If it's a hallucination, I don't mind.

Shortly before we returned home, our passports and plane tickets back in our possession, I realized it had been a while since I had talked to my parents. Getting a call through was not easy. Often you had to place the call a day ahead of time, and my schedule made that even tougher.

At last, this one day I was able to get through and my parents answered on different extensions. "Lionel, so good to hear from you," my mom spoke first, relief in her voice.

"Son," my dad said next, with a tinge of annoyance, as if to ask why I hadn't called sooner.

For three summers, I had been away from home and had survived. The time had come to announce that I no longer needed permission.

"Dad," I began, thinking he'd understand if I used code. "Do you remember all the things you told me that were bad for me?"

"Yes, son."

"I like 'em."

Immediately, my dad said, "Alberta, get off the phone."

Mom hung up. My father and I had never talked about my experiences with the opposite sex, and he may have wondered whether I was even into women. In this time, friends of the family had sons who had come out as gay. Maybe he thought that's where this conversation was headed.

To be sure, he asked, "Boy, what, um, what are you talking about?"

"You know, Dad, there are two girls that like me. So I'm hanging with both of them."

My dad chuckled. No kidding. Oh, and there was more. "You know, boy, let me tell you, your mother, she's a fine woman. But, you know, back in the War, your dad knew of a ménage à 'trey' in Germany." He pronounced it like that: *trey*.

"Yeah?"

"Your dad can speak a little *voulez-vous*, you know . . ." he carried on, cracking me up.

All the hard-ass stuff began to peel away. We started being able to talk about anything, like guys, and, though it took a few more years, I slowly got to know the dad who became my best friend in life.

The change for us was more than "now we could talk about man stuff." It was also about me accepting that I didn't need his approval to make my own decisions, right or wrong, about my life and who I wanted to be in it.

And that, I learned, is the *ultimate* golden ticket.

Liftoff

(1970–1982)

The thing I am to do and the way of doing it are
revealed to me. I never have to grope for methods.
The method is revealed to me the moment I am
inspired to create something new. Without God
to draw aside the curtain I would be helpless.

—GEORGE WASHINGTON CARVER (1864–1943),
REMARKS DELIVERED NOVEMBER 18, 1924,
MARBLE COLLEGIATE CHURCH IN NEW YORK CITY

7

Jackson 5

THERE'S A POINT IN TIME that sticks out, circa Thanksgiving 1970, when I sensed something *big* was around the corner.

The Commodores had arrived back to campus in late September, weeks after classes started. Most of us cut our course load with some independent study so that we didn't have to worry about flunking out. My plan for senior year was to complete enough credits to graduate the following spring with the class of 1971.

I was still plagued by occasional flashbacks, but my coping mechanism was to try to be . . . *cool*.

Besides, this was my favorite time of year in Tuskegee. Football weather. Late fall, early winter. Barely a chill yet.

The season was changing along with everything else. The sixties had come and gone, and now, welcome to the seventies. *Boom*. The Civil Rights Movement, fueled by a worldwide cultural embrace of "Black is beautiful," was still revving up. Anti-war sentiment was intensifying, moving to Main Street. And, man, free love was starting to happen—not just in the South of France but, bit by bit, in the USA too.

Some of the "*voulez-vous coucher avec moi*" stuff was much too out there for the serious activists in Tuskegee. Me, I still had my tam and glove—I mean, of course. But now I was Mr. Worldly Musician, back from Europe with my brothers in our latest custom-made uniforms: flared tie-dye pants and mile-high platform shoes, not to mention my competitively oversize Afro. We'd returned looking like the last gigolos out of the South of France.

My dear friend, Wilma Jones, the campus embodiment of Black awareness, stopped in her tracks to check us out, and just said, "What the *hell* is wrong with you guys?"

Us? We were clueless that we were back in American reality, so out of place.

Alabama took a while to catch up to Saint-Tropez, but before long the vibe was best captured in "Love the One You're With" by Stephen Stills, released in November 1970 (when he left Crosby, Stills, Nash, and Young to do a solo album). The Commodores, staying current, decided to include it in our all-genres repertoire.

There's a skill to learning how to feel famous before you ever get to be famous. On campus we were major celebrities—still figuring out how to get the world to catch up.

Benny was working on it. Days before Thanksgiving, in fact, he'd gotten us a last-minute gig at Lloyd Price's Turntable, a club in Midtown, on Broadway, between Fifty-Second and Fifty-Third.

We'd made this trip so many dang times, we figured we'd drive the seventeen hours straight through and arrive early enough to set up, change, have a bite to eat, and play.

One hitch: We did not plan for a snowstorm.

A blanket of sleet and snow hit us on the New Jersey Turnpike, then one of the van's tires blew and we skidded and slid over to the shoulder, barely missing a semitruck that jackknifed in front of us.

After changing the tire, we set off again, hoping to get to NYC on fumes, but were stopped at a tollbooth that took only coins that we did not have.

Mercifully, the tollbooth lady paid our toll and directed us to a service station, where we were about to trade equipment for a tank of gas when we called Benny, who promised to send money to the attendant for "loaning" us a quarter tank—enough to get us to Lloyd Price's Turntable and onto the stage for our slot. Only fifteen minutes late.

Like I said, *You can't make this shit up!*

We had one of our best shows ever. This was the original Birdland, named for the Jazz legend Charlie Parker. There was history in that downstairs room, which had the feel of a speakeasy, a hidden grotto.

By the wee hours, we finally made it to Benny's in Harlem, where I camped out in my regular spot under his dining room table. We slept until the evening, when Benny returned from Thanksgiving dinner—with big news.

THE SUBTITLE OF Benny's account was *It's a Small World.*

Benny had gone to the home of his sister, Miriam Walker, who lived in the upscale Harlem neighborhood of Sugar Hill.

Some of us knew Miriam from when we visited Martha's Vineyard. One of her closest friends was Eunice Brown de Passe, whose family also owned a home on the Vineyard, and whose daughter, Suzanne, now in her early twenties, had grown up, like Benny, in the same Harlem / Oak Bluffs / East Chop social set.

In fact, he was *Uncle* Benny to her.

This was fate. Why? Because Benny had been trying to find a smooth angle to tell Suzanne, who worked in the record business, about the Commodores.

Benny had our attention. Then he told us that Suzanne used to book talent at the Cheetah Club, before she happened to meet Berry Gordy—the founder of Motown, the record company he named for the Motor City, a.k.a. Detroit, Michigan.

Suzanne complained to Mr. Gordy that she was having trouble getting her calls returned when she tried to book Motown artists. She brashly told him, "The people who work for you are losing you money."

Berry Gordy asked if she could do a better job, and she said she could try. He hired her, sensing she had a feel for talent, and told her never to hold back from coming to him with honest input, even if it meant being critical, because, he said, "I pay people for their ideas, not mine."

Maybe that's why, Benny told us, Gordy listened when Suzanne chased him down—about a year later—as he was on his way into the Detroit high-rise where Motown had its business offices. She wanted to set up an audition for a group of five brothers, ages nine to sixteen, from Gary, Indiana.

Suzanne gave her report to Mr. Gordy in a literal elevator pitch. He was wary of kid groups—the chaperones, the tutors, the short-lived novelty—but Suzanne had his ear and promised he would feel differently about these Jackson kids. Within the week the audition was set, and Mr. Gordy signed them in the room.

Suzanne at the time was already working closely with Diana Ross—who would soon be launching her solo career. In addition, she was put in charge of everything Jackson 5—other than their records. Pulling out the stops, Berry Gordy assembled the hottest teams of songwriters and producers, and he joined in as well. Over the period of one year, from late 1969 to late 1970, the Motown machine gave the J-5 four consecutive

#1 hits—"I Want You Back," "ABC," "The Love You Save," and "I'll Be There."

Unprecedented.

In no time, the J-5 took their place beside the other giants of Motown: Diana Ross and the Supremes, Smokey Robinson and the Miracles, Marvin Gaye, Stevie Wonder, the Four Tops, the Temptations, Gladys Knight, and the list went on.

The Jackson 5 was to be the last group birthed in Detroit and the first to be raised in Los Angeles—where Motown was moving. The move to LA, setting up a West Coast studio, and getting into film and TV—all of that was part of Suzanne's responsibilities, along with a pressing need for opening acts for the latest tours. "Know anybody?" she asked Benny.

"I do," he answered immediately. "They're all asleep at my apartment, including under the dining room table." He set the audition for the next day.

WE ARE HALFWAY through what might be the biggest break of our lives, downstairs at Lloyd Price's Turntable.

The trick is to play our climactic Commodores "Showtime!" set for a small group in winter wear in this dark cavern as if the joint is jumping and we're casting a spell over everyone.

From the first note, we're smokin' hot.

Out in the dark of the club, I can see Suzanne glance at Benny, giving him a tentative nod.

With only a couple songs to go, I know it's my turn to sing lead. A trickle of sweat begins. I fight the panic as I prepare to go to the mic center stage and then lean into it and sing, "I am a lineman for the county . . ."

I'm terrified, but the thought that I could blow this for the guys helps me calm down.

I begin the song, as I always do, in character. I am the lineman who will now become the storyteller. I lose myself for the duration of the song and then—*snap!*—come back into the moment.

Applause, applause.

After our last song, Suzanne jumps to her feet, impressed. With her, as I'll soon learn, is Tony Jones, her cousin, recently hired by Motown to help her on the tour, looking wowed. Also in their group, smiling, is Skip Miller, about to start his Motown rise to top radio promotion executive. Suzanne shakes our hands, asks us each our names, and thanks Benny for putting it together.

We are about to leave when Suzanne makes an executive decision. "You know," she says, "we need an opening act tomorrow night." She informs us that it's in Rochester, New York, at an arena with a seating capacity of over twelve thousand—bigger than any venue we've played. Suzanne doesn't say who the headliner is. Like we'd say no. "Your set has to be forty minutes exactly," she adds. "Not a minute less or more."

We spent the rest of the day making sure we had bolted down a forty-minute set that would kill anytime, anywhere.

For the next several decades, I was convinced that Suzanne de Passe fell in love with the Commodores because she saw we already looked and performed like pros—and that we were musically versatile. And that was what she saw in us, for sure.

The part I didn't know was that the tipping point at the audition was my solo. Forty years later, she remembered that what grabbed her was when "this guy comes out and sings a Jimmy Webb song."

But no one told me that at the time.

Suzanne was surprised, she'd say, by how emotional and beautiful my version of the song was. And that was her connection to us and to me. "I will always believe after seeing this guy singing 'Wichita Lineman' that his crooning voice is everything." She sensed, before many others did, that doing ballads held promise, because as she said, "That is where I think the seductive power of Lionel Richie's voice lives."

At age twenty-one, I would never have put myself in the same sentence as the words *seductive* and *power*. Never.

I was just grateful to be along for the ride.

We were all in fine spirits as we passed through the Rochester city limits and approached the Community War Memorial, our destination.

Ronald LaPread, best-natured human you'd be lucky to know, cussed under his breath when we came around to the front of the arena and read the marquee: TONIGHT ONLY! THE JACKSON 5 WITH SPECIAL GUESTS—THE COMMODORES.

We had suspected this as a remote possibility. Until we saw our name as special guests, though, we had no idea how that would feel. My first thought was *Thank God we play Top 40*. That didn't stop us from *freaking* out.

Maybe it was better that nobody told us we'd be playing for an arena full of children *screaming* for the J-5 so loud we couldn't hear ourselves. Rochester had the Jackson 5 fever and all we could do was have fun, do our thing, and capture their interest for forty fleeting minutes.

That night, before we heard any reports of how we did, we watched from the wings as the members of the J-5 took the stage with a command that was shocking. Their covers were flawless and their up-tempo hits "I Want You Back" and "ABC" had the entire arena on their feet going wild. I mean, wild. And Michael, twelve years old, mesmerized everyone with their ballads—"I'll Be There" and "Never Can Say Goodbye." It wasn't only the purity of his voice but the feeling underneath the lyrics.

Only an old soul, as Michael was, could have told those stories with such heartfelt emotion. The same maturity was true of his brothers—Marlon (thirteen), Jermaine (almost sixteen), Tito (seventeen), and Jackie (nineteen).

After the show backstage—as we waited for security to clear the exits because of all the fans trying to get backstage—the Jackson brothers ambled over to say hello and compliment us. Everybody introduced themselves and then, naturally, started jabbering about regular stuff that kids of our respective ages might talk about.

One of the Commodores, in a thick Alabama accent, said, "And this is Lio*nel* Richie," and noted that I was shy.

I believe that Michael, who had his own form of shyness when he was offstage, said, "Nice to meet you Lion-*nel* Richie." From that day forward, for the next thirty-nine years, Michael pronounced my name like he too was born and bred in Tuskegee.

With that, the Jacksons were whisked out with their security detail. Suzanne and Benny came back and informed us that we were hired.

We were now the opening act for the Jackson 5 on their world tour that was scheduled to include a stop in every single one of the fifty states in the USA.

[|||||||]

THE PLAN WAS to ease into part one of the tour for a few months with a handful of dates—starting in December 1970—so all the various kinks could be worked out.

The schedule made it possible for us to get back to Tuskegee during the week and then perform on the weekends. Our first dates took us to North Carolina—Charlotte and Greensboro—followed by Nashville, Tennessee. Right away, the difference in scale was bracing. These were arenas and colosseums, mostly anywhere from six thousand to nine thousand seats. Sold out by the Jackson 5.

We had cut our teeth playing clubs, clubs, and mo' clubs. For the past year we'd been an in-demand band on university campuses, occasionally playing theaters like the Apollo in Harlem and the Fox in Atlanta. Going from 4,500 max to 12,000 just didn't faze us.

We were fortunate to have a front-row seat to the coaching of the J-5 on how to kill with every performance, even how to handle the press and television appearances. Very valuable information. Onstage they were technicians. You wanted to watch, you wanted to listen.

The Jacksons were unusually aware of their responsibility to deliver.

Whenever Motown executives attended rehearsals, I'd hover, soaking up every tidbit I could learn about record releases, radio play, and concert promotion. Mainly, I was eager to understand the Business: *What's involved in radio promotion? Wait, are you telling me you have one executive to promote records to Black DJs and somebody else to promote to white radio?*

Mostly this was an effort to take my future as an artist more seriously. At the same time, the fearful part of me still thought I could use a plan B and find a place in the Record Business—in case for whatever reason I was no longer in the Commodores.

J-5 rehearsals ran like clockwork. Their punctuality and discipline were ironclad.

We soon learned that "Thou shalt be on time" was a real commandment at Motown. People told stories about the all-important Quality Control meetings (where the next record releases were chosen) and how Berry Gordy used to lock out latecomers, even top producers. Or fine them heavily. The Commodores instituted our own policy for fining each other over lateness.

Watching the Jacksons work with a choreographer, I'd think, *These kids must have been born dancing.* You only had to show Michael something once and he nailed it. This kid could do three *frick'n* pirouettes, come out, do a split, come up, put the coat on his shoulder, and keep singing. At twelve years old.

Shockingly, once the Jacksons left the stage, they'd turn back into regular-ass kids who wanted to hang with us.

We were like their college cousins, not so much older, and hilariously, we could be just as silly as them. The J-5 excelled in practical jokes. They were relentless. If we left our shoes out to be shined, they'd put ice cubes in them. They'd sneak up and put itching powder in our hair. Ronald LaPread got pranked so bad one time. Early one morning there was a knock at our hotel door, and he went to answer it—only to be doused with a bucket of ice water.

We were all completely juvenile. At one point, we decided to take them on—with the pillow fight of life: The Jackson 5 versus the Commodores. No one knew but us. We set a time, picked a room at the hotel where we were all staying, and brought in extra pillows. As soon as we began, we realized they had a strategy—the older, taller Jacksons lined up behind their younger brothers, Michael and Marlon. The assumption was, obviously, nobody would take a swipe at the younger Jacksons—especially Michael, the star of the whole show. As soon as we backed off, Jackie, Jermaine, and Tito jumped out and started swinging hard. Gotta hand it to those kids, their strategy worked. That is, until we were in the heat of the action and I swung a pillow at Michael—and knocked his ass right off his feet. *Yes!* He wasn't hurt at all, but when word got out, I was *the* problem.

Suzanne de Passe went off. "What were you thinking? You could have broken his leg! Or worse!" I apologized, naturally. Of course, we got those kids good and they respected us for it.

We started to form alliances along common interests. Jermaine, who played bass, bonded with Ronald, our bass player. And Tito, who played guitar, bonded with Thomas, our guitar player. This happened with all of us. I think Michael and I struck up a friendship because he was a kid and could sense that so was I.

I have a vivid memory of a night on our tour that year when we were about to open the show at Madison Square Garden. I was twenty-two and he was about to turn thirteen.

"Lion-*nel*, look!" Michael said ten minutes before the show was to start. He waved me over to a spot in the wings, at a corner of the stage, where we both could see what a crowd of more than nineteen thousand youngsters and their parents looked like.

The building was shaking before we even played a note. Michael, in awe of this feat, said to me all-knowingly, "Lion-*nel*, can you believe that? *We* sold out Madison Square Garden!"

"Nah, we didn't sell out *nuth'n*, you sold it out." I meant him and his brothers.

"*We* did." He meant all of us, I assumed.

He used "we" whenever he looked into the future, always with plans to keep topping himself and promising, "*We* are gonna be bigger than big, Lion-*nel*."

The sight of a sold-out Madison Square Garden was a sight I will never, ever forget. Walking out on that stage for the first time felt like floating on air, with a view from the crow's nest of a ship—fitting for a member of a band that had named itself the Commodores.

I couldn't see how on earth any of this could get any bigger than that, but I promise you that Michael Jackson could.

LET ME REWIND for a moment. Somebody—I can't remember who it was—had a brainstorm for the Commodores to enjoy some after-hours escapades in the early days of our tour.

After Harlem and the South of France, you would have thought that I was Mr. Ladies' Man of the century.

Not by a long shot.

What we had learned was that seeing someone holding a mic or an instrument can be as much of a turn-on as watching an athlete spike the football. We decided to test this premise in every town. After playing every arena, we'd hit every after-hours bar or club or party with the finest girls across the nation and wreak havoc. We didn't have to go to bed with everyone, or at all. Whether it was a drink, a kiss, or whatever. Ladies' choice.

Here we go.

We're new at the game, as a band opening for the J-5, getting our professional tour legs under us, and we begin in Atlanta (for example). And we *kill*. After the show, we take over the clubs all night. Party the next day. We meet every imaginable beauty Atlanta has to offer then drive to the next city. We are not driving the van much anymore because our equipment and wardrobe are on the truck with the J-5's stuff. Now the difference is that the Jacksons are flying and being driven in limos to the better hotels. We are in a couple of our own cars, or taking the bus, or an occasional airplane, and staying mostly in motels.

That does not slow us down when we get to Charleston, South Carolina, where the flowers are in bloom. (It's a metaphor—interpret as you will.) We throw down at this show and go out, party all night, stumble back to our motel, sleep a couple hours, and then drive to Washington, DC. We do the show—*bam*, we kill it. Knowing we have a day off, we buy more partying time. Phew. Now I'm exhausted. Only, guess what?

We have a show in New York City, and we know the clubs in every borough. We roll out of there, and there ain't a girl left for anybody else to flirt with.

The plan hit a snag in Philadelphia. Why? *Welllll*, I missed the party after the show because I was tired.

And then we went to Boston. Shit. I missed the party again. I was a little hoarse and still hungover from New York. Our next date was in Pittsburgh, and I was already done. No more parties. No more rampaging. In sum, it took five and a half cities to convince a late bloomer that it was absolutely impossible to seduce your way across a tour. You cannot, it will not happen. You can't sing a show, party all night, drink your ass under the table, maybe screw, and then make the next show the next night. I don't care if you are in your absolute prime, you may have those kind of dreams, but you don't have that kind of testosterone.

The learning curve is too steep. I could manage, "Hi, I'm Lionel. Um, are you hungry for breakfast?" but I couldn't start with, "Let's get naked."

I'm too polite.

I tell you this ahead of time. Whatever you have heard, it's grossly exaggerated. And some of it's true.

Yes, I said it—*Some of it's true.*

If that is shocking to anyone who thinks, *Oh, my, this can't be, Lionel's so pure*, let me jump ahead and respond. *Pure?* My ass.

Listen, y'all, I survived my impurity.

Okay, I'm talking about later, during the wild partying excesses of the 1980s when I was trying to keep up with the likes of Rick James. I loved Rick. He was crazy and fun and over-the-top talented. You couldn't hang with him. Nobody could. Rick wanted to party every day and night. I used to try to hang with the Funkadelics. Couldn't do it. Hanging with George Clinton—who I love and who is still a friend—was an

E ticket ride. But, no, I couldn't hang with him or any of the Parliament Funkadelic crew.

At some point, I got to know Teddy Pendergrass. You cannot hang. You don't want to try. You will die from trying to be so much of a chameleon that you think you are him. You've got to go home.

My survival can be attributed to two words, the two most boring words that I was going to have to learn, not only in Show Business but certainly in having a semblance of a meaningful love life. Those two words are: "Good night."

Part of maturity, for me, was paying attention in the early going, when I could, to the truth that I had a choice. You either hang or you sing the show the next night. I'm stating this from years into the future, of course, because I was, as we know, slow on the maturity track.

People tell me, "If I were you, I would have had more restraint."

My response has been, "If you were me, you would have been dead by now."

There is no prep course for how to grow up when given attention you've never had. Expecting someone unprepared to handle sudden fame is like giving a baby a Ferrari. That's a surefire crash.

The Commodores' short-lived worldwide seduction effort served as a cautionary preview. When you win, you win the girls. When you win, you're in the money. If you want drugs, you get all the drugs. And if you want twenty-four-hour partying, they give you forty-eight-hour partying.

Now, let me tell you what you can't handle. *All* of that. It was by divine intervention that I learned this ahead of flying too close to the sun. If you understand that this is a life and death dance, early on in your career—before the rocket ship has lost contact with ground control—you stand a chance at survival. The moral of this story: Man must know his limitations.

SOMEWHERE, DURING A break in the action, when I was back on campus, I had spotted *her*—twirling her baton, moving gracefully in formation with her fellow Piperettes. They were out on the practice field rehearsing their routine with Tuskegee's Crimson Pipers, the oldest high-stepping, musically gifted marching band of any HBCU in the country.

She had been sent from central casting to play the part of Major Love Interest in the movie I'd been dreaming for my life. She was gorgeous, the girl next door, soulful, and—because I saw her laughing—apparently funny. She looked so carefree.

Who was she? Too shy to introduce myself, I enlisted friends to make introductions. She was Brenda Harvey, a freshman, from a small town in Alabama, the daughter of a military father and a schoolteacher mother. The answer was "No" to the question, *Could you miss her?* It was that simple.

I didn't know how it would feel to have someone genuinely care about me, to dig below the surface.

Enter Brenda. From the start, we had a lot in common—both raised with the values of family, church, community, and the almighty importance of getting a college education. We also had differences—more than her being a freshman when I was a senior. Where I avoided confrontation, Brenda had no problem speaking her mind. She was *direct*.

For our first date, I didn't want to go overboard. Nothing too intimate. And I had to stay within my budget.

Did I say *budget*? My nickname was still Jack Benny.

People assumed that because the Commodores were starting to make it, that meant we were rolling in the money.

Nope. Same old story. Opening for the Jackson 5 was impressive, but we split the money with six guys and paid a cut to a manager—far from living large.

Fortunately, my thrifty proposal—"We could go for a couple of milkshakes."—was kindly received.

"Dairy Queen?"

Brenda's eyes brightened and she said yes. Only one condition: "I'm bringing my roommate with me." She was referring to Janet Warren (later Janet Shorter), her best friend forever. Oldest trick in the book! Brenda was gonna drag Janet along to chaperone our date and check out my references.

"Oh, okay," I said. But now I had a cash flow problem.

I was a senior, a Commodore, famous (on campus), playing a few tour dates, and she was a freshman I wanted to impress. Except . . . what the hell, I was gonna be on tap for *three* milkshakes?

On the way up to the counter, I came up with the solution—which led to the joke that, later, Brenda and Janet and everyone who heard it never stopped telling: "Lionel was so tight, he bought me and Janet one milkshake with two straws."

True story.

Then and now, I make no apology. The three of us drank our shakes, theirs with the two straws, and mine with my one straw, and neither Brenda nor Janet commented. After the date was over, as both would tell me, Janet turned to Brenda and warned, "This brother's broke. This brother's so cheap."

That could have been the end.

Later, in the throes of success, whenever anyone asked where I was in my career when I met Brenda, the answer was—*Back when I could only afford two milkshakes.* If anyone ever suggested that Brenda Harvey fell for me for my money, I'd correct that assumption. "Nope, I don't think so."

The Dairy Queen anecdote was told all over campus and spread over time—*Lionel was so tight, he out–Jack Benny'd Jack Benny!*

And you know what? I loved every minute of it. Every other man on the hunt had to flash the cash. How lame. In an act of noble individuality, I went the other way and sent a clear message: *Just letting y'all know, up front, there is no cash, and if that's what you need, it's not gonna happen, babes.*

Not for a while.

You'd think after a first date like that, there might never be a second date. Luckily, Brenda did not count me out. She thought I was funny. I made her laugh.

(If you are taking notes, you'll recall that's what my mother said about why she married my dad.)

Brenda always listened to me like I was amazing. That's a heady potion. She became my number one fan. Everything that was about to happen would be on her watch. With or without success, she cared about *me*.

I'd asked myself, *Well, what other girls cared about you before Brenda?* Not too many.

The clincher was the intangible of, *You get me, you understand me, and you're willing to wait for me to grow up? Because that could be a long wait.*

My limited knowledge of relationships was raggedy, stitched together from hearsay. I'd later understand why you need to have the failures—because they prepare you for the inevitable strains that come with the ties that bind. Meaning—I had a lot to learn.

THERE WERE TWO opening acts on the J-5 tour—the Commodores and recently signed Motown artist Yvonne Fair. We'd open the show with our five songs and then remain on-stage to back Yvonne when she came out.

Smart. This saved Motown from having to hire another band for the road.

Our set list, selected for us, was about as mainstream (white) as you could get: "Love the One You're With" (Stephen Stills), "Liar" (Argent, covered by Three Dog Night), "You've Got A Friend" (Carole King, covered by James Taylor), with the occasional "Wichita Lineman." The only Black group we covered was Sly and the Family Stone with "Dance to the Music." No real Funk to be had.

R&B and downright Soul was the domain of Yvonne Fair—who could sing her ass off. She had previously sung backup with James Brown and had a raucous delivery. After our first couple of shows, Suzanne pulled me aside and said, "We want you to sing with Yvonne." They chose two duets—Ike and Tina Turner's "River Deep, Mountain High" and "Proud Mary."

What a gift to be mentored onstage by an artist who'd been mentored by James Brown. Yvonne taught me that if you worry about hitting the big notes and doing the dazzling vocal runs, you forget the most important element—the feeling, the emotion of the song.

Yvonne was a light. She was only twenty-eight years old and yet she had seen some real life, which came through in her delivery. Later, in the mid-seventies, she tore it up with one of the greatest torch songs ever sung on a record—"It Should Have Been Me" by Norman Whitfield and Mickey Stevenson.

Offstage, Yvonne was kind of like Mama to all of us. She offered us worldly wisdom that usually began, "Honey, let me tell you what's really happening . . ."

Our biggest problem early in the tour was that we'd never played to audiences who were mostly six to twelve years old. Still, we were being well received, and we started to worry that we might make the J-5 feel like we were stealing their thunder.

The Commodores called a meeting. The consensus was: "Our job is just to warm up, not to take over the night." That's why opening acts do fewer songs and the reason that the volume and lights are set lower.

At the next show, we didn't go full-out and even tamped down our "Showtime!" intro. Backstage during intermission, the brothers Jackson didn't react, but when they went out for their set, the five of them killed like never before, doubling their output.

Yvonne saw the shock on our faces. "Honey, let me tell you what's really happening . . ." she began, and then said our choice was to either be Mickey Mouse in our flashy red jumpsuits *or* accept that we were really playing for the mothers and fathers of the kids.

Ohhhhh . . .

No need to tone down. We went even harder, performing as if we were the main attraction. No one seemed to mind. *Except* . . . maybe Joe Jackson—who was friendly but not one to compliment anybody who might take the focus off his sons.

Don't get me wrong, opening for the J-5 was a dream come true. The only issue was that we were grown-ups.

After a while, we admitted to Yvonne that we were going stir-crazy. If we wanted to meet anyone and go out for a drink, we couldn't date the fans who were moms of the kids. Besides, as far as I could see, "These ain't no club folk, these are church folks."

Yvonne had cabin fever too. She was the only woman on the tour other than Suzanne, and they weren't going to the clubs either. For consolation, we'd grab Yvonne, go out, and grab a drink or two at the hotel bar.

One night, after a couple of drinks, all six of us and Yvonne went up to our rooms. We said good night in the hall, and the rest of us went to hang out in one of our suites. We were about ready to head off to bed, at about 2:30 or 3:00 a.m., when we all heard a woman calling out, "Somebody! Somebody!"

We ran out to the hall and saw Yvonne, clearly having had too much to drink.

She looked at all of us and said, "Somebody come and get me. Come and get me."

We all fell out. Yvonne was serious. Then she sighed and added, "I am so sick and tired of six-to-twelve-year-olds!"

MICHAEL JACKSON MUST have known I had this Other Side where I'd hear stuff or where I'd go to daydream.

We never talked about it, but he had it too. We talked about everything else. After a rehearsal or before the show, we'd sit on the edge of the stage or get to talking as we walked.

Michael had a way of looking up into the lights, far off, and then looking back at me, making sure I saw what he saw. And whatever he saw for himself, he saw for me too.

In a softish voice, he asked me one night, during the first leg of the tour, "Lion-*nel*, do you know? Do you know what bigger than big is?"

I nodded. Did I? He was pushing me.

I was given a chance to hear this kid's inner child talk about how big he *wanted* to be. He let me glimpse how he saw this vision of celebrity. And it was *gigantic*.

Could I see it? The way he put it, yes. My inner child couldn't see it for me on my own, but when thirteen-year-old Michael Jackson and I hung out after a show on the edge of the stage and looked into any empty auditorium—suddenly I could believe.

Man, this little kid, if he was a motivational speaker, he'd have you walking on coals before you realized, *What the fuck am I doing walking on these coals?*

His career never surprised me because it was all there with

the lights in his eyes. In less than a year after our tour, Motown released his first solo single, "Got to Be There," and his solo album debut of the same name. For a time, he remained with his brothers as well, continuing as a part of the J-5.

The story had been foretold long ago. He went from the novelty of the group before long to . . . *I need to move on from the group*. No surprise. There are a handful of artists who have that larger-than-life quality that takes over. And that was him, as gigantic as the vision he had for himself. Always.

Michael and I were both escape artists. The tour allowed me to accept that playing music and being onstage, fears and all, was the greatest escape ever. Michael had always known that.

The difference was that while I was escaping the unknown world and not being sure of where the hell I fit in, Michael was escaping the pressures of the world he was entrenched in—the entertainment industry, his fans, and a difficult family dynamic I didn't understand.

He kept that turmoil a secret for a long time. We only knew that Joe Jackson was a disciplinarian. What was evident was that Joe loved his children, his family, and was out to protect their best interests, but that he had to have control.

Michael didn't talk to me about his father making him self-conscious for his big nose or holding a strap during practice, though I heard those stories.

He would say publicly, "My childhood was completely taken away from me." Many who start careers at a young age feel the same. I had to give up a college life. Did I miss it? In the end, no—because I chose it. Michael desperately missed what he never had.

And he never had a shot. He was this little boy whose every waking hour was regimented—no regular social life or every-day fun at a playground or park.

The studio became his playground. And it happened soooo

fast. When we were painting our fantasy of being bigger than big, I thought we were just talking some shit. Turned out, *I* was talking some shit but Michael was already *on* it.

If he taught me anything, it was the lesson that, if you are going to build a dream, you must learn to plan—to be pre-meditated. If there was a roadblock of any kind up ahead, he'd say, "Lion-*nel*, now what are *we* gonna do here?" Or if he saw an opportunity for me, he'd ask, "And what are *you* gonna do now, Lion-*nel*? How are *you* gonna fix it?"

Michael was a forecaster. Whatever was in front of him, you better believe he had the script written by the time he got to it.

To learn from the best, he asked everyone he admired—producers, writers, arrangers, musicians, dancers, movie directors. He'd call up famous people he'd never met, put on an accent, and get them to laugh and then ask if they would work with him.

When we all saw the iconic image of him on his toes, pelvis thrust, hat tipped, and head bowed, we knew that was inspired by everything he learned from adopting the moves of the Nicholas Brothers, Sammy Davis Jr., Gene Kelly and Fred Astaire, and Gregory Hines. Oh, and Baryshnikov. "Lion-*nel*," he'd later call and ask, "can you come to the ballet this weekend with me and Elizabeth Taylor?"

And thankfully I happened to be in LA and was able to witness the most unforgettable guest performance by Mikhail Baryshnikov with the Los Angeles Ballet—the hottest ticket in town and what was billed as one of his last performances. Never could I have imagined that Baryshnikov would be meaningful to my own story and career later on.

Michael also paid attention to the street, to kids who were breakdancing and gliding in their sneakers—and that was the moonwalk. He didn't invent the moves, but he combined them, and, like a magician, made them his own and brought them to the masses. And that is *everything*.

Michael and I were just kids, nine years apart, him in his early teens, me in my early twenties, talking how he would be bigger than Elvis while "my" band would be bigger than the Beatles. We'd talk about the perils and harsh realities too—about Jimi Hendrix, Janis Joplin, and Jim Morrison, all in their twenties, all who died from drug overdoses.

We considered other Show Business pitfalls—jealousy, infighting, making it rich and losing it all, and how good luck can go wrong. We talked about how we'd avoid the traps, the way kids talk about slaying dragons.

Whenever we spoke of the tragedies, Michael, the lights in his eyes, would only shake his head with complete confidence and say, "*We're* never gonna let that happen to us, Lion-*nel*. Never."

Who was I to argue?

That was then. But life doesn't work that way. Celebrity doesn't work that way. Everybody falls into unseen traps. Everybody. Shit happens that you didn't plan, it just does.

You didn't plan on the accident, or the illness, or the depression, or the loss. You didn't fall in love to fall out of love. You didn't get married to get a divorce. You didn't plan on hurting somebody. You didn't plan on having kids who resent you. You didn't plan on joining a band and then hearing the call of opportunities elsewhere. You didn't plan on being a prisoner of your fame or wishing you could have planned differently.

It is a heavy burden to carry a piece of so many friends whose lives touched mine and accept that I am here, and that they are not. We didn't plan on that. We were all once young, like me and Michael, two kids, aware of the hazards but promising ourselves, "*We're* never gonna let that happen to us. *Never.*"

8

What Are You Gonna Do?

I WAS *SMITTEN*.

Los Angeles. City of Angels. California, the Capital of Cool. It was just like in the movies. Come to think of it . . . this was Hollywood, y'all, and it *was* the movies.

In March 1971, we had a travel break from the J-5 tour and found ourselves in LA for a little time off. We were all seduced.

Let's talk about the weather. Zero humidity. Just palm trees, balmy breezes, and blue skies. I'd never seen so many varieties of cacti and flowering succulents. And I fell in love with the bougainvillea vines popping their blossoms of red, purple, and pink—even in winter.

In Beverly Hills we saw mansions the size of city blocks, with magnificent sculpted hedges, swimming pools, and backyard tennis courts.

From Hollywood Boulevard to Rodeo Drive to the Boardwalk at Venice Beach, everywhere we looked, there were the most ridiculously beautiful people, every age, everybody out and about like the whole town was on a movie set.

Everybody looked like somebody.

We drove the Sunset Strip, past the Whisky a Go Go and the other Rock 'n' Roll clubs. We slowed way down to check out the windows of Tower Records—with posters outside of the latest album releases by everybody from Miles Davis and Marvin Gaye to Elton John and Bob Dylan.

In the scheme of things, we had clocked a lot of miles in our three years as the Commodores. Maybe the windows of Tower Records would be next. Some of the guys were getting impatient. The silent loner in our bunch, Milan Williams, for one. And Thomas McClary, kind of an out-there guy who was always trying to elevate our position, was sure that not enough was being done to get our name and music to the masses.

Just before we all headed back home to Tuskegee for spring break, Suzanne informed us, without any advance word, "We have an audition for you at the studio tomorrow. Be ready."

A record label deal would change our lives. I'll never forget seeing the J-5 getting handed a check for $180,000—for one night of work. We were making a thimbleful of that. The math was simple: When you sell records, you sell out arenas. The only thing missing for us was having a recording home.

Cue the band. And bring on the crowd.

The next day we went early to set up at MoWest—Motown's new recording studio near Formosa Avenue and Santa Monica Boulevard in Hollywood that was still under construction. The downstairs studio was completed, totally state-of-the-art, but the interior of the upstairs wasn't done.

Yeah, I thought, *this is literally getting in on the ground floor out here.*

Many of Motown's executives had moved from Detroit to Los Angeles and were at our audition. Berry Gordy, now in his forties, was not in attendance, but we understood that Suzanne would oversee the process and confer with him.

Mr. Gordy had made the move primarily to pursue opportunities for Motown artists to expand into film and TV. He was met with skepticism. A lot of Hollywood folks were up in arms when suddenly deals were in the works for Motown's leading lady, Diana Ross, who had never acted before, to star as Billie Holiday in *Lady Sings the Blues* with Gordy as executive producer. The critics scoffed, *Who are these record people trying to break into the movie business?*

That sentiment fired me up. To think—we had an opportunity to be with a Black-owned entertainment company, a mouse that had already roared as the most successful independent record label of the 1960s.

The other memorable aspect of our audition—which we frankly enjoyed because we were playing for adults—was that I recognized Billy Preston, a keyboardist and singer who was working on something at the studio. Billy Preston had played with the Beatles, which made him the true Black Beatle. We were starstruck.

Suzanne immediately called Berry Gordy with the verdict: "I think we should sign them."

She had earned the credibility, even at twenty-five years old, to make the call.

Within a day, Benny got the news that we would be recording for the newly minted MoWest label—under Motown of course. The big push was to sign acts that were "self-contained"—the Business word for groups who played, sang, and could bring their own hits to the table.

Benny came by to give us the lowdown. We were each going to be making up to $100,000 a year. We were stupefied.

Before our contracts were drawn up, the Motown lawyers asked us each to say what we played and did in the band. We told them. Then they asked, "And who are the writers?"

We looked at each other and shrugged. It wasn't me. One song attempt didn't count. None of us were writers. Did that matter? We assumed that getting signed meant you were stars now and then they gave you hits.

The minute I signed the contract and looked at the upcoming schedule, an alarm went off—*Oh, shit, I'm a frickin' college student!*

ON THE FIVE-MINUTE walk from Grandma Foster's house to the administration building on Old Montgomery Road, I focused on my mission—to explain my situation to Dean Carter and ask for an exception to the rules for determining our grades.

This was March 1971, three months before I was supposed to graduate. For the past three and a half years, I had managed to take makeup exams and had turned in extra-credit papers. Overall, I technically had a B average. The problem was that if you missed so many hours of classes, you'd lose one or two letter grades. So now, with only elective credits to go, I found myself with a D average. Without a rule change, I would either flunk out my last semester or be forced to quit the band if I wanted to graduate with the rest of my class.

I had the greatest respect for Dean Carter, who was in the same social circle as my parents. He greeted me cordially, asking after Alberta and Lyonel, and my grandmother and sister too. He took a seat behind his desk and gestured for me to have a seat across from him.

Well. I took a deep breath and asked for an exception to the rules for hours required to graduate. I did emphasize why I missed the hours—because I was learning a professional trade in a band called the Commodores.

Dean Carter couldn't change the rules. It would open the door to requests for other exceptions. But then, as he thought about it, he said, "This band you are in . . . are you making any money?"

"Yes." When he asked how much I told him, "Between $75,000 and $100,000 a year."

Dean Carter instantly said, "You make that kind of money? *I* don't make that kind of money. *We* don't make that kind of money." He meant his fellow administrators and instructors.

I wasn't sure how to respond.

"Listen," he said, as he lowered his voice and leaned across the desk, "let me give you some advice. And don't tell your folks I said it . . . Your best choice is to get out of here and go make that money. You can always come back and make up the last semester."

Wait. I took that to mean he was advising me to drop out.

I imagined saying "I'm dropping out of college" to my parents and it was not a pretty sound.

Dean Carter reassured me, "You go make that money and see what happens. You'll never know if you don't try. You can find the time later to get your degree."

"It's just one semester."

He smiled and shrugged, as if to say, *Or longer?* He noted that, as long as I had satisfied requirements for my major, if the band had some success, the Tuskegee powers that be might even wind up waiving the remaining electives.

And that was *it*.

No matter how many times I practiced versions of how to break the news to my family, I came up with *nuth'n*. Maybe if I tried to speak to their hearts, they'd listen—*I don't love accounting or mergers and acquisitions, but I'm in love with playing music, and I have this paper that says I get paid to do that.*

I knew better. The failure to earn a degree would be a mark of dishonor on the Richie family value system.

My stomach hurt.

Grandma was *mortified*. Who got paid to play music without formal training? The world had lost its mind.

I called Mom next and she was in total shock. "Well, Lionel, if that's what you think is best." She wasn't comforted by my saying, "I'll just stay out for a semester." She might have been most upset over how Dad would react.

My fear was that he might drive to Tuskegee to get me to change my mind. That's why I told Grandma and Mom first—so they could warn me in case I was about to get killed.

Out of love for the memory of my father, I will not repeat the words he said over the phone. He sure could cuss. He found words I didn't even know he knew, or at least that I'd never heard him say as the good Christian man he was.

Maybe, in his own original way, Dad was shaking me up, the way you do when you send someone into combat. If this was my path, he put me on notice, there was no room for failure.

Dad may have overreacted because he had watched his brother go through the ups and downs of being in the Music Business. I don't think he stopped cussing until I had a few hits under my belt. But I'll get to that.

The next person I called was Brenda Harvey.

I liked her. I liked her a lot. And she liked me. Brenda's reaction to our getting signed was, "Oh, that's amazing! And about time." And me dropping out of college was no big deal to her either.

Before we settled into any kind of college sweetheart groove, I was *gone*. For the next eighteen months, the Commodores were either on tour or coming back home for a minute or, as was the case one time, driving off to Martha's Vineyard—where we went for eight days to prepare for the launch of the major part of the J-5 tour. One of the highlights of that stay on the island was discovering that James Taylor was there at the same time, recording and rehearsing.

Every now and then we'd hear music coming from his barn, and I was in awe. This was James Taylor! His "Fire and Rain" was already a classic at the time and he was getting ready to release a smash #1 hit cover of Carole King's "You've Got a Friend"—which, in early 1971, she had recorded and released on her *Tapestry* album, one of the biggest albums of the year. I loved these artists—James Taylor, Carole King, and Carly Simon. And they were all on Martha's Vineyard when we were.

This wasn't the ideal way to begin a college romance. Brenda and I kind of got to know each other in installments from the road—whenever I could find a pay phone. She became a confidante. I could vent at length, and she could vent louder and longer on my behalf. Or I could tell her that I *killed* on a given night and she'd cheer me on.

The fact that I could be myself and that was enough was mind-blowing. But did I know who "myself" even was?

NO SOONER HAD I become a college dropout than I woke up in the middle of the night in a panic, realizing I was no longer safe from being drafted.

This was now the summer of 1971, the beginning of a prolonged drawdown of American troops. The ceasefire wouldn't happen until 1973.

After the lottery of December 1969, I had decided that I wasn't at risk until I was out of school. What I knew was that the lower the number associated with your birthday in the lottery, the more likely it was you had to go. You wouldn't know if it was high enough until the call came, depending on the need for fresh boots on the ground.

With this life-and-death roll of the dice, I decided that if my number got called, I'd go to Canada. Year by year, I'd seen what was coming back, and nobody, not one person, even if they survived life-threatening injuries, came back in their right mind.

June 19 of my year received a #104, and June 21 received a #60. *Terrifying.* As I recall, my draft number, for those with a June 20 birthday, was #360. *Thank you, Lawd!*

The year that I dropped out of college, they were only drafting up to #195. The following year it was even lower. And in 1973, the Vietnam War draft came to an end.

Either I must be the luckiest sonuvabitch on the planet or divine guidance intervened. We can call it a draw.

What happened to our servicemen and servicewomen when they came back home and were treated without honor is a wrong that has never been made right. I say that after witnessing everything that was taken from my friend and mentor Michael Gilbert—and from Harold Boone's brother and from countless of my other friends.

We got together with Mike in Tuskegee as soon as we heard he was back in the early summer of 1971. He came over to the house and we piled up around him, like the puppies that got lost in the woods and were reunited with their pack leader.

Michael was so proud and excited about everything we had coming up. He knew he had left us in good hands with Benny. He kept saying to each of us, *That was all part of the plan.* He didn't say, *Look, I have PTSD bad, and I'd appreciate it if you didn't ask me about what's happened.* He didn't need to say that. His eyes said everything.

After talking to Benny, the guys and I were able to arrange a job for Michael, basically, as part of our crew. We wanted to do *something.* If I remember that short stint, I think it made sense, at first, having him drive, getting us to gigs.

Soon, I could see this was killing him. He'd start to say, "You know what kept me alive over there, every day, every hour? Thinking about getting back . . ." before his voice tapered off. He meant being the lead singer, playing bass, and starting back up where we had been when he was marched off in handcuffs.

We all knew, Mike included, that it wasn't possible to just rewind the clock. The harsh truth I'd face at various stages of maturity is that not everybody who matters in your life gets to go the distance with you.

Mike drove us to New York to board the SS *France*, which would take us once again to the French Riviera. He alluded to some medical issues he had to address. The malaria he had caught in the jungles had never been resolved and a full-on hospitalization at the VA was in order. After he was released, with a permanent disability, he went on to work in the tech sector, ahead of his time as always, eventually settling in Memphis, Tennessee. Many years in the future, I'd finally catch up to him and get to tell his story to a sold-out crowd, who gave a standing ovation to Michael Gilbert, the true founder of the Commodores, without whom there would not be a Lionel Richie.

CHRISTIAN CABAZAR, THE French promoter we knew, had booked this three-day engagement at the Hotel Byblos Saint-Tropez, on the Côte d'Azur in Provence. We were to play in honor of the birthday of the daughter of a Paris city official. Oh, *mais oui*, we were oh so sophisticated and so in demand now. That's one show, but you get the idea.

On the SS *France*—the most famous ship afloat—we would be enjoying first-class accommodations. In exchange, we were to entertain our four thousand fellow passengers, but only for one night on the six-day trip over and then another night on the six-day trip back.

What could go wrong?

Well . . . the first thing was not a crisis but a slight misunderstanding. We had been told that there was only a formal dining room, and we would need to dress for dinner. On the SS *France*, it turned out, that meant tuxedos—which we did not have with us. We improvised. Our Alabama version of dressing for dinner was, to put it mildly, quite unique. Even though they weren't tuxedos in the traditional sense, they were colorful and we passed the test of formal.

At our first dinner, the six of us were taken to our table, just across from J. Paul Getty Jr., a philanthropist and book collector, and son of the oil man who was in 1971 the wealthiest American alive. We found out that he hated to fly and so he was a regular, you could say, on the SS *France*.

All six of us Commodores tried to blend in as we passed by other passengers, smiling and nodding hello, causing something of a stir. We took our seats as a band of waiters, in white gloves, came around the table, each with a little napkin over one arm, and each with a bowl holding water and a segment of lemon.

As they stood there, the bowls of water and lemon in their outstretched hands, we all looked down and into the bowls and then at each other. I figured it out, I thought, and nodded to the guys.

Taking the bowl from the waiter, I put it on the table, squeezed the lemon, added some sugar to the bowl, stirred the sugar up, and drank up the bowl of this . . . beverage.

I handed the bowl back to the man, took the towel, and wiped my mouth. The rest of the Commodores followed in turn. We all did this ritual.

My waiter didn't react. I thanked him and he replied simply, after a pause: "*Monsieur.*" And he walked off, followed by the other waiters, muttering something that sounded like "*merde.*"

I shrugged. Ronald LaPread just said, "Funny glasses for lemonade."

We did not know until five nights later, our last day, that we had committed the cardinal sin of etiquette. The water was for washing your hands at the table, then adding a squeeze of lemon to your fingers afterward.

Luckily, we were given a free pass for not knowing. What do you expect? We were from Alabama.

What can I say? We were the only Black folks on this boat, maybe among the few who'd ever been on it. We were in some high cotton alright, on the way to being hifalutin.

We laugh about that lemonade to this day.

We had almost *nuth'n* in common with the four thousand or so passengers on the SS *France*. We felt that way until the night of our performance. By the time we finished our intro—*You are about to be exposed to the supersensitive soulful sounds of the Commodores . . . and you will never ever again be the same*—it didn't matter that we came from different worlds. Passengers were *transformed*. The Funk was officially on the SS *France*.

All of this was the funny and fun part of the cruise.

Now let's talk about the life-and-death part of the cruise. It's called the Irish Sea. Everything on the ship had to be bolted down. We were sicker than dogs and praying to heaven that we would not sink like the *Titanic*. At one point I was praying that we would sink to put us out of our misery. That Irish Sea gave me a recurrence of panic attacks.

We assumed we'd be the main entertainment in Saint-Tropez—the fishing village that was a hub for celebrities from the literary and art worlds—only to find out that Mick and Bianca Jagger were getting married there. Which meant an army of paparazzi arrived. So much for secrecy.

The guest list was Rock 'n' Roll royalty, along with the high society of New York, Paris, and London—each wedding guest more beautiful and iconic than the last.

Later that night, during our last set at the Hotel Byblos—after a very successful party for the Paris official's daughter—guess who showed up? Mick Jagger with most of his wedding guests.

Apparently, there wasn't enough room at the Café des Arts (where we'd played before), and Mick was trying to get everyone back to the Byblos nightclub that was emptying. From the bandstand, we couldn't tell exactly what was going on at the bar, but we kept getting reports that it was wild—everyone having the time of their lives. We kept on playing until our last set was over.

The Stones probably had no idea who we were when we crossed paths that night. But about four years later, to show you how divine guidance works in mysterious ways, the Commodores were hired to open for them on tour. How 'bout that?

JACKSONMANIA WAS AT full throttle when we continued the tour in the fall of 1971 and early 1972. We began to attract a different kind of attention. One of the New York newspapers picked up on the push we were getting from Motown, calling the J-5 concert a chance to show off "soul sister" Yvonne Fair and us, "a dynamite group from Alabama."

The press got better, especially after the next Jackson 5 show on August 21, a Saturday night, at the Cow Palace in Daly City, just outside of San Francisco. The energy and engagement were at the highest level we'd seen. The exposition arena, which had in fact been built for massive livestock shows back in the day, sat about seventeen thousand.

We were now set to play the Hollywood Bowl, a dream come true. Everyone told us, "Ain't *nuth'n* like playing the Bowl under the stars."

Early Sunday afternoon, as we're stumbling around, after a late-night drive from San Francisco to Los Angeles, Thomas brings in a handful of newspapers with reviews of the show the night before, that all say, basically: *The Jacksons were good, but the surprise of the evening was the Commodores*. All the reviews give us raves.

In great spirits, we arrive at the Bowl and settle into our greenroom above the stage.

Before the gates open to ticket holders, we go to the stage to do our sound check and . . . *Where's our equipment? Where are our instruments? Where are our uniforms?* None of it is there. You don't have a show without those things. It's impossible that our stuff's not there.

We have a powwow. We know everything was on the truck the night before because our stuff is always loaded last and unloaded first. We talk to the roadies.

Nobody knows *nuth'n*.

We all have an idea as to who might be responsible, yet nobody wants to say it out loud. Then as we're scrambling, Joe Jackson, who has an intense stare anyway, strolls onto the stage, surveys the scene, sees all of us looking bewildered, and says, "Hey, I heard your equipment is late. Man, that's rough. Sorry to hear about that."

We exchange glances. Suspicions confirmed.

Turns out, we learn after much ado, our stuff is back outside the Cow Palace, right where they left it.

Good that we located everything, but there is no way to get it before the show.

Michael's important question rings in my ears: *What are you gonna do?*

We find most of the Jackson brothers in their dressing room.

They're genuinely concerned seeing how upset we are. Nobody wants us to have to cancel our appearance at the Bowl—even if we are not the main attraction.

"Hey," Jermaine offers, "why don't you play our instruments?" His brothers echo him, one by one.

We are left without a sax or a trumpet because nobody in the J-5 played horns, but WAK and I decide to improvise and beef up our choreography, and—Are you ready for this?— *hum* our horn parts.

The uniform situation is more challenging. We have our tops—form-fitting bodysuits that you step into like women's bathing suits, that we kept with us. So we decide that is going to be our look—to go onstage *without* our pants and without our boots. Oh, yeah, barelegged and barefoot, with only our bodysuit tops.

It was so traumatic, I probably passed out, and when I woke up, they told us we did fantastic. The word was that we damn near stole the show and grabbed most of the headlines for our look that was way ahead of its time. The Motown creative executives who were there called it the greatest Hollywood Bowl debut they'd ever seen.

Ironically, the stunt pulled on us was a chance for us to pass a pressure test, making possible the moment of our liftoff. Call it our lemons-into-lemonade hurrah.

Right there at the Hollywood Bowl, August 22, 1971, was when all systems went to GO.

The big talk afterward was, "We can't wait to get you guys into the studio."

By Thanksgiving, give or take—a year after our audition at the Turntable—we were checking ourselves into the Tropicana Hotel in West Hollywood, waiting to record.

News flash: Um, no, we couldn't get into the studio to record because we were at the bottom of the roster. Number 58. The only way to become a priority was for your last record to be a hit. How does that work when you don't have a record? Well, late at night when there was an open slot at the studio, we'd go in and sing on tracks brought to us by a few top Motown producers, including Hal Davis and Jeffrey Bowen. We were still low on the totem pole.

What do we do? I wasn't a writer yet. None of us were. We began to get restless.

And then something terrible happened. We were told, "If you're lucky, you might get a Temptations track. Or a Four Tops track." Meaning—we could do covers or try to record a song that had been rejected.

We were insulted. We loved the Tempts and the Tops, but those were songs written for *them*. "We don't want those tracks, we're the mighty Commodores."

They heard us. "Well, alright then, but we gotta ask you one simple question: What do you sound like?"

The answer was: "We don't know."

And that's when the adventure began—with a crash education I didn't see coming.

9

Motown University

THE COMMODORES WERE IN NO rush to pull up stakes and leave Tuskegee.

Most of us had girlfriends back home, some were getting married, and whatever we did, we were all going to do it together. Why go broke in LA when the cost of living was sky-high and the fast lane could actually slow us down?

Los Angeles also required wheels and I hadn't gotten around to buying myself a car yet. We'd been signed to Motown a year and a half but hadn't scored even a modest hit. I mean, sure, it was probably time to get a fun, economical car—but I hadn't found anything that fit the bill.

Besides, where was I going? Some of the Commodores had cars, and I could ride with them.

The lack of a car suddenly became a problem when I decided, after months of talking to Brenda Harvey on the phone, that I should take her on a real date, our first, and splurge.

"How would you like to go see a concert with me?" I said,

and gave her the details—University of Alabama, Tuscaloosa, a two-and-a-half-hour drive.

She was thrilled, then asked, "You don't mind if Janet comes with us, do you?"

Here comes that roommate again. The Dairy Queen all over! "Oh, no, I don't mind," I answered, wanting to be a gentleman. If I remember correctly, I then invited William King to join us. There was still a transportation issue.

Sheepishly, I asked if Brenda would mind driving. Silence. "Or, I could drive your car," I offered quickly. She did not mind.

So I bought four tickets to see Elton John, whose biggest hit of the moment was "Crocodile Rock," and we set off for Tuscaloosa in Brenda's yellow VW bug.

We got up to our arena seats—way up in the back, but so what? And I looked around and thought, *Hmm, there's about six Black people in this whole place, and four of them are us.*

The most incredible show followed. Elton played all my favorite songs—"Rocket Man," "Your Song," "Levon," and "Country Comfort." And Elton, in his flamboyant costume and Mad Hatter hat and glasses, was the ultimate entertainer. WAK agreed. Then I glanced over at Brenda and Janet to get their reactions. I can't tell you how it felt to see the two of them, fast asleep. Shocking!

As we were getting up to leave, I muttered, "I can't believe y'all fell asleep at an Elton John concert." Brenda and Janet looked puzzled.

Their comeback was, "Who the hell is Elton John?"

They just wanted to come along to do something I wanted to do.

One other thing I want to mention about Elton John. Many times when you meet someone famous, they can fall short of their public persona. Not Elton. When I later met him in person, he was so gracious, down-to-earth, and wonderful, I realized, *That's how to treat your fans*, and took a note.

The people who worked for Elton reflected his character as well. That night, after the concert, the four of us were following the herd trying to leave the building. A young man with credentials tapped me on the shoulder, "If you guys want to get out faster, that side door right there is open."

Ten years later, I needed a new promoter and I met this same man, Howard Rose. We got to talking and he said he worked for Elton and I remembered him! Small world, again. A short time later, I wound up hiring Howard. It gets better. Before we left Elton's concert that night, Howard waved to a guy in a cowboy hat. "Chris, show these folks how to get out."

That guy was Chris Lamb. At the time, he was Elton's crew chief, and in another fateful turnabout, Chris Lamb later became my crew chief. Ten years later. He came in wearing a cowboy hat and I still recognized him. I couldn't believe it. I said, "I know you don't remember, but you were the one that showed me how to get out that side door."

The point to my young friends is: Be frugal, but don't miss the concert. Take the drive. Buy the tickets. Take the girl. Or the boy. Borrow their car if you must. Trust divine guidance.

WHENEVER WE WENT to LA to work, the Commodores mostly stayed in Hollywood at the Tropicana Hotel on Santa Monica Boulevard. All kinds of Music Business folks stayed at the Tropicana—where the walls of its diner, Duke's, were papered with the headshots of everybody who was anybody in Rock 'n' Roll.

Just as cool, it was less than a ten-minute walk to the MoWest studio near Formosa and Santa Monica. Or, if I wanted to pop in at Motown's corporate offices at 6464 Sunset Boulevard it too was within walking distance.

From the early to mid-seventies, I made those walks so often I wore grooves in the sidewalk. This was my golden triangle of learning at Motown University, as many called it.

At the corporate offices, I didn't need an excuse to show up and go check in with Suzanne, Tony Jones, or Skip Miller. Even if they weren't there, I'd snoop around, especially on the third floor, which was the business nerve center.

My inner monologue still gnawed at me: *In case you get fired, or the band doesn't work out, learn the ropes of becoming a businessman in this industry.* Insecurity often isn't logical. Then again, we had no hit records, and none in sight. A backup plan seemed the wise thing to have.

So I'm up and down the hall, trying to interview executives— *How do I read royalty statements? What about publishing pay?*— but getting pushback.

"The name of your group is . . . The Commodores you say? We don't have any royalty statements under that name."

"Oh, no, sir. We don't have any records yet, but I'm learning now for when we do."

Everyone wondered, *Who is this twenty-three/twenty-four-year-old kid with the big Afro and a gift of gab snooping around on the third floor?*

Suzanne would vouch for me.

One of the questions I asked everyone was, "Any chance I could meet Mr. Gordy?" He never seemed to be there. He was away or on a TV set for a Diana Ross special or at Paramount Studios looking at dailies of *Lady Sings the Blues*. Or he was holding meetings at his house.

The more elusive he was in those early months, the more he took on the dimensions of the Great and Mighty Oz. And that only made me want to meet him more. How many Black businessmen who had defied the odds offered a textbook of accomplishment at the level that Gordy had—that you could study from?

Next to none. Close to zero.

My first opportunity to meet Mr. Gordy was not at the office but at a company party he hosted at his home in Bel Air. The property was an estate with a panoramic view of Los Angeles that went all the way to the sea.

After our car followed a long winding driveway up a hill that went by a tennis court, we were dropped at a roundabout where a team of valet parkers pointed us toward a wing of the mansion.

Suzanne, Tony, and Skip ushered us inside. It was like walking into a palace. Everywhere we looked were photographs of Motown royalty—lots of Diana Ross and the Supremes, Smokey and the Miracles, Stevie, Marvin, the Jackson 5, movie stars like Sidney Poitier, Harry Belafonte, Sammy Davis Jr., and Civil Rights leaders, including a photograph of Berry Gordy walking with Dr. King. I remember hearing that Mr. Gordy had offered, at his own expense, to put Dr. King's speeches on record—one of the reasons those speeches are so well preserved. After Dr. King's death, Motown bequeathed the masters to the King family.

Finally, when Mr. Gordy walked into this sitting area, looking younger than his forty-three years of age, I could see that he had the power of presence. I'd been told, "Whatever you do, do not ever, ever make a reference in any way, shape, or form to his height."

To be fair, he was not tall. But his demeanor negated that reality. He had been a boxer in his teens and it showed in how he walked—like a prizefighter. Even if he was . . . not tall.

He was not in a dapper suit or leather jacket or bell-bottoms and a fringe vest. Nope, he was wearing tennis shorts and a casual polo shirt, much like his later uniform of a Fila tracksuit. Not the intimidating maestro of Motown I expected, he had an infectious smile as he welcomed everyone.

"BG," Suzanne said, "meet the Commodores."

He smiled, telling us, "We're expecting big things," and then nodded as Suzanne went down the line introducing us.

She added, "William King and Lionel Richie here are both avid tennis players."

"Wow!" he grinned, and invited us to bring our rackets to play. We accepted and said we'd be honored.

Then there was a momentary lull, and I took it upon myself to fill the silence—or, rather, to insert my foot in my mouth—when, as only an idiot could, I looked around in admiration and said, "Wow, if this is Berry Gordy's house, you know the Temptations' and the Supremes' houses must be even bigger."

Mr. Gordy grinned. I had no clue this was not a good thing. But I found out fast. Suzanne, Tony, and Skip immediately exited me out of a side door, barking out in unison, "Don't you ever say something that stupid again as long as you live!"

I'd assumed that the artists were more popular and more famous than the chairman of the board and the owner of the company, because, after all, they were the ones making the most money selling the records. Wrong. House rules: The company owners were the ones making the most money.

Fortunately, I never made the mistake of blurting out something so clueless with Berry Gordy again ever.

There was one incident, unfortunately, that I thought would end me at Motown, and it came later in the 1970s when the Commodores were riding high and my parents flew out for a visit. In early preparation for what I expected would be an introduction to Mr. Gordy, I went into literal rehearsals with my father.

"Dad, listen, there are only two lines you have to remember."

First, I would practice the cue, which would be "Dad, this is Berry Gordy."

And Lyonel Sr. was to say, "Great to meet you, Mr. Gordy."

The second cue that we went over many times was the standard comment from the head of a music label, along the lines of, "I'm sure you are proud of your son." That was the cue.

"And your answer, Dad, is 'That's right, sir,' and don't say another word!"

One other thing. I gave my father explicit directions to refrain from making any reference to Berry Gordy's height. Dad brushed me off, insulted, as in, *Do you take me for a fool?*

Shortly after my folks arrived in California for their first visit, I took Lyonel Sr. for a tour of the recording studios. We walked around the first floor, and I showed him the two studios, Sunrise and Sunset, and was about to take the elevator up to the second floor to see Twilight, the third studio, when, just after I pressed the button, the elevator arrived.

The door slid open, and standing there was none other than Berry Gordy, accompanied by security. He was rarely, if ever, at the studios. Immediately, I smiled and said, "This is my father. And this is Mr. Gordy."

For a split-second, I saw my father give the head of Motown, my bread and butter, the once-over. *Oh shit.* It was a car crash about to happen, and I couldn't move fast enough to stop Dad from taking a step back and saying, "*Huh.* You're shorter than I thought you were going to be."

It was at that point, I believe my soul left my body. You know that part in the movie where the sound goes silent and the clouds gather over everything? Was my life and career at Motown over?

To his lasting credit, thank you *Lawd*, Berry Gordy just fell out laughing at my father's near disaster of a comment, and then let it go. This was not the last time I would suffer through a loved one's comments made to Mr. Gordy—it would happen again in an even more traumatic context. We will arrive at that story soon enough.

In the meantime, what I learned from watching Berry Gordy and his aura of power—his ultimate teaching tool—was everything.

NOT ONLY WERE there artists stopping in at 6464 Sunset, but just as important, if not more so, there was the regular presence of Motown's most prolific chart-topping writer/producers—who, I now knew, were chief among the reasons why a song did or did not become a hit.

On any given day, I could look from right to left, and there, up close and in person, would be any one of the Motown stars—some of whom were entertainers who also wrote and produced. Marvin Gaye, Stevie Wonder, and Smokey Robinson all had offices there. In the studio, they'd invite you to sit in on sessions and see how the magic happened.

The first time I went to hear the latest from Marvin's new album—*Trouble Man*—he was taking a break while getting a massage from two masseuses. He waved me over, directing me to a seat near him. My kick at that time was to write a research paper that could allow me to earn my degree, after all. My interest was how artists dealt with taxes in the entertainment industry. Here I had someone who had just made a load of money, so who better to ask?

"Marvin, how do you deal with taxes?"

"Brother, I told the government to go fuck themselves, and they haven't bothered me since."

When I went back and reported my interview with Marvin Gaye himself and pitched that approach to my accounting teacher at Tuskegee, he said, "Mr. Richie, I don't think that would work." My instructor, I would soon learn, was correct. In fact, the IRS later took a substantial amount of everything Marvin owned.

When I asked others their key to success, "Pay your taxes" was the number one mantra.

An education was at my fingertips and I wanted to learn it all. For instance, one reason Berry Gordy decided to open his first recording studio—Hitsville, USA—was because in 1959 Detroit was busting at the seams with pure, raw talent.

I heard this story over and over from everyone who had come up in the formative years of Motown. To build his hit factory, Berry Gordy borrowed principles learned from a stint working on the assembly line at Ford Motors, where he watched the frame of a car go down the line until it came out a brand-new shiny automobile. At Hitsville, he believed any kid with raw talent but little experience could walk in one door, go through the stages of development, and come out the other door a star.

Teams of writers/producers competed for who "could get a hit on" whom, as the saying went. There were dance instructors, experts in hair and wardrobe, teachers of etiquette, not to mention sales, marketing, and promotion teams, along with tour and booking reps. Hitsville became a mecca not just for singers and musicians but also for others hoping to get their start behind the scenes—in the offices or as sound engineers, arrangers, writers, and producers.

One such young writer/producer who used to hang out at Hitsville always asking questions was a tall kid with a big Afro and a gift for gab. Sound like someone?

That was nineteen-year-old Norman Whitfield, who, at first, couldn't catch a break to get into the studio to record until he cowrote "Pride and Joy" with Marvin Gaye, giving Marvin his first Top 10 Pop hit, which peaked at #2 R&B. Norman then began a winning collaboration with Barrett Strong (the artist who sang Berry Gordy's classic hit, "Money"), culminating with the Whitfield/Strong almighty song of life, "I Heard It Through the Grapevine." Norman produced it first for Gladys Knight, giving her a monster hit in 1967. A year later, he recorded the same song with Marvin Gaye. A megahit, it flew to #1 on the Hot 100 and stayed for seven weeks. Until 1981, that record ruled as Motown's top-selling single of all time.

What happened in 1981? Hold that question. We'll get there.

Norman's early breakthrough resulted from Motown's unique system. When two producers had records with the same artist, whoever scored the biggest hit would get the next release on that artist. The battle for the Tempts was won by Norman's "Ain't Too Proud to Beg" (#1 R&B, #13 Pop) versus Smokey's "Get Ready" (#1 R&B, #29 Pop). Soon Norman locked up the Temptations with one smash after another—from "Cloud Nine" to "Ball of Confusion" and "Papa Was a Rollin' Stone."

Every Commodore knew who Norman Whitfield was. He was the shit. Badass in every way. Of everyone that I wanted to meet, he would have been the last person that I thought I'd *get* to meet.

And then, one day while waiting to talk to Suzanne—circa early 1972—I looked up to see Norman walking by me. In the flesh. He gave me a look that said, *Do I know you?*

I nervously introduced myself, and then—*inspiration!*—like we talked all the time, I asked, "Whatcha work'n on right now?"

That's all it took. The seas parted. Next thing I know he's telling me about new stuff he's got going for Edwin Starr. Earlier, Norman wrote and produced Starr's "War"—a #1 on the Hot 100 and a timeless protest song.

Norman was nine years older than me, in his early thirties, and he didn't mind passing along some of what he knew. The next time I ran into Norman, he picked up from the last conversation and just free-flowed. "Hey, Lionel, did I tell you about how we wrote . . ."

I mastered the potent phrase, *Really? No way!*

That's all it took to get Norman telling stories. More than just a kid in the hallway, he saw me as an eager sponge for his wisdom.

The biggest lesson he shared was classic—*If at first you don't succeed, try, try again.*

We had a bond. Or I felt that we did, though I couldn't prove it.

THE COMMODORES WEREN'T sitting idle. Throughout 1972, we were still opening for the Jackson 5 and then hustling back to Tuskegee, home base, or jaunting out to Los Angeles to get our names onto the hit board.

We were still driving a lot more than flying, but what made it cool for us was this hot new trend in radio communication on the road called CBs. "Breaker, breaker . . ." We could make CB references onstage and audiences loved that we had this Americana trucker element to our identity. When we picked our CB handles, the rest of the guys insisted on Jack Benny for me.

Thank you very much.

The big question we'd been asked—"*What* do you sound like?"—was now, "*Who* do you sound like?" Some suggested we were Motown's answer to Sly and the Family Stone. Or they compared us to groups like Kool and the Gang or the Ohio Players.

Suzanne de Passe was now head of A&R, as well as being even more involved with film and TV, and she started to push writers/producers to bring us fresh material. Finally, in early 1972, the Commodores excitedly drove the three and a half hours from Tuskegee to Sheffield, Alabama, to the famed Muscle Shoals Sound Studio. We were there to record what would be our first single release on the MoWest label, "The Zoo (The Human Zoo)," written and produced by hitmakers Pam Sawyer and Gloria Jones.

The studio felt like church. Everybody recorded here—from Aretha and Bob Dylan to the Rolling Stones to Willie Nelson. Pam and Gloria were high-energy, creative, and they dug us. Pam heard me on a backing vocal and said, "I'd like to hear your voice more." That was the first time I heard myself coming through so clearly on a state-of-the-art recording system. Sounded pretty good. A few of the guys said, "You should have more songs." Clyde was our lead singer though, so I shrugged them off.

The record had some eclectic elements, but there was nothing about "The Zoo" that helped us identify our sound or our story. It didn't sell either. The same thing happened with "Don't You Be Worried," a second effort for us by Tom Baird, a young staff writer who had written/produced for Rare Earth and for Diana Ross.

We did start to worry.

Most labels would have dropped a band that hadn't made a dent in the marketplace after a year. Motown was different. Mr. Gordy reminded Suzanne of his position—*If the Commodores don't have a hit yet, it's the label's responsibility to see that they do.* The unspoken example was the four years it took for the "no-hit" Supremes to break through and become the top-selling Motown act of all time. HDH (Eddie Holland, Lamont Dozier, and Brian Holland) figured out the elixir with their breakthrough #1 "Where Did Our Love Go"—that light-sweet bouncy Pop formula with bells. (Everyone did bells from then on.)

The more I thought about it, the more I started to question why we were waiting for a superhero to deliver us our hit formula. Why couldn't we deliver it for ourselves?

"HEY, LIONEL," I heard as I arrived at the studio one day, just to check out the action. I turned around to see Norman Whitfield coming down the hall. "What are you doing this afternoon?"

"*Nuth'n.*"

"Come on and go with me to Disneyland."

Was he kidding? No, he loved the rides. "Let's go," was all I could say.

So, Norman and his then-girlfriend drove me from Hollywood down to Anaheim, and we spent the day walking and talking. No matter how many questions I asked about cracking the code of songwriting and hitmaking, Norman had answers. He said, "Write from experience"—your own or somebody else's.

"Really? No way!"

It was nighttime when I returned to the Tropicana—where all of us Commodores were staying—and the guys were concerned. "Where were you all day?"

When I told them, they said, "C'mon man, stop bullshitting." *Disneyland? You gotta be joking! You went with who????*

Imagine the shock, down the road, when they found out I was telling the truth!

There was a tug-of-war in my brain that Norman (and others) helped settle. The desire to try my hand at songwriting was starting to well up inside, and that was amazing. Two problems: 1) I didn't understand how to get the music I was hearing in my head from the Other Side and put it down on paper or play it. 2) Worse, I was under the impression that the most successful songwriters had studied how to read and play music. I asked Norman about how he learned to read.

"*Read* music? Nah, I never learned." Did he play an instrument? "Nah, I can't play shit."

I was relieved but confused. How do you compose music and not read or play? The answer was—*You need an arranger.*

It wasn't just Norman. I did a survey. Half of Motown's top writers and producers didn't write down the music. Sometimes they'd work out a melody on the piano or they'd hum or scat with *la-la*s or *da-da*s, or sing lyrics. Then they used arrangers. There were a bunch of great ones walking around the studio with pens and score sheets.

Hello to the future Lionel Richie.

Marvin Gaye laughed when I asked, "What music conservatory did you go to?"

"What the fuck you talk'n about? Conservatory, what's that?"

"Like music school, where you study composition."

He had started his career as a drummer, and played piano too, but he was not trained to read or write music. He composed the songs on the piano and then along came other people, including the arranger or the concert master or the engineer, and they put the music to the page.

Smokey, one of the most prolific and poetic writers ever, had one word for whether he studied formally or if he was proficient at reading or writing music: "No."

Smokey carried a notebook at all times for writing down lyrics and song ideas. Berry Gordy as a child took piano lessons from an uncle, enough to play a little Boogie-Woogie, but he couldn't really read or write music in the formal sense. Yet he could hear the song, and he could hear a hit. It's called a gift.

Stevie Wonder, blind, didn't read or write in the traditional sense either. Still, he could outplay anybody in the room. He could play multiple instruments, sometimes at the same time. What amazes me about Stevie is how visual his lyrics are, how he sees the world and transmits it to music, as in "You Are the Sunshine of My Life."

The first time I met Stevie he was coming down the hallway at 6464 Sunset with his assistant as I sat waiting for Suzanne. Before I could introduce myself, Stevie paused—as if being told, *It's that kid from Tuskegee who's always hanging around*. All I knew, to my amazement, was he then called to me, "Commodore! Lionel, right?" Next thing I knew, Stevie Wonder invited me to drop by the studio anytime.

I'd been studying songwriters for years—the lyrical genius of Bob Dylan, the gigantic body of work of John Lennon and Paul McCartney, and the masterful Neil Diamond. What I loved about Neil was that he was a pied piper, writing songs that set you up to sing along. Standards like "I Am . . . I Said" and "Sweet Caroline" were the kind of songs I wanted to write.

How could I do that?

All I can do is ask Norman Whitfield—"Tell me the secret."

"No, man, no," he says, "I can't." He gets quiet and says nothing. After a beat, "Well, can you hear it?"

I listen. Yeah, there's something low and persistent coming from offshore, from the Other Side. I hear the beat. Like always. But how does he know and is that what he means?

Norman nods in time to his own frequency that's there for him, not me. He explains, "If you hear it, you listen. If you can't hear it, then you don't have a song."

So I start listening and trying to re-create it on the piano in made-up chords. Norman listens and comes over and hits one note on the keyboards and begins to talk-sing, adding melody but just playing that one note. "See?" He shows me: *You can be what you want to be, you ain't got no responsibility . . .*

Overnight the mantra of "Either you hear it or you don't" told me that I could be a writer. I was excited out of my mind. I'd been hearing something since I was six years old! There were still a few issues—mainly, *How do I access everything I'm hearing and play it?*

Marvin leaned out of the studio one day and said, "Hey, little brother, come and sit in the studio with me and watch us put this song together."

Holy shit.

That was the day I found out I'm not the only hummer. Marvin's secret was, "Now either God is talking to you or he's not."

Marvin started tapping on the table. And he said, "Now, if you hear me just tapping on the table, you're not a songwriter." He said, "But if you hear a song from the beat from just tapping on the table, you're a songwriter."

Best music lesson I ever got in my life. My next question, "Well, how do you write it down?"

"Get a tape recorder and hum into the damn thing." The assembly line for creating hits was hummers talking to players, and players talking to arrangers, and arrangers talking to producers, then producers talking to the artists and to the record company.

That's what the West Coast Motown University was like— where Detroit graduates became the teachers. The Commodores arrived already cultivated as artists, and instrumentally self-contained. Luckily, a few of us caught the songwriting bug and could learn from the Greats.

What we called Motown University went by another name back in Detroit. They must have called it Heaven.

"THERE'S A SONG in My Heart" was my first composition to appear on vinyl in April 1973. It was chosen as the B side of the Commodores' third single release, "Are You Happy" (written by Jesse Boyce and produced by Clayton Ivey and Terry Woodford).

When neither side went anywhere, once again we were stuck not being able to get studio time. During the wait, I was churning out songs. When the day came that we were ready to record, I had two years' worth of material. One of those songs was my first to be submitted for publishing (which I forgot until years later) and was called "Superman." The story was written from the point of view of a character, prompted by the image of a Black Jagger:

> *Watch out for Filthy McNasty*
> *He'll try to cross my lines*
> *From kryptonite to TNT*
> *He'll try to blow my mind*
> *But I fight him with my goodness*
> *I fight him with my strength*
> *If that don't work, my good friends*
> *I'll hit him, hit him with the kitchen sink.*

This was not a future indication of who I was to become as a songwriter, but it was a validation that, okay now, I can be a lyricist and put words and melody together. The sword had been pulled out of the stone. I had more to say.

One of the next songs I wrote was "This Is Your Life." It was a ballad, a melancholy love song about the need for freedom to travel one's own path, no matter how lonely. This felt like it was my authentic songwriting voice, even if it wasn't the more up-tempo Commodores sound the company wanted.

When I wrote a song, it wasn't to feature me as the lead vocalist. If it worked for Clyde's voice on lead, I was happy. Or I could sing it. The goal was to sound like the Commodores.

Then I wrote a song with the other guys in the band and producer Jeffrey Bowen that had more of the sexy, funky vibe we'd been trying for. "I Feel Sanctified" was a character song, a confession about being spiritually blessed after a night of lovemaking. Later, when it was included on our first album and came out as a single, "I Feel Sanctified" broke into the Hot 100 at #75 and went all the way to #12 on the R&B charts.

As soon as it got out that I was sitting on some songs that might not be bad, the suggestion was made that I should be a Motown writer. Jeffrey Bowen asked, "Could you write a song for the Temptations?" The Tempts had gone ice-cold and needed new material.

We took elements of "I Feel Sanctified," turned the track around so it was a different song, and wrote "Happy People" together, and the Commodores played on the track. The record went to #1 on the R&B chart for the Temptations while also hitting at #11 on the Disco/Dance chart.

Suddenly, I began hearing from various sources, "Okay, we need some more songs from you." The incentive to write for others was that you'd be paid songwriting royalties and if that group had a hit with the song, the money could really add up—from record sales, radio play, and publishing royalties.

Then it dawned on me that I was being asked to service other artists' careers. My response was, "If you want any more songs, I'm in a group called the Commodores. I write songs for the Commodores."

Benny Ashburn decided that we should go and make a case for more studio time with Ewart Abner, who was the president of Motown Records. Berry Gordy oversaw Motown as chairman of the board, and Abner, as he was known, reported directly to Mr. Gordy.

We all went up and sat outside Abner's office to say we'd like a meeting. Abner had no time. He came in and went out, came in and went out, much too busy for us to schedule a meeting.

This went on for days until finally, one morning, Abner came out of his office and said, "Let me tell you something, guys. You want to have a meeting with me? Sell records. I'll have a meeting with you every day." In fact, he said, "When you have hit records, I'll come to Tuskegee and have a meeting there if you like."

That brought me down to earth. He was right. If we wanted studio time, we were gonna have to earn it. But *how?*

Like every great play, this was a drama that would have a few memorable entrances and exits. Drumroll please. Enter James Anthony Carmichael.

He had arrived not a moment too soon, saving us from being stuck as a house band or session musicians.

James Anthony Carmichael, sent to us by Suzanne, wasn't known as a producer yet, though he had produced. He was an arranger. One of the best around. His great aspiration was to graduate to producing Diana Ross, the leading lady of Motown, the top priority in the studio.

Now, we didn't hear this story. We heard, "You're going to be working with a world-class arranger, James Anthony Carmichael, who is going to be your producer."

We found out later that right out of the gate he didn't want anything to do with us.

We weren't exactly thrilled at the start either, because he treated us like a singing group.

Excuse us, we're a band.

"Let's talk about harmonies. Who's the tenor, who's the bass . . . ?"

We didn't think like that. We sang with one voice, though we knew how to harmonize. Like you do in a band.

There was something down-home about James Carmichael though that put us at ease. He was from Alabama originally, a gentleman with wizardlike diplomatic skills who had been to a music conservatory in LA.

Once we got into the studio, we realized we had hit the jackpot. We had in James Anthony Carmichael a brilliant arranger/producer who was there to bring out our sound, not invent it or tell us what we should sound like. We were no longer in search of a musical identity. It had been there all along.

James recognized right off that if I brought in a song that I wrote, I was the one to sing it, even if that wasn't my intent. My vocal phrasing just fit better with the flow of the music.

He also agreed with Milan Williams, who didn't want to play keyboards on my song "This Is Your Life."

What? "Milan, you're our keyboard player, c'mon man!" Everybody in the band played other folks' stuff.

Milan dug in. "No. I'm not gonna play it. You're gonna play it. 'Cause I don't play like you."

James shot me a look that said, *My point exactly.*

Stubbornly, I didn't understand why we wouldn't want Milan's intricate synthesizer sound that hooked a listener. But he did me a favor by forcing me to develop another facet of myself on keyboard. This helped me phrase my vocals around how I played and develop my own style.

Most keyboard players will fill up all the spaces underneath their vocals. I would hold that chord until I finished my phrase, and then I'd change it, and then I'd change, then I'd change. That let me take the emotional ride that chord changes are all about and my voice could rest in that emotion.

James would say to me, "Don't get impressed with the band. We're gonna put you on and build the band around you."

Wouldn't we want to bring the full band for a rousing sound?

"No, no, no. We're gonna put down three pieces, four pieces, and get you and your melody on. And then we'll build the sound around your vocal." Whenever we recorded my songs, he told everybody else, "If you find yourself playing when Brother Richie's singing, lay out."

Arrangements and production depended on the song. When Milan played us a song he'd written, melody and lyrics, called "The Ram," James Carmichael loved the infectious keyboard track but not the lyrics. "Let's record it as an instrumental," he argued. We were skeptical but loved the electronic staccato sounds of the clavinet on the song.

Suzanne de Passe, head of the creative division, aware that the bean counters were urging the company to drop us, listened to the demo and believed in it so much she grabbed a plane to go play it for Berry Gordy, who was, inconveniently, at a backgammon tournament on the island of Saint Martin.

When Suzanne returned, she said that after playing the song for BG, "He loved the effect of the clavinet . . ." We could hear a "But" coming.

Suzanne went on, "But after listening, he said, 'Sounds like a machine gun.'" BG wanted to call it "Machine Gun."

That was it. We changed the name. Years went by before we found out how close we had come to getting the boot.

Saved by the clavinet!

We rush into the studio, inspired, getting "Machine Gun" ready for release. Right at the end, late at night in the middle of the do-or-die process of mixing the record, in walks none other than Norman Whitfield. He says, "I don't want to disturb anybody. I'll just have a seat over here."

Norman sits off to the side quietly, arms folded, no expression.

James Carmichael asks, "Is . . . oh, that's Norm Whit—"

"Yeah," I confirm, "that's my friend Norman."

James and Whit know each other and exchange small talk. Everyone looks surprised.

I go around the room, introducing the Commodores individually to my friend Norman Whitfield.

The guys all act cool. "Hey, good to meet you, Norman . . ." They're in shock.

"I told you we hung out," I say under my breath. "Remember, we went to Disneyland."

Norman doesn't say much more, other than he doesn't want to get in the way but he'll just be over in the corner observing. Of course, he's not gonna go around Carmichael, who has his hands full with six of us getting in our mixing ideas.

And then the beauty happens. After watching us labor for two hours, Norman stands up and says, "Guys, do me a favor, let me help. You got a hit record and you're 'bout to fuck it up." With that, Norman showed us the way to do what we'd been trying to do but just didn't know how. In a short amount of time, he helped us tremendously with his mixing brilliance.

"Machine Gun" quickly went to #7 on the R&B charts and #22 Pop. Fittingly, Milan Williams—who had started back with Michael Gilbert before we were even the Commodores—had scored us our first hit.

The success of "Machine Gun" was shared by all of us. *Except* . . . we learned that for the songwriter a hit record brings with it a change in status and money.

Milan was paid an additional $35,000 cash the first time he got paid. There was much more to come for him as the sole writer, but if I needed any incentive to take my writing more seriously, that first check spoke to me. What it said was—*Sure, you're putzing around tryin' to write songs, but it's time to switch to laser focus.* This could be the ticket to "I told you so" to my parents.

It would validate my choices. Not to mention that the money was like—*damnnnn*. Next we heard, "Oh, Milan is flying to New York for a gig we have coming up and the rest of us are driving."

Hmmm, I thought, *he could have at least bought us a plane ticket.*

And there it was—that little sick feeling in your throat called envy.

You think it will go away and you try not to acknowledge it because you're really happy for Milan, and for the group, right? But Milan got $35,000, we didn't.

I didn't forget how I felt when he was getting the win. And later, when it was me, there was almost some embarrassment.

We had always thought that everybody would split everything equally, and I was just finding out how naive that was.

Bottom line: As a committed capitalist, I felt a new surge of motivation. My competitive streak was apparently alive and well.

WHEN WE STARTED to select tracks for our first album release in July 1974—also named *Machine Gun*—"I Feel Sanctified" was chosen as the second single. Because I shared writing credit on it, this wasn't the big payday Milan had received as sole writer of "Machine Gun."

But wait. When I contributed two additional songs as album cuts—my early compositions "There's a Song in My Heart" and "Superman"—I earned additional writing royalties. I also realized that if I wanted to make sure I got a song on the album, I had to go against the grain.

If everybody's bringing in a fast song or a funky song, I gotta bring in the slow song. That's at least guaranteed one song on the album. The strategy gave me an edge—love ballads.

For our next album, *Caught in the Act*, released in the spring of 1975, almost everybody had their own cut and their own writing credit. This time, Thomas McClary and I had the first single, "Slippery When Wet," which delivered us a #1 R&B hit. The second single—which I sang lead on—was my song "This Is Your Life."

"Who wrote that song right there?" Norman Whitfield had said when he first heard it, after I played him a few different tracks we'd been working on.

"I did."

"You got any more? Because that's a hit."

That was a huge moment. My reaction was, *Yeah, maybe I do have more.*

It hit #13 on the R&B charts, and the reviewers used a term I'd never heard before when they called it a true "Funk ballad."

Whit, by now, had begun to stop by whenever we were working on my songs. He was the silent "bad cop" to James Carmichael's "good cop." If I was pushing too hard or being lazy with the vocal, all I had to do was look over at Whit. I'd turn to James and ask, "Should we try it again?" Then I'd focus and nail it.

The first slight nod of approval came after Norman heard the playback of "Sweet Love." Maybe my songwriting education was about to pay off.

"Sweet Love" gave us our biggest hit yet (#2 R&B and #5 Pop, our first to break into the Top 10 of the Hot 100). The story was for every man who wanted to reveal his heart but didn't have the words to do so. Maybe my suffering had not been in vain.

With the next single I wrote for the Commodores, I went for broke. It was "Just to Be Close to You" (#1 R&B and #7 Pop).

Norman Whitfield gave me an actual grin when he stopped by the studio to have a listen.

Looking back, I'm surprised by my boldness—especially by the spoken intro that was my gift to the shy guys in the world who needed some of my pent-up poetry:

> *You know I've been through so many changes in my life girl*
> *Aw I've been up real high where I*
> *thought I didn't need anybody*
> *Aw and then again I've been down real low where*
> *There was no one in my life who needed me . . .*
>
> *There was a lonely man*
> *A man with no direction, with no purpose*
> *With no one to love and no one to love me for, for me*
> *Aw girl then you, then you came into my life*
> *You made my jagged edges smooth . . .*
> *You became my purpose my reason for livin' girl*

My mother called me the minute she heard the song. I could tell she was not happy.

"Lionel Junior" Mom said, "you know you don't talk like that."

"Mom, it's not me. I'm playing a character. I'm telling a story."

My mother, the English teacher, insisted she didn't raise me to sound like someone trying to be slick.

And what could I say? Other than, "Yes, Mom, you are right."

As for Lyonel Brockman Richie Sr., well, he had a different reaction. It was, believe it or not, my redemption in his eyes—a ready-made classic. Dad finally accepted that this was the path I was always meant to be on.

He embraced "Just to Be Close to You" with all the love and fervor of his soul. That was his song.

Every morning when he shaved, instead of singing, "Oh, Danny Boy," from then on for the rest of his life, he would sing, in his deepest, loudest, most resonant voice, "Just to Be Close to You."

And if that ain't proud, I don't know what is.

10

Easy

WHY, I CAN'T SAY, BUT starting in 1975—as the distractions mounted and the dates we played tripled—I couldn't wait to get back to LA, to the Holiday Inn at Hollywood and Highland. At my upgraded home away from home, I wrote feverishly.

I didn't really grasp how quickly our fortunes would change as "Machine Gun" raised our profile worldwide. Discos and dance floors everywhere had that record on constant rotation. Benny began hearing from promoters in the Philippines and Japan with dates that kept us very busy. Then he got an offer we could never have predicted a mere four years earlier when we crossed paths with Mick Jagger at the Hotel Byblos. Apparently, Mick and the other Stones loved "Machine Gun"—great!—and they wanted the Commodores to open for them on their upcoming Tour of the Americas extravaganza, for the two first nights in Philadelphia.

We met Mick before our show and he was cool. I mean, really cool. No mention was made of his wild wedding celebration when we had seen him last. Had he mellowed in such a short time?

You be the judge. This was the tour where Mick Jagger rode onto the stage astride a giant penis. A madman but a true showman. Our "Showtime" magic paled in contrast to the production values of a Stones concert. As we listened to every number, I realized—*Oh, this is what is known as a body of work.* "Honky Tonk Women," "Jumpin' Jack Flash," "Wild Horses," "Brown Sugar," and "Angie." Those are forever hits. That's what we needed.

How do you write some of those? That's all I could think about.

Occasionally, the question came up about whether we should consider moving to LA. Nobody in the band thought that was necessary.

What was it that Andy in Harlem had said? *When you're trying to make it, you can't break a group up with dynamite.* We did see it that way. We genuinely liked one another. We bought houses in Tuskegee next to one another, and our girlfriends became close friends too. None of them, as far as we knew, were pushing to move to California.

If we're just gonna wait for y'all to come back and leave on tour again, we might as well do it in Alabama.

Brenda had never given up on me. Even with long breaks, a month or two at a time, we stuck it out—talking on the phone a lot. Brenda had spent her college years cheering me on, while shining as a sociology major and winning one beauty contest after another.

In the spring of 1974, Brenda graduated from Tuskegee Institute. In this same period, I was awarded my undergraduate degree—true to Dean Carter's prediction that they'd claim me if I had some success.

Brenda never faltered as my number one fan and number one majorette. She was there as I went through the most dramatic learning curve, from when I was just getting used to girls screaming when we walked onstage, to getting signed, to learning I could write songs too. She stayed for every stage— from *Who am I? What am I doing? Where am I going?* to *Oh, my God, this is a great feeling!*

She almost never complained about the band being gone so much.

There was one instance when the Commodore girlfriends (some were wives) called a meeting with us guys to express concerns about the girls who threw themselves at us when we were on the road. The rest of the guys and I sat and listened stoically. Brenda was the ringleader. She began, "Y'all are so stupid. The only reason these girls even bother with you is they think you're rich and famous—because you have songs on the radio. Don't you know, if you didn't have hit records, they wouldn't pay attention to you one bit."

The other ladies backed her up, "That's right!"

And then we gave the worst answer possible: "And what's your point?"

Once some of the other Commodores started getting married, I could see the logic. Whenever I was with Brenda, it was like seeing her the first time—twirling her baton, laughing. I didn't want to lose the girlfriend who had been so steadfast. She was so strong, authentic, selfless, and up for the adventure. And we had the same values of family and community.

My feeling was, *Better solidify what we have.* We were a team and we loved each other. Why not? That's when I proposed.

A short while later, I overheard a conversation that my dad probably wanted me to hear. He and three of his friends, army buddies, were talking about me, almost in a call-and-answer routine.

"You know that Lionel Junior is good lookin' . . ." *Yeah, yeah.*

"He makes money." *Yeah, yeah.*

"Travels all over the world." *Yeah, yeah.*

Then someone had to tag it with, "Shame he is just as dumb as the rest of us." They joked about how you fell in love with the girl of your dreams and you also knew that you could count on two checks coming in. But if you didn't need two checks, why get married? They carried on, shooting the shit about settling down young when there was no rush. They were really happy for me, but they were ribbing me and enjoying the fact that I was just like them.

Did I pause to question if they had a point? If I did, I let that go.

I was twenty-six and Brenda twenty-three—we had some sense, after all.

And so, the only issue when I asked her to marry me was: *When?* We didn't set the date, because of my schedule, but we made the commitment. Getting married didn't have to be a big deal. My expectation was, *Hey, let's just continue on our easy roll.*

Anyone could have told me, nothing was gonna be easy, not when you're on a rocket. Brenda had come out on tour a couple of times, and, I will say, there was an ease to having her along. But a shift was coming. She would no longer be the girl-friend, she would be the wife, along not just for the perks, but for every painful, wonderful, heartbreaking, mind-altering unimaginable fantasy ahead, and she would stand in the turbulence of those crosscurrents. For better and for worse.

We agreed to set the date for some time in the fall of 1975. Then I was off and running on our latest tour to promote *Caught in the Act* in Japan.

I called Brenda from an airport pay phone to say I'd be back in five or six days, depending on logistics. We were playing Osaka as well as Tokyo, but Benny had pulled strings to have our album submitted for an award at the Tokyo Music Festival. Brenda wished me luck, as always, reminding me, "Don't forget to call when you land."

THIS WAS NOT the Commodores' first visit to Japan. Earlier in the year we toured to sold-out shows. With "Machine Gun" all the rage, we arrived in July to Commodore mania. Then, at the end of the trip, we received the bronze award at the Tokyo Music Festival.

What was I feeling? Exhausted, elated, revved up.

The rest of the guys chose to fly all the way back from Japan and continue straight home to Tuskegee.

"I'm not gonna do that," I said. I needed to be quiet for a minute. The plan was that I'd get off the plane in Los Angeles, stay a few days, write, see friends, check in at the studio, and then go home.

Everybody knew I wouldn't stay long in LA because, as treasurer of the Commodores, I was carrying a cash deposit that had to get into the general slush fund at the bank to pay for bills coming up.

The band had two main bank accounts that we shared. One of them was in New York, set up in our early days, and the other was in Tuskegee. On this trip, a Japanese promoter had paid us in cash, a sizable amount, most of which I had with me wherever we went, well stowed in our Bank of Tuskegee zippered blue pouch. By "sizable," I mean fifteen thousand dollars.

That was then a scandalous amount of money to be carrying on your person. I'm talkin' *scandalous*.

On the flight back to Los Angeles, I had a close call or two where I'd panic and then remember I had the pouch safely tucked away in a bag next to me. All I had to do was reach in and pat it to know it was there.

And so, after a long flight, I landed in sunny and hot Los

Angeles, grabbed a cab, and it dropped me at my crib—yeah, the Holiday Inn overlooking Hollywood Boulevard. First thing, I go to the front counter and I check in, pouch in my hands, and send my bags up to my room. Before I head up, I go over to a row of pay phones, dig out some coins from the bottom of the pouch, and I make a few calls. One is to Brenda.

Just the usual scat. "Hey babe, I'm in California, be home in a couple of days. Love you darlin', can't wait to see ya. Oh, yeah, we won the bronze."

She's singin' back. "That's amazing! Love you, can't want to see you too."

I call a couple of the guys in Tuskegee and leave messages with their answering services or girlfriends to let them know where I am and what's up.

Feeling grimy from the heat and the travel, I hurry up to my room to take a shower. I've been under the water for less than four minutes when I have a major panic attack because I suddenly can't recall—*Where is the pouch?*

Like a crazy person, I start patting myself. You know how that happens, when you start patting your body up and down, even knowing there ain't *nuth'n* to find because you're in the tub naked with the shower going? *Oh shit, oh shit, oh shit.*

Cut to: The lobby of the Holiday Inn and people trying not to stare as a brother comes galloping out of the elevator, with his Afro wet and flat to one side, and the other side wild and out of control, in some wet clothes, with water dripping all over the lobby floor.

I am describing this as if I saw it through my own eyes.

You know how when something like this happens, that you are 100 percent sure you left the pouch on top of the pay phone you used. And—*Oh, hallelujah*—as you turn the corner, you can see the exact phone.

You run gratefully, arms outstretched, but no, as you feared, you can see there is no blue Bank of Tuskegee pouch on top of that thing.

As a man who is delirious and wet and jet-lagged, I do the only thing a desperate man can do. I walk over to put my hand on top of the pay telephone and pat it, to make sure it's not there, because it might be invisible. And it might appear by the time I get there.

My hand confirms it is not there.

A bell goes off. I got it! *It's on the bank of telephones behind me on the other wall.*

You don't see any blue pouch, but you go and touch the top of each pay telephone on the other bank. And then reality sets in.

I recheck the tops of all the pay telephones. I do this exercise for fifteen minutes, back and forth, back and forth, walking up and down touching the phones on one bank and then over to the other, like any one of the poor crazy folks who have come up from Hollywood Boulevard.

Punch drunk, I'm so miserable. My Afro is fucked up. Everything is wrong. And all I can think is, *How am I going to tell the Commodores I just lost fifteen thousand dollars?*

Not five, not ten, but almost fifteen thousand dollars!?! And some loose change.

By about the sixth time performing my ritual, touching every phone, with total delirium on my face, I notice two young blond teenage girls—tourists, perhaps from the Midwest—who are sitting in the lobby watching me walk back and forth.

One of them pipes up. "Excuse me, are you looking for something?"

And by this time I'm almost manic.

"Am I looking for something? Hahaha, yes, I am, I am looking for something." Are the little girls making fun of me or just really nosy?

The girl who hasn't said anything asks, "Can you describe what you're looking for?"

I question her question but go ahead with, "Uh, you know . . . I don't want to be a bother, but it's a little blue pouch about this big . . ." I show them. "It has BANK OF TUSKEGEE written on the thing."

The two Midwest teenage girls exchange looks. One says, "Uh-huh, would you come with us?"

She points toward the front desk as I follow. The other asks the manager, "Could we have our safety deposit box?" She turns back to me and says, "We have it."

I wanted to cry. Can you even believe what I'm here to report? Of all the people who would have been in the Holiday Inn off Hollywood Boulevard to find this pouch that I left on top of a pay phone and forgot while making a phone call, how perfect was it that these two Good Samaritan girls from Idaho, as it turned out, on a church trip no less, were the ones? They could have kept it or just turned it in and gone on their merry way, but instead they put it in the safety deposit box, and they sat and waited to see if somebody came looking.

I got the pouch back, opened it up, and pulled out a one-hundred-dollar bill.

"No, sir, we cannot take it," the older of the two girls said. "God made sure that you got it back."

Nothing I could say would change their minds, so all I had was, "Thank you. God bless you. God bless you."

And that's when I realized that God will go to the greatest lengths to get you to enjoy and appreciate not just the big splashy miracles and the hit records and the fame and fortune, but the kindness of strangers who do the right thing just because it's the right thing.

God is so powerful. He returned eyesight to the blind. And

he returned money to Lionel Richie that he had lost in the lobby of the Holiday Inn.

People always ask, "When did you realize how blessed you've always been, every day of your breathing?" And I can't ever list all the moments. But this had to be one of them.

Can you say *hallelujah*?

THERE IS A dividing line that runs through my early career. That was the song "Easy." I could look back at that period and see how much *easier* life was *before* "Easy" and how quickly the altitude and the speed increased *after* "Easy."

We never appreciate the *before* enough, when you're just coming into your own and feeling that power boost that comes from a little success. We don't know that all of it comes with some kind of cost. The *before* ends up being addictive because it's wild and crazy and all things feel possible.

Creatively, emotionally, and professionally, I loved my days staying and writing at the Holiday Inn at Hollywood and Highland. Nearby was the iconic Capitol Records Tower— what they called the "House that Nat Built," where Nat King Cole had his recording home.

I never took for granted that the gates of Hollywood would never have been open to any of my generation if not for the giants on whose shoulders we stood: Nat, Sammy Davis Jr., Harry Belafonte, Sidney Poitier, Dorothy Dandridge, Lena Horne, a handful of others. Maybe that's why I promised myself never to be shy if I had a chance to thank anyone whose contribution had made possible any opportunity that came my way.

My first chance meeting of a hero was in the Holiday Inn

lobby, where I was scribbling notes for lyrics and noticed Little Richard walking up to the front desk.

He looked alarmed as I came flying over.

"Excuse me, I just have to shake your hand and thank you." Something like that.

I had to tell him that "Tutti Frutti" did more to integrate the music charts than any other record, in my view. He laughed. I told him that if it wasn't for him, Chuck Berry, Fats Domino, and a few others, there would be no such thing as Rock 'n' Roll, and every Black artist getting their music played on the radio owed him their careers. Of course, so did every white artist who copied what the Black creators had started.

Little Richard and I were friends from then on.

What I loved about these days was being able to move around Los Angeles freely. People were starting to know our songs, but they didn't see us on the street and go, "Oh, you are the Commodores!" They weren't screaming like we were John, Paul, Ringo, or George. If anything, now and then, it was "Commodore!"

You'll be glad to hear that I broke down finally and went to the dealership in Montgomery and bought myself the sweetest ride, a silver Datsun 280Z 2+2. What I wanted was a Jaguar—way too pricey—but the silver Z kinda had the same vibe. I bought it on low monthly payments to build up good credit. Best decision I ever made. Over the next two years, after having it shipped out, me and that Z were famous.

In LA, nobody stops you on the street unless you are *really* big. Otherwise, you're just in the category of *trying* to make it. There were unwritten rules that said if you're in Hollywood, east of La Brea Boulevard, driving west to Beverly Hills is ill-advised, especially if you're Black.

If you defy the "who's who" patrol and make it to Fairfax, well, fine, but then turn around and go back. Let's say you are on the verge of becoming famous. They might let you go to Doheny—on the border of Beverly Hills. That's it. Once you are there, you have to turn your ass around and return to your hotel in Hollywood. Doheny is the cutoff. Now go back to where you came from.

I'm being facetious, of course, but there's a built-in attitude to keep you in your place.

Nobody told me. On one trip to LA, we were having some recent success, with a healthy royalty check, and I convinced a couple of the guys to come with me, like pioneers of old, to cross Doheny and drive all the way to the heart of Beverly Hills—Rodeo Drive—where rich and famous folks go to shop.

We were halfway down the street, window-shopping, when a finely dressed fellow, a manager, came out from Gucci and called to me, "Lionel, how are you?" He added, "Commodores!"

He knew us? I said, "Oh, yes . . . doin' fine." The guys echoed me.

He continued with what was the least likely question that became the line that would forever mark the beginning of my new adventure. This gentleman said, "Lionel, have you seen Sammy lately?"

Sammy? Was he referring to Sammy Davis Jr.? Sammy wouldn't have known me from Adam's house cat, if that was who he meant, but I only said, "Not lately."

The man from Gucci said, "Would you tell him his watch is ready? When you see him."

Clearly, to some people, all Black folks who walk down Rodeo Drive must know each other. What was the response? "Okay. Will do."

Then he called, "Lionel, would you like to see the watch?" He wanted me to see it—as if maybe I was planning on having dinner with Sammy that very night. Or maybe I was planning on buying one myself. The answer to that—with all those diamonds—was clearly no.

It was a killer watch. Just killer.

And that was my introduction to Rodeo Drive in the days *before* "Easy" and *before* Sammy Davis Jr.—Mr. D., as I always called him—became my dearest friend and guidance counselor, rabbi and, appropriately, one of my greatest mentors. That is, in the time *after* "Easy."

HOW DO YOU know when you've made it?

The last people you should ask are your friends from back home. There was a reason, as a matter of fact, why in my early days as a Commodore I told my family members and class-mates, "I don't want y'all in the front row." Why? Because I was just learning how to get sexy onstage.

Here I am grabbin' my crotch, walkin' sexy across the stage, doin' my provocative moves, and the last thing I need to see are people I know like my Home-Boys or Wilma Jones, all of them doubled-over, laughing their heads off. *That ain't Skeet!*

Eventually, I convinced them this was just another form of acting, of being a character. That was the point. Onstage, I could escape my shyness and be somebody else. Well, you can imagine how excited I was to actually try my hand at profes-sional acting when the Commodores were hired to do a TV movie starring Billy Dee Williams about the life of Scott Joplin.

I had visions of grandeur. *Our first film, this is only the be-ginning.*

We'd been hired to play wandering minstrels. We had one scene we were going to improvise. No problem. On our shoot date, we rolled through the movie studio's pearly gates at 7 a.m. and were sent to makeup.

As soon as we were done, someone called, "Breakfast!"

Then we waited. Touch up, touch up, more makeup. Lunch break. We waited.

Finally at 4 p.m., the director walked over. "Okay, Commodores, you're up."

Ready.

"Now, here's the scene, guys." He described the camera angle and how there would be music, and then, "We'll pan, pan, pan to you guys, and then you do that thing you guys always do together."

Was I hearing this correctly?

"You know, you guys do the thing you do all together. And then the camera goes to Billy Dee."

"Excuse me," I said, politely but seriously. "What is that thing we always do together?"

"You know, you singing groups. You know—" Oh, he meant dancing?

I said, "We're not the Temptations."

The other guys gave me sideways looks.

I went on, "What is 'that thing' that Black folks do together?" This was not me talking. This was an out of body attack. My mouth had run off with my thoughts. Was this guy telling me all Black groups had "that thing" that we do together? And then I paused to come back to my senses. I still wanted to be in the movie. I explained that, normally, "The drummer, Clyde, doesn't do any dances with us, and neither does the keyboard player, Milan. So, it's just the four of us." As in me, Thomas, Ronald, and WAK.

Clyde, so diplomatic, offered, "Listen guys, I don't have to be in it." And Milan—with his Mississippi drawl—piped up, "Y'all just do it."

"Whoa," I came back. "We're the Commodores." All for one and one for all.

I wanted to be in this movie, but this was injustice. I mentioned to the director that we'd been here all day and could have been working on a routine if anyone had asked.

Maybe they assumed that all Black people kind of danced together.

After a rehearsal or two, we improvised and we did "that thing" we do. It was painful and it was ugly.

The director didn't know this could seem racist to us.

The way those words came out of his mouth so easily, so casually, reminded me of playing the frat houses and hearing, "Oh, we got some Soul Men playing for us tonight." Kinda like the movie *Animal House*.

They didn't know what they were saying was racist. They thought they were open-minded for hiring a Black group.

I had a similar discomfort meeting the white family that employed my grandmother, Frances Richie, in South Carolina. Grandma Frances, my father's mother, took care of the children of that family and raised them. And they called her Mama.

I knew that was a compliment, but she was a domestic worker. It was endearing, because they did love my grandma to death, and they were trying to show that they loved her as we did, but they called her Mama—yet didn't know anything about her life or her journey or her difficulties or joys. They knew her because she remained in the role to which she had been assigned—Mama.

After our one movie experience, especially after waiting all day for a scene that lasted fifteen seconds, I saw there was little glamour in the acting thing. And I also had a new appreciation for what actors and actresses of color have had to survive. Thankfully, the job didn't hurt our recording careers, and we went on to do a couple of other cameos in movies that didn't feel like they were setting our race back one hundred years.

ONE OF OUR smartest investments was to set up our own re-cording studio in Tuskegee. Instead of commuting to LA and back, we'd fly out James Anthony Carmichael, as well as our brilliant engineer, Motown veteran Cal Harris (not to be con-fused with the DJ Calvin Harris), and other personnel. We saved money and time, and then got to enjoy ourselves at home with our wives whenever we came off the road.

In the fall of 1975, ladies and gentlemen, I happily became a married man. Brenda and I had gotten up one morning when I happened to be at home in Alabama, and we had a conver-sation that went from "Do you love me?" to "I love you, do you love me?" to us eloping. We jumped in the car and drove to Auburn—where we were quietly married by a justice of the peace. That night, we returned home, excited to give our fam-ilies our news, proud to have spared everyone the expense of a big wedding.

The Richies and Harveys—robbed of a celebration—were furious. And so, a couple of months later, we threw the big wedding bash at the Holiday Inn in Tuskegee, the only spot that could hold everyone. We did it right.

Within the year, we bought a house next to where the other Commodores and their wives had bought houses. We had a compound, an extended family.

This was as close to a charmed life as I could imagine—like a fairy tale unfolding.

But then—in the winter of late 1976 or early 1977—without warning, we faced a tragedy. The Commodores had just left for a series of dates when Ronald LaPread's wife, Kathy Faye, suddenly became gravely ill with cancer. We could have kept our engagements when Pread left to be at her side, but we decided to reschedule the rest of the tour and hurry home to be there for Pread and for Kathy, the most angelic young woman you'd ever want to know.

The return to Tuskegee meant we could also get into the studio to finish up our fifth album, *Commodores*, which we hoped would be our biggest yet. I'd been working on lyrics for a new song that felt important—but wasn't sure what to do with them next.

Our immediate concern, of course, was to go see Ronald at his house. Almost stoic, he told us that Kathy was terminal—not expected to live more than two months. We sat in shock and denial, and all broke down. She was twenty-three. It happened so fast.

The five of us left and held an impromptu meeting. We came to a group decision—*The Commodores are gonna pay for her treatment. That's it.*

We went right back to Pread's house, and I began, "Look, the guys and I, we talked, and we got money. Tell the doctors to fix it. Just make it happen."

Ronald LaPread's face went through a range of reactions—from gratitude to sorrow. He repeated what the doctors had said. "No, fellas, you don't understand. There's nothing we can do."

Money couldn't stop the cancer. The doctors had tried aggressive and experimental treatments, but the prognosis was the same.

Pread knew. His heart was broken because he knew. All we could do was go through it with him—as his brothers. We were going to help find meaning in the time Kathy had left. Somehow.

Then Pread told me, "I've been at the piano trying to write a song." He had a melody but that was all. Kathy sat with him at first and kept saying, "Don't go down, go up." He wasn't sure what she meant but he kept working on it, hoping to finish it for her.

Kathy's condition worsened. She had to be hospitalized. Pread called me from the hospital and asked me to meet him at his house. I rushed over and he went to the piano, saying "Richie, I'm begging you, help me, man." He played what he had so far, and it was beautiful. Kathy was right, in the melody the notes descended. No lyrics.

I had something that I'd been working on, I promised him, that I thought could work.

Pread wanted to be in the studio and would come in briefly, just to get a break, and then run back to the hospital. The next day or so, probably in the very early hours of the morning, I brought in my take on the melody and played what I had, and then played the melody Pread had given me.

James Carmichael suggested, "During the lunch break, you two need to see each other." We melded the two melodies together, his that was on a descent and mine that built up. Pread rushed back to the hospital, and I continued, fitting my lyrics to what we had. Later that night, Pread came walking into the studio and I told him it was done.

Everyone listened as I talk-sang the words. When I got toward the end, we were all crying like babies:

> *Whoa, I'd like to greet the sun each morning*
> *And walk amongst the stars at night*
> *I'd like to know the taste of honey*
> *In my life, in my life*
>
> *Well, I've shared so many pains*
> *And I've played so many games*
> *Ah, but everyone finds the right way*
> *Somehow, somewhere, someday*

Whoa, ʒoom, I'd like to fly far away from here
Where my mind can be fresh and clear
And I'll find the love that I long to see
Where people can be what they want to be . . .

I wish the world they call freedom
Someday would come, someday would come, baby

Whoa, ʒoom, I'd like to fly far away from here.

The song was "Zoom." Carmichael gave us such a fantastic arrangement. And all of us felt Kathy's spirit when we recorded it. Though it was never released as a single in the United States—because Motown execs had other choices—"Zoom" would become a phenomenon over the years, some even calling it the Black national anthem. Fans of all backgrounds could relate to the desire to transcend the weight of the world.

In March 1977, we dedicated the album to Kathy Faye LaPread, who passed away days before *Commodores* was released. Ronald LaPread went back on tour with us soon afterward.

I didn't know how he did it. I couldn't imagine losing my partner at such a young age. But he made it through and found healing within the Brothers Commodore.

BENNY ASHBURN'S TOUGHEST job as our manager was to keep everything fair and equal between six artists who were at different earning levels. He became the pseudo marriage counselor, diffusing any squabbles among band members. At first his position was, "Lionel has a hit record, but don't worry, you can get a hit record too." Soon it was out of hand with, "Lionel's got four hit records." Benny had to reassure everyone that nobody was missing out.

I hate to be the bearer of bad tidings, but *equal* is a word that messes up every group in the world.

We developed a system of deciding what songs got on an album. In Tuskegee we'd have a band meeting and try to agree on what were the best songs. Benny would have the final word. With *Commodores* every single one of us had writing credits. The album gave us what would have been our first Platinum certification—meaning, it sold a million copies. Motown wasn't yet using the RIAA certification process, but this was still a huge deal.

The first single was my song "Easy," and the second was "Brick House"—written by the Commodores, inspired by an idea from Walter "Clyde" Orange, who was also the singer of it.

When Clyde brought the concept into the meeting, we all loved it and started pitching in on the lyrics. With everyone sharing credit for writing—something I wish that we would have done more of—we went to town on that song. I knew the expression "built like a brick shithouse"—a reference to . . . can you say a woman's "voluptuous" figure? Guys used to describe a girl as so "stacked" she could just fall over, but if she's built strong, ain't no knocking her over. Clyde shortened it to "She's a brick [beat] house."

Not everyone would know the meaning. The person I worried about knowing was Adelaide Foster. I could see Grandma listening to the song on the radio and being disgusted.

And, man, was she ever. Grandma refused to go to church for two weeks out of embarrassment. At some point, the song became such a hit, she got past her fear of religious persecution or of God's wrath raining down on her—as if she would be held to account for her grandson's transgression.

"Brick House" soared to #4 R&B and #5 Pop, a killer crossover and a party-anthem-forever song.

When we were in the Motown studio (what used to be MoWest) recording it and were adding in all the bells and whistles, Stevie Wonder happened to drop by and wouldn't leave.

"You like it, Stevie?" I asked.

"Lionel, I love it!"

Stevie's assistant kept coming over and saying, "Stevie, Stevie, we gotta go to your rehearsal. We're late. They're waiting on you." Apparently, his rehearsal was supposed to start at 11 p.m., and it was 10:30.

Finally at about 1 a.m., as they were heading out the door, I looked at the clock and said to Stevie's assistant, "Oh shit, he's at least two hours late."

No, he was not two hours late. The rehearsal was in New York City, and here he was in LA. So he was one day and two hours late.

Stevie is a genius and one of the most loving human beings on the planet, but he is notoriously late. With my ADHD, I've been known to be late, but not Stevie Wonder late. In defense of both of us as creative human beings, sometimes late just comes with the artist. And mostly it's worth it. Yes, we were late. Yes, we were terrible on budgets. But we would give you a classic smash-hit record like you hadn't heard before. And the fact is that when he shows up, he's going to be Stevie Wonder, he's going to move mountains and part seas.

In fact, in the year we were working on our fifth album, Stevie was riding high on his eighteenth, released in September 1976, and it was a masterpiece on steroids. *Songs in the Key of Life* included such singles as "I Wish" and "Isn't She Lovely" and remains his top-selling and most critically acclaimed album.

Stevie Wonder late? Who cares.

Anyone who has spent any time with Stevie knows that he is a notorious practical joker. He got me every time. Remember, he is blind. Undisputedly, legally blind. Yet, somehow, he'd detect me from down the hallway if I happened to be up at the Motown offices—maybe hearing my voice—and he'd call, "Hey Commodore! Lionel Richie, is that you?"

I'll never forget being over at Stevie's house one night when he brought up a new song he wanted me to hear that was in his car. "C'mon I'll play it for you," he said, and had me follow him to the door.

Outside, Stevie escorted me to the passenger side of a luxury automobile parked at the top of the driveway and kindly said, "Get in, Lionel." He ran around to the driver's side, opened the door for himself, and slid in behind the wheel. Skipping no beats, he put the key in the ignition and *cranked* the car up. Ladies and gentlemen, I *repeat*: Stevie Wonder *cranked that sonuvabitch up*! Next, he popped the cassette into the console tape player, pushed play, turned up the volume, and then . . . wait for it . . . put the car in reverse, put his arm over the seat rest, and turned his head over his shoulder as he began to back down the driveway.

At that point, I lost it completely and screamed, "Stevie, what the fuck are you doing!?!" whereupon he started laughing hysterically. He got me. He reveled in the satisfaction of having completely freaked my ass out. So much so, and to his lasting enjoyment, it took me days to recover. I couldn't remember the song now if I wanted to.

ONE OF THE secrets of going to the Other Side, as I had learned, is that you can't force the magic. I wasn't the kind of writer who would write a love song because I was in love or a sad song when I was sad. Often, I'd write an up-tempo song when I was down or a sad song when I was on top of the world.

The first flash of "Easy" came faster than usual. I'd just been handed a binder of close to 365 pages that detailed my schedule for the next year. *Where was my life?* My immediate reaction was to take out a pen and write directly on the binder:

> *Why in the world*
> *Would anybody put chains on me?*
> *I've paid my dues to make it*
> *Everybody wants me to be*
> *What they want me to be*
> *I'm not happy when I try to fake it! No!*

My feeling was *please, leave me alone*. What was this? What did it sound like? What was the story I had to tell? First off, I had to hum and walk around before I went out of body. Some compare it to going into a darkened cave where all the secret feelings are stored. This was something I'd just been learning to accept, that I could go into the inner room, through the doorway, and not worry about having trouble getting back again. The door had begun to stay open.

Now, you go in and get "Sweet Love." The next time you've got to go a little deeper and you get "Just to Be Close to You." The deeper you go into the room, you go deeper into yourself, and you get "Zoom." The next time, you go even further, and you have to take a corner, and you keep going until you find the music and the rest of the lyrics for "Easy."

Then it gets scary because two things happen: 1) You feel like you are the master of the Universe. Like, *Well, nobody's humming this to me, but it's clear as a bell*. And 2) You discover that the only thing that can make the room go away is doubt. As soon as you think, *I can't do this*, the door shuts.

As the King of Doubt, I worried, *How do I control this?*

Marvin Gaye, like James Carmichael, advised, "Keep going in that room and don't think about anything else, but just get the stuff out."

How do you know when you've struck gold? Marvin said, "The minute you think you know how to write a hit, you kill the magic." Seriously? "Don't think about it. Just receive. Hopefully, you never know the answer."

That is the mystery. Songwriters are storytellers, but we're also detectives of our own inner lives. We are having therapy and so are you.

Creativity is in the silence.

Going through the portal is often painful. For me to be able to write the lyrics or to feel the melody, I'd have to go to a place in my life where I had felt the hurt. Sometimes after the elation of finding that song and giving birth to it, there is a letdown, even a depression. It's like being a Wichita lineman.

"Easy" was not an easy song to write. Not a simple love song at all, it was musically complicated—*So what is the hook and which is the chorus, Lionel, and do you need one more verse?*

The story was complicated. It was a song about breaking up, not about goin' along to get along—like you might think. And that twist made the lyrics complicated. I got stuck when I wrote the line, "I'm easy-ay-ay, easy like . . ." Easy like *da-dah-da-dah*. Easy like *what?*

What? The question I had to ask was what easy used to feel like in my life. To a country boy growing up in Tuskegee, what was that feeling? Then I remembered how I used to hear folks say that the easiest day of the week was Sunday. There it was. Filling in the *dah-dahs*, I had it: *Easy like a Sunday morning.*

Nothing logical or obvious. The key was not to think about it. You have to wait for it. In the silence came the answer. Everybody understood that feeling even if they hadn't heard the phrase before. That's when I knew where to find all the greatest lyrics in the silence on the Other Side. I just had to quiet my brain and *listen*.

The beauty of getting to write a song like "Easy" is that you become a bridge into another person's life, especially when you start to hear, "Hey, Lionel, I just wanted to tell you, man, I'm going through the same problem you went through, man."

One thing we songwriters have in common is the desire for listeners to hear their stories in our stories, to make their discoveries in our discoveries, to feel that we are saying to them, "I know how you feel."

We are now having group therapy. What follows is an emotional bond, even if you come from completely different backgrounds.

"Easy" was an instant smash. Usually, we'd see movement on the R&B charts and then, once that was moving, we'd see how we did on the Pop charts—a "crossover" hit. "Easy" started moving on the Pop chart right away, eventually peaking at #4 and at #1 R&B.

From the earliest days of the record business, the charts were basically devices for segregating music sales. Record stores reported sales, and Pop was supposed to be white buyers and R&B was assumed to be Black buyers. Motown had blurred the lines, but divisions remained.

The methods for tracking airplay by *Billboard* and *Cashbox*, among others, varied. What mattered was that your records got played up and down the dial, preferably at peak drive time.

Skip Miller (Motown's head of Pop promotion, which is an oxymoron) and Miller London (who promoted to R&B stations) let us know we could help our odds immensely if we'd go meet with DJs at radio stations or conferences. If we carried the record into the room, most of the time the DJs would listen for a minute and say, "R&B, you got it. But it's too Black for Pop."

This was actually said to us.

That didn't happen with "Easy."

Pop stations put that record right on the air and the request lines lit up. But some DJs decided the record was too white for R&B. Suddenly, the game was different. Not so easy.

In 1977, at the Jack the Rapper convention—where Black DJs came together to bolster support for Black artists in all the changing formats and Funk was alive—I started to get additional scrutiny from DJs who were looking at me like I wasn't passing the Funk litmus test.

Skip Miller saw my discomfort, as I bent myself into a pretzel trying to be Black enough for R&B and accessible enough with program directors in Pop radio. Skip and I had known each other from the time of the Commodores audition at the Turntable, right when he was getting his start at Motown.

Everybody in Pop radio knew Skip Miller and loved him. He sat me down. "Here's what I want you to do," he said. "You write anything you want to write, and I'll get it played." That was all.

Between him and Miller London, the point person with the Black DJs, that's what they did. And that was the birth of Lionel Richie.

The promotion team caught hell getting songs played like "Easy," "Three Times a Lady," and "Sail On." They didn't follow form. The songs were going Pop, they were going Country, they were misbehaving, and they weren't going R&B. We had crossed over alright, but we couldn't cross back. Or as detractors in my own community later put it, "Lionel Richie crossed over and he can't get Black."

Ridiculous. Why be mad that a white fan of a Soul song that had the feel of Country and Pop and Rock could relate to a Black Funk R&B artist? What made me mad was when bean counters at my own record label decided they had to test-market "Sail On" before it was released.

Part of what I loved about not staying in our lane was that we were becoming provocative. We didn't have to get buck naked onstage, but we definitely got folks to talk. We were breaking the rules, writing songs that made people go, "What the fuck? What are these Black guys trying to do?"

This thinking helped me let go and let the buyers and the listeners tell us what was hit-worthy or not. When we appeared on Dick Clark's American Bandstand the first time—right after "Machine Gun"—he gave us that advice. He cautioned us not to lose our accents, to stay true to the values that had raised us, and never to forget the fans who were the ones most responsible for getting us to where we were.

Amen to that, always and forever.

THE THING ABOUT the Commodores is that we were educated, not stereotypical country boys. We were a cast of six characters, each with our own quirks and eccentricities. Thomas McClary won the prize in that department.

I have a vivid memory of when we opened a huge Rock festival in Germany. Queen was the headliner. The die-hard Rock fans started booing and throwing drinks at us and then began beating up our fans. We were just about to leave the stage when, suddenly, what did Thomas do? He got this crazy gleam in his eye as he went to the edge of the ramp all the way to the end—like his whole life had led him to that moment— and he fired up his guitar with a showstopping "Star-Spangled Banner" à la Jimi Hendrix.

The crowd stopped throwing things at us and began to cheer. The press raved about that moment. Thomas saved the day.

Then there was the incident with Thomas in Baton Rouge, Louisiana, where we were starting a tour. When we arrived, the mayor of Baton Rouge welcomed us and asked about what activities we enjoyed.

I said, "Tennis." WAK said, "Tennis." Milan wanted to play golf. Clyde said he wanted to go on a boat. Pread said he wanted to go four-wheel driving.

Thomas had a long answer. He went on to say how, when he had time off, he liked to ride his horses. He may have mentioned the five-thousand-acre farm he owned in Colorado.

Impressed, the mayor invited a prominent local man to bring his two-million-dollar stallion to the grounds of the Colosseum for Commodore Thomas McClary to ride. How did that go?

We had to rely on the report given to us by Ronald LaPread, who met us when WAK and I got back from playing tennis, and said, "You ain't gonna believe what happened!" He had shown up at the Colosseum, back from his four-wheel driving, to join the mayor and a group of local officials and fans to witness our bandmate go for an easy ride on this athletic specimen.

Pread—who knew a lot about horses—could see right way that the stallion was a powerhouse only a top rider could control. He warned Thomas, "Don't get on that horse. I'm telling you, that horse has got too much funk and you can't handle it."

Ignoring him, Thomas said, "I got it," and climbed up. He was barely in the saddle before the horse immediately took off running toward the exit of the Colosseum grounds. Everybody started to chase the wild-eyed horse, including the owner, with Thomas holding on for dear life.

Pread told us it got worse. Much worse. The more everyone screamed, "Pull up the reins!" the faster the stallion ran.

Where was he going? Like in a disaster movie the horse bolted headlong onto the interstate, into oncoming traffic!

The owner went absolutely ballistic. He threw his hat, crying, "My horse, my horse!"

The horse then somehow jumped over the divider—there were no cars thankfully—and came thundering back on the other side of the motorway toward the Colosseum.

Before anyone could exhale, Pread said, "At the last second, he turns and gallops off down to the beach."

Everybody at that point ran down onto the sand as the horse went straight for the water! Pread described seeing Thomas still clinging onto the swimming horse's back. The horse got so far from shore, Pread said Thomas's head was like a fly on the horizon.

We listened in misery until Pread concluded his account. The horse, having calmed down from his swim, came back to shore with Thomas in the saddle, dripping wet. Our fellow Commodore dismounted, pleased as hell with himself, and that was the end of that.

Cue up our theme song: *You can't make this shit up.*

IN LATE 1978, we held a group meeting. As our savings account had grown considerably, we voted unanimously to buy ourselves Christmas gifts. Right before the holidays, I was given the job of going to Montgomery, Alabama, to order seven brand-new luxury-model cars—one for each Commodore and one for Benny—and to make sure they were delivered by Christmas Eve.

After two years with my Z, which I had just paid off, I was ready to live a little. Six of us were each going to be getting a Mercedes, various colors and models—mine was to be a silver 450 SEL—and one of us was getting a Jaguar.

Just before closing time, I walked into Jack Ingram Motors in my proud Afro and a pair of bell-bottoms. Christmas was only a few days away, and the salespeople were focused on helping a couple of customers in the showroom, which was decorated for the season. Nobody from sales bothered to ask me anything, so I went to the main office and took a seat outside a door with the name JACK INGRAM on it. I could hear an older man having a loud phone conversation in his good ole boy twang.

Finally, Jack Ingram hung up and came out of his office and saw me there. "Can I do something for you, son?"

"Yes, sir," I began. "I'd like to purchase six Mercedes and one Jaguar." I rattled off the colors and models.

"Six Mercedes and one Jaguar? Would you please step into my office, son?" There he sat behind his desk, and I took a seat across from him. "And what is your name?" he asked, taking a notepad out.

"Lionel Richie."

"Nice to meet you, Mr. Rickey." He smiled, but seemed doubtful as to whether I was capable of making such a purchase. In a pleasant Southern accent, he proceeded to ask the most obvious question. "Uh, how do you plan on paying for the seven cars?"

"I'm going to pay with one check," I answered, and started to take it out of my wallet.

"Do you have anyone to verify your ability to pay for this?"

"Yes, sir." I pulled out a card, and said, "Please call this number for the president of Chase Manhattan Bank in New York City."

He placed the call. The bank president picked up as I gathered from what I could hear. Jack Ingram said, "Now, sorry to bother you, I have a Li-nell Rickey in my office who says he's with a band called the Commanders and he wants to buy seven cars. Can you verify if this fella . . ."

With the phone in his hand, he stopped midsentence and listened, then looked up at me with a sudden warmth. "Oh, yes, right away sir. Oh, well, yes, . . . uh-huh, oh, I see . . . Very well, and thank you." And then he hung up the phone.

Wearing a Cheshire cat grin that could have reached all the way to Atlanta, Georgia, Jack Ingram now knew my name. "Mr. Richie, let me get right on this. You sit here for a minute." With that, he got up and went to his office door, where he stood and spoke these words: "Ladies and gentlemen, may I have your attention, please? Jackie Ingram Motors is closed until the first of the year. Thank you very much, we'll see you after Christmas." He waited a beat before adding, "I'd like to see all the sales-people in my office in five minutes!"

Next thing, a group of sales guys came in grumbling about the two deals they just lost.

Their boss said, "Don't worry about the deals. God is sitting in my office." He needed the entire sales force to get on the phone, fly, and drive, to locate the specific cars, and to have six delivered to Tuskegee and one to Harlem in time. As he escorted me out to my 280Z, he reassured me, "We'll get it done, Li-nell, don't you worry."

True to Mr. Ingram's word, on the afternoon of Christmas Eve, a huge truck carrying six brand-new luxury cars—five Mercedes and a Jaguar—pulled into the center of our home-town. One by one, those cars were offloaded from the truck, ready to roll. And I do believe that was when the word went out to the entire city of Tuskegee, Alabama, that the Commodores had really made it.

11

Flying High

NO ONE CAN PREPARE TO be famous. There's not a course or a class you can pass or fail. My word to the wise, borrowed from several sources, is simple: Money, power, and fame does not change you, it only magnifies you.

If you're a little nice person, you're gonna be a big nice person. If you are little asshole, you're gonna be a big asshole. And if you have vices that can kill you, you're dead. Fame doesn't fix you, it just makes you more of who you already are.

Fame didn't cure me of worrying. Even though the light was green, I worried it might turn red at any minute. So, I pushed harder. Once we got to 1978/1979 we were flying. The songs were coming, the public was coming, the band-name awareness was coming, and the hits just kept on coming.

We had started work on our sixth studio album, *Natural High*, and I leaned into collaborations more than ever. Milan Williams and I both had cuts on the album with sole writing credits. My song was called "Three Times a Lady."

The story about how the record ever came to light taught

me a lesson—that sometimes the hit you're looking for is right there in your back pocket. It was not well known that I had a secret stash of songs from my early days when I thought I might get kicked out of the band, before we had any hits, when I was just learning how to write. One of those songs was inspired by a toast given by my father, Lyonel Richie Sr.—who, as we all knew, could hold a crowd spellbound. In this case, as he stood up at a family gathering, Dad delivered a most heartfelt, warm, affectionate, and succinct toast to Mom.

There was no special occasion to my knowledge—which led me and my sister to think he might have been feeling guilty about something. Deborah and I glanced at each other as our father became very sentimental. As in, "Dad, you okay?"

He ignored us and proceeded to describe his gratitude to our mother for always being there for him, through the ups and downs. And he acknowledged he had never taken the time to say, "Thank you, Alberta, for the years you've spent with me and struggled with me."

He asked us all to raise our glass to her, to honor her, because, "She's a great lady, she's a great mother, and she's a great friend."

The rhythm of the words and the moving toast left such an impression that I wanted to capture it in a song that I duly called, "Three Times a Lady," and that title led to a waltz signature—*one*-two-three, *one*-two-three. R&B/Funk it was probably not. The song was not for the Commodores though. No, it needed to be sung by someone with more gravitas, someone iconic. To be precise, I wrote it for Frank Sinatra. Nobody but Frank would do.

The only problem was I didn't know Frank and had no way to get the song to him, much less convince him to record it. I tucked the song away and forgot about it.

Cut to: Around the spring of 1978, or there about, the

First solo tour in 1983.

At the 1982 Academy Awards show, performing "Endless Love" with Diana Ross— the only time we ever sang it as a duet together, live and in person.

(ABC Photo Archives / Getty Images.)

With the amazing Tina Turner, the Queen of Rock (around 1985). What an electrifying moment.

At the Rosemont Horizon in Illinois on the horn on my solo tour.

Here we go. After five Grammy nominations and five nos, in 1983, I won with "Truly"!

Two icons I was blessed to call mentors, Sammy Davis Jr. and Frank Sinatra, who both called me "the Kid" (1982, Thalians Ball in Los Angeles).

Singing "All Night Long" at the 1984 LA Summer Olympics for two billion viewers globally. This close-up moment made me recognizable around the world from then on.

At the Waldorf Hotel in 1985 with Brenda and our daughter, Nicole.

Onstage at Madison Square Garden.

One magical night—January 28, 1985, at A&M Studios in Hollywood—when a gathering of some of the most generous artists in Pop music checked their egos at the door to record "We Are the World."

Michael and I putting the finishing touches on writing
"We Are the World."

At the 58th Academy Awards in 1986—when, yes, hallelujah, I won the Oscar for Best Original Song ("Say You, Say Me," featured in *White Nights*).

Commodores were in Tuskegee recording, and I asked James Anthony Carmichael to come by my house so I could play him something I'd written for Frank Sinatra. Maybe the time had come to get it to him.

After I finished playing him the song, James said, "Brother Richie, that is not gonna make it to Sinatra. That's gonna be on the Commodores."

"It doesn't fit the Commodores," I argued.

James put his hand on my shoulder. "Some songs fit the moment," he said, "and other songs make the moment." This was in the latter category.

Worth a shot, I guessed. We were in the studio back in LA working on the vocals when Norman Whitfield dropped by. He found his usual seat in the corner and sat down.

Norman never said much. Maybe a smile or a nod. "Easy" got me a thumbs-up. Not this time. After a couple takes, I went over and asked him, "What do you think, Whit?"

He had the weirdest expression. "What the fuck are you doing?"

"What do you mean?"

"Richie, that's a waltz! What the fuck are you doing?" He didn't let me answer. He just shook his head and muttered, something like—*First "Easy" and now a waltz, what's next?*

That's when I stopped doubting. Norman was saying to me that I knew what I was doing, going against the grain.

Others had severe doubts. They knew that Berry Gordy did not like waltzes, and they went so far as to tell me "Three Times a Lady" was *going to ruin my career.* The magic phrase. It was like I'd heard with "Easy" but a hundredfold.

Let me cut to the chase. "Three Times a Lady" gave the Commodores our first #1 on the *Billboard* Hot 100 (Pop), where it stayed on top for two weeks. It went to #1 R&B and #1 Country. The fact that it had an appeal to a Country audience didn't surprise me because the waltz timing goes back to hill-billy music. But in case anyone forgot, I grew up Black in the country. The part that did surprise me was the appeal it had as if it was a standard. It was our first true worldwide hit. It went everywhere. Although it was never covered by Frank Sinatra, "Three Times a Lady" became one of the most covered singles of any of my songs—with covers by more than forty artists. And counting. There was no rhyme or reason as to who covered it—everybody from Conway Twitty to Johnny Mathis, from Isaac Hayes to Andre Kostelanetz and the entire Top of the Pops symphony orchestra.

The publishing royalties for having a song covered to this extent were pretty amazing. I mean, my career was going just fine.

And so, from then on, whenever I was looking for a song for the Commodores, James Anthony Carmichael's standard line became, "Brother Richie, do you have any more of those songs you are planning on giving to other artists?" The other lesson was that whenever I heard that my creative choices were going to end my career, I could take it as an endorsement for disrupting the norm.

The fact that I was able to dedicate the song to my mother made her feel wonderful, of course. And I included Brenda in that dedication, naturally, because without her in my chaotic life, I wouldn't have been able to sing the song with a personal point of view. Grandma was pleased, as you would expect. As for my father, well, the story in our family was that when the Commodores went on Johnny Carson and I told how the song was inspired, Dad commented afterward, a little sarcastically, "Son, I'm very happy to have inspired that song but does it come with a check?"

That became a running joke.

The other lesson learned about having that song stowed

away—until I pulled it out and played it for our producer—was that everything you do in life has its meant-to-be time. And that's where divine intervention comes in.

The greatest irony is that, right in this same time frame, who did I meet? Of course—Frank Sinatra.

▌▌▌│▌▌

WHEN YOU DRIVE west on Sunset and you pass Doheny, you'll soon spot the Beverly Hills Hotel. Back in the day, you couldn't see much of the pink hotel with the private bungalows in the back because of the palm trees and the hedges that kept all the looky-loos out. You would miss it if not for the iconic green sign with the white script lettering out front.

In the mid to late 1970s as the Commodores were starting to make a name for ourselves, *the* place to have lunch was at the Polo Lounge at the Beverly Hills Hotel. Only the most elite celebrities could get a table. Like it was a private dining room for stars and studio heads. Certain people had their own booths reserved, even if they weren't there, and the big deal was that each booth had its own telephone. Before there were cell phones, this was a great way to go have lunch and not miss your calls.

The Polo Lounge was a world unto itself.

Want to test whether you're famous? Go at eleven thirty. If they don't let you in, you ain't made it yet.

For a few years I didn't even bother driving up to the valet: 1) because I'd have to tip and I was planning on paying for the meal, and 2) because I might not even get in. So I would park on a side street and jog around to the front and walk in. That way, if I tried to get a table and heard, "Sorry, sir, it's closed until three o'clock," I wouldn't have parked at the valet in vain or wasted the tip.

One day, in the whirl of the "Three Times a Lady" era, let's call it late 1978, I was in LA, taking a break from a studio session, so I thought, *What the heck, let me test my clout.*

At the Polo Lounge door, to my amazement, the maître d' said, "C'mon in." Me and my Afro just walked right in. *Holy shit.* This was major.

As I walk by the bar, heading toward the back part of the Polo Lounge, I hear somebody go, "Hey, hey, hey, here comes the kid now. There's the kid. There's the kid."

I look into the VIP dining area and see the guy pointing me out is the comedian Buddy Hackett. He's at a table talking to Sammy Davis Jr.—a social acquaintance I'd recently met at a charity event. Brenda was with me for that occasion and together we had met Mr. D. and his wife, Altovise. The Davises instantly took the Richies under their wings.

As I say hello to Buddy, Mr. D. gets up from the table where he's sitting next to Frank Sinatra. Frank's talking to a nearby group of men who run the town. Mr. D. says to me, "Hey Lionel, Frank's over there and he wants to meet you."

Frank Sinatra wants to meet me?

I'm confused but I awkwardly walk over to where Frank Sinatra has just stood up. I've barely introduced myself, when suddenly Frank's talking to me. He has a smile on his face but it seems he has something serious to say.

In what is a completely surreal moment, Frank says, "You know, kid, I like you."

I feel total relief. "Thhhhankk you very much."

"No, kid, I like you." He explains, "There's a lot of shit out there."

I nod in agreement. I'm twenty-nine years old. Sinatra, handsome at sixty-three, Old Blue Eyes, has barely aged, even with his drinking and smoking.

Then he makes his point. "Listen, kid, if you get yourself

one song in this business that people ask you to play over and over, for the rest of your life, you've got yourself a career."

We are standing, eye to eye, nose to nose, as if he wants to be sure I'm paying attention.

Suddenly, to make doubly sure, he takes his open hand and lightly smacks me on my cheek. For further emphasis, he proceeds to pinch me on the same cheek as he says, "You, you lucky son of a bitch. Not only do you have one song, you've got more than one. But not only that, you wrote 'em all." He laughs. And then he says, "Alright—"

With that, Frank Sinatra turns and walks away from me like we didn't even have a conversation.

I probably made a joke to Sammy along the lines of, "Did I just get beat up with people smiling, or was that a compliment?" Actually, it was an endearing smack on the cheek.

From then on, I could go to lunch at the Polo Lounge, where I was known for decades as "the kid." The Rat Pack—Mr. D., Frank Sinatra, Dean Martin—and the comedians like Milton Berle and Buddy Hackett, and so many of that generation of some of the greatest entertainers all called me that and welcomed me into their circle.

What I learned about Frank is that he adored songwriters. Before performing a song, he would name the writers and the arrangers and then sing. That's what happened before he met me. He had done his homework. He heard the songs and had asked, "Who wrote that song?" *That kid wrote that song.* "Well, who wrote that other song?" *That kid wrote that song too.* "Well, who is this kid? Where's the kid?"

All of that happened before Mr. D. told me, "Frank wants to see you."

FLASHBACK: THE WINTER of 1970, Lloyd Price's Turntable, New York City. On my way to the stage, after our break, my path is blocked by a mountain in a leather coat. Unmovable. And—I'll never forget—I look up and it's Muhammad Ali. He grins. I say, "Hey, Champ."

In that hush of a voice that can make anything sound poetic, he says something like, "How you doin', little Brother?" *End of memory.*

Cut to: Nine years or so later. I get a call at the place where I'm staying in LA at the time. In a familiar, raspy voice, the person on the phone says, "I want to speak to Lionel Richie."

"Speaking."

"This is the heavyweight champion of the world. Come to my house right now." *Click.*

What to do? I call Benny Ashburn, who's in town and knows where Ali lives in Hancock Park. Two hours later we pull up to the main check-in for this gated community and are told, "The champ is waiting for you."

As we pull up to his house, I look over to his front lawn and see him standing there, his arms folded, waiting. Perfectly still. Like a fucking statue.

You can probably imagine what his first words are when I jump out of the car. Of course, he glares at me and says, "You're late!"

Without further ado, Ali ushers me inside and takes me on a tour of his house. In one spot we pass by a baby grand and he says, "Can you play piano?"

"Of course I can play piano."

"You write songs?"

I'm catching the drift that he's pranking me, but you have to be ready. So I play along. "Well, I do write songs." He wants to know if I can sing. I tell him, "I sing."

"Can you play my favorite song?"

"Sure, what is it?"

"Can you play 'Once, Twice, Three Times a Champion'?"

Ah, that was the setup. He was three times a champion, that's three comebacks. And I happily adapted the song as I sang it to him. This was his way of meeting me and vetting me. After that, we sat down and he told me his struggle, how no one expected him to come back. "They all thought I was out and then I was on my way back because I'm the greatest."

I had a chance to tell him how he had been a beacon, a placeholder in my brain that told me there could be a mentally and physically strong hero who could stand up to everything thrown at him. More important, I could tell the champ what that meant when I was starting to write, to have an example of how to fight through the word *no*.

He accepted my praise about how fearless he was. He had the charm, he had the wit. But most important, he had the grit. He could back up his mouth.

"I have to ask you," he said before I left that day. "You know what we have in common?" I didn't know. He told me, "We're pretty." He went into a riff. Ali said, "You can almost be as pretty as me, but you're not." From then on, every time we met, that's what he'd say: "*We're* pretty, but you ain't as pretty as me."

ROBERT BURNS, A Scottish songwriter and poet of the late 1700s, was the person who wrote, "The best-laid plans of mice and men often go awry." The quote was longer, but the short version has stuck around for us to use as a reminder that there is much we do not control, no matter how well we plot and scheme and strategize.

Well, the best-laid plans of the Commodores started to collide with reality. Everything was in motion, going faster, and the fear I had, for my part, was that if I took a break, the whole thing would come crashing down.

Got another song, Lionel? "Yeah." *Got another song, Lionel?* "Yeah."

The only place where I could hide was at the studio. Imagine how that must have felt to my wife, who'd waited until I got off the road, looking forward to us taking a vacation together, and all I wanted to do was rest for a day or two and then go back to work.

And then I started to feel friction with the guys. I was used to hearing most of them say, "I'm writing with Richie." If I had the hot hand, and it was a better payday, why not? Then, as more and more records started coming out that I'd written, alone or as a collaborator, the wealth was not being spread across the board. Yes, we all made money from being on the record, and we split that six ways. But if you wrote the hit song, that was your own annuity. Again, we were all doing phenomenally well. Nobody was suffering. If there was resentment, I just saw it as growing pains.

The harder part was the added attention shown me by the press. Some outlets began calling us Lionel Richie and the Commodores. Clyde and I had become co-lead singers, true, but putting the light on me incorrectly must have felt terrible to him and to everyone.

The other brewing drama was that our wives, a team of their own, were becoming jealous wives. I could imagine the pillow talk. One guy would say his wife was upset because Lionel's wife is walking around showing off what Lionel bought her. Another wife was showing off her stuff even more. We all entered a reality show called *Keeping Up with the Commodores*.

The next fracture was that some of the guys had kids and assumed it was cool to bring them to our rehearsals. It was and it wasn't. We now had to watch how we joked. If Milan's kid, Jason, was in the rehearsal hall, we couldn't call Milan names or give him shit, part of our process, because Jason would be confused by that.

Brenda and I had not started a family yet. It hadn't happened and that was understandable, given how often I was away. We weren't in a hurry either, but I'm sure it was uncomfortable for her when most of the conversation with the other wives was about the joys and challenges of being moms or moms-to-be.

We sought out top fertility specialists. The ups and downs of fertility treatments added another challenging dynamic for us both.

There was nothing overt about any tension I may have sensed with my bandmates. There was definitely a competitive undercurrent, but to think it was anything that could break us up was sacrilege. The code we had set for ourselves was never to think of "I" and "me" but to always speak in terms of "we" and "us." We were the mighty, mighty Commodores—forever.

Occasionally I'd recall the warning from Andy at Smalls Paradise: *When you're trying to make it, you can't break a group up with dynamite. When you make it, you can separate the group with a butter knife.*

That ain't us, I reassured myself.

WHATEVER WASN'T WORKING, I believed, could be fixed by what always worked for the Commodores. *Midnight Magic,* our seventh album, proved that.

We all scored big. Everybody had at least one album cut with either sole or cowriting credit. *Midnight Magic* soared to #1 R&B and #3 Pop on *Billboard*'s album charts.

The first two single releases were mine—songs inspired by stories that friends and strangers increasingly confided in me.

At thirty years old, I wanted to understand love as it seasons—how couples react when they go through change.

"Still" came from a couple I knew. Separately, they recalled how their relationship fell apart. Tragic. Both expressed regret and remorse but couldn't save their marriage:

> *We lost what we both had found*
> *You know we let each other down*
> *But then most of all*
> *I do love you*
> *Still*

This was one of those songs that was me saying, "I know how you feel." "Still" also gave the Commodores our second #1 hit on the *Billboard* Hot 100 (Pop), as well as being #1 R&B and #6 Country.

"Sail On" was the record that threw everybody into a tizzy because it followed no rules. On the *Cashbox* Top 100 it hit #1 Pop (#4 on the *Billboard* Hot 100), was #8 on the *Billboard* R&B, and made waves on Country radio. "Sail On" was again inspired by a friend who was going through a divorce, written to help him in the letting go:

> *And I don't mind*
> *About the things you're gonna say*
> *Lord, I gave all my money and my time*
> *I know it's a shame*
> *But I'm giving you back your name*
> *Guess I'll be on my way . . .*
> *I'm looking for a good time*

"Sail On" was another song I originally wrote thinking it would be recorded by a Country artist but that James

Carmichael insisted had to be on the Commodores. It became known over time as the ultimate breakup song. What few figured out was how much of an eff-you to an ex there was buried under all that healing. My theory, and I only confessed this many years later, is that one of the reasons I could go into hostile, war-torn places and be embraced by both sides was because I had devised a method for expressing anger peacefully through melody.

Way into the era of Rap and Hip-Hop, I was surprised to get a call from comedian Chris Rock, who wanted to talk about "Sail On." Chris said, "Dude, I've been listening to the lyrics. Lionel, that's the most gangsta song ever written!" Ah! He was on to me.

Chris went on to talk about how resolved and at peace the music felt to him, and how the lyrics could be read that way too, only the "I'm giving you back your name" snuck in the cold finality of "And I am done with your ass." Chris Rock was amazed that a song written in 1979 could still be relevant forty years later.

What we all learn, as I did after "Sail On," is that very few relationships—marital or professional—can withstand change taking place at a constant and high clip. The friction at home for me was hard to ignore, though overshadowed by a chilling atmosphere with the band.

Get the knife. We were becoming butter.

HOW DOES A dream come true turn into a tragedy? I tried to deny that could ever happen—the Commodores tragedy.

Benny, in his efforts to massage egos and resolve conflicts, decided he was not going to commission us like a manager. He would be an advisor, helping run the business, Commodores

Entertainment Corporation. It was the worst mistake, but he did it to be fair, explaining that he was getting his percentage off the gross and then splitting what was left six ways. Instead of taking money off the top, he said, "I'll tell you what, guys. I'll just be a seventh Commodore."

In other words, Benny gave up the managerial veto vote. When we'd sit down to have a meeting, instead of him being the wise old bird to say, "Guys, this is bullshit, let Clyde do this" or "Lionel should have a say," he no longer had clout.

In choosing songs for our next album, *Heroes*, our eighth, I had a stack of contenders, a lot of them ballads, some more up-tempo tunes and possible collaborations, and a very personal Gospel/church song called "Jesus Is Love."

I'd learned by now not to bring in finished songs because I'd run the risk of starting to play a song and in five seconds hearing, "No, not that song, next song." If you took all day and all night to finish it, you just wasted time and you're going to be mad because they threw it away. Instead, I came prepared with only the tops of tunes. If we liked it, we'd keep it in the mix. I'd finish it later. Or we'd chuck it and move on.

Right away, before I showed my stuff, one of the guys announced, "We don't want any more ballads on this album."

Kinda took the wind out of my sails, no pun intended. I didn't say much. There was some discomfort in the room and then a more up-tempo song I pitched was accepted for a collaboration, along with "Jesus Is Love"—which turned out to be the surprise breakout song. In the end, I had four songs on the album, but no love ballads.

During the rehearsal period for this tour, I got over my slightly bruised ego. The guys didn't want ballads. So be it. No reason to be mad.

Rrrrinnnggg!

You'll never believe who called.

Kenny Rogers.

What?! We had been introduced at some awards shows, but I didn't know him well, only that I was a fan. He was Mr. Personality, a Texan with Soul. Charismatic like you can't believe. You couldn't not like Kenny Rogers.

With his husky, warm voice and friendly twang, Kenny wasted no time telling me, "I need a Lionel Richie song, a ballad."

Now, ever since "Three Times a Lady," I'd been getting such calls frequently from managers and labels and artists too. I'd never said yes, but that was then. My band didn't want ballads and I had a ballad that I loved with a little scat going called "Baby." I didn't have much other than, "Baby, I'm a da-da-da-da . . . and I love you, dah-dah-dah-dah."

Kenny's situation was that he had a greatest hits album coming out in the fall and they needed something new to be a big hit out of the box.

Damn timing. Man, I was honored, but I had to say, "Well, Kenny, I can't make it." My schedule was impossible until late in the summer with the Commodores' next tour. "But when I come off the road, if you need something then, I'll see if I can put a song together for you."

Tours in this period were required for album promotion, and had to begin four weeks after the album hit the record stores and radio stations. At rehearsal in Tuskegee, shortly before the tour began, we received a phone call that Clyde was in the hospital after falling off his motorcycle.

We went from *Omigod, is he alive?* "Yes." To *What the hell was he thinking?*

The doctors said he would need several weeks of recovery. Thankfully, the prognosis was good. We were unanimous in deciding to postpone our tour until he was better.

Without missing a step, I called Kenny and told him about the change in my schedule. "You still want that song?"

Without taking a breath he says, "Meet me in Vegas."

A day later I fly to Las Vegas and sit down to get to know Kenny, who spends thirty minutes telling me about Marianne, his wife.

He is over the moon. "Oh, my God, I just married a *lady*," is what he says. "Me, Kenny Rogers. Can you believe it? I'm a Southern Texas guy—Houston, you know . . ." And he tells me stories of the rough ride of his life and career and how she is full of grace and elegance. Kenny says again, "How did I end up so lucky? I married a lady, like a real lady."

I'm listening but thinking on my feet.

"Oh," Kenny goes, "what was the name of the song you have for me?"

And, complete poker face, I say, "Lady."

That's how my scat "Baby" became "Lady."

Did I change it on the spot? Dead on, I did. I was no fool. Man, we'd just spent the last half hour talking about his lady, and I wasn't going to call it "Baby."

Kenny couldn't believe it. He was fired up. "Okay, play me the song."

We went over to a piano in his suite, and I sat down and began to play and sing: "Lady, I'm your knight in shining armor, and I love you, bah-bah-bah-bah . . ." I stopped after a few more notes, took my hands off the keys, and waited for his response. And turned around, asking, "You like the song?"

"What's the rest of it?"

I said, "What, you like that? Because if you like it, I'll finish it."

Clearly, he'd never heard anyone pitch a song with half of a verse and a hook. And I'd never pitched a song to anyone outside the Commodores before. That was how we did it. Kenny took a long beat to make up his mind. He could have said no but just went for it. Later, he confessed the only reason he said yes—I had a track record. "Okay," he said, "I'll do it." And added, "Can you meet me in LA next Thursday? I'll put my vocal on."

Five days to write the song? "See you in LA."

Before I left, he asked an unexpected question. "By the way, who's going to be the producer?"

And I said, "Me."

Oh shit. What have I done?

I had never produced a song by myself.

The next person I called was James Anthony Carmichael, screaming on the phone, "Are you ready for this? The two of us are going to produce for Kenny Rogers. He wants to record 'Lady,' you know, the song 'Baby' that the Commodores turned down. What do you think?"

This was about to be a fateful conversation. I had assumed he'd love nothing more than to be the copilot on my first producing flight. No, no, no. James had news for me. He began, "Brother Richie, remember I told you that a time was gonna come when you won't need me? Well, you don't need me."

But no . . . I don't . . . I can't do this on my own . . .

"You produce this song for Kenny yourself. You have all the goods."

James Anthony Carmichael gave me permission to fly on my own.

We completed the record in August 1980, and then I scrambled to leave in time on the *Heroes* tour with the Commodores. Clyde was good to go. All was well. For the time being.

WE RETURNED TO Madison Square Garden—for two nights as headliners. I looked over and saw the spot where, nine years earlier, twelve-year-old Michael Jackson showed me the crowd and said, "Lion-*nel*, *we* sold out Madison Square Garden!"

Another memorable Commodores gig at the Garden had been a few years earlier. We found out that everyone wanted to claim us as homeboys, thanks to those first Harlem summers. Going in, we thought nobody could rock the Garden like us, but we learned a thing or two about that from our opening act—Bob Marley and the Wailers. They had *asked* if they could be our opening act and we were thrilled.

I will never forget—I went down to Bob's dressing room before they went on to celebrate getting to do a show together.

One interesting facet of the night was that, before the Wailers came out, there were a couple of numbers performed by an artist named Kurtis Blow—whose single "The Breaks" was being featured as this new music trend called Rap and who had an album coming out soon. Bob and I talked about the influence of the roots of Reggae in the house parties up in the Bronx and other New York boroughs where DJs were rapping over music samples. Artists like Kurtis Blow and the Sugarhill Gang ("Rapper's Delight") were stirring something up.

Bob Marley had a presence, an aura, that made me feel like we'd been friends forever. Before I left his dressing room, with the rest of the Commodores, Bob began to roll a joint, a paper bag filled with weed that he lit on fire. The smoke fumigated his whole dressing room. It was *nuth'n* to him. I, on the other hand, inhaled a cloud of the smoke and stumbled out and don't remember anything else about that night.

The fog lifted a week later, the day "Lady" was released.

Oh. My. God.

"Lady" was on every station, in every cab, pouring out of windows and in bars and restaurants. We were still on tour when it peaked at #1 on Country and #1 on the Hot 100 Pop chart (Kenny's first single to do so), where it remained for an unimagined six weeks, and it also became an unexpected #1 R&B hit. The album was eventually certified Diamond and sold in the range of twenty-one million copies.

For inquiring minds, let me explain that my contract with Motown didn't extend to any outside writing and producing I did for other artists and record labels. There was no exclusivity. When I was a Commodore, my publishing was split fifty-fifty with Jobete (Motown's publishing company). Any writing I did for anyone other than the Commodores, it turned out I owned 100 percent. For math folks trying to calculate royalties for a runaway massive smash single on twenty-one million copies of a hit album, let me put it this way: *Someone back the Brink's truck up to the front door.*

AN ARTICLE IN *The New York Times* in this era hailed the Commodores as probably the most successful current Black crossover group—by virtue of our having scored hits in Pop, R&B, and Country. What the newspaper didn't report was the ongoing struggle faced by our promotion team to get us airplay on Black radio.

We had been shown so much love from Black DJs in our early years, but at the height of disco, they'd listen to thirty seconds of "Three Times a Lady" and some would say, "Not R&B, but we'll let the listeners decide," while others were more cut-and-dried: "We don't put on that white shit."

I was scared of these guys and their power, but I grew to love them later, and vice versa. The shift began at a Black Radio Entertainment convention where I was expected to make some flattering remarks and leave the stage.

Well, something possessed me to ask, "If Mozart were

Black, would he be Mozart?" Nobody said anything, so I forged ahead. "The answer is no. Because he wasn't funky enough and you wouldn't have played him. But you just killed the Black Mozart."

My fellow Commodores had their mouths wide open. What was Lionel doing?

I said, "I'm not trying to be liked. I'm trying to be Mozart. And you're either going to help me get there—and not only me, but every other Black Mozart that wants to be somebody different than Funk—or you're gonna kill a generation and a genre that's never going to see the light of day."

They were won over and became my defenders. If R&B program directors didn't want to play my songs, the disc jockeys in my corner would say, "Fine, you've just killed Black Mozart."

I still had my detractors. You bet they were up in arms over Kenny Rogers singing my song. "Can you believe it? Lionel done lost his mind and gave 'Lady' to a white guy who's taking credit for it."

Skip Miller called them up and read them the riot act. Unheard of. Skip, a Black promotion guy from Motown, promoted to Pop radio. "Lady" was on another label. Why should he care?

Skip told them, "We have to make this a hit record on R&B, Pop, Country, Crossover, everything else, because the guy who wrote the song is Lionel Richie. That's our Mozart."

I WAS STILL on tour with the Commodores when I received a call from Kenny Rogers's manager, Ken Kragen—a very accessible, smart, and down-to-earth veteran of the entertainment industry whose management clients ran the gamut from the Bee Gees to Olivia Newton-John, among numerous others.

Wasting no time, he congratulated me on "Lady" and said that Kenny needed to start work right away on his next album. "And we want you to produce it."

In complete shock that after one song I was being asked to produce a whole album, of course, I said, "Yes!" They were hoping too that I'd write some songs for the album.

The best part was that alongside the creative alliance was the gift of my friendship with Kenny for life.

Next came the leap to hyperspace—with the jangling of a phone. *Ringgggg!*

The office of Jon Peters called. A celebrity hairdresser who'd been Barbra Streisand's boyfriend, Jon Peters had joined Peter Guber, a music industry honcho, to head up PolyGram Pictures. They had a project with Keith Barish and Dyson Lovell, along with director Franco Zeffirelli, and wanted to know if I would be interested in composing an instrumental title song for their new movie—an adaptation of a bestselling novel about young love.

I didn't know much about writing that kind of a song but I said, "Well, sure, I'm honored." I put down the phone, and went to ask Brenda, "What do you know about this book called *Endless Love?*"

12

Endless Love

FAME, MONEY, AND POWER DO not buy immortality. Being a legend doesn't make you less mortal.

That was shown to the world in December 1980, when forty-year-old John Lennon was murdered. A crazed fan had approached Lennon and had gotten an autograph on an album, only to come back later that evening as John and Yoko walked from their car to the front door of the Dakota, in New York City, after being in the studio. The fan pled guilty after shooting Lennon, once his idol, in the back, because, he said, "He was phony."

In May 1981 came more proof that being a musical prophet of peace and love, as embodied by Bob Marley, does not prevent you from succumbing to disease, for him a rare form of skin cancer. He was thirty-six years old.

I was thirty-one, almost thirty-two. These deaths should have shown me that I too was human and that I should try to slow down. But it's impossible when you're young and you don't ever think it could happen to you. I just pushed harder.

Early that year, after starting work on the next album from the Commodores, *In the Pocket*, which was due June 1981, and producing Kenny's album, *Share Your Love*, also due in June, Brenda and I realized we had to find a temporary living situation in Los Angeles. Rather than rushing to find the right home, we accepted Kenny's generous offer, "Why don't y'all come stay in one of our guesthouses?"

Kenny had recently bought the eleven-acre hilltop estate known as the Knoll up on Schuyler Road in Bel Air. It was fit for royalty—a magnificent thirty-five-room Georgian-style mansion. Brenda and I fell in love with the guesthouse, an elegant two-bedroom bungalow with a view of the gardens and pool—perfect for writing and creating.

We were just getting settled when I had my meeting to pitch my idea for the instrumental title song for *Endless Love*. Prior to going in, I had screened a rough cut without any music.

No one suggested that this was an audition but the minute I walked into the waiting area, who came out?

Marvin Hamlisch.

Are you kidding me right now? Marvin Hamlisch—the iconic conductor, arranger, composer/songwriter with hit records, Broadway show tunes, and even Oscars for everything from *The Sting* to *The Way We Were*—was my competition?!

I don't stand a snowball's chance.

I'm ushered into the inner office and wait for the axe to fall. Introductions are made. Franco Zeffirelli stands as he speaks with big gestures, as he says, "The music must be soaring, Lionel, soaring so we feel the passion! Soaring!"

The main producers nod. Jon Peters and Peter Guber nod too, but not as much.

"Well, Lionel," someone asks, "did you see the movie?"

"Yeah, I saw the movie." I say this like a doctor, as in—*Yes, I have examined the patient.*

"And?"

"And," I begin, take a breath, and continue, "let me tell you what you need here."

They wait.

"It's simple. This is young love. This is two young people."

They nod.

"It's almost like *Love Story*, you know?" And I hum that unforgettable opening of the *Love Story* theme. *Bah-ba-ba, ba-Bah-ba* . . . Then I say "You want a melody like that. It needs to be something like . . ." and I hum, *Bah, Bah, ba-bah-ba-bah-ba-ba-ba* . . .

Everyone says, "That's it?"

I smile. "Yeah, simple, something like that."

"Thank you very much," one of the producers says, giving me my exit cue. Off I hurry to other pressing concerns.

Two days later, producer Dyson Lovell called to ask, "Say, Lionel, you got the rest of that *bah-bah* song?"

"Yeah, I got it."

That's how I got the job. Though I had a lot on my plate, I figured, *Hey, it's only an instrumental theme song.* I'll hum it and bring in all the pros I know to help record it.

Leaving *nuth'n* to chance, I put myself on a very strict schedule at three different studios. The Kenny Rogers album was on from 10 a.m. to 6 p.m. at Lion Share Studios in West Hollywood, the Commodores was 6 p.m. to midnight at Motown Studio, and the slot for "Endless Love" was 1 a.m. to 4 a.m. at a recording studio in the San Fernando Valley.

Everything was set to release in June—the albums and the movie. Zero wiggle room.

Okay, we got this.

The filmmakers had a new idea. They loved the melody and they called to relay an additional part: "Can you just write us a first verse because in the middle of the movie the girl is going to sing it to the guy."

"Oh, sure, no problem." Here we go:

> *My love*
> *There's only you in my life*
> *The only thing that's right*
>
> *My first love*
> *You're every breath that I take*
> *You're every step I make*

No sweat. I recorded it on a cassette and had it delivered to them.

They *loved* it. They loved it so much they wanted lyrics for a full song and then had another new idea: "We're thinking of a duet. Who do you suggest for the duet?"

In my self-doubting way, I wondered if they wanted Kenny Rogers. "No, no," they assured me. I was their only choice for the male singer.

My first thought for the female voice was Dionne Warwick. Over the years, I'd gotten to know Dionne. Soul and grace personified, Dionne's haunting, rich voice was perfect for this movie, I thought. And she had sung other movie songs.

Before I even suggested Dionne, guess what? They said, "We want Diana Ross."

They assumed getting Diana Ross was something I could pull off because, after all, the single would be released on Motown.

I could have set them straight by urging them to go with Dionne. They apparently had no idea what had just happened with Diana Ross, that after twenty years as the leading lady and

Queen of Motown, Diana took off her crown and announced her departure for RCA Records, after signing with them for an unprecedented twenty million dollars.

Motown was already in a state of upheaval. The seventies had seen the departures of Michael Jackson, most of the J-5, the Four Tops, Gladys Knight, the Temptations, and others. By the early eighties, even Marvin Gaye would leave. Independent record companies like Motown no longer had the resources to compete with major labels that were now corporate conglomerates making offers to established stars that they couldn't refuse.

The Commodores, thankfully, had no reason to seek better terms. Why would we leave? With everybody gone, after waiting all this time, we had just become a priority!

What Berry Gordy was going through had to be *crushing*. He had been Diana's mentor from the beginning and her love interest for many of those years.

Mr. Gordy, when asked how he felt about Diana leaving, had said, "I don't wish her any harm, I just wish her distance."

The producers of *Endless Love* apparently didn't see why this was the worst time ever to assign me the job of asking Motown for the favor of getting Diana on the theme song.

My reaction was—*I ain't touching this with a nine-hundred-foot pole!* That's what I told Brenda after my ranting woke her in the middle of the night. She listened as I explained that the only person who could get Diana Ross to sing on "Endless Love" was Berry Gordy. "And they want me to ask him?!" I went off. "Why do I have to grovel for him to call her?"

Besides, I was terrible at difficult conversations. Not Brenda. She had no problem speaking her mind—or sometimes mine. Brenda tried to placate me, then went back to bed.

When I got up, Brenda wasn't there. My assistant was there, however, and when I asked if he had seen her, he said, yes, and "She told me to tell you she's going to Berry Gordy's house."

No . . . It was all over. How long would it take before Berry Gordy decided to take my name off of Motown's roster forever? The man was going through hell, and the last thing he needed was Brenda bringing up anything about Diana Ross. This was going to set him on fire.

I had given Brenda enough fuel and kerosene to blow up the whole thing.

Two nerve-racking hours go by. The phone rings. It's a direct call from Mr. Gordy. He begins, "Ah, did you know your wife is here?"

"Jesus Christ," I say, in a tone of "Oh, so the rumors are true?"

"I want you to come up here right now."

I imagine everything just short of being shot at the gate.

It's a tragically short drive to Mr. Gordy's estate. As I get to the call box, I'm told he's waiting for me. As I pull up the driveway and get to the top, pulling into the courtyard in front of his house, I glimpse a terrifying sight. It's Berry Gordy standing alone. Waiting.

In his Fila tracksuit, ladies and gentlemen. In the history of Motown, both in Detroit, Michigan, and in Bel Air, California, Berry Gordy has never waited for anyone out front.

Shit, I tell myself, *it's not bad. It's really bad.*

Drenched in sweat, I park, get out slowly, with what must be a nervous look on my face, dreading the conversation that's about to come, and then I walk a few steps to where he is standing.

Mr. Gordy then says these words: "Lionel, no one, no one has *ever* spoken to me the way your wife has spoken to me. No one has said words like that to me ever in my life . . . *except* my daughter, Hazel."

This is where I stop breathing, unprepared for a sudden wild-hair turn.

"You are very lucky" are the next words he has to say. There is a pause. And then, he explains, "You have someone fighting for you. I wish I had someone to fight for me like your wife is fighting for you. She's right. It's not about Diana Ross. She's not signed to me, but you are. Brenda's right. You're trying to get a break with a movie song, and you need my help, and whatever my relationship is with Diana does not matter in this case, because she needs this hit record as much as you do."

I hadn't thought of her needing a hit until he said it. Mr. Gordy led me into the house where we were joined now by Brenda—who was looking quite confident even though neither of us knew what was to happen next.

"We're going to call Diana right now," said Berry Gordy, sending a jolt through me.

Then he got on the phone in his den, right away, and called the superstar whose career he had shaped from the start, who had just left the only recording home she'd ever known, and left him, the visionary whom she had once promised, "If you can dream it, I can do it." And on the phone he convinced her to do one more song, a duet with me, as a final bow on the Motown label.

With thanks forever to Brenda, the "Endless Love" phenomenon was about to unfold.

THEN SHIT GOT crazy. There was a ticking clock.

DIANA'S PEOPLE: Lionel, we need you to fly to New York. Diana can't do it in LA.

ME: Well, guys, I'm in the studio doing Kenny Rogers from ten to six, Commodores from six to twelve. I can't do it.

Meanwhile, Zeffirelli was frantic that I understand the action to unfold on-screen so I could time the theme song to the drama to be more soaring. Jon Peters and Peter Guber were calling me and saying, "We have the utmost respect for Zeffirelli, but don't pay any attention to him. We want a hit record." So did I, but I was adamant that I could not go to New York to record the song with Diana.

At my wit's end, I decided to call Quincy Jones, sure he would agree that I should not give in. I had met Quincy in our early days and then had gotten to know him when he produced Michael's *Off the Wall* album at Epic. The two were about to get started on the next album, which would turn out to be *Thriller*. It went on to be the #1 all-time greatest-selling album at an estimated seventy million copies.

"You know, there's no respect," I complained. "I'm not gonna bend over backward."

"Well, good for you." Quincy added, "Now, the artist named Lionel Richie feels real good about that."

"Yeah! I damn well do."

"Well, let me tell you who's pissed at you."

"Who?"

"The writer Lionel Richie is pissed off. The producer Lionel Richie and the publisher Lionel Richie—they're pissed off."

I got quiet.

He said, "Let me teach you a word about being a producer. The answer is yes. You'll worry about your feelings later." End of story.

Diana's people and I, with the help of Suzanne de Passe, reached a compromise. We could work in a small sixteen-track studio in Reno, Nevada, after her show in Lake Tahoe. That was a two-hour flight for me. To keep everything running smoothly, Suzanne and her chief colleague, Suzanne Coston, flew to Reno, took a limo forty miles to Tahoe to pick up Diana, and rode with her back to Reno.

I had gone up early before her show so I could be ready. Thinking I had enough time to take a quick nap, I went to the hotel and fell into a deep sleep, only to be awakened by a call from the studio with the horrifying news: "Miss Ross is here waiting on you." I had overslept! I was probably a half hour late.

The two Suzannes greeted me with expressions of "You are in for it," as I profusely apologized and made some jokes at my own expense. I took Diana's hands, smiled, and said, "Thank you, Diana, for your patience, and, more than that, thank you for doing this after your show, and for making the effort to come all the way here."

She smiled and said, in effect, "You're welcome."

At that point, she warmed up and was ready to go to work. Later there were comments in the press that we didn't get along while working on this recording. That wasn't my experience, although I know she wasn't happy about my being late and she certainly had a point.

Now, the exhaustion and the pressure were building and getting to me. Did I mention I had to get a part of the song synched with a movie trailer ready, like, the next day?

We didn't sing the duet together. The objective was to put her on tape and then I'd record my vocals separately. Man, I had to be so sure that we had the best possible vocal, we put her on every track we could. Even the drum track.

Diana Ross has a tough-as-nails work ethic, and I appreciated it. I also saw that she was tough on herself, in an endearing way. On one of the takes on the line "I don't mind, I don't mind . . ." she made a comment with a laugh, "*Huh* . . . I can't do this" or something like that. That *huh*, though, I loved and I ended up keeping it. We managed to capture every Diana vocal nuance and expression to be had, and on the initial play-back we all heard that it worked—gorgeous and emotional.

That was a wrap. The two Suzannes whisked Miss Ross off into the early morning light. My engineer and I hurried to pack everything up and get to the airport in time.

By midmorning, back in the studio in LA, our big job was to comp (short for compile) the Diana Ross vocals from multiple tracks and merge those many takes all onto one reel. Then we would comp my vocal reel and we'd put the two of us together, so I could mix the song for the movie trailer due in three hours.

I left the setup to our brilliant engineer, Reggie Dozier, and went to grab coffee from the coffee machine, where I was joined by Suzee Ikeda, the multitalented ace production manager who was keeping everything moving on schedule. Suzee and I were laughing and celebrating the successful recording session with Diana when I turned around and saw a freaked-out Reggie.

"We have a problem," he said. Before I could ask, Reggie took a breath and told us, "The SMPTE code . . ." Now alarm bells went off. "Somehow in putting Diana on her reel, the SMPTE code got erased. In putting her on all those tracks, it's gone . . ." This was the technical term for the time code that allowed the comp to happen, and that would let us connect Diana's reel with my reel.

"Erased" as in . . . without the translation code, the sound on different reels can't speak to each other. Fuck.

And that was when desperation and panic would normally take over. We now had less than three hours for a mix of the song—parts of it—to be synched with the movie trailer. I was due in two hours at another studio to start mixing for Kenny.

In my delirium, in the face of Reggie's wide-eyed freak-out, I made a decision that could only have sounded like a man in denial. I said, "I am going to breakfast. I will bring you back something to eat. When I get back, I want you to have Diana Ross and Lionel Richie singing together."

That was my passive-aggressive way of saying, "It's your problem, you fix it." My other message was, "I'm gonna leave God here with you to figure it out. You got this." I don't know if I believed that, but the goal was to make Reggie believe.

All I can say is: God came to visit while I was away having breakfast. Reggie used an oscillator, where you bring two sound waves together. He created a new SMPTE code.

When we finally aligned the reels into one, we listened to the playback on every speaker in the studio—and it sounded *amazing*. If you didn't know, you wouldn't have known that Diana Ross and Lionel Richie had never sung it together for real, standing up and looking into each other's eyes. I then scrambled to mix the song for the movie trailer. Hallelujah. Done.

Then, over the next ten nail-biting days, we had to create and complete the hit record—for the movie and for Motown to release to the world. Everything up until this point had been a warm-up, but we all lived, including me.

I've often been asked if I knew the impact "Endless Love" would have. The truth is that you always hope the song that you have birthed out of the depths of yourself will be well received, but you don't really know. "Endless Love" freed a part of me when I wrote it—an end of suffering for the kid I had longed to heal. It was a song for hire, yes, but it made me feel worthy of being the messenger of love. And then people—in hearing it, singing it, falling in love, and getting married to it—just confirmed that belief.

The song was released on June 26, 1981. It rose to #1 on the Hot 100 Pop chart, where it remained for an astonishing nine weeks, and hit #1 R&B and #1 on the newer category of Adult

Contemporary. "Endless Love" stayed on the charts for twenty-seven weeks and became Motown's all-time highest-charting and most-successful single, a distinction held up until that time by Marvin Gaye's "I Heard It Through the Grapevine"—produced, as you recall, by Norman Whitfield, written by Whit and Barrett Strong.

The movie didn't catch fire, sadly, though the song wound up being nominated for an Oscar for Best Original Song—ultimately losing to "Arthur's Theme" by Burt Bacharach and Christopher Cross. But the coup of that evening was that, finally, at the Academy Awards ceremony, Diana and I performed "Endless Love" as a bona fide duet.

Up until that performance, I wasn't sure how she felt about the song . . . or me, for that matter. At rehearsal, she could not have been more gracious. We hugged, we rehearsed, we related to each other as if from our younger teenage selves. There are some artists who keep their energy in reserve and wait for the lights and the cameras to turn on, and then they are *on*. That's Diana Ross. That's what the world saw at the Oscars. After walking offstage, we congratulated each other, and that was it.

The record to this day remains—so I am told—the most successful single of both of our careers.

Superstitiously, I told myself that this embarrassment of riches all banging at the same time was some momentary fluke—a lucky streak. It was as if I fell asleep and woke up to hear, "Oh, you hit three home runs."

It was completely surreal. Kenny's *Share Your Love* album, released June 1981, went Platinum, #1 Country, #6 Pop. The Commodores' *In the Pocket* became our third-best-selling album.

After so much soaring and rising to this crescendo, I expected a leveling off, a calming. But everything kept soaring faster. No longer was I in the part of the rocket where I could hang with the other Commodores, trying to enjoy the view. No, I was on the nose of the rocket. Alone. Couldn't see shit. Couldn't remember what just happened. No control. Flying blind.

I was euphoric, proud, and grateful, but also unsure and scared to death because I couldn't see where I was going. The taste of victory was beginning to be bittersweet.

Motown had been pushing for me to do a solo album, but I'd said no, repeatedly. My thinking had changed. First the guys turned down "Baby," which became "Lady," and then, after I proposed including "Endless Love" on a Commodores album, they didn't go for that either. Maybe it was a sign to do that solo album of mine.

The plan was to do that while still promoting the Commodores' album and starting work on the next one at the same time.

So much for best-laid plans.

13

Sail On

IF I'D BEEN ONE OF the other Commodores, I'd have been ready to show that Lionel Richie guy the door starting with "Lady."

Forget our brotherhood. Forget the family, forget that they had told me no more ballads and that I'd taken some of my marbles to go play somewhere else. Secretly, I'd worry, *Why go solo?* Then I'd hear them say, "Yeah, you should do a solo album," like, "Why don't you jump off a cliff."

I didn't blame them. Not after "Lady."

"Lady" was everywhere. "Lady" was enough to kill the group dead. To be fair, Kenny Rogers loved the Commodores, and the success of a hit like that cast its magic not only on me but on the group. It was good for us all but it was great for Lionel. That part was the killer.

Then "Endless Love" came along, and there's Lionel going to Oscar-ville and freaking out—*Hey guys can you believe it? I met Henry Mancini!*

How could you not be sick of him already? In fact, I was sick of me, it was so awkward.

Now, hold on. In my thinking, I'd been given opportunities to grow and learn as a songwriter and producer and I had the chance to stretch by doing my own album. Putting together my own band—not named the Commodores—was sobering, but between everyone I'd met working on several projects at the same time, I assembled some of the greatest musicians working in the Business.

This was not forever. My plan was to continue to be in the Commodores but go on a brief sabbatical, then return to the mother ship and it was all going to be fine.

In the excitement of it, I didn't realize that doing this kind of a one-off could be the beginning of an uncoupling. That possibility was just unthinkable. Public perception was another new problem. During that same week when we were in New York playing Radio City Music Hall, the press was featuring me more and more in our group interviews. One reporter would ask, "So tell us, Lionel, how you started the Commodores."

"No, I didn't . . ." I'd correct them. I'd talk about the Mystics and the Jays. Nobody cared.

"Okay, Lionel, as the leader of the band, how do you choose what songs—?"

"No, I'm not the leader of the band, and we all choose the songs . . ." Then I'd try to inject humor and explain that I was really the saxophone holder who sang on some of the songs, but the glue and the lead singer of the band was really Walter "Clyde" Orange. The sniping and the weirdness became more frequent.

It got more painful. The reviews describing our live shows had references to ballads, including "Endless Love," which we had in our show now, and they said, "Finally, at long last, Lionel Richie sits down at the piano and plays his hits."

The review that drove the stake in the heart was, "What's

a guy like Lionel Richie doing in a Funk band like the Commodores?"

Pause. *Did you hear that?*

Now, go back and try to have a rehearsal after that review.

In my well-intentioned attempt to avoid hogging the spotlight, I thought up an oh-so-clever tactic. I decided to show up to the interview thirty minutes late and give the guys a chance to get more attention. The reaction I got was, "You think you're so good, you don't need to be there to do interviews?"

No, no, no. Guys!

Clearly, no good intention goes unpunished. It was terrible to watch. Terrible.

These were the rumblings of Greek tragedy—but I refused to accept that a rupture was inevitable. Little did I know, this was a dark tale written forever ago.

[IIII|II]

BRENDA HAD TO deal with fallout from the other Commodore wives (who saw her as the antagonist in my ear), but I couldn't hear it. So, I reverted to being an escape artist in the studio, totally in isolation with my dear friend the piano.

One day, in the late afternoon—at Kenny Rogers's guest house—I was tinkering on something in my home studio there when James Anthony Carmichael stopped by to see what I was working on. As soon as I heard him come in, I hit three chords and sang to him, "Hello, is it me you're looking for?"

He immediately said, "Brother Richie, finish that song."

Hmmmm? "I was just bullshitting."

"Finish that song."

I proceeded per his direction to write the song that became "Hello."

After I finished it and we brought my band in to record it

with me, when I listened, I hated it, like it was the corniest shit I could ever think of.

James disagreed. I pushed back, "I don't want it." When I threw it off the album and tried to decide what to include instead, he asked me if maybe I had one of those songs lying around that I'd written for someone else.

Before I could answer him, I received an urgent call from Suzanne de Passe who said, "Mr. Gordy wants to have a breakfast meeting with you tomorrow at 7 a.m. At the beach."

The next morning, after little sleep, I sped up the Pacific Coast Highway to Malibu to Berry Gordy's beach house, announced myself at the call box, waited for the gates to slide open, and drove in. A security fellow directed me to an area where I could park and then pointed toward the backyard.

I spotted Mr. Gordy past the swimming pool, seated at a little table set with coffee and breakfast items. The ocean view was breathtaking.

He asked how things were going, and I did not hold back.

Lemme tell you what they're doing to me . . . And it's ridiculous . . . And all I'm doing is trying to do this one album . . . and they're treating me like I'm the bad guy, and being ice-cold . . . or taking little jabs about me being selfish . . . I mean, c'mon. Am I doing that to them? No . . . Have I insulted or demeaned them? No . . .

He let me go on and on. Weirdly, the whole time he had this little smile. The humor escaped me.

Then it was his time to talk. He said, "Uh, you could be Diana Ross and the Supremes." Okay. "You could be David Ruffin and the Temptations. You can be Smokey Robinson and the Miracles." He could see I didn't get it, so he said, "You're not doing anything new, it's just your time to do it."

I nodded but hoped he was wrong.

"Now, the problem is *what* are you going to do?" Going solo had been done before, he repeated.

"But I don't want to go solo."

"Many have tried to avoid leaving but have been very un-successful." He hinted that leaving was inevitable. He had seen this movie many times.

I had to make the point that the Commodores were different from other groups. We were a *we* and not a lot of *me*s.

"Okay, Lionel" was all he said. We left it there.

My attempts to avoid the inevitable went nowhere. The ge-nie was coming out of the bottle and the tragedy was that he was not planning to go back in.

In a last-ditch effort, I arranged a meeting for all of us with Sandy Gallin, a dear friend and the manager of a long list of stars of that era, and David Geffen—the music mogul with a management background and two major record labels (Asylum and Geffen Records). Sandy recommended we talk to David who was smart, tough, and honest.

All six Commodores met with David and Sandy at David's house in Beverly Hills. David calmly asked each of us to an-swer the question, "Where do you see yourselves, individu-ally, years from now?" In other words, he was asking where we hoped that being part of the Commodores would one day take us.

Each of the guys spoke up and answered honestly about our highest goals for ourselves.

David said, in effect, "Okay, if you genuinely want to real-ize your goals, the person who is the vehicle to get you there is that guy right there—Lionel." David made it sound matter-of-fact. "If you know what you want, the way to get there is to line up behind Lionel."

Pause. *Kaboom.*

Of course, he wasn't telling us, "Get a divorce, there's no hope." He wasn't telling the guys to be a backup band, but that most groups end up with one person at the center. The solution was, *Hey, if you want to keep the marriage between the six of you together, don't let ego and resentment rule the day.* Nobody wanted to hear that.

We were not built to adapt to a different band formation. I felt pushed out. It was like in a marriage when someone says, "You know, I might want to see other people on the side."

"You what? You want to break up?"

"No, I want to stay. Do you want to break up?"

"I do if you want to have someone on the side."

The hurt snowballed.

When I wrote "Sail On" about a relationship breakup, I didn't know that it would be prophetic for me, or that it would apply to other kinds of separations. I had heard somewhere that in almost every dissolution there is one party that feels guilty and another that feels angry and hurt. Everybody loses something in the process.

I couldn't accept a future in which I was no longer a Commodore. My feeling to this day is that I would have stayed had I not felt that I was being shown the door.

Everybody else knew that I was leaving before I could accept it had already happened.

"HEY, BABES. HEY, babes. What are you doing, babes?" The voice talking to me is Mr. D., Sammy Davis Jr.

It's three in the morning. When the call comes in, I'm at Kenny Rogers's guesthouse, either writing, playing *Pac-Man*, or watching TV. Or all three.

"Mr. D., hello, oh, not doin' much."

"Hey, babes, I want to talk to you. Come over to my house right now, we're waiting on you, and bring your wife with you."

Sounds like he has something important to say, so I get Brenda and we drive over.

We arrive at 4:00 or 4:30 a.m., and Sammy has me follow him into one room and the ladies go off in a different direction.

Sammy sits me down. "Hey, kid, you've got a career that's about to go through the roof."

Coming from him, I'm reassured. "How do you know?"

"The cats have been talking."

Who are the cats? They turn out to be his people, his circle. "Cats" is Rat Pack speak and I'm all ears. They are not Mafia but maybe they know those guys—the ones who've got power and some money, and run casinos or are involved in the entertainment arena.

Sammy calls off names of guys I've never heard of before. "Lionel, the guy from Jersey is going to call you. And the guy from New York. And the guy from Miami. And listen, babes"—as he calls me—"These guys are going to offer you everything. You got the support, the backing, everything you need."

"Wow, this is amazing."

Sammy becomes very stern, and he says these words: "Your answer to everything they offer you is no."

"Mr. D., why?"

"Because I said yes. And I don't want you to make the same mistakes I made."

Now, I just gave you the crux of this entire conversation because I didn't hear anything else. After that, a hum came into my ear.

His warning was—*Don't throw your future in with just anyone who promises to invest millions because they will own you and your career.*

"I'm Sammy Davis, but I sacrificed a lot." At the time there had been nowhere else to go.

Sammy talked about how he had to come in through the back door of the kitchen to perform in top nightclubs. A Black man could not come in the front door.

Who made it easier? Frank Sinatra, his godfather. Frank was his passage.

The cats were white, Black, Jewish, Catholic, Baptist, no calling cards. He wanted to pass the baton to me so that whatever I would go through would make it easier for someone who could accept the baton from me.

Later on, when it was a miracle that I survived, people would say, "Oh my God, Lionel, it's amazing how you navigated your career."

I didn't navigate my career. I had a cheat sheet. The first thing I do even to this day, if I have a chance to talk to anybody who's been in the war of life, is ask them, "Tell me about the war. Tell me where the pits are."

You don't have to fall into them if you listen to the cats when they're talking.

THE CLOSER IT got to October 1982, when my solo album was coming out, the darker the clouds became for me and the Commodores—of which I was still a member. By midsummer I was practically living at A&M Studios, where I was working with James Carmichael and a new group of studio musicians, recording feverishly. The rumors that I was leaving the Commodores were everywhere.

Everything moved at warp speed. I was freaking out, everyone was freaking out around me. And my marriage was in trouble. My side was, *We need counseling but there's no time, and oh, by the way, you know I'm going through some shit?* Brenda's was, *We need counseling and we have to make time and you know I'm going through some shit too?*

I hated it when I heard people say the guys were assholes for making snide remarks about my being an asshole, because— *Those are my bandmates and only I can call them assholes.*

Nothing was glued down.

In a burst of practicality, I came up with a desperate plan for how to keep the Commodores intact. The idea was that Ken Kragen (Kenny Rogers's manager) and Benny Ashburn could manage the Commodores together.

This could be a win-win. Yeah, but Benny could be an overbearing, difficult personality at times. I didn't think he'd really go for it.

That summer, on August 15, I was at A&M Studios and got a call from Benny, who was checking in. He was out of town but was going to be back soon and had some thoughts.

Point-blank, Benny said, "You're gonna leave the group, aren't you, killer?"

"No, I'm not leaving the group."

Benny had been hands-off until now. Maybe he assumed the rift would pass. He was not the official manager after becoming the seventh Commodore, but he felt the need to say something. "Killer, I know you. You know, it's the only logical thing to do."

I told him he was wrong.

"Damn, you're smart." He hinted that I was conniving, wanting things to work out for me.

And I kept saying, "I'm not trying to be smart, Benny. This shit is happening and it hurts."

The conniving suggestion made me feel deeply misunderstood. Later, I'd hear the Commodores say things like, "It wasn't *what* Lionel did but *how* he did it." Probably no one felt worse than WAK, because of how close we had been, or Clyde, because he had been the lead singer. The hardest for me was the innuendo that this was my plan and it was all great for me.

"Listen, Benny," I said. "Put it in your head that this is not something I feel good about, because these are my brothers."

Benny agreed that we'd talk in a day or so.

I hoped there would be a change in the weather, and in a few months I'd do another album with the guys. That would fix everything, and we'd let bygones be bygones.

Two days after I talked to Benny, I was in the studio at A&M, where I was called to the phone. Brenda's best friend, Janet—and my friend—asked, "Did you hear the news?"

"What news?"

"Benny just died, baby. Of a massive heart attack." The room started to spin. He had been found dead in his apartment. Benny was fifty-four years old.

The tragedy was overwhelming. And I went through the stages of grief and guilt. *Did I break his heart?*

Benny loved us. He loved the family of us. There was nothing ever on this earth that Benny wanted more than to make his mark as the Man of the Town in Harlem, with the glamour, the success, and the badass don't-mess-with-me edge. Being the manager of the Commodores gave that to him, along with the joys of being one of us, of having girls scream at him too.

I'd been counting on Benny, the logical one, to come up with a solution so I didn't have to leave the band. With his death, I couldn't find a way back.

The funeral was held in a Harlem church overflowing with folks from every walk of Benny's life—high and low. All the Commodores were there. For the first time in a while, after our bickering and issues that seemed miniscule on this day, we all came together as brothers. After this day, our parting of the ways became just ridiculous, which was inevitable, but that afternoon we were there to celebrate Benny.

We were putting to rest our steadfast champion, our cornerman, our leading fan, our manager, our brother, our dad.

We kept saying to each other, "I can't believe he's dead."

The minister, an older Black gentleman, began the eulogy in a manner that told us he may not have known Benny at all. Not to say that Benny was not a churchgoer, but this funeral may have been one of the only times he was in a church.

"Benny Ashburn was a good soul," was the opening. "He was just a good man. A good man who was kind. All I can say is that when Benny walked down the street, he smiled, and was gentle. Very gentle."

I whispered to the guys, "Now I know Benny's dead." Otherwise, he would have jumped out of that box and smacked that preacher upside the head.

The minister ended, "Yes, that was Benny, a common man, just a plain old Black boy."

We all hid our faces to control the laughter. Everyone else sank into a stunned silence. Suddenly, from the front row, Benny's girlfriend began to cry, "Oh Benny, oh Benny . . ."

That was his woman. Moments later, we heard another girl's voice, as she too, said, "Oh Benny, Benny . . ." And yet again, from over on the side, another girl, louder, started up, "Oh Benny, oh Benny . . ."

He had gotten his wish to have lots of female attention alright, never planning for them to all show up at his funeral and find out about one another. When it was my turn to go up to Benny's casket and to have a word, I leaned in and told him, "Lay there, brother. Stay dead, Benny. You do not want to wake up for this nightmare."

After that, I went around, paid my respects to family, cried and laughed, and walked out of the church like I was leaving a whole lifetime as a Commodore behind me forever. The lesson I'd have to accept was that what comes with growth is outgrowing. We outgrew one another.

Two months later came the release of my album and a statement from Motown that I had left the Commodores to pursue a solo career—what felt like the end of the world. I kept thinking of Berry Gordy's words: *You're not doing anything new, it's just your time to do it.*

Flying Solo

(1982–1999)

Sometimes you've got to let *everything* go—purge
yourself . . . If you are unhappy with anything . . .
whatever is bringing you down, get rid of it.
Because you'll find that when you're free, your
true creativity, your true self comes out.

—TINA TURNER (1939–2023), INTERVIEW
IN *EBONY*, NOVEMBER 1986

14

Truly

MY MANTRA BECAME "NO EXCUSES."

At age thirty-three, I realized that it was going to be 100 percent on me if the solo album, not so originally titled *Lionel Richie*, didn't succeed. If it did, then I'd be grateful to everybody who worked on it with me, who believed in me. But if the album bombed or fans rejected me or the forces of radio refused to play the singles because they weren't *this* or *that* enough, then the failure would be mine.

When you're in a group, if you don't succeed, you have the others to blame. *Yeah, I told 'em not to do that!* Going solo taught me that if a project wins, glory, hallelujah, you can claim the victory. But, man, if it loses, you have to own every part of the defeat.

For thirteen years, I'd been one vote among six on every decision. Now I was in charge. Nothing had prepared me. One day it was, *Look at me, I'm King of the World!* The next day it was, *Oh, shit, nobody showed me how to fly this thing!*

Going solo was the most liberating thing ever. And also scary as hell.

My brain hurt from having to pay the most acute attention to every decision.

Remember the messages sent to me as a kid—"Lionel, would you care to join the class?" My attention deficit was not fixed. Anything that wasn't me doing the thing I most loved, being in that creative space and discovering the goods, messed me up. But now that I was writing for just me, I wasn't sure I could trust the process.

James Anthony Carmichael steadied me. He understood the Other Side and felt I could go deeper. "Brother Richie, you came out of the room too fast. Go back in there again, you're almost there."

Sometimes I'd resist. "C'mon, James, I'm looking for a word. What is it? Give it to me."

"Brother Richie, if God was talking to me, I would have given it to you by now. But He's only talking to you. And my job is to sit here until you tell me what God told you."

Something amazing happened next. The act of collaborating with God taught me to listen more closely to my own voice. In fact, when I went to the Other Side, I talked to myself, and sometimes, as a technique, I set up a mirror in the studio for a dialogue to take place. I could stand and look into the mirror, knowing I am the *I AM* on One Side, and I am the person in the mirror on the Other Side.

It sounds strange but it worked. By trusting that voice, writing and recording became a bliss state, like being possessed. *Nuth'n* better. A few peers I knew were like me in this way: Elton John, Bruce Springsteen, Stevie Wonder. And they would agree that when you're in the zone, there is a moment when you could cough and that's a song.

It's not necessarily fun living with someone in an altered state. There are times as an artist when you appear not to pay attention to others. You are lost in the creativity.

You hear, "You're so selfish." Inside, your childlike voice says, "Yeah?" but you ignore the criticism. That's when the guilt comes in. Because you were taught that selfish is bad.

Whenever I disagreed with James Anthony Carmichael about what would go on the album—like my telling him I thought "Hello" was corny—he didn't argue. That was until I played him parts of an unfinished song called "Truly," and he insisted it should be the lead single.

"Nah, I wrote this for Barbra Streisand." Nobody could deliver it like Barbra. I could just hear her nailing those long sustained high notes:

Because I'm truly
Truly in love with you . . .
I'm truly head over heels with your love
I need you, and with your love I'm free

James convinced me to finish it and then decide. Every time I thought, *Done!* he'd give me that look of *Nope, not there yet.* He must have sent me back three times, and then he had me rewrite the second verse. *Three* times—to where I complained, "C'mon, James, give me a break!"

He only came back with, "Brother Richie, we're not looking for *good*, we're looking for *greatness*." It got to the point that I was absolutely annoyed.

And out of that annoyance, I listened to my own voice and knew "Truly" had to be my first single. In the studio, I listened to other voices too. We developed a routine where we'd have the James Anthony Carmichael mix, the Cal Harris mix, and the Lionel Richie mix. Then we'd contrast and compare.

My gauge was hearing how the song's movement—melody, lyrics, and the full production—made me feel emotionally. The curse of hypersensitivity was paying off!

WITH THE ALBUM nearing completion, I had an interesting first meeting with Ken Kragen, now my official manager. We knew each other from the work I'd done for Kenny Rogers, of course, but I had no idea how his management of me as an artist would compare to Benny's approach.

Why not be direct, right? Boldly, I walked into his office, took a seat, and asked, "Tell me, what are you gonna do for my career that's new?"

Ken calmly said, "Nothing new. We aren't going to change anything you've been doing. Just keep doing it." *Except* . . . he thought a few minor fixes could make a big difference.

That sounded a little vague.

Ken explained that we had a small challenge. "Your songs are more famous than you are." The "minor fix" needed was to do more to connect my face to my name and to the hits.

More meant instead of being known from having my songs *heard* on the radio, there had to be a *visual* that went with the name—what Ken described as "having you stand next to your songs." The way to do that was television, by getting me on every awards show, TV special, and late-night talk show, you name it.

Ken's gift for planning ahead gave us the theme for most of our meetings—especially whenever a new album was about to come out. Later on, we had a memorable exchange that came at the end of a planning session mostly about logistics.

There's this moment, right before I leave, that changes the vibe. I can see Ken mulling something over. Then he says, "I want to ask you a question."

"Sure." I'm about to hear a question very few artists get asked.

"How famous do you want to be?"

I try to buy some time. "Why?"

"Because I have a couple things in the works that, if I do them, you'll never be able to *not* be Lionel Richie, where you could go and have a normal life—where you'll never be recognized. If you want to be able to go unrecognized, then I won't do certain things. But if you want to be famous everywhere you go for the rest of your life, then I will plan for it."

The way he says it, like a sorcerer offering a potion I can never undrink, I get wary. Then I say, "Well, I'll call you back tomorrow but it's probably going to be the same answer, which is . . . *do it.*"

All night, I was wide awake, questioning if I could give up any possibility of one day having a normal life.

Listen, I was not new to this rodeo. For over a decade I had been given a front-row seat to the perks and pitfalls of being a spotlit celebrity. Michael Jackson was a case study. He couldn't return to a normal life because being larger than life was the vision, and at this time in 1982 he'd been famous for most of his twenty-four years.

In this period, Michael had been working intensively on his sixth studio album with Quincy Jones producing. Right before the release date, the two of them sat down to listen and Quincy felt the album wasn't ready. He went so far as to throw off some of the songs and send everybody back to the drawing board. There was a cut on the album called "Starlight" by Rod Temperton that was then rewritten to reflect Michael's love for horror movies. That song became "Thriller"—the last single to be released off the album also titled *Thriller*.

After *Thriller*, there was nowhere on the planet where Michael could go and walk around like an everyday regular person—other than going in disguise. Could I handle that? Maybe not, I worried.

But then, I thought of the Hollywood legends and well-recognized celebrities I'd been fortunate to meet and how they managed their fame—somehow staying real. The first time I met Elizabeth Taylor, the oxygen left the room. She was *that* radiant, that unbelievably beautiful, but she knew there would be several seconds of hyperventilation. Once I caught my breath, I saw that Elizabeth had a gift for letting you into her aura, the embrace of her energy. That's how I got past my awe. Yet there was a boundary, a self-protection.

When Elizabeth became Michael Jackson's godmother, I got it—given their similar experiences with stardom. She had been a child actress. She was always in the public eye, always in the news with headlines about her eight marriages or other scandals and crises. Actually, neither of their lives were ever normal.

In my role as big brother to Michael, I could offer my honest opinions—but our journeys were different. Elizabeth Taylor was one of the few who could advise him on his various life stages—from boy to adolescent to adult to global celebrity to crash and burn.

Perhaps, I decided, the way to handle fame was to stay truly *you*. I saw that in Kenny Rogers—who was one of the biggest superstars of the early 1980s. Kenny made being famous look, well, like an adventure. Maybe he handled the loss of privacy better because he had struggled to make it, starting life in a Houston housing project, one of eight kids.

My conclusion, after a long night's deliberation, was that the only way to make it happen and find out how famous I wanted to be was . . . *I gotta try it.*

The next day, I called Ken Kragen, and told him to pull out the stops.

"Good," he said. He spelled out three initial goals—for me to win both a Grammy and an Oscar, and to be chosen to host the American Music Awards. Sounded fantastic. The stuff of dreams.

Even so, let me tell you that there is nothing to prepare you for that part about never being able to go anywhere unrecognized again for the rest of your life. Nothing.

THE RECORD BUSINESS was in a state of rapid change. Many independent labels had gone under, unable to compete with companies now a part of the all-powerful entertainment conglomerates. Midsize labels were also being bought up by the corporations, as were radio stations. The fight to get played was that much harder for artists who crossed different genres. Illegal payola—"paying for play"—was running rampant.

Sales of vinyl records had declined, and 8-tracks had given way to cassettes. The Sony Walkman and its knockoffs that played cassettes were changing how and where you could hear music. Now we had to create music that you could not only dance to, drive to, and make love to, but that you could also run and skate and do aerobics to. By the mid-eighties, CDs came in, resulting in yet another format.

Suddenly, home stereo systems changed. Consumers were willing to spend money replacing their records with the same music in different formats—which led to a boom in compilation and greatest hits albums. Just when we adapted to those changes, bam—by the end of the 1990s we would hit a massive iceberg called file sharing and MP3 players. Music downloading—hits on demand—would collapse everything.

The first big change I remember confronting was this new cable TV outlet for music—which debuted in 1981. The first time I saw an ad showing the MTV flag being planted on the moon, I knew music videos would take over. They could make or break your record.

Everything cost so much more. This was the go-go eighties, y'all. It was bigger, better, best. And when it came to selling and promoting a new album, nothing was as important as performing live. Stage shows had to be as dazzling as the music videos—from lighting to pianos on turning platforms, all the bells and whistles.

My solo tour was to begin in Las Vegas with a nightclub act at the Aladdin. Between Ken Kragen and Suzanne de Passe, recently promoted to president of Motown Productions, the film and TV division, a stellar production team was assembled. Heading it up as director was Broadway veteran Joe Layton—who I'd watched years earlier direct the Jackson 5. Joe had directed and choreographed major productions for stage and screen, working on huge touring concerts for everybody from Barbara Streisand to Diana Ross and Bette Midler.

Joe had his work cut out for him with me. The thought of commanding the stage by myself—without the Commodores— struck terror in my heart! I'd joke, "Well, if it's a bust, I can always pursue the priesthood after all," but people in my inner circle knew I was uneasy—big time.

During rehearsals, it helped just having fun with the members of my new band.

Joe Layton could see I was trying to add Commodore-style banter. He didn't approve. My job, he said, was to act like a lead singer.

At one point, during a run-through at a rented auditorium in LA, I cracked a joke before starting a song, and the band members looked at each other like, *He's funny*.

Waving a raised hand, Joe screamed from the back of the auditorium, "Lionel!"

We all stopped. Joe blasted the band, asking, "What are you guys looking at?"

These were my new guys.

Joe told them, at full volume, "Every chance you get, you don't take your eye off the reason we are here. Look at Lionel. And if Lionel wants to wink at you, you wink back. If you miss his wink, you're fired."

What the hell?

I had never heard words like that. But I learned something that day: If you want the crown, you must be willing to wear it.

Joe Layton challenged my vision of doing a version of the Commodores' "showtime" opening—how we'd hype the show beforehand and then kick into three big-ass up-tempo numbers. Joe insisted that I open my debut Vegas show with— *What?*—a ballad.

This can't be right. We don't want to reinvent the wheel here.

Joe sounded to me like a crazy man when he repeated that I was going to begin the show by singing my new ballad "Truly"—which was already #1 on the Pop charts and cranking up to #2 R&B, right behind Marvin Gaye's "Sexual Healing." Joe said I should trust my ability to tell a story and let the song cast a spell.

And then he told me what I thought was the silliest idea ever. He wanted me to start my entrance, from out in the audience, toward the back of the showroom, singing and winding through the tables and down the aisle until I got to the stage and hit the spotlight at the exact moment when I finally sang the word *truly*.

Walking through the crowd? "I'll get mobbed," I joked. But not really.

Joe said, "No one will touch you." It was all about having an aura. "Trust me, Lionel, it's a winner. It's not what the audience expects."

Four days before the show, we all traveled to Vegas and went into intense rehearsals. Of course, I was no stranger to preshow nerves but this was at a whole new level. To try to head it off at the pass, I was given a great exercise to try by Bobby Adams—head of my security—whom I'd met when he was working on the Jackson 5's tour. Bobby reassured me that stage fright was common.

"More like mic fright," I admitted.

Bobby said something along the lines of, "Just stare the mic down." He was referring to a short little piece of writing he had given me that was a parable about a lion. The lesson was that if you run from the lion (what you fear), the lion will chase you, but if you stand still and face the lion, it will run away. In other words, if I walked out and grabbed the mic, the lion would leave.

I began to see that the nightmare of waiting in the wings before a show was no different from the terrible anxiety I used to have as a kid taking tests. The worry and thinking about everything that could go wrong vanished once I got to the exam. The same was true of the show. You couldn't think about it once the lights went down and the curtain rose.

Over our four days of rehearsal, Joe Layton used another strategy to get me to feel comfortable with my entrance.

The first time we try it, instead of telling me where to go, he walks with me as I sing, starting from the side toward the back of the showroom. He stays at my side as he walks me easily down the stairs to get to the aisle, and then up to the stage all the way to where I hit the mark and sing the line on cue. On the second day, he walks in front of me as we go through the audience—where they'll be sitting—and he shows me the route that leads back up to the stage. He does the same thing for the next two days, leading me, keeping the pace, going over the blocking, going with me all the way to the stage for the killer moment.

Now, it's the night of the show and I'm nervous as hell. All my techniques have gone out the window. Joe comes to the dressing room, gives me a nod, and walks me over to where the curtains are on the side of the room—where I'm supposed to enter and go out into the audience to start my walk when I sing, "Forever, I will be your lover . . ."

And we go through the curtains, both of us, and I'm waiting for Joe to walk in front of me so I can begin, like we rehearsed it. The music begins, and I'm standing there, waiting for him to step in front of me, at which point, he doesn't. Instead, Joe Layton nods for me to go ahead, and then leans into my ear and says, "Enjoy your career."

Everything flowed from that moment on. It was an amazing opening.

Family came, friends came, the Motown brass came. Tuskegee was in the house, you better believe—including most of the Home-Boy Association. After the show, I was congratulated by all my people. Everybody was backstage celebrating—except one person.

Strangely enough, though I knew Mr. D. had been at the show, I didn't see him afterward. I felt great about the night but wanted his honest assessment.

We caught up later in the week, back in LA on the phone. I had to ask him, "What do you think, Mr. D.?"

He sounded puzzled. "I don't really know what to think, Lionel."

Oh, shit. I must have fucked up bad.

It wasn't about me. He was actually comparing his experience back in the day to what he had witnessed. "Let me tell you," he said, recalling his start in Las Vegas, "not only did they require me to enter the showrooms through the kitchen, but they had a rule you couldn't go past two feet before the edge of the stage."

The rule applied to all Black performers. The thought was crushing. *Two feet?*

"That's your lane. Don't go to the edge of the stage. Don't bend over. And don't touch anybody." In the forties and fifties, Black entertainers, even the highest paid, couldn't stay in the same hotels where their names were on the marquee.

"Whenever I finished a show," Sammy said, "I went out through the kitchen, through the back door, got in my car, and was driven back to where I was staying."

I knew that Sammy Davis Jr. had helped integrate Vegas, breaking multiple barriers for Black entertainers and patrons. We were all in his debt.

He wasn't sure if he could trust the changes. Mr. D. said, "I saw men of all colors bringing their ladies up to the front of the stage. You would touch them, you would kiss them, and then you would throw them back in the audience. And they screamed the entire show." He asked, "What on earth were you thinking?"

"Well, Mr. D., I thought if Elvis did it, why couldn't I?"

"Bless you, kid," he sighed. "Maybe times really have changed."

Later, during a low point for me, Mr. D. was the one mentor I asked, "How do you know if you are winning or losing?"

"Unfortunately, Lionel, you don't know whether you won or you lost until the end of your life, and then you go back and add up the wins and the losses, and then you'll know if you did it alright."

The moral was to play the long game, to let your story unfold. If you define yourself only by the wins, you miss what the losses can teach. You become addicted to the juice of winning. Highs get too high and lows get too low. The day when you're winning, that's the best day of your life, and the day you're losing, you never want to see that day again.

But c'mon, if given a choice, I'll always take the win.

IN MY EARLY career, the teaching was, "It's not what you know but who you know." Then I learned the advanced version: "It's not who you know but who knows you."

How people knew me was a mystery. But somehow, in moments of severe angst, I'd be about to stumble, when, suddenly, a guide would appear.

Quincy Jones—who'd been popping in with advice for years—knew me well enough to adapt my nickname to "Skeets."

During my painful deliberation over whether to go solo or not, he checked in, saying, "Skeets, I need to tell you a little story. You feel like you are fighting the woes of the world?"

"You hit it on the head," I admitted.

"I know how you feel. I've been there." Quincy revealed that back in the day, he had a disastrous experience with his Jazz band when they were on the road. They were playing a concert far from their hotel, and the band hadn't been paid yet, and after the show, his manager split in the limo. They were stranded with nowhere to stay, with no way to get the band paid. "I didn't think I could survive," he recalled. His homelife was bad too. "Nothing was good. And I didn't know what to do."

At his wit's end, Quincy told me he looked across the street and saw a cross and a marquee belonging to a corner church. On the marquee was the subject for the coming Sunday sermon, and it read, WORRY IS A BY-PRODUCT OF INDECISION.

Made sense, but was it that simple?

"Skeets, you just have to decide. And then the Universe will take care of the rest." He had made a phone call he wanted to avoid but that got him paid and put the wheels into motion for an even better destiny.

The power to make my own decisions became a lifeline, as long as I owned my actions.

Q gave me powerful wisdom about winning awards. Starting in 1978, it seemed like I'd run into Quincy whenever I was up for an award. Every year at the Grammys, in particular, I'd arrive in high spirits, feeling confident, only to walk away empty-handed. Quincy would console me—"Man, I know how you feel, this is just par for the course."

Yeah, yeah. Still, that year it was two nominations for "Easy" and one for "Brick House." Huge hits, great songs, fantastic performances. We all felt robbed.

The next year we went in with another three nominations (including two for "Three Times a Lady") and once again didn't win. The following year "Sail On" was nominated for Best Pop Vocal Performance (Group), and the band was nominated for our R&B performance on the album *Midnight Magic*. Nada, zilch. In 1981, I arrived feeling more confident than ever, knowing this had to be a breakthrough year— with two performance nominations ("Jesus Is Love" and the whole *Heroes* album) *and* two nominations for Kenny Rogers's "Lady" (one for writing and one for producing).

When that night ended without one award, I spotted Quincy coming my way and tried to laugh off the disappointment. He gave me the same pep talk, reminding me that the Grammy voters "just have to get to know you," but not to give up.

This was not feeling good to me at all. What kind of conspiracy was this shit?

Then came the big year—1982! And I show up with a total of six Grammy nominations, four of which were for "Endless Love" (as writer, performer of a duet, producer of the single, and the album). The grand total for five years so far is eighteen nominations. I mean, "Endless Love" topping the charts for nine weeks? This is a no-brainer.

The night is a disaster. I lose six times. I try to put on a smile that says, "I'm alright." But I'm not. In fact, after the show, while going backstage to clean out my dressing room, I lose it when I cross paths with a music industry guy I don't know but who apparently knows me.

The guy says, "Lionel, you know what I like about you? You're a good loser. You're really good at losing."

The most uncharacteristic fit of temper possesses me. Years of cowardice fall away and I decide I'm now gonna kick his ass. *Weird*. This industry executive who was only paying me what he thought was a compliment has no idea he has knocked the chip off my shoulder from years of being bullied. But just as I'm about to lunge, I feel a hand grab my arm and pull me away. Guess who?

Yep, Quincy Jones.

Quincy pulls me over to the side and says, "Skeets, let me have a word." I fold my arms and half listen. He says, "You think you lost tonight? You just got told no—it happens. And something else happens, you got it?"

I try to tune out the looky-loos in tuxedos and gowns, gawking like they wish they could hear Quincy's word to the wise.

"I got told no so many times I lost count," he tells me. The number he cites is like twenty-six or thirty-four times or more before winning his first Grammy. (The late Quincy Jones ended up with twenty-eight Grammy wins and *eighty* nominations.) "Skeets!" he goes on, "you know how grateful I am for every single no?" Each fed his will to get a yes.

"But . . ."

Quincy nudges me to the exit, so he can adapt the PG version of his message—what we call real talk that only Quincy could deliver. "Do you understand why you have the catalog you have? Because they keep telling you no! If they give it to you on 'Easy' or 'Sail On,' you might just hang up the writing and feel like you can bask in the sun." Then he gives it to me in Quincy language.

"You know why you keep calling the girl? Because she won't give you the . . ." I can't hear but I know what he's saying. Classic. "Once she gives it to you, next thing you don't call her anymore."

End of story. The Grammys withheld favors like the hard-to-get girl.

What a timely lesson—be thankful for the *no*s. Be thankful for it all. That mindset helped me combat my fear that without the Commodores I'd never have another hit. And I wound up with three strong single selections—"Truly" (which dropped in September), "You Are" (an up-tempo ballad released three months later), and "My Love" (a slower ballad, for release the following spring). With award season on the horizon, we were about to test Quincy's theory.

⸻

KEN KRAGEN DIDN'T mess around.

"Did you say . . . I'm going on *SNL*?"

Ken had worked his magic, booking me on *Saturday Night Live*, then in its eighth season, on December 11—with Nick Nolte hosting. This was when Eddie Murphy, twenty-one years old and with only two years on the *SNL* cast, was already hotter than hell after making his film debut with Nolte in *48 Hrs*. This was *huge*.

At the last minute, Nolte had to cancel, and Eddie became the host—the first and only time a current cast member hosted the show. His opening monologue gave millions of *SNL* viewers a chance to see Eddie do stand-up. He was fall-on-the-floor *hilarious*. The show felt like my own record launch party—live on network TV!

As a very good sign, that same Saturday, the album *Lionel Richie* hit #1 on the *Cashbox* chart. There were three main outfits that did rankings: *Billboard*, *Cashbox*, and *Record World*. Everybody used similar sources to tally sales and airplay, though results might vary. Who cared which was more prestigious? A hit is a hit is a hit.

The overnight reaction to *SNL* was phenomenal. Radio play went through the roof. A couple weeks later we released "You Are"—the first song performed on the show that the public had never heard—and it shot up to #4 Pop and #2 R&B. The second song for *SNL* was "Truly" (already at #1 Pop, #2 R&B, and #1 Adult Contemporary). With the later release of a third hit single, "My Love" (#5 Pop, #6 R&B, #1 Adult Contemporary), album sales picked up even more, eventually reaching five million copies.

No matter how many years have passed, whenever I perform "Truly," I'm taken back to this period, to the feeling of awe that this was how I made my living. The best part of the adventure was that I had no idea what would happen next.

FOR MANY YEARS the Music Business's award season kicked off every January with the American Music Awards—which had been the brainchild of Dick Clark in 1974 when ABC lost the contract to CBS for the Grammy Awards.

Dick Clark, one of the smartest entrepreneurs in Hollywood, was another mentor who saw the potential of who I could become before I ever did. The very first time we met on the set of *American Bandstand*, however, I committed the sin of saying, "Mr. Clark, I've watched your show since I was a little kid and kind of grew up with you. To think I've followed you from the time I was a baby and now here I am face to face with you."

"Go to hell, Lionel, I'm not *that* old" was Dick Clark's instant response. Then he laughed. Lucky for me. I mean, his whole image was youthful exuberance, and I'd shattered that myth in one introduction.

Dick was more than his image, though. He was a maverick, carving out his own lane by showcasing up-and-coming artists, while quietly building a media empire. He was not flashy—though he had one indulgence, which I discovered when Brenda and I were invited to his house in Malibu one night.

When the gate opened, we saw a row of cars and assumed they belonged to the other guests. No, it was just us for dinner. Those were his cars. All of them. He was a car collector. And the ones parked out front were his favorites.

When Dick founded the AMAs as a competitor to the Grammys, he created a less formal atmosphere, with voting based less on the choices of industry insiders but more from airplay and sales. The show moved at a faster clip—meaning shorter speeches, as I reminded myself on my way along the red carpet outside LA's Shrine Auditorium in January 1983. I was excited. This was my year. Unlike the Grammys sending me home empty-handed for years, my reception at the AMAs as a Commodore had been warmer. Out of seven nominations, the band had won two awards: Favorite Pop/Rock Song for "Three Times a Lady" (1979) and Favorite Soul/R&B Band, Duo or Group (1980).

That history helped, except I was no longer a Commodore. The first of my two nominations was Favorite Soul/R&B Male Artist, while the second was for "Truly" for Favorite Pop/Rock Song. (Whatever those categories were supposed to mean.) Holding my breath when nominees were announced for the first category, I had a tiny flash of *Me?* and then I heard that the winner was, in fact, *me*. Like a nervous rabbit in a rocking chair, I bolted to the stage, trying to be cool, like it was no big deal. After I rattled off thanks to James Anthony Carmichael and Calvin Harris and Ken Kragen, I ended with a sincere thank-you to Brenda.

My main competition for Favorite Pop/Rock Song? None other than Stevie Wonder *and* Paul McCartney for "Ebony and Ivory," which was massive. Was that even fair? Only—can you believe it?—"Truly" won! *Holy cow!* What was going on? With no speech prepared, I ran up and just said how amazing it was to get an award for doing what I loved to do. Short and sweet.

My relief from winning lasted about a month before I started to agonize all over again.

Cut to: February 23, 1983, back at the Shrine, this time for the twenty-fifth annual Grammy Awards. With only one nomination, Best Pop Male Vocal ("Truly"), I'm already in a sweat.

Hell, the Rolling Stones hadn't won a Grammy. And neither had Marvin Gaye—so ridiculous after his groundbreaking protest album, *What's Going On*—although he is also up for two awards this year.

The running bit of the night is Eddie Murphy saying he isn't going to leave without a Grammy—after he lost to Richard Pryor in the category of Best Comedy Album. I laugh when he says it, little guessing that Eddie is serious.

Using reverse psychology, I'm sitting there pretending not to care—with no speech prepared. It's like pitching a song. Why spend the time to write it if I'm not going to give it? Besides, I'm not great reading off the page—or from a teleprompter.

A few years prior, the great Ed McMahon saw me struggling with cue cards during an appearance on *The Tonight Show*. Ed worked with me after the show and taught me how to take small bites of words. I couldn't have ever been a candidate for hosting a show without that skill. Still, I usually did better at accepting awards by speaking from the heart.

At the Grammys, my main competition is Elton John for "Blue Eyes"—one of his bigger hits since the 1976 breakup of his legendary writing partnership with Bernie Taupin. Not lost on me is the fact that Elton, up to this time, has also never won a Grammy.

I think it was Elton who once described artists like us as "egotistical maniacs with inferiority complexes." Agreed.

Then comes the moment when I hear the names of the nominees, including mine. I smile for the camera—with thirty-one million viewers watching—and get that hum in my ear, where I hear *nuth'n*. My brain fails to grasp I've won until I hear Brenda scream.

What in the hell just happened?

I come back to earth to realize they called my name. And then I run up onstage to thunderous applause.

Thunderous, I tell you.

The Grammy statue is placed in my hands—*Oh, my God, it felt amazing*—and I'm now having a mini panic attack as I go to the mic to give my off-the-cuff speech. As I step to it, out of the corner of my eye, I see a streak of somebody running at me. Next, a guy in a tuxedo grabs my Grammy and runs off the stage!

You'll never guess who stole my Grammy. Or maybe you will. Mr. Eddie Murphy has made good on his pledge not to leave without a Grammy so he's taking mine home.

It was one of the funniest, most unexpected moments of my public life. I laughed so hard I had to walk away from the mic, lean over, catch my breath, wipe my eyes, and turn around to see how the audience was reacting. The sight of six thousand or more glamorous attendees in hysterics and falling out of their seats was the most beautiful sight I could have seen. After many minutes, still laughing, I began my thanks. First, I confessed that after years of being asked how I felt about losing and answering, "I really don't mind," I could now state without reservation: "There is nothing like winning."

I thanked my Motown family for sticking with me— Berry Gordy, Tony Jones, Suzanne de Passe, and Skip Miller (someone, I said, I'd never want to work without). And then I got to the Commodores, my brothers/mothers/fathers and everything else to me, saying, "Thank you for fifteen wonderful years."

And, yes, I was able to pay homage to the small town of Tuskegee, Alabama. I thanked my new family, including Ken Kragen, again, and finally, I was able to thank someone who was not there but who had been with me for fifteen years, Benny Ashburn. My message was, "We finally made it."

As I was being escorted off the stage, I chuckled thinking that Quincy was right about how good you feel once the Grammys gives you some you-know-what. Just the thought of it set off a small explosion in my head—*Oh, eff me, I'm a dead man. I forgot to thank Brenda!*

How was I going to live this down? Could I blame Eddie Murphy for distracting me, even though my Grammy and I were soon reunited? My apology era was about to begin.

No time to bask in glory. As always. I had to get the next album ready so that when I left later in the year on a nonstop world tour, I would have two albums worth of new material.

Anything could go awry, but for the first solo outing, it was all systems go.

15

Happy People

I DON'T WANT YOU TO think that Brenda and I just moved into the guesthouse at the Knoll to mooch off of Kenny and Marianne Rogers. The story has more nuance.

I insisted to Kenny, "Let me pay rent. I have to pay for utilities, something."

Kenny grumbled. The fact is, he was almost never home and liked having me around to keep him posted on the six-million-dollar renovation of the Knoll—a massive undertaking. We settled on something like four thousand dollars a month, major money but so worth it.

Knowing that Kenny and Marianne would be eager to sell the Knoll once the renovation was done, we casually started house shopping but I was in no hurry to leave.

Brenda and I were still adjusting to a different dynamic now that I was no longer in a band. One change I resisted came from how Ken Kragen spoke about "Lionel and Brenda" just as he talked about "Kenny and Marianne" in connection to every aspect of career management.

After years of following rules for the band—and walking on eggshells worrying about members and five other wives—I didn't know the rules yet for a solo artist. My assumption was that the next part would be a cakewalk, and we could just be happy people. Did we even need to own a big ole house to be happy?

Not right away. So my question was, *Why can't we just hang right here in this guest house for as long as possible?* How to negotiate that?

You just never know until the opportunity arises, that's how. Sometimes it comes in unexpected ways.

Here we go. One afternoon, before going to the studio, I decided to grab a little Bel Air sunshine and give a good wash and a wax to my prized silver Commodore Mercedes 450 SEL. Kenny and Marianne weren't in town, as usual.

The guesthouses were actually tucked away on a road outside the gates of the Knoll. Kenny and I learned early in our friendship that we shared a love for architecture and landscaping. I told him my backup job was architect or horticulturist—"In case this music thing doesn't last."

"Funny!" Kenny said. He had no clue I was serious.

Outside, washing my car, I didn't hear the sound of a limo pulling up behind me. What startled me was the shadow cast by someone who stepped out of the limo—a towering figure close to six foot four and three hundred pounds. I knew this had to be Marvin Davis, the Colorado oilman turned entertainment mogul who had recently bought 20th Century Fox.

In a loud voice, Mr. Davis stated he had come to see the property but the real estate agent was late.

"If you'd like, I can show you around," I offered, and proceeded to put in the codes at the gate and give a deluxe tour.

As we wrapped up, Mr. Davis asked, "Hey, Lionel, do you think I should buy this place?"

Because we had bonded, he seemed to trust my opinion. In all sincerity, I answered, "I think you should buy it. You are the only one who could buy this house and be believable in it."

A few days later, Kenny called and was over the moon. "Lionel, I think Marvin Davis wants to buy the Knoll!"

"Wow," I said, happy for Kenny and Marianne, though, again, I didn't want to move yet. My new joke was, "Oh, well, if the music thing fizzles, I can go into real estate." Kenny assured me we would have some time before the sale was finalized, if it happened at all.

FOR MANY MONTHS I hear rumblings of a possible sale of the Knoll. Nothing is definitive until one evening around dinnertime when Brenda calls me at the studio. She is at the guesthouse, where an urgent call has come in from Marianne Rogers. Marvin and Barbara Davis are there, at the Knoll, and are getting ready to sit down to dinner with Kenny and Marianne—to seal the deal they are about to sign for the sale. But there is a problem.

Marvin has thrown everyone for a loop. Apparently when he arrived, he immediately asked, "Where's Lionel?"

It's become an emergency. Brenda explains, "They want us to come to dinner. Now."

"Brenda, I'm trying to finish the album. You know how behind I am." I tell her to please send my regrets but it's impossible.

Ten minutes later, the studio phone rings again, and this time it's Marianne—who is frantic. She is referring to me by my first and last names, as Southern women tend to do when they're wound up. Marianne whispers, "*Lionel* Richie, *Lionel* Richie,

Marvin Davis does not want to have dinner unless you are here. You have to come now. He will not eat until you get here."

"Okay," I give in, but warn her, "I gotta change. I'll get there as soon as I can."

"Hurry, Lio*nel* Richie."

In just under an hour, I walk through the front door. There in the sunroom is Marvin Davis, sitting with his lovely wife, Barbara, tending to him, and Kenny and Marianne, pacing nervously, though they are relieved that I have finally shown up, and my wife, trying to smile through total anxiety. Eight other guests are there in the room waiting for dinner. The tension is thick as molasses.

Marvin takes one look at me, stands up, and starts walking toward me as he says in a booming voice, "You got a lot of nerve, Lionel! I can't believe you had me waiting for dinner!"

Kenny and Marianne look like it's all they can do to keep from passing out.

Nobody says a word. And that's my cue. In the loudest voice I can muster, I blast him back, "Marvin! I told you to have dinner without me!"

Everybody looks at their feet. Everybody, that is, except for me and Marvin Davis. He grins and hugs me and winks. Kenny pipes up, "For God's sake, let's sit down and eat then."

In the dining room, we all take our seats at a long formal dining table—with Kenny and Marianne sitting together at the head of the table, the Davises and the Richies on either side of them, and the others in the rest of the seats. Drinks arrive and the salad is served. Gone is the usual small talk. The atmosphere is prim, proper, and downright stiff.

The silence is killing me. So, I roll the dice and ask this wildcatter from Colorado who has done well for himself, "Marvin, I heard you struck oil in Denver. How much money does that represent?"

Marianne loses it. She lets out a sound like "Aghhhh!" as her soul attempts to run from her body. She can only say, "Lio*nel* Richie, who asks a question like that?"

Kenny throws in a nervous laugh like—"Hah-hah, oh, Lionel."

An awkward silence. Marvin shrugs. "Well, Lionel, I think I made a couple hundred million, hard to say."

My question came from a genuine desire to understand what made a person successful, not just rich and powerful and famous, but happy in themselves, being able to say, *I made it!*

The room warmed after that. The tension vanished because it became clear that Marvin Davis was a prankster, I understood his humor, and he understood mine. Marvin could be intimidating but really in a big teddy bear kind of way. Soon we were chatting, everybody enjoying the dinner and the company. That was when Marvin leaned forward and asked me point blank, "You really think I should buy this place?"

My opportunity had arrived. "I do," I said. "Definitely." Everyone breathed a sigh of relief, and we were good. That's when I added, "I just want you and Mrs. Davis to know that Brenda and I come with the house."

Marianne couldn't hold back. "Lio*nel* Richie, what on earth do you mean?!"

"I'm not leaving the guesthouse. Brenda and I are perfectly happy, and we see no reason to leave."

That was that. Marvin and his wife accepted our negotiated terms. I bought us enough time to go on tour and come back and then purchase the house that would become the Richies' version of the Alabama mansion in Beverly Hills, which was in need of extensive renovation for the next few years.

AMONG THE RECORDS that came out of me for my second solo album were five hit singles. All were in the Top 10 of the Hot 100. Two went to #1. One of them was the song that I'd thrown off the first album, "Hello."

Norman Whitfield—who had left Motown some years earlier to start his own label—had the strangest reaction when he happened to be in the studio the day I was dubbing in "Hello."

I got to the second chorus at the end when I glanced at him for a reaction, after the line "Tell me how to win your heart / For I *haventh* got a clue."

Stopping it there, I asked, "What do you think, Whit?"

He shrugged and did this gesture, throwing his hands up like "what the hell" and then walked out of the studio. James Carmichael had his back to Whit and didn't see that response.

Telling James, "Let me take a break," I ran out to catch Norman in the hall. He was waiting for me. "What do you think?" I asked again.

He shook his head. "It ain't about me anymore." He laughed. "I don't know where you are now, but it's way past my vision. I just want to sit here and watch, to see where the hell you're going."

Is this good or bad?

He closed his eyes and played back to me what he had just heard: "'Tell me how to win your heart, for I haven*th* got a clue.'" Then he opened his eyes and said, "Brother, that's some Shakespeare shit."

With that, Norman Whitfield gave me the nod of approval. I couldn't hide my grin. It was me trying for Shakespeare, no doubt.

That was a milestone. I had just gotten the confirmation of life that I was on my rightful path—from one of my most important mentors. And that's happiness.

KEEPING UP WITH the Joneses in Tuskegee was one thing. Keeping up with the Commodores was another thing. Keeping up with the folks in Beverly Hills was ridiculous. Forget just keeping up. What about helping out?

It was no secret that I had a tendency to want to help fix the problems of friends and strangers. If someone told me a tragic story about their life, the kind that would make me want to go write a song about it—and sometimes I did—I was happy to try to offer a solution.

In Alabama, if the problem was money-related, and a matter of a couple hundred dollars—Hey, you got it. But in LA, the numbers multiplied. You want to borrow how much? Unfortunately, because I was in the habit of loaning money, I had trouble saying no. My business manager, Len Freedman, became alarmed, insisting that if I wanted to loan money to someone to come to him first.

Each time, I'd give him the situation, such as, "Len, this guy's a famous producer, he wants me to loan him twenty thousand dollars, and he's going to put up the recording equipment as collateral."

"Lionel, that's fine," Len said.

"Okay. It is?"

"Here's what I'll do," Len explained. "If for whatever reason he doesn't pay you back, I'll take twenty thousand of my own money and put it in your account. You can't lose money."

Wow. What a deal. He was taking on the risk and any loss.

Sure enough, the twenty thousand wasn't repaid and Len gave me the money.

There was another loan request for seven thousand dollars. Same thing happened.

A third guy came along and asked to borrow ten thousand dollars.

Frankly, I didn't want to lose Len's money. But I went to Len first, told him the situation, and said, "Look, I don't think I want to loan it to him because I don't want you to lose any more money. And frankly, I don't think he's gonna pay the money back."

And Len said, "Thank God, it took three times for you to come to that realization. I was going broke." The lesson was, simply, that if you loan a friend some money, you lose money *and* a friend. Oh, and, by the way, I put the money back into Len's account. From then on Jack Benny had no issue with saying no to anyone wanting to borrow money. I had learned a very important lesson.

Another discovery I made was that the biggest challenges for Hollywood marriages came from fast growth, fame, and money. The irony was that the faster you grew, the more stress there was that came with success. At one point, during a rough patch, I called my pastor in Tuskegee for some advice. What I said was, "Father Jones, I need some counseling. I think Brenda and I might be getting a divorce."

He said the oddest thing ever. He told me, "Lionel, I'm really not a good candidate to give you counseling about divorce." Why not? Because, in his experience, no one in Tuskegee, or at St. Andrew's specifically, got divorced. He did say, "I can only encourage you to stay together."

He was just telling it like it was—because the Hollywood marriage is a beast unto itself.

When I was getting my start in LA, my first reaction was, *How stupid are these people?* They get married and divorced every week. That's not to say love wasn't involved. It's just that you're a star and you have a long line of candidates wanting to be your next one and only.

In Tuskegee, if you met someone at a party, all you had to say was, "I'm married," and the woman would be, "Oh, sorry, I didn't know," and back away.

In California, the dance was different. Even before hit songs, I was out somewhere in LA and a girl was hitting on me, and I politely said, "I'm sorry, but I must let you know I'm married."

She came back with a question I didn't expect. "Is she with you?"

"No."

She said, "Then there's no problem."

Yes, I was successful in fending off the advance with "That's flattering, but wait, wait, wait now."

Imagine this—you fall in love and probably get married, maybe to the first girl who says, "I love you." Now, when you're new in the Business, magnify that with it happening over and over, every day, and think how it feels like every time someone walks up, and you hear, "Oh, my God, I love you." It's confusing.

Wait . . . You love me. You do?

In this atmosphere, "I love you" then becomes the least trustworthy phrase in life. In the Business of fame and entertainment, it loses its magic fast.

The part that I hated most was that this word that I use as my religion could become a throwaway phrase.

When I write, "I love you," and when somebody plays that record, that's an emotional moment. When a man or a woman says, "I love you, still," after everything, that's an emotional moment. Naive as I was, it took me some time to see that everybody that says "I love you" to you when you're famous, that's something they say, not something they feel.

Over time, even when writing emotional love songs, I began to distrust "I love you."

How did that happen?

They don't teach you in Alabama how to tell the real one from the fake. My observations were through the lens of a perpetual college student. I imagined how others had to feel after falling for temptation but thought I was immune. Or wished that I was.

WHENEVER I NEEDED a reminder of the values that raised me, I went back to Alabama—where I was seen as the hometown boy done good. Most in the community expected that of a graduate of Tuskegee University (as it was known by the 1980s), not to mention a member of Alpha Phi Alpha Fraternity—whose noted members include Thurgood Marshall and Martin Luther King Jr.

To some, I was the luckiest sonuvabitch in town. *Can you believe that's Skeet?*

That boy could never sit still, how in the world did he ever write those songs? Some folks back home didn't even know who I was—which was sometimes a relief.

In fact, earlier when Brenda and I bought a house in Tuskegee, the one I chose was away from campus—for privacy. This modern home, only about five years old, was near the Tuskegee Lake in an area where, rumor had it, members of the Klan were around back in the day.

We didn't know if any of that was true because there had never been any Black folks over there to find out.

The closest neighbor was Bill—we'll call him—whose little girl always waved at me whenever I came or left.

This was not a "go visiting" type situation. That is, until one night when Mrs. Willis, my housekeeper, inadvertently changed the combination on my alarm system without telling me.

Unsuspecting, after flying from LA to Atlanta and driving to Tuskegee, I arrive home at about four in the morning, I open the door, and the frickin' alarm goes off, and I can't shut it off.

Up from the driveway comes Bill and his granddaddy with two shotguns over their shoulders. Bill calls, "You alright, Lionel?"

Under normal circumstances, two white guys at 4 a.m. walking up with shotguns would freak my ass out. But in this case, I am happy to see them. Bill and his granddaddy wait as the police officer arrives, and then radios the station to get the code from Mrs. Willis. So much for a guy trying to sneak into town.

I told a few people about the incident, and they shook their heads and lowered their voices, muttering—*Somethin' somethin'* about *the Klan*.

I dismissed it. Bill came by one day, and my life in California came up and I mentioned that my wife and I stayed in the guesthouse belonging to Kenny Rogers.

"Kenny Rogers? You . . . know Kenny Rogers?"

"He's one of my best friends." I hesitated about mentioning I wrote the song "Lady."

Bill was beside himself. He probably didn't believe me.

There was only one thing to do—invite Kenny to come and visit. Can you even imagine the look on Bill's face after Kenny Rogers flew to Tuskegee for a visit and we went down and knocked on Bill's door?

I swear to God, Bill just stood there as if Kenny had arrived in a golden chariot sent from heaven. We visited and then Kenny left, and I was now Bill's most worthy up-the-hill neighbor.

So, I got to talking to him one evening, and because we were getting along so well, I had to ask, "Bill, do you know the mayor of Tuskegee?"

"Oh, hell no, I don't know him," he said, an indication that this was taboo territory. Going further I asked if he'd ever met any community leaders, like the president of the university. He said, "Oh, no, I don't know anybody up there, Lio*nel*."

When I invited him to come over with his little girl for a Sunday in my backyard, he agreed. We'd swim in my swimming pool, and he could meet the mayor and Mr. Logan, the university's head of finance.

When Sunday came around, Bill showed up. And I found out what everybody was drinking. It was Tanqueray gin, Mr. Logan's choice. And we sat there in the pool, the little jacuzzi part, and we were all sitting there laughing and joking, telling stories.

It was a Sunday in the backyard in Tuskegee.

Mr. Logan left, and the mayor left.

And I looked over at Bill, who had the most puzzled expression. He said, "Lio*nel*, I got a problem."

"What is it, Bill?"

"I had a great time, Lio*nel*."

"Well, thank you Bill."

He said, "I gotta tell you, I'm a little confused. I feel like I been lied to."

"No, Bill," I said. "You haven't been lied to." How could I explain this to him? Here is what I offered: "You're just the first of your generation that can see it for yourself and not fall for the stories that you've heard about Black folks."

He took this in.

"You're the first to know." I said, "Maybe nobody in your family had a chance to know for themselves before."

This was the dawning of my knowledge of a plan for my life that I'd missed up until now.

I saw it with Bill—that if you don't talk to people with assumptions about you, then they can only fall for the stories they've been told. If they don't talk to you, then you will only fall for the stories you've been told.

Bill had never planned on this day. But now he had shared quality time with community leaders, during an afternoon with family and stories about plain old stuff we all had in common. As I pointed out, "You met them. Now you know who they are. And they know you." He listened quietly. "Bill, you have now been educated for the next generation to understand. But you can't go back and accuse your kinfolk of lying to you because they were only repeating what they were taught."

This was not an easy conversation, and he was deeply, deeply disturbed by it. How had he really taken it in?

About a week and a half later, I heard a knock at the door and looked out but didn't see anything until I opened the door, and there was Bill's little girl with a face full of blood.

Oh my God.

Just then, I looked up and saw this deer in the back of the truck, upside down, and Bill was up in the back proudly waving me over. "She killed her first buck. Come over here, Lio*nel*, and cut yourself a piece of this venison off."

The visuals haunted me—the god-awful sight of a man cutting off the side of a deer, and a little girl's face full of blood.

Bill asked, "Now, you got a garbage bag? Put it in the garbage bag, and have Big Mama"—talking about my Brenda—"cook it up for ya. This is some mighty good venison right here."

Let me tell you, it took every ounce of my willpower not to throw up as I grabbed the bag and carried it full of that deer flesh and brought it out onto the back porch. You know, I realized then that, no, we were not the same, me and Bill, and we weren't supposed to be. Yet, we didn't have to fear and disrespect the other. We could be friends.

Bill and I never stopped being friends, until later in the eighties when he moved away and we lost touch. Those words of his—"I feel like I been lied to"—lived on and rang forever in my head. How many of us have been lied to? The lesson forever explained my values to me—*that until you have spoken to someone, you don't know who that person is, and they don't know who you are.*

▓▌▐▌▐▌

SAY WHAT YOU will about how phony people can be out in the land of Hollywood, but let me tell you that, in my research, I discovered that many of the most famous stars were also the most down-to-earth, kindest, and most generous people I've ever known.

The perfect example? Gregory Peck. When we met in the late 1970s, he was in his sixties and as handsome and youthful as he was in the films that had earned him legendary stature. His most famous role, of course, was as Atticus Finch in *To Kill a Mockingbird* in 1962—as a small-town white lawyer who defends a young Black man accused of a crime he didn't commit. He taught me in that portrayal how acting can be a lot like going to the Other Side, where you find the voice of the character that speaks through you. In his own right, Gregory Peck had the same courage and decency as Atticus Finch.

Gregory and his wife, Veronique—French, elegant, with a fantastic sense of humor—were so gracious to me and Brenda, almost parental. Imagine having Atticus Finch and his wife cheering for you when you're coming into your success.

The first time that we were invited to dinner at the Pecks', I couldn't believe that they had included us in their circle—with the likes of Liza Minnelli and Elizabeth Taylor—as well as our mutual friend, Michael Jackson.

As soon as we pulled up to the Peck estate and rang at the gate, we heard a familiar voice—"Lionel, is that you?"

Was that the guard or valet, or was Mr. Peck passing by when we rang?

"Oh, it's Lionel, yes. The Richies are here, yes."

The gate opened. We pulled up a long driveway. There, at the top of the hill, stood a valet, I assumed, who was helping park the cars.

Oh damn, looks like Mr. Peck.

He smiled and welcomed us. "Park right over there, Lionel. Good to see you." Obviously, his usual valet was off for the night.

After we had a chance to greet the others, Mr. Peck turned and said, "Lionel, would you like a drink? And Brenda?"

Oh. Mr. Peck was now the bartender. We didn't see any household help at all until a lady came from the balcony and said, "Dinner is served."

We all went outside, took our seats at a table under the stars, and had a beautiful dinner.

At one point Mr. Peck said, "Is anyone cold?" Veronique replied that yes, it was chilly. Thank God she said that. Michael and I were freezing to death.

Within minutes, we turned around and there was Mr. Peck with his arms full of his very large sweaters he had bought down from upstairs for us to put on. And he started passing them around.

Brenda and I were quiet on the way home as I mentally replayed the night. The Pecks were visibly happy but obviously regular. They didn't need all the trappings, with people waiting on them in every way. They were home and we were home with them. It wasn't a show. It was pure downhome hospitality— with a French twist. I guessed that the only thing he didn't do was cut his own grass, although he probably did that when the gate closed, and nobody knew about it.

As my career took off, I never forgot that feeling and was determined to entertain with that down-to-earth graciousness—when at last Brenda and I moved into our house.

We had barely begun the process when we had a request from Elizabeth Taylor for a get-together. She saw me at a gala and said, "Why don't we screen a movie at your house? I'll bring a date."

Are you kidding me?

In a frantic frenzy of preparation, Brenda asks a critical question: "What does she eat?"

I call Elizabeth, who says not to cook. "Do you know Maurice's Snack 'n Chat on Pico?" *Did I know it? It was my hangout.* "Well, call Maurice and tell her the order is for me."

Maurice, owner and chef of one of the best soul food spots around, knows what to send—fried chicken, collard greens, and candied yams. Rice and gravy. And apple pie and peach cobbler. And don't forget the macaroni and cheese. (Oh damn, now I'm starting to wonder if Elizabeth Taylor could be Black!) The night arrives, with dinner set at 6 p.m. Brenda and I decide we'll set up TV trays and watch the movie while we eat. No sign of them at 6:00 or 6:30. At 7:00 p.m. we begin to worry.

Finally, over an hour late, the limousine pulls up through the gate and the first person to step out is the mystery date—the ever-so-dashing and notoriously tan George Hamilton, dressed in an immaculate summer jacket and an ascot. Elizabeth follows next, looking like a naughty kid in her Fila-type tracksuit and her hair pulled back like Cleopatra.

That's when George tells us why they're late—mainly because they stopped at the 7–Eleven for lottery tickets—the scratch-off kind. They were in the limo scratching off at the 7–Eleven, in case any were winners. *Can you imagine?*

They're giggling now like children, which they're supposed to be as creative people. And that's *it*—the secret to protecting the creative part of yourself in the middle of the gravity of success. For all the complaints I'd heard about artists being immature, I discovered a truth—*Yes, we are*. Back to the lessons of the sandbox.

"YOU HAVE TO meet this young drummer I saw last night," I heard Brenda say one morning.

Half asleep, I didn't want to ignore my wife, who had great instincts about talent. "Cool," I said. "What's his name?"

Her name was Sheila Escovedo, and Brenda raved about this beautiful, young, incredibly talented percussionist. "She's a star. Hire her for your band."

Turned out that Sheila and her brother, Pete, also a percussionist, had grown up in Northern California, the kids of the well-known Latin percussionist, also Pete Escovedo. Sheila started performing with her dad's band at fifteen. The first time I went to hear her, I admired her—knowing that as a woman she had to fight to be taken seriously. And then I watched her go to work.

Unbelievable. A showwoman, she was all joy, no fear. Not only did I hire Sheila as my percussionist for different legs of my tour, but she opened for me in early 1984. In getting to know Sheila, I also met her brother, Pete, who became, at other points, my percussionist. When I met him, he was in the middle of a breakup (as I later learned) with a young woman who worked as a wardrobe person for Prince.

In this period, Sheila E. (as she became known) was either already with Prince romantically or soon to be. Sheila was naturally funny as hell, and the two of us could riff on any subject and crack each other up. She used to call me up just for us to get a routine going by asking questions—supposedly about me and what I was up to. Nuth'n seemed weird until I realized

Prince was with her, listening on the other line. Finally, I said, "Sheila, if Prince wants to talk to me, tell him to stop by the studio."

Prince knew me. The two of us had met a few years earlier when I was working on the mix for "Endless Love." He had stopped by Motown studios and was fascinated by the process our engineer used to bring up Diana's voice on the track.

Sheila must have given Prince the message because, probably the next day, he dropped by the studio. Prince, very serious, said—"Is that your Rolls-Royce parked outside?"

For some crazy reason, Kenny Rogers had just given the Rolls to Brenda. "It's my wife's," I told Prince. "But, hey, you want to drive it? You can come up to the house. I've got sweet potato pie. We can hang out."

He looked like the seas had parted and the two of us had become fellow escapees from the land of bondage. He drove the Rolls up to our house, I drove Brenda, and we put out the sweet potato pie. We were there just in time for Prince to pull up in the Rolls, with Sheila, followed by more cars carrying the rest of his entourage. Luckily, we had extra pie in the freezer.

From then on, Prince and I were thick as thieves.

We talked music. I was enthralled with how he played every instrument and could run an entire session from the board, on his own. I never saw anyone who could hear melody and move through octaves like an Olympian diving off the high dive and plunging down low. He surrounded himself with superstars— Sheila E., Jimmy Jam and Terry Lewis, and Wendy and Lisa. A musical melting pot.

When Sheila E. opened for me on my solo tour, we played Minneapolis—Prince's hometown and home base. And I wasn't surprised that during Sheila's set, Prince came out and started playing with her—with his whole band. The crowd went wild. This continued until I walked up onto the corner of the stage and gestured—like, *Get your ass off.* He knew he'd taken over and it was Sheila's show, so he left, sheepishly. Sheila picked right up and the crowd went completely crazy.

Moments later Prince stopped by my dressing room and said, "You know I wasn't going to stay on that long."

"Oh, yes you were!" I laughed. He laughed even louder.

That same night, after my show—and he was right in the front, like a fan—Prince threw a party for me. The kicker was that he put on some recorded music—all my songs. The vocals were mine, for sure, but, amazingly, he had remixed the music with tracks of his own! He had prepared for days or weeks. That was the greatest compliment from any fellow musician.

We were, as the saying goes, members of a mutual admiration society.

I HAVE A hazy memory of attending a Prince concert, around the same time that *Purple Rain* was getting ready to hit movie screens. On the stage of this concert was an unusual sight—an adorable little girl, barely three years old, playing a tambourine, by herself.

Who is supervising her? Is this where she is supposed to be?

I couldn't stop wondering about her walking around onstage, and had to ask Brenda, "Who the hell is this little girl?"

She had no idea, but we began to ask if anyone else knew. The story we tracked down was that when Pete Escovedo broke up with his girlfriend, she was pregnant, and that they were the parents of this enchanting little girl, Nicole Camille Escovedo. Everyone called her Nikki.

Her parents were touring, not together, and we weren't sure who was in charge of her care. We didn't want to jump to conclusions. As I recall, it took months to put the pieces of the puzzle together. Nobody wanted to shame the parents—who were having problems. And our asking may have been seen as none of our business. We didn't want to be intrusive.

When Nikki was about four, from what we heard, there still wasn't any stability. Clearly, they loved her and were trying hard, but it was an uncertain time. Other family members volunteered to take charge. The reality was that whenever I crossed paths with the little angel, no adult was nearby.

"This can't be in Nikki's best interest," I said to Brenda.

The suggestion came from Brenda that maybe we could be foster parents, until her birth parents were in a better situation. Our focus would be on giving love to Nikki and letting her know that she was in a safe space.

Brenda put Nicole front and center in her life. She told me, "While you're on the road, I'm not going with you. This little girl is staying at our house and I'm staying here with her."

The timing was such that I was back in the studio and not away as much. And what happened next was that, in short order, this little girl became the light of my life. We just connected so naturally that I felt—as hard as it may be to understand—it was me and Nikki against the world. She was a version of me, the people-pleasing little person who only wanted to be loved and accepted. She was the cutest, most adorable little girl, and whoever walked in the room, she would see you and do whatever she had to do to steal your heart.

Whenever I was away, I couldn't wait to get back to make sure she knew that she could count on me and Brenda, no matter what. It killed me to think that she had to carry so much baggage at her age. Yet that is not what she projected. On the contrary, Nikki looked at me as if she'd come along to help me rid myself of my load.

She was literally my comic relief, as I was hers. All I had to do to entertain us was pick her up and tickle the bottom of her feet. And out would come the deepest belly laugh. She'd lean in and crack me up even more, saying, "You got a face on you!" *A face?* We laughed ourselves to Silly-ville daily.

Nikki had my number. She had this one expression that said, *Oh, you think you are the adult in this relationship? You are the kid here, I'm just here to validate that part of you.*

Eventually, Brenda and I arranged to be Nikki's legal guardians. She was at home with us. We wanted what was in her best interest, though we knew it wasn't easy for the family. Above all, she had to know she belonged somewhere.

Worrying that she felt as if she didn't belong just wrecked me. To the point of killing me—watching the uncertainty on her face that seemed to say, *Well, what's wrong with me? If I'm so adorable, what's wrong with me?*

Even as issues at home became complicated for me and Brenda, the one thing that never changed was how devoted we both were to Nicole—who, in the process, proceeded to blossom.

No matter what doubts anyone else projected, I made her a promise. I will never forget looking at her straight in the face, telling her, "Okay, now we're going to prove everybody wrong. Whatever happens, one thing I want you to know for sure, we are never going to leave you."

I made that deal with her. "Right, you get it?" Nikki understood.

"We are never going to leave you" was the promise I made without knowing that everything in my life was about to be thrown upside down.

The deal was forever and always.

And we've had that relationship from that day forward.

Her life had not been given a fair start. As much as I would have wanted to, I couldn't change what had already happened.

She opened my eyes to the responsibility of becoming a dad. I began to understand a phenomenon I'd noticed once I became a solo artist—that whenever Brenda's father, Marshall Harvey, and my dad were around, a lot of the musicians in my band gravitated to them.

On the road, if Dad and Marshall had come to see my show and were staying at the same hotel as the band members, I'd find everyone up in my father's room. Dad even asked me, "Now, why are these band members in my room?" Other times, some of the guys would even call to ask Marshall and my dad for advice—"What would you do if you were in my shoes?"

My drummer explained that most of the band members hadn't grown up with fathers. "Where we come from," he said, "if you have a dad, we're all adopting your dad."

Lyonel Sr. and Marshall didn't take their roles as adopted fathers lightly. Neither did I when we formally adopted Nicole at age nine.

Brenda was her mom and I was her dad. She was our daughter. For life.

And, in the process of becoming a dad, I finally began to grow up. A little.

What Nicole gave me, over time, was the strength to trust myself—because I was her father, and I couldn't let her down. Over time, my daughter taught me the truth of myself—that in the depths of who I am is a profound need to love something more than anything. She taught me to honor my need to care about someone without condition.

Nicole didn't need me to prove myself worthy enough to be her father, despite my shortcomings. She only required love.

What I required, she gave in abundance—purpose.

16

All Night Long

"I NEED A DAMN HOOK," I call over to James Anthony Carmichael, my ever-present producer/mentor.

Hunkered down at the studio—A&M Records in Hollywood—I'm churning out songs for my second solo album. And for the first time in maybe forever, I don't have a hook.

C'mon, I know how to find a hook. But I can't find this one for the life of me. Something is wrong. All I have is a melody, a beat, and an intro:

> *Well, my friends, the time has come*
> *To raise the roof and have some fun*
> *Throw away the work to be done*
> *Let the music play on*
> *(Play on, play on)*
>
> *Everybody sing, everybody dance*
> *Lose yourself in wild romance*
> *We're going to party*

Karamu, fiesta, forever
Come on and sing along . . .

Uhhhhh . . . What? This is drivin' me crazy. James Carmichael has no suggestion. Of all the songs I've written, I have never started without a hook first. For a moment, I flash on Mom, the English instructor, giving me the rules of composition—how you start every essay with a subject, and then you write about that. Somehow, I'm doing this song backwards—a vibe and a verse. But no title (the same as the hook for me) and no sense of my character for the song.

There are two clear themes in my music now. The main theme brings out the moody ballads of *I love you, I need you, I'm leaving you, I will still love you forever.* The other theme is for the guy who can't sit still and wants to know, *Where da party at?*

With the infectious beat I've already got—almost Calypso, definitely funky—I feel a party song brewing. It's just the universal vibe of every vacation you've ever been on.

Maybe the hook is—*We're gonna have a good time?*

Nah, nuth'n. You know what I really need? A break!

Just in time to go meet the family for dinner at the home of dear friends Dr. Lloyd Greig—a distinguished, Jamaican-born Beverly Hills gynecologist—and his wonderful wife, Sally.

As soon as I walk into the Greigs' house, everybody is talking like we are on the island of Jamaica. The *Ya, mons* are thick in the air, along with a hint of Patois. The atmosphere is so full of Jamaican accents you could cut 'em with a knife.

Is this the right place or what to take a break from the studio? *Ya, mon!*

We're having a great time. Around nine thirty, though, I know it's time to go, and as I'm leaving, I start to sing out my goodbye, announcing, "There's work to be done, I gotta get back to the studio, *mon.*"

"So soon? You gotta go back to the studio *tonight?* You workin' late, *mon!*"

I keep singing, "I gotta go back to work all night long, *mon.* Goin' to be workin' all night long . . ."

Holy shit! What did I just say? That's it. The hook! The title! I stop in my tracks and repeat, "All night long. All night . . ." singing it in my new-found Jamaican accent. Lionel Richie Marley has just been born.

And so has "All Night Long (All Night)."

From there, I went back to the studio and almost finished the song. Now that I had the hook, it was a matter of stacking and layering the perfect island character for the delivery.

There was only one problem left. I wanted a breakdown in the song where I could go into an African dialect that would suggest a call-out to a spontaneous party. Bob Marley would include lines like that—not Jamaican Patois but, I assumed, a well-known African dialect—like a tribal chant. That's what I had to have.

Through a friend, I was given a contact at one of the African consulates, and after I reached an official and described what I was looking for, he asked, "Mr. Richie, what tribe? What region?" When I sounded confused, he informed me there were more than a thousand dialects. Of those that were most common, with over a million speakers, he explained, "Mr. Richie, there are at least one hundred and one."

"Let me get this straight. One tribe has no clue what the other tribes are saying?"

"In some cases," he confirmed. The dialects were that different.

My next call was to my dear friend, Dr. Lloyd Greig, and I gave him my best rendition of Bob Marley's use of an African dialect. "So, Doc, what is he saying?"

Dr. Greig said, "Absolutely nothing." The words had no literal translation. That's all I needed to know to come up with my own words:

> *Tam bo li de, say de moi ya. Yeah jambo jambo*
> *Way to party oh we're going, oh, jambali*
> *Tam bo li de, say de moi ya.*

Wow. Apparently, I had now created the 102nd (major) African dialect . . . with a hint of Jamaican Patois.

In August 1983, Motown released it as the lead single, six weeks before the album, *Can't Slow Down*, was released. There was a story I'd later hear about a meeting with Berry Gordy where an executive had heard the record—"It's Calypso!"—and predicted it would bomb. Berry said, "I haven't heard it but if it's Lionel Richie, it's a smash. Put it out."

I was still on my world tour for the first album in November when "All Night Long" hit #1 in the US with a *Billboard* trifecta of Pop, R&B, and Adult Contemporary, and it stayed on the charts for twenty-four weeks. The video, released in September, did something I'd never experienced before and made the single an instant global hit.

Timing was optimal. MTV had just loosened its rule of only showing Rock videos—which had been a middle finger to Black artists like Prince, Michael Jackson, and me, plus others who didn't pass the Rock purity test. What got MTV to reconsider? They did a very normal thing . . . they asked the viewers what videos they wanted to see. And by popular demand, the rules changed. First, in 1982, Prince made it onto MTV with "1999," then Michael Jackson's "Billie Jean" went into heavy rotation, followed by my "All Night Long" video, leading up to the *mutha* of all videos of this era—the fourteen-minute-long video for "Thriller."

Nobody, anywhere in the world, cared what label you stuck on "All Night Long." They cared not a shred that they were singing along to foreign or made-up words. Nobody cared if it was Rock or the Blues or whatever. It was a monster hit, an anthem.

Even Grandma loved that song and started calling to report how it was doing on the charts. Dad couldn't contain his pride. Mom was the only one who wasn't into the hoopla. For her, the English teacher, the lyrics didn't make sense. Her refrain was, "Why would you say that? You don't talk like that."

As soon as "All Night Long" hit the airwaves in Jamaica, Dr. Greig started hearing from friends who knew he and I were pals. He told the story of how I got the hook at his house.

Now everybody hounded him. "Doc, congratulations! I know you made a lot of money off that song, right?"

No matter how hard he protested—"No, I didn't write it. Lionel just made it up at my house"—they felt he should get a piece.

"How could you let Lionel Richie do that to you, *mon*?"

We have laughed about it to this day.

AS KEN KRAGEN had promised, he managed to get me booked as the host of the 1984 American Music Awards on January 16, 1984. In the blur of it all, I came off of one leg of my tour and barely arrived home before changing into a tux, jumping into a limo, and hoping I'd get to the Shrine Auditorium in time to go over my cues. If all else failed—improv!

After years of using comedy to cover up my shyness, I had tried borrowing a tactic used by Michael Jackson and Prince—both of whom were very shy. Michael and Prince could be funny sometimes, but they had another coping mechanism—mystery.

Why not give up Mr. Funny Lionel Richie and go into Mr. Mysterious Richie? So I went to my dear friend, Howard Kenney, fellow member of the Home-Boy Association, and I said, "I've decided to be quiet and mysterious, what do you think?"

Howard shook his head and said, "Lionel, if you become quiet and mysterious, folks will think something is wrong with your ass for real." He pressed his point. It was too late to stop being silly, talkative, and funny. "I hate to break it to you, but you're doomed to be who you are now forever. Don't even think of changing. Ever."

And that was the end of my attempt to be the moody guy. Good thing—because as a host of a TV show, the looser and the sillier I could be, the better.

The beautiful thing about the American Music Awards that year was witnessing the dreams of a young Michael Jackson come to fruition—with the eight awards he won, a feat only matched a decade later by Whitney Houston.

I forgot completely that I had been nominated for three awards, two of which I lost to Michael. No surprise. The only award I think he lost that night was shockingly to me, when "Billie Jean" was up against "All Night Long" in the category of Favorite Soul/R&B Song.

A month later, I lost again at the Grammys after being nominated for five awards. And in September, at the inaugural MTV Video Music Awards at Radio City Music Hall, I lost Best Male Video to David Bowie's "China Girl."

How did I feel? Are you kidding me? Did I even lose? My name was next to David Bowie. C'mon. The nomination in that instance was me winning like a big dog.

While all this was going on, with *Can't Slow Down*, there wasn't a second to celebrate one single before the next was coming out. Late in 1983 it was "Running with the Night"

(#7 Pop, #6 R&B, #6 Adult Contemporary) and then, knocking that out of the way, we released that once-discarded song, "Hello," in February 1984.

The video told the story of me as an acting teacher in love with his student, a blind girl who also takes dance and pottery. Then she sculpts a bust of him and it is revealed that she loves him too. During rehearsal for the scene, I hounded our director, Bob Giraldi, with a concern about the clay bust. I kept saying, "Bob, it looks *nuth'n* like me."

"Lionel," he said, "she's blind."

My answer? "Oh . . ." Now and then, to this day, someone will ask if I have that bust. And I just say no. The truth is I got rid of it after the shoot—because it didn't look like me!

The video was in heavy rotation just as the single of "Hello" was released in record stores and on the radio. The record was a trifecta (#1 Pop, R&B, and Adult Contemporary) and became another worldwide smash. The fourth single, "Stuck on You" (released in June 1984), and the fifth, "Penny Lover" (September 1984), were both #1 in Adult Contemporary, also both Top 10 Pop and R&B. "Stuck on You" was another song inspired by me being nosy, listening to a guy I met on tour who told me about the love of his life he couldn't forget. In "Penny Lover" I included the line that "when a man's in love he's only got one story"—a truth about how it feels when you find the person of your dreams.

Can't Slow Down would quickly go on to sell ten million copies—the equivalent of being certified *ten times* Platinum or what the RIAA would later designate as Diamond certification. Well, the crazy thing is, before long *Can't Slow Down* became the earliest certified Diamond album. Earlier albums by other artists surely reached the same sales threshold, but somehow it was my luck to have been officially certified before them.

Can't Slow Down would go on in time to sell well over twenty million copies worldwide. It stayed in the Top 10 for fifty-nine weeks and on the Hot 200 for three years. It was a #1 album on all charts, here and in almost every other country in the world where rankings are kept.

THE *CAN'T SLOW DOWN* tour topped anything my team and I had ever attempted. We touched down in twenty-six states of the US and made three stops in Canada. Wherever we went, I witnessed the truth that no community is exactly like another. But everybody—everywhere—has two things in common: 1) a desire to have their feelings about love and life understood, and 2) a desire to bask in the glow of the healing powers of music.

Opening for me in this era were the Pointer Sisters—high-energy, super happening, and hip preacher's daughters from Oakland, California. When they took off to headline their own tour, I was joined by the one and only Tina Turner—no longer with Ike and promoting her debut solo album, *Private Dancer.*

Tina became one of my closest friends in the Business. I admired her for how she fought at every turn to get industry recognition as the Queen of Rock—on her own terms. In 1991, the Rock & Roll Hall of Fame tried to induct her with Ike Turner but she wouldn't show, not willing to share the award with her well-known abusive ex.

Tina had *presence*—at an electric level that would have been intimidating if not for her sultry warmth. We bonded over our refusal to be put in a box musically. Tina was always hearing she wasn't R&B enough, to some, but not Rock 'n' Roll enough because she was Black.

She had unwittingly stoked the resentment of Black activists because she played South Africa in the middle of apartheid. Her critics suggested she go out on an "I'm Sorry" tour. She wasn't ready. She said, "Can you believe it? Black folks are demanding an apology from me." Nobody knew that Tina couldn't get booked anywhere else when she took the work in South Africa. The only way she could perform in front of Black South Africans was to accept the designation of Honorary White Person required for her to perform there. Later she officially apologized. I know that was hard baggage.

My observation in 1984 was that she was still scared to death Ike might try to come after her.

Onstage Tina Turner was a force of nature, an energetic sexual powerhouse, a beast. In our duets together—like "Three Times a Lady" and "Hot Legs"—she talked to me while we were singing, pushing, teaching me how to be present in every performance. In between singing our parts, Tina kept in my face, talking to me in a low voice, almost hissing, "Lionel, c'mon, give it to me, sing it to me baby, you got more than that, Lionel, c'mon!" She was the shit, man, never phoning it in, always turning it up. She was amazing.

We'd walk offstage and, with the PTSD of a battered woman, she'd shrink and wouldn't calm down until she was in her room.

On this tour, or on a later one, we were supposed to play in St. Louis, where she had lived before, and she had warned me, ahead of time, "I don't think I can play there." I reassured her that we'd have security with her 24/7, but I could tell as soon as the show was over, she was totally freaked out. Normally, because Tina was on a bus tour, if we weren't in a hotel, she would leave on the bus after the show and drive right to our next stop. Backstage throughout our show, I saw how visibly frightened Tina was—as if Ike would appear and kill her right there. She was that broken.

We arranged on the spot for her to leave on my plane after our show, and I could have it come back for me. That's how PTSD works, even for someone as powerful as Tina in almost every other way.

Another dramatic story on that same tour happened in Philadelphia. When we arrived at our hotel, we were met by a group of Black promoters and DJs and their representatives, along with local Black community activists, all threatening to boycott the tour. Why? Not only did they want Tina to apologize for going to South Africa, but they were also unhappy with Lionel Richie because my promoter Howard Rose was white, as was my manager Ken Kragen.

Even before we came to Philadelphia, the phrase I heard was "You have to water your roots"—and I understood. However, when the suggestion was made that we cancel our show, I refused.

We go up to my hotel room, where Tina goes off—pacing, venting to me but talking to these guys as if they're with us. She's stomping around, saying, "Where were you when I was struggling? Where were you when I didn't have a roof to stay under?"

I listen.

"You know what," she says, pointing to an imaginary accuser. "I was a ho to you. And here I am, Tina Turner. And who am I still to you? A ho. And you want me to apologize?" She turns, ready to leave, to go and curse the guys out herself—including the leader of the local Nation of Islam branch.

Oh, shit. I convince Tina to let me go talk to them.

On the road with us is Ken Kragen, who is Jewish, and he ain't going down there. "Lionel, are you sure?"

"I got this," I say, and for the record, I'm not that nervous. Maybe I should be, but I had seen Tina be vulnerable about her fears—which made me want to step up and, instead of avoiding a confrontation, just stand up for us both.

Then again, it's a crapshoot. I'm betting that if I can get the two leaders up to my room, it will be less hostile than down in the lobby.

The two guys come in and thank me for meeting with them. One of them says, "Before we get started, I have a little story I want you to hear."

This is not what I'm expecting. "Okay . . ."

"Back in 1972, Benny Ashburn, your manager, a dear friend of mine, offered me a piece of the Commodores."

"Wow." Again, not what I'm expecting.

"The one thing I regret to this day is I didn't say yes. But it's a pleasure to meet you. Congratulations on your success. How can we clear up this problem?"

From there, it is just people talking. And I explain Tina's situation—that she is getting on her feet, but will clarify her support for ending apartheid soon. My concern is that a boycott of a tour of two Black artists will hurt the causes we all care about.

They agree. The other gentleman lets me know, "You are loved in the Muslim community. As you're loved in the Philadelphia community."

Sometimes people just need to be heard. But there is something else.

The Muslim leader says, "The reason I came up here to meet you was that before Benny died, I told him that if there was anything I could ever do to help, please call me." He and the community leader had our backs!

Nuth'n like a sign to let me know Benny Ashburn was still pulling strings.

Tina never stopped thanking me for intervening in Philly, as well as for asking her to open for me. Incredibly, when she came off our tour, "What's Love Got to Do with It?" was a smash, soon to hit #1 on the Hot 100, the biggest single of her career.

Back in LA, Tina and I went for lunch at the Ivy Restaurant on Robertson Boulevard in Beverly Hills to celebrate. In every era, the Ivy was always just the best—with its New Orleans decor, crab cakes and corn chowder, the red brick patio, and the white picket fence that let passersby gawk at all the celebrities out in the California sunshine.

Tina and I got to talking about why we loved getting to perform night after night, doing the same songs, same shows, and I had a startling realization. I realized that every time I sang the same song to a new audience, it was a brand-new adventure, a brand-new love affair. Tina said the same for herself. When you can get people in a crowd to connect to one another—that is the high of all highs.

As we were waiting for the check, we overheard some of the waitstaff talking about how the restaurant was going to close because the landlord was selling the building. Tina and I asked a few questions about how much they were selling the building for.

I had a thought. "I like this restaurant," I said.

"Me too," Tina said, and looked at me like she was having the same thought. "Well," she said, "I guess we're buying a building together."

And that's what we did.

[|||| |||]

CERTAIN EVENTS IN life strike without warning, like earthquakes, and forever after you remember where you were when you were shaken to your core.

That's how it was on April 1, 1984, when I was at the studio and calls started pouring in with the news that Marvin Gaye, age forty-four, one day before his forty-fifth birthday, had been shot and killed by his father. At first, fans refused to accept that he was dead and called it an ugly April Fool's joke.

Within the hour we had verification, and I cut the rehearsal short. Marvin had been my friend and teacher—who had convinced me that my inability to read music would not hold me back, and that if I could hum it, somebody else could write it down. Marvin understood the Other Side.

The world grew darker that day. Certain artists and human beings are like comets. They burn bright and streak across the sky, giving us parts of themselves that change us forever. And then they are gone.

The idea for me to write a song about Marvin came about in an unusual way. Three or four years earlier, when Diana Ross agreed to record "Endless Love" as a duet with me, she asked if I would be willing to write a song for her—at some time in the future. And I had said, "Of course."

Not long after Marvin's sudden death, I heard from Diana—who was working on an album and wanted to include a song from me on it. Pleased to fulfill my promise, I said yes and then asked her what she might want to say in a song.

Diana brought up Marvin. The two of them had recorded duets together and had been there in Detroit at Hitsville in the early days, like a sister and brother. Diana said, "I loved Marvin very much and I miss him so, so much. I would love to record a song about the tragedy that he left us."

I approached writing and producing "Missing You" personally, of course, as a fan, and someone blessed enough to have had Marvin as a mentor. Knowing him had changed me. He was a master instructor who helped me overcome my insecurities and fears. And I felt the loss because of that deep connection, because of the songwriting wisdom he passed on to me, and the courage he gave me to just be free. That's what I was missing. More than anything, I had lost a beautiful friend who was gone too soon.

Diana's vocal on "Missing You" is so poignant and haunting— no one could have delivered the line, "Tell me why the road turns" better. I rarely perform the song because it's not my song, it's Diana's.

As the years have passed, I hear more and more in Marvin's records—things I missed when he was with us. He had a voice and a presence that to this day have survived his death. That's not the case with every artist who moves on. You hear a vibrancy, a hugeness of spirit and connection that always made him seem otherworldly. We were just lucky to have had him here for as long as we did.

‖‖‖‖

April 28, 1984
The SHARE Boomtown Gala
Pauley Pavilion, UCLA Campus, Westwood

Here I am, posing for photos, dressed up in a combination of Native American and cowboy gear, because the theme of the Boomtown Gala is the whole Western thing. I'm standing with Brenda, a knockout in her blue satin cowgirl ensemble.

The irony, I must confess, is that this is the last place I wanted to be. On a night that was supposed to be a momentary break in the crazy ongoing tour for promoting *Can't Slow Down*, I was corralled into coming.

Every year this major charity event includes a show produced and directed by the legendary George Schlatter (famous for comedy variety specials and hit series like *Laugh-In*). Every year the closing act is the Rat Pack—whose wives are members of SHARE, an organization that benefits programs for special needs children.

See, what they don't teach you in "How to Be Famous" class

is that at a certain point you begin to be flooded by requests for your time from folks you don't know. Only they don't come after you. They come after your mom, your dad, your wife, your kids, your friends. You are the commodity, but the way it works is, soon, so are your loved ones. It's hard enough to sell yourself, which comes with your job, but when members of a family are involved, you lose all privacy and control. And what happens is that your family can now deliver you—whether it's to a dinner party or a wedding or any number of charity luncheons and galas.

Brenda, a new member of SHARE, has earned major brownie points—like all the members who have delivered their husbands—because she has delivered Lionel to play his latest hit, "All Night Long." That's what happens when family become deliverers. No matter how much you want a night off, you can't say no to your wife.

At least I'm not the only one. Everybody is usually expected to show up with their wives—Kenny Rogers, Johnny Carson, Sammy Davis Jr., Frank Sinatra, Dean Martin, Bob Hope, and the rest of the who's who of the Golden Age of Hollywood.

I'm scheduled next to last, but George Schlatter is worried I'll upstage the Rat Pack. He goes over to Sammy, Frank, and Dean, and says, "You might not want to follow Lionel."

I can't hear what they say, but I'm sure it's some version of, *Do you know who the hell we are? We close the show every year. The kid's the new flavor on the block, but he can't touch us!*

The show begins. Everybody's having a great time, spending money on an important cause, making their wives happy, drinking, and joking about not having to wear tuxedos.

It's finally time for the next-to-last act, me and my band, and I hear my name announced. To my surprise, as I walk onstage, there is a major eruption. A standing O. And I haven't started playing yet. What the hell is going on? I look around at the faces of movie stars I've watched all my life, wondering if there is a mistake.

I'm a nervous wreck too, by the way. We hit the first notes of "All Night Long," and some guy down in front is losing his mind, yelling, "I want to see you after the show! I want to see you after the show!"

Okay, let me just finish the song.

This guy—whose name I'll soon learn is David Wolper—continues applauding and waving.

This is surreal but I play on, play on, play on. Everybody's singing and dancing. The place has exploded. They are not just standing on their feet but are up on their chairs and on their tables. I'm having an out-of-body experience. Brenda's beaming and all the SHARE ladies are screaming and it's absolute pandemonium.

It's the biggest Boomtown Gala ever. Another standing O follows. This is beyond gratifying. Only three people are mad at me: Sammy, Frank, and Dean. I wouldn't have wanted to follow me either.

Before I could grab Brenda to try to leave, the guy I didn't know headed me off at the pass. David Wolper introduced himself and quickly told me that he, too, had been dragged here by his wife. He rattled off some stats, how he was a film and TV producer, and mentioned he had produced the series *Roots. Okay, now we were family.*

Now I listened. He had something he needed me for in August.

"Okay?" Maybe I laughed.

Wolper was in charge of producing the closing ceremonies for the Games of the XXIII Olympiad in Los Angeles. Everything was gearing up to begin for the summer, but there was no talent hired to perform, and no idea for what the finale was going to be . . . until this very night.

Stone-cold serious, he explained, "You're the closing act of the Olympics. I'm going to use the song 'All Night Long' with or without you."

The reality hit. Yes, it's uncomfortable when loved ones are deliverers, but because I said yes this time, I landed in the perfect place. Sometimes the places where you don't want to go and the things you don't want to do are the blessings in your life.

TO THIS DAY, there are viewers who saw the closing ceremonies—the ninety-two thousand at the LA Coliseum and the 2.6 billion people watching *live* from around the world— and still recall the giant spacecraft hovering over the entire field. Music by John Williams blared as an eight-foot alien came down to guard center stage, while shooting stars filled the stadium. Then, like in the movie *E.T.*, the spaceship began to play chords of universal harmony before it lifted up and away, followed by fireworks and incredible fanfare—leaving me on a platform that rose up under the biggest spotlight ever to capture me. Two hundred breakdancers and hundreds more acrobats and dancers were part of the spectacle that was like nothing ever attempted on this scale.

How does the kid who was so scared of being onstage that he walked off with the curtain now perform for 2.6 billion people? It makes no sense. Somebody in the Bureau of Fate must have switched scripts.

Yet, there I was, in my white pants and blue spangled jacket over a white shirt, arms akimbo, taking it all in, and figuring I might as well get over my terror or miss out.

Let me rewind a few weeks to when we started rehearsals on a football field somewhere in Anaheim. Some significant things happened.

One of the things didn't seem significant at the time. On the first day of practice, we began with auditions for the dancers. As they were lining up to learn choreography, I had just jumped onto a lift—which was how I was getting up on the plexiglass platform we had for this rehearsal. And as I was going up, I looked down at one of the dancers—right at her. My reaction was just a feeling of *wow*, a feeling of, *What an incredibly beautiful young lady.* With long, dark hair, she struck me in that moment as shy, or mysterious, and my guess was that she was Greek or Italian; turned out her name was Diane and she was part Greek. Nothing happened. It was just a moment of forgetting myself.

Lionel, could you please join the class . . . er . . . the rehearsal?

That was that at the time.

The other significant thing that happened while we were rehearsing was that we practiced all day long but we never had a night practice. No one thought, *Oh, in this part of the hemisphere, the dew gathers in the late afternoon and peaks at seven or eight o'clock at night.*

Why would that matter? Well, we found out on the Big Night as soon as the actual closing ceremonies began.

What we didn't calculate was how the dew would affect the entire surface of the plexiglass platform stage. During the day when we rehearsed with the choreography, no problem, little guessing that once the dew fell, we'd all find ourselves on a surface as slick as an ice-skating rink. All around me on this slick surface were acrobats and breakdancers sliding around, even in sneakers. Being pros, they adapted, and toned down their big moves. My strategy for not dying was to dance from the waist up.

Even scarier were the terror threats announced just before my entrance. The plan had been for President Ronald Reagan to come to the middle of the field for a speech. We knew he had arrived earlier because four Black Hawk helicopters had silently come into view—securing the airspace so nothing could pass over or around the stadium, preventing the threat of an invasion being mounted from above. At the last minute, though, the security experts decided the field was too open for the president of the United States.

Somehow, the powers that be determined that I, Lionel Richie, would give the speech instead—a draft of which was delivered to me not long before I went to take my place.

Oh, you want to protect the president, but you don't give a shit about me?

Then I looked at the speech and got a hum in my ears that made me forget all the reasons to be afraid. How many times in your life do you get a chance to say words along the lines of, "I know I speak on behalf of all the people of America and around the world to say how proud we are of these amazing athletes."

Nobody gets to speak on behalf of the whole world. Nobody.

My speech and performance on that sheet of ice was an out-of-body experience. *Saturday Night Live* had been a walk in the park. There were no cell phones recording, no social media sharing. There was only the world that tuned in—2.6 billion people.

With hyperfocus, I made an imprint on my brain of everything I'd witnessed that night so that I'd never forget. Then I ran out the back, hopped into a car, left, and went home.

The next day, I needed to get away, just to chill and to quiet my mind. At this point, instead of trying to hide out in the recording studio, my car had become the sandbox where the escape artist could go, free to cruise the streets of Los Angeles to my heart's content. Sometimes I'd grab a stack of cassettes of music I'd been working on, or I'd listen to the radio, turning up the volume and flying up the Pacific Coast Highway, forgetting everything about my life. Sometimes I'd head downtown or cruise into Hollywood.

That's how I found myself driving down Sunset Boulevard, no music playing, when I hit a patch of slow traffic. The light turned red up ahead. About four cars from the light, I could see people crossing the street at the crosswalk. Just another day in Hollywood.

And then something unbelievable happens. Suddenly, I see folks in cars next to me rolling down their windows and other drivers waving in their rearview mirrors. People are turning as they cross the street, and others pause to stare from the sidewalk, or they lean out of doorways, like a neon sign has begun to flash over my life, with everyone trying to get my attention. They're chanting, "Lionel Richie, 'All Night Long.' Lionel Richie, 'All Night Long' . . ."

Holy frickin' crap.

What just happened? I went from "Your songs are more famous than you are" to an overnight transformation where horns are honking up and down Sunset Boulevard, and tourists in car rentals are screaming, and I can never cross the street again without being visible.

I was now no longer the invisible man. Ever again.

17

We Are the World

January 28, 1985
The Shrine Auditorium
The American Music Awards Broadcast, 4:40 p.m.

"Twenty minutes," I hear someone from Dick Clark Productions say, as I wait backstage for the start of the five o'clock live broadcast of the AMAs—which I am hosting for the second year in a row. Panic is setting in.

This has already been one crazy, long-ass day, starting with an early morning arrival here at the Shrine. Besides needing to familiarize myself with the final script—enough so that I can put everything they've written into my own words—my biggest concern has been making sure we rehearse the cues for every single transition. Nobody has to tell me that if I miss any cue, it will throw off lighting, sound, the orchestra, the music performances, not to mention the entrances and exits. We're talkin' about a trainwreck of epic proportions.

Let me tell you, as loose as the AMAs can feel, Dick Clark and his people run a tight ship.

By the way, this is not the only source of my freak-out. As if hosting this show and performing "Running with the Night" as the opening number aren't enough to worry about, there is also this other plot unfolding—a top-secret recording session for a charity single, never before attempted on this scale in the history of Pop music, that's supposed to happen immediately after the AMAs.

Over the last several hours, I've been getting phone calls at the Shrine from Quincy Jones, among others, reminding me that only at the last minute can any of the artists, over forty-five of the biggest stars in the Business, know *where* this session is happening. At the most strategic moment, I'm supposed to turn into James Bond and make sure to secretly tell this group of artists to go directly from the Shrine downtown to A&M Studios on La Brea in Hollywood. If anyone else finds out ahead of time, the avalanche of paparazzi will descend and none of the stars will show. And if they don't, then this record, "We Are the World," will most certainly never happen.

Oh my God. How in the hell did I get myself into this impossible position in the first place?

KINDLY BACKTRACK WITH ME.

A month and a few days earlier, I received a call from Ken Kragen—which was the first time I ever heard of this project. To be precise, Ken said, "I had an interesting call with Harry Belafonte. He's looking for you."

My response to the opening line for everything to come was, basically, "Oh, Harry's looking for me?"

Ken said, "He has an idea for a charity, something about famine relief. Very interesting. Harry wants to explain it to you."

That's all Ken needed to say for me to say, "Of course." There aren't enough superlatives to properly sing the praises of Harry Belafonte—as an artist, as an actor and entertainer, and as a human rights icon who broke down more barriers in the Music Business than I can count. Harry, a friend who I admired greatly, had, in fact, been the first Black artist to sell a million records.

Another couple of days went by before Harry and I connected, but when we did, he spoke about the devastating news coverage we'd been seeing of the famine in Ethiopia.

An estimated one million people were believed to have died from starvation—with no end in sight. Harry believed action had to be taken to raise awareness and money to bring aid to Africa. He also felt it was important that Black artists take the lead on such a project. The way he put it was, in effect, "We got white folks saving Black folks, we ain't got enough Black folks saving Black folks, and that's why I'm calling you. We need to step up."

Harry first thought about a concert, but then the idea of a record came up. The example was Bob Geldof, who had started Band Aid with mostly white artists in the UK. They had recorded a song called "Do They Know It's Christmas?" that had just been released.

During that initial conversation, we floated the possibility of me maybe writing a song with Stevie Wonder. Sounded amazing to me. Stevie had recently moved mountains with his single "Happy Birthday"—a song he'd written for the cause of a national holiday to honor the birthday of the Reverend Martin Luther King Jr. Incredibly, Stevie fired up so much activism that President Ronald Reagan went and signed a federal law celebrating Martin Luther King Jr. Day every year on the third Monday in January (which would begin in 1986). That is the wonder of Stevie Wonder.

Now, bear in mind, this was almost Christmas and not an easy time to track down Stevie, who could have been anywhere in the world moving other mountains. Even so, I immediately put in a call to Stevie and left word that I wanted to talk to him about something important. There was no date set about when we had to get a song written and recorded, although I knew there was a humanitarian tragedy unfolding in Ethiopia. And the sooner we talked, the better.

The next thing I knew—about 3 a.m. that next morning, which is when I talked to Quincy Jones daily—I was telling Quincy about my conversation with Harry. Quincy was totally into it. A few days later, he checked in, wanting to know, "Hey, Skeets, any luck reaching Stevie?"

When I told him we hadn't connected yet and I was concerned because time was starting to be of the essence, Quincy mentioned he could talk to Michael Jackson later as the two were recording at the time. I loved the idea.

Long story short, a core team rapidly assembled itself— Quincy to produce, with writing and singing from me and Michael. This had the feeling of being meant-to-be.

A dozen years had passed since the Commodores had last opened for the J-5, and as much as our lives and careers had changed, Michael and I remained close. Sometimes I played big brother to him or we switched roles and he became the wise counsel to me. What I had just come through—with the Olympics—he had been going through since he was nine years old.

Michael was very close with his family, but once he went solo, making these monster albums, movies, and videos, he was in charge of his own ship. His day-to-day life was what you could call eccentric and extremely chaotic.

Quincy used to tease him with the nickname "Smelly." Michael would laugh too, realizing that he was oblivious to the fact that he hadn't changed or washed his clothes for a couple of days. Or so. We all have our quirks. Michael didn't buy clothes like you or me. He couldn't just go to department stores or Beverly Hills boutiques. He was on tour performing in the elaborate costumes made for him by his stylists, or he was in his pajama bottoms and slippers in the studio, or he was in his going-out attire. Or he was at home in something loose and comfortable so he could practice his dance moves and play with his menagerie of pets.

Some of his thrown-together looks—white socks and black loafers, say—became global fashion statements. Those loafers were fantastic for moonwalking or going up on pointe.

Whenever Michael came to visit me, he was wearing whatever—jeans and a T-shirt. And the jeans were either falling off him or too short to even be jeans and, well, smelly.

"Where'd you get those jeans, Michael?"

"Lion-*nel*, I walked by a store in the Valley. The owner came out and gave me a free pair."

I'd suggest he go back and get a pair that fit.

On the road, if Michael sent his clothes to the hotel cleaners, only half of the items would come back. Everything else was kept for souvenirs. He just got into the habit of wearing the same pants until they were unwearable.

We teased him, but it was out of love so he didn't mind. He teased me and Q about our quirks right back, like my attention deficits and how fast I could break into a sweat if my nerves kicked in, or how Quincy would tell great Jazz stories from way back in the day (and you had to listen), or how Q could cuss—words that weren't even in Michael's vocabulary.

Whenever Michael visited me, I usually went to pick him up. That was because he didn't want a driver all the time, but if he drove himself, who knew how long it would take? First of all, he wouldn't drive on the freeway, because everybody drove too fast and he'd get recognized and it would be a whole traffic situation. He only drove certain back streets you've never heard of. Think about it: Michael Jackson driving a car, alone. Sounds like the setup to a great joke. Not gonna happen.

One day, soon after I left the Commodores, he came over—after I picked him up—and when we walked in my house, I noticed the jeans were dingy.

"Man, where'd you get those jeans?"

"You don't like them?"

"They could use a washing."

I took him upstairs to my dressing area and went and got him a pair of my Commodore jeans—we had once put out our own line—that I probably had worn one time. They were a little large but he could grow into them, and I gave him a brand-new pair of underwear—still in the package. You heard that right. And I repeated to Michael, "They are brand-new, you just have to take them out of the package." After that, I pointed him to my bedroom where he could change and told him to meet me downstairs, where he soon joined me. So much better! Later, I drove him home, on his back streets, and he was sweet and thankful.

As soon as I got home, I went upstairs to get something from my bedroom, and as soon as I walked in, I noticed that there, on the carpet, was the pair of Michael Jackson's discarded underwear and his old ratty jeans. Just lying there like roadkill.

What do I do but laugh? MJ was here.

In his daily comings and goings, that kid was winging it every minute, but creatively, musically, Michael had a feel for detail that was disarming.

Right after Christmas, 1984, he and I went to work on the as-of-yet untitled benefit record.

MY THINKING WAS—*Let's get the Michael Jackson flow going at his place, where he's comfortable.*

We began by sitting down in the dining room off the kitchen to talk about the concept of the song. But there were interruptions. There was a dog barking and a person screaming at the dog. It went on and on—the dog barking and barking, and the person screaming, "Shut up! Shut up!" at the dog.

"Michael, what is goin' on back there?"

"Oh, Lion-*nel*," he said, "the mynah bird is having an argument with the dog." I went to look and that was exactly what was happening.

We talked some more, and then Michael smiled and asked, "Do you want to say hello to Bubbles?" He was about to go get his chimpanzee.

"No, Michael, I don't want to say hello to Bubbles."

We got back to the song concept. Did we want Pop, R&B, what? We wanted an anthem. Like "The Star Spangled Banner." Almost Roman, we thought, with bass drums and drama.

We wanted this to be big, even bombastic. We started humming every national anthem we knew. By our second or third session we landed on a pattern from "Rule, Britannia!" that gave us a template for our rhythm that led to *da-duh-duh-duh*, the intro. We didn't have the title, melody, or lyrics yet, but this was a start.

A week or so went by. I got a call from Ken Kragen, who was supporting the project and providing guidance if we needed anything. He was breathless. "Kenny Rogers wants to do the record."

Oh my God, I love Kenny. That's great.

There was no song yet. We didn't stop to think that we had

just gone from the two of us singing to three of us. But we kept going.

Michael and I worked similarly by starting with a feeling, with melody. We both were hummers. We were taping ourselves. Humming.

We had cassette tapes all over the floor in the little music room where we were working. Humming, listening, taking pieces from this and from that.

At our next session we continued with melody for a chorus and a verse. It was Michael who always used the word *we* to describe his vision. He and I knew it should definitely start with a *we*. And then we came up with several titles, one of which was "We Are the World."

Two calls came in right then. First, Ken Kragen took us by great surprise when he called to say that Bruce Springsteen had agreed to be a part of this song. Wow! And so had Bob Dylan. Wow again! We didn't know that this was part of the plan at all. Suddenly the project was taking on a life of its own. Ken rattled off another five or six artists who were asking for details. "How soon will you have something to show?"

"Soon." I told Ken the title. He loved it.

The next call was from Quincy, who liked the title and then announced the shocker: "We're going to do it the night of the American Music Awards because all the artists are going to be in town."

Wait a minute. We didn't have the song finished at all. And that was a little less than two weeks away. And what did he mean "*all* the artists are going to be in town."

With Springsteen basically confirmed, the number of participants began to snowball. Ken Kragen, the master of not keeping a secret, had made this into a cast of thousands. What happened to the magic of Quincy, Michael, and me? What was supposed to be a nice collaboration was turning into a mega *what the hell are we getting ourselves into?*

Now we had to grind. Once we found our story—that we can't ignore the suffering of others because we are all part of the same human family—most of the lyrics wrote themselves.

Every few hours we'd get an update—Billy Joel was a yes, Diana Ross was too. Ray Charles would be there. Smokey Robinson. Tina Turner, Dionne Warwick. Harry Belafonte of course was going to join us. Paul Simon, Hall and Oates, Willie Nelson, Al Jarreau, James Ingram, Bette Midler, Kenny Loggins, and Steve Perry. Cyndi Lauper was on the list. Huey Lewis was in. Kim Carnes was as well. Sheila E. said yes, as did the Pointer Sisters. Waylon Jennings, Jeffrey Osborne, Lindsey Buckingham, most of the Jackson siblings, and a handful of others signed up. Dan Aykroyd, a friend of Ken Kragen's—hot on *SNL* and the *Blues Brothers* movie—was on the list.

At some point, apparently a discussion came up as to who was missing. One superstar was Madonna. I have felt badly for years that she was not included. There was a thought in the planning that you couldn't have her in the same room with some of her competition. Maybe it wasn't even on her radar. To be clear, Michael and I, God bless us both, had so much to worry about with writing and our backs against the wall, we had little idea who was supposed to be there or not.

Was this a record or a party? We would find out.

We eventually had forty-five artists, some of whom sang only on the chorus. Fifty artists were said to have been turned away.

With a week to go, on Monday, January 21, we had hours not days to finish the song because we had to go into the studio to record a demo so all these pros could hear it and learn it. We were about 80 percent done but stalled. I will never forget to the day I die what it felt like as I was sitting on the floor of Michael's little music room—or was it a bedroom without a bed and he just slept on the floor? There were shelves of record albums lining the walls and a carpet and small bench.

The first line needed a little something and then we tried, "There comes a time" and that fixed that. Suddenly over my shoulder I heard a *loud* hissing sound.

"Michael what is that?" I asked, but before he could answer, the shelves started shaking and albums were falling everywhere, and I turned my head and saw a boa constrictor or anaconda or python—some frickin' big-ass, ugly-ass snake—slithering toward me.

I jumped up and screamed.

Michael was euphoric. He beamed and said, "There he is, Lion-*nel*, we found him. He was hiding behind the albums. We knew he was here somewhere." Michael added, "He heard your voice. He wants to meet you."

Pause.

Did you hear what the man told me? He had lost the god-damn horror movie snake in his room. They don't have snakes like this in Alabama. Michael knew better than to ask me if I wanted to pet the boa.

Once I calmed down, an hour later, we basically finished the lyrics—with a couple of stray words here and there to work out later.

Our job the next night in the studio was to record the track with the musicians and Quincy—for the top-secret cassette to be rushed to the artists. In the middle of the session, Stevie arrived! Somehow he had heard about the project and he was in. He was on beautiful Stevie time, wanting to know, "Ready to write?"

Lawd, have mercy, was all I could think. Quincy said, "Great, he's here."

Too late for Stevie to help write, but right on time for singing on the demo with us.

Quincy brought in masterful arranger Tom Bahler—to

suggest which artists should sing what and be able to kill it on just one half a line.

I've been asked many times how the artists were selected to do solos on only half a line. The beauty of each vocalist selected is that they would be instantly identifiable on that half of a line. I believe there are singers and stylists. And this was to be a circle of stylists.

On the demo we traded off singing the different parts to give the feeling of how that could flow. The next day we entered the hellscape of finalizing the list for principal voices and for the chorus. This process was surely what inspired Q on the night of the actual session to put up a sign on the entrance of the recording studio that read, "Check Your Egos at the Door."

Ken Kragen and Harriet Sternberg—his in-house PR / personal assistant / powerhouse get-it-done person—duplicated the demo cassettes. Everything had to be packaged, marked, and addressed individually—only to be opened by the addressee to preserve secrecy.

The next night we met to create a floor plan where everyone would stand, flowing around the room in a circle. We had to guess who would harmonize well with others and who wouldn't.

Ken Kragen and his team offered to set up a couple of viewing/listening rooms at A&M Studios for friends and family. That meant all forty-six or so participants could invite their people, which turned into some crazy five hundred more folks. Only at the last minute would they get coded messages about where the secret session was being held.

Every single added variable made it more likely this was to be a historic failure. We were moving at warp speed and nobody had done anything on this scale before. But when I read the note that Quincy sent with the cassettes, it put everything in perspective. He said that, in the future, when anyone who chose to give their time on this night was asked by their children what they did to stop world hunger, they could point to this as their contribution.

IT'S NOW LESS than ten minutes to the live broadcast of the AMAs at the Shrine, and I'm suffering from an acute case of sensory overload. Too much going on. I haven't rehearsed all the cues. They keep changing the copy. And I gotta sing the opening. This is my second year hosting so it should be easier, but the pressure is overwhelming. My choice is to find another part of myself that I don't know exists. Or I can bail.

My leg is shaking, my arm is cramping, and I'm already in a full sweat.

Larry Klein, the high-energy head of production, hurries over to check my mic, reassuring me, "Lionel, you are having a case of the nerves. You are gonna have the best night."

I just don't think so. And so I make a beeline for Dick Clark because earlier he had said if I had a problem, to go to him. It's only fair that I warn him now. "I just don't think I can do it," I say.

We have five minutes before the broadcast is to begin. Dick doesn't waste a second. "Lionel, look at that sign over there, what does it say?"

"American Music Awards."

"No, above that."

"Dick Clark Productions."

"*I'm* Dick Clark," he emphasizes. "You know, you schoolboys are all the same. You think you need a diploma to be able to do something. And if you really think you need a diploma, I will give you one after the show. What you need to understand is that you are hosting this show not because I think maybe you can do it."

Dick is walking and talking—not listening at all as I continue, "You gotta have someone to cover for me"—and just nodding his head with an "unh-huh" or two, seeming to be in no hurry, as he calmly positions me (without me realizing it) for the first number.

"Lionel, you are hosting because you are the only one who can do it, the only one with your talent, your charm, your humor, and your ability to deliver to my highest expectations. I wouldn't tell you that if I didn't know it to be true. And keep in the back of your mind . . . it's my show. Now, if you still want to discuss any of this, we can talk after the show . . ." Without a breath, he continues, "In five . . . four . . . three . . . two . . . one!"

And the broadcast began.

The night would be forever remembered for the performance of "Purple Rain" by Prince—possibly the most unforgettable performance at any awards show. Prince was still a holdout for taking part in "We Are the World," although we hadn't given up on him. Many of the artists who would be joining us later also ended up winning awards—Cyndi Lauper, Hall and Oates, Bruce Springsteen, Huey Lewis, Tina Turner, the Pointer Sisters, Kenny Rogers, and Willie Nelson. My wins were *outrageous*—considering that I won as Favorite Pop/Rock Male Artist (over Prince and Springsteen), Favorite Soul/R&B Male Artist (over Michael Jackson and Prince), Favorite Pop/Rock Male Video Artist, Favorite Soul/R&B Video Artist, Favorite Pop/Rock Video for "Hello," and Favorite Soul/R&B Video for "Hello."

My refusal to be put in a box had paid off.

Outrageous.

The awards and the excitement of the show went so amazingly that I was sure it was all a setup for the chaos that was about to happen once we all started to arrive at A&M Studios.

And I guess I was right and wrong.

WHAT I SAW that night, from my unique vantage point as that guy who sang the first line to get it out of the way, and then just ran around to make sure everybody was alright, was a room full of massive talent and huge heart.

Every recording studio has an energy and a resonance of its own, but this one, owned at this time by the label started by Herb Alpert and Jerry Moss, the *A* and the *M* of A&M, had some of the most beautiful acoustics around. Walking into it empty or without many people in it can feel like walking into church. When it's full of some of the greatest voices in the world, it was like walking onto holy ground.

I was so revved up, I thought there were sparks flying out of me.

Of course, there was the tension of *What do you want me to do?* and *Why do I have to sing that part?* And it was kind of like all these superstars who didn't really know each other that well were getting sent to camp for a night—where the counselor was Quincy Jones.

When we practiced the chorus in unison, everyone was a soloist. Q began to rein it in. A few artists just had to try to showcase their voices, and some of the artist/producers in the room couldn't help suggesting tweaks. Really, it was like a bunch of big unruly kids with ADHD who all needed to focus.

Somehow, I became Mr. Hyperfocus, quietly running around putting out fires—like hiding the bottles of white wine stashed around the studio by Al Jarreau. I have to hand it to Al, though. After Quincy got us ready to record the chorus, first by thanking the organizers and especially Harry Belafonte who had spearheaded the record from the start, Al broke the ice. As soon as the applause wound down, Al Jarreau took that moment to look over at Harry Belafonte and began to sing, "Day-o, day-ay-ay-o . . ."

Everyone understood. This was Belafonte's signature song.

It was a call to action, like we were all being summoned to our higher purpose.

Voices started joining in. "Daylight come and me wan' go home . . ." Al took us to church.

We went back to work on the chorus to "We Are the World." After about three tries, there was a subtle shift, and Q led us off again, and it was electric. I looked at Michael to see if he was hearing it.

So far so good.

Michael's vocals on "We Are the World" would live forever as perfection. At some point, either the day before or earlier, he had come to the studio to hear how he sounded on the track we had just finished. He was not leaving his part to chance.

We banked the chorus. It sounded amazing.

We had to then make sure everyone had their right scripts and rehearsed their individual parts. Done. We were getting ready to begin. At the start of the night, Quincy had *explicitly* told me, Michael, and our recording engineer, the brilliant Humberto Gatica, that for this session there was one question that the four of us could not ask, whatsoever, at any time, which was, "I'm not sure about this, what do you guys think?" We understood. In a room full of the most gifted artists in the world, asking that question would lead to a Pandora's box of different insights and approaches.

Here we go.

Just as we were ready to begin, Stevie made a very important comment we loved. He thought we should have some kind of African dialect in the verse and suggested a line. We all gave it a shot. Except for Waylon Jennings. He said, "This ole Country boy is outta here." And sure enough Waylon walked right out of the session.

We worked through the new line and to most of us it sounded great, but then, after all that, we decided not to use it.

Quincy, the maestro, got us back on track.

Earlier there had been an unforgettable exchange when the consensus was we needed a break. Ray Charles, talking to Stevie, said, "Honey, we gotta stop. I gotta go to the bathroom."

Stevie said, "Oh yeah, you go out the door and turn to the right and it's down the hallway."

Ray nodded along, saying to Stevie, "Let me get this straight, honey, let me get this straight. You go out the door, down the hall . . ."

Stevie stood up and said, "C'mon, Ray, I'll show you where it is."

And Stevie Wonder took Ray Charles by the arm, and they walked out the door.

The whole room picked up on the end of their conversation and everybody busted out laughing. Billy Joel may have been the first person to say, "Did anybody see that? The blind really is leading the blind."

Later in the night when Bob Dylan started to rehearse his part and was awkwardly unsure how to do it, Stevie went to the piano and started to play and sing with his best Bob Dylan impression—a pitch-perfect demonstration for Dylan that all he had to do was to be Bob Dylan.

Nothing in my experience had ever brought together this many monumental artists who all showed up *alone* in a room—without name tags, without managers or assistants, without top-billing, without knowledge of expectations. It was unbelievably intimidating, like the first day of preschool without your mom or dad. Bob Dylan was already a legend and someone who rarely put in public appearances at all. So, kudos to him and to Stevie for giving him permission to be Bob Dylan. When you hear, "There's a choice we're making / We're saving our own lives"—you can't mistake the voice.

There was another moment everyone talked about with

Dylan and Diana Ross, who bonded earlier in the night when she decided to just plop down on his lap in greeting.

Bruce Springsteen had flown in after the culmination of the latest leg of his tour, directly from his most recent show. He had a flight delay, and he was exhausted and concerned that his voice was hoarse. It did not matter. Bruce never fails to show up when it matters, and that's part of why I love him. The Boss blew the roof off.

We had never written Prince off entirely and had hoped he'd change his mind. We had even assigned him a line, but when it looked like he definitely wouldn't show, Kenny Loggins suggested that Huey Lewis could do it.

Huey's comment when he heard he was doing Prince's line was a classic, "Who me?" He was so nervous his legs were shaking, but after a couple of rehearsals, he killed it.

One of the last artists to leave, believe it or not, was Diana Ross. She was in one of the last pieces of video footage shot that night, just saying on camera she didn't want the experience to have to end.

When I left that morning, there was a refrain in my head of "daylight come and I want to go home" as in "Day-O." Slowly, everyone else did go home or off to breakfast. By 8:30 or 9:00 a.m. the studio was more or less empty. Looking around and trying to imprint everything we'd been through, I had a moment of catharsis. You know what? Dick Clark had shaken some sense into me. Maybe, I didn't have to suffer from impostor syndrome after all.

"WE ARE THE WORLD" changed my life. It made me ask, *Well, if I'm in my championship season, what good can I do with it?*

On March 7, 1985, six weeks after we recorded "We Are the

World," it hit the airwaves. I remember hearing the song on my car radio the first time while taking a drive into Hollywood.

Everywhere I went, I heard it playing. Driving down Sunset, I heard people singing along with it out their open car windows, and it sounded so beautiful. I thought about all the different paths I could have chosen and how grateful I was this one had chosen me.

A month or so after we released "We Are the World," I received a letter. The return address was Tuskegee, Alabama, and to the best of my recollection, the sender's name was Father Vernon Jones. How many years earlier had I gone to him to say that I didn't think the Episcopalian priesthood was for me? A brief note was enclosed. As I recall, the message was this:

> Lionel, there are two types of ministers. Those that preach on the corner of every street and in every community across the nation and around the world, and those that preach to the masses. After "We Are the World," I believe your ministry is doing quite well.

It had taken me all this time to learn how to put my sermons into songs—and hopefully uplift other people's lives.

The record sold eight hundred thousand copies in three days. We went on to raise eighty million dollars and built the infrastructure for more fundraising that was spearheaded by Ken Kragen and, coincidentally, Dr. Lloyd Greig, along with Jay Cooper—the attorney who had been the sole lawyer for "We Are the World" and who dealt with all the legal entities around the world, which he did for free. Distributed by Columbia Records, our charity single eventually sold well over twenty million copies and became the fastest-selling US Pop release in history.

At this writing, forty years later, I can tell you in all my travels, I have found that the spirit of "We Are the World" lives on. We see so much division, hate, greed, and fear of the "other" and yet what do most of the people on the planet want? Love over fear, hate, and war. The opportunity to flourish. The means to get help and to give it.

Yes, at my most cynical times, I question whether we could ever do again what we did that night. The jury is still out. But we can't stop trying.

Sometimes I grieve that the world has forgotten how interconnected we all are. And then I think back to the words Quincy Jones reminded me and Michael to include when we were finishing up the lyrics. He wanted us to use the word *choice*. "There's a choice we're making, we're saving our own lives . . . So, let's start giving."

The good we do really is a choice. Recognizing that we are family, that we are the world, is a choice.

When I watch the footage captured of the greatest night in Pop—and I cry like my momma died every time I do—I'm struck by how young and hopeful we all were. Was the world younger then and less hard?

My next reaction is sadness for the ones so present on that night but who are gone.

Everybody who was there left a part of themselves in that studio and on that record. Too many of them aren't here anymore—Harry Belafonte, Ray Charles, Kenny Rogers, Tina Turner, Anita Pointer and June Pointer, Al Jarreau, James Ingram, and Waylon Jennings. Prince, who wasn't there, but almost was, is no longer here. Ken Kragen is no longer here. Quincy Jones is no longer here. And Michael Jackson is no longer here.

When you get a chance though, listen to the song, and speak their names out loud, because as the saying goes, no one is truly dead until the last person says their name.

18

Out of Body

EVEN IN EARLY 1985—WHEN I was riding high—I felt a collision coming.

Every day there was a soaring soundtrack of more hits, more awards, more fame, more stature. Nobody told me about the PTSD that comes from the highs too. A sixth sense told me that when too many things go right, something's gotta go wrong. The question was how bad. But I distracted myself thinking, *How can I top this?*

Only one month after the epic night of recording "We Are the World," I was back at the Grammys, rolling in with four nominations—trying to quiet the fears that I'd go home empty-handed. This was a memorable night for Prince and Tina Turner, who each won three awards—and I was thrilled for them both. But I could see how the picks were trending.

It went without saying that the Grammys hadn't always shown me love—with one exception. Could this year be different? My best shot, I thought, was for Best Pop Vocal Performance, Male—for "Hello." I braced myself when the category came up and heard that the Grammy was going to . . . Phil Collins for "Against All Odds (Take a Look at Me Now)."

This didn't bode well for the second category—which was Producer of the Year (Non-Classical) for *Can't Slow Down*, up against Prince and the Revolution, among others.

And the award goes to . . . "It's a tie!" What do you know? James Anthony Carmichael and I tied with David Foster for Chicago's *17* album. The winning felt good, need I say? Then came the category of Song of the Year, the award for song-writing. I held my breath and instead of hearing "Hello" I had to feel great with the winner—"What's Love Got to Do with It." Tina was on a roll. Everything came to a crescendo with the fourth category, Album of the Year. The competition was insane—Prince, Tina Turner, Cyndi Lauper, and Bruce Springsteen. I felt hopeful at seeing the presenters—Joni Mitchell (my next-door neighbor and the GOAT personified) and Dionne Warwick (with her almighty musical gifts and one of my favorite people). The thrill of hearing I'd won felt like a jolt of electricity. When I went up to accept, I took the Grammy from Joni Mitchell's hands and kissed an icon for all to see. And I liked it.

All I could do was look out at the room and tell everyone that I needed to take some breaths so the beating of my heart could slow down.

That night was one of the most gratifying awards expe-riences I've ever had. And I'd love to say I left there—after two nos and two yeses—convinced I had to ease up. But that wasn't the story. Instead, I ignored the warning light trying to tell me, *If you don't lighten the pace, this shit will kill you.*

My concession was to tour less, especially with Nikki having entered our lives at this point.

Now, I could hunker down in the studio and finish the

next album—already six months behind. The scary part, if the rumors were true, was that Motown could be gone by the time I delivered. For Berry Gordy, holding on to the company was becoming financially unsustainable. Other than newer artists like Rick James and Teena Marie, there was just a handful of us—Smokey Robinson, Stevie Wonder, and me—whose albums could earn the millions needed to pay the bills.

But if Motown would no longer be Black-owned, many felt the legacy of David conquering Goliath would be at risk. Berry Gordy was like a matador ready to put down his cape and leave the arena. My prayer was, *Just give him one more bull.*

All I could do was push myself to deliver the goods, the hit albums that had fueled Motown from the start and could continue to do so.

RING!

I am not answering no phone! is what I think, really loudly to myself, and put the pillow over my head.

It's three in the morning, and I've got a jam-packed day ahead that could wipe out an Olympic athlete. Thirty minutes earlier, I arrived home from the studio, and I've just crashed. There is no debate. *I ain't talk'n to nobody.*

I am done. Cooked. Barbeque. Sleep is what I need.

I pick up and don't say anything. It's the guard at the gate, who tells me, "Sir, I've got Quincy Jones on the line, he says it's an emergency."

"Tell Quincy I just got in and I need a couple of hours of sleep. I'll call him when I wake up." And I hang up.

Ring, ring, ring! (Not even fifteen seconds later.)

The guard apologizes. "Mr. Jones says if you don't take

his call, he's driving here and coming over the wall." I don't question that possibility. Quincy lives close to walking distance from my house and it's not unusual for him to call at this hour because I typically go to bed at 5 or 6 a.m.

Sigh. "Okay I'll take the call."

Quincy Jones growls with a "Skeets, listen, I got a big problem on this one song for *The Color Purple*." Still half asleep, at least I remember that he's talking about the score he's composing. This is the major movie production being directed by Steven Spielberg, an adaptation of the Pulitzer Prize–winning novel by Alice Walker.

"Oh," I say, not sure where this is going. "What's the problem?"

"I just ran the lyrics for 'Miss Celie's Blues' by Spielberg and Alice Walker, and they don't like the lyrics we've got." He goes on to say that he and Rod Temperton have been working all night and are stuck. He gets right to the point, telling me, "Skeets, we need you to come over to my house and write the lyrics to 'Miss Celie's Blues.' Quick."

"Well, Q," I say, "send the cassette and I'll get you something tomorrow or the next day."

That's not soon enough, he explains, because they're shooting the scene this very day at 2 p.m.

Just as I'm about to say it's impossible, Brenda wakes up and says, "Who the hell are you talking to?" I cover the mouthpiece on the phone and tell her it's Q and "He wants me to help with lyrics for a song on *The Color Purple* . . . now."

And, because she had heard me trying to say no, Brenda said the smartest thing. She asked, "Do you know how many people are waiting for that call in this town?"

How do you argue with that? "You're right," I said to Brenda, and told Quincy, "I'll be right over."

Before I got off the phone and dragged myself out of bed, he asked me a simple question. "You read the book, didn't you? *The Color Purple?*"

"Yeah, yeah." Let me clear about that answer: *I lied*.

"Okay, it's the scene where Shug—"

"Got it." I had no idea what the fricking book was about.

By the grace of the good Lord, Brenda had read the goddamn book, and while I was getting in the shower, she gave me the storyline and read the pertinent scenes to me.

I arrived at 5 a.m., and as soon as I walked in Quincy's door, I saw two of the most tired, worn out talented human beings I've ever seen in my life sitting there waiting for a recruit with fresh ideas. We skipped the small talk and sat down to listen to the tape of the music track Q and Rod Temperton had written, a sultry Blues. Quincy then asked, "What's the lyrics, Skeets?"

After working together on the first verse that was in need of serious repair, we finished the rest of it two hours later, including the sassiest ending:

> *So let me tell you somethin' sister*
> *Remember your name*
> *No twister*
> *Gonna steal your stuff away*
> *My sister*
> *Sho' ain't got a whole lot of time*
> *So shake your shimmy*
> *Sister*
> *'Cause honey this 'shug*
> *Is feelin' fine*

They were now ready to film at 2 p.m. And I was so blessed Quincy believed in me enough to give me the chance to rise to the occasion. Even if it meant missing out on some desperately needed sleep.

IN MANY WAYS, 1985 was the gift that kept on giving.

Are you ready? To my own shock, Pepsi signed me to the most lucrative soft drink sponsorship deal up to that time.

Outrageous!

The deal included an immediate shoot for a three-minute commercial. And the concept for the shoot in LA was to re-create the backyard of my grandmother's house in Alabama—with a cameo starring Grandma!

Am I hallucinating?

The first person I called about the deal was my father. Just to get in a dig that I was right to run off with the band, after all, and check him with my old standby—"You don't want to be a tool of the Man, Dad, kissing a lot of ass." He would always come back and check me with, "Son, sometimes you have to kiss ass for the privilege to kick ass."

After years, though, I figured we'd finalized that debate.

To let him see me in action as the face of the New Pepsi Generation, I invited Dad to my concert in Chicago. With my new deal, whenever I performed, a VIP room was set up for the Pepsi-Cola execs and all the top bottlers in the area.

The Chicago show was huge. Afterward, I took Dad with me to the suite for the meet and greet. I cracked jokes, took the photos with the executives, shook hands, kissed the ladies, hugged the babies, and made sure everyone was satisfied.

Dad took all this in, and I knew he had to be busting with pride. During a pause, he walked over to me and said these words: "You sure are kissing a lot of ass."

Stung, I said, "What the hell are you talking about?"

He gave me a slight smile and went on, "Congratulations, you've figured it out. It's your paycheck. Now you've answered your question why I was kissing so much ass." Could he have just gotten me back?

He delivered the last word. And that was the genius of my father, who could wait decades to win his point.

You can call this a draw. I had proven him wrong by being a success in Show Business, yet he proved me wrong with a lesson about survival I had not yet learned.

A FERRARI? I don't know what I was thinking.

In the aftermath of the Olympics, late 1984 or early 1985, a high-end car broker sends over a black Ferrari for me to test-drive.

In my logic, I'm supposed to be more "incog-negro" and a Ferrari clearly doesn't help.

Me in a Ferrari is like a billboard on wheels. But I decide to take it for a spin and drive myself to Motown studios in West Hollywood near Formosa, below Santa Monica Boulevard, which has been renamed Hitsville, USA.

I'm kind of excited because I've been asked to write another movie theme song. When I first heard from director Taylor Hackford, I was excited. "What's the name of the movie?" I asked. He told me it was *White Nights*. There was no such thing in my book as a hit song called "White Nights" by a Black guy.

Happily, Taylor Hackford decided it wasn't the title song so I could call it what I wanted. The good news was that I had something cooking that I thought might work. The great news, not yet known to me, was that this was to be another Oscar shot. All thanks to Taylor Hackford.

In a fine mood, I'm driving down the street about to turn onto Formosa and I see a yellow Volkswagen Bug next to me at the light.

Holy shit, it's that girl from the Olympics.

I see her, she sees me. We both roll down our windows.

"Oh my God, how are you? Uh . . ."

"Diane." she laughs. "Good." And that's almost it, but then, "Where are you going?"

"Right over here, to the studio." I point.

Then I think she might like being a guest. Before the light turns green, I invite her to come listen.

This is not anything scandalous. This is just an aha moment in a serendipitous life. Diane comes in, she stays for about two hours. And then she's got to go.

"Thank you very much, Lionel."

"Nice to see you, Diane. Bye-bye."

That's it. *The world is a small place*, is what I think. And I go back to work.

Forty-five minutes later, Diane walks back into the studio, dazed.

"Wow, hey, did you forget something?"

No, she explained, after turning back onto Santa Monica, out of nowhere a car hit and totaled her car. She was alright but the VW Bug was undrivable. I felt so bad, I offered to drive her home. It was far. Somewhere out in the middle of the Valley.

As we drove, she told me that she lived with her folks. We talked about her interests, not just in dance but also in design. She was not Show Biz in the least. Not even trying to be.

The further we went, the more I realized that we were outside of LA, in another town.

"Keep going? Is it much further?"

"Yeah, keep going. It's only a little further."

By the time we pulled into her driveway, I knew that the black Ferrari wasn't for me, because when I stopped at her house, suddenly three police cars arrived.

"You okay, Diane?" one of the cops called out. Apparently, everybody knew everybody.

"Fine!"

Another cop came over to look inside the Ferrari and said, "Oh, it's Lionel Richie."

All three officers got on their speakers in their squad cars. "I've got Lionel Richie at Diane's house."

So much for trying to fly under the radar.

This was nothing. Or so I told myself.

For a while, I avoided doing anything to jeopardize my marriage, my homelife, my world. And I kept on writing.

AT SOME POINT I must have left my body because when I woke up it was early 1986 and it was award season again. The new album wasn't ready yet but the song I wrote for the movie *White Nights*, which I called "Say You, Say Me," had been released as a single in October 1985. James Carmichael and I loved the musical changes in the song, but the DJs had trouble with it, and many execs at Motown were on the fence. The big concern was that it sped up in the middle. *Why do that?* My answer was simply, "Well, the Beatles did it, why can't I?"

They used the magic words—*This is going to ruin your career.* That told me it was a hit, but I never expected it to skyrocket to #1 Pop, R&B, and Adult Contemporary.

And then along came nominations for the Golden Globe for Best Original Song—Motion Picture and the Oscar for Best Original Song.

The film was about a Russian ballet dancer, white, Mikhail Baryshnikov, and an American tap dancer, Black, Gregory Hines, and how they develop an unlikely friendship to escape the oppressive regime of the Soviet Union. Everyone thought at first it was a romantic song, though I would say, "You can interpret it that way . . . but if you listen, there is another story whispering at you under the surface." It was about trust, about two people from two walks of life having one thing in common—the desire for freedom. And the only way to achieve it was working together. The song was also a metaphor for what we in the world should do together:

> *Say you, say me*
> *Say it for always*
> *That's the way it should be . . .*
> *I had a dream, I had an awesome dream*
> *People in the park playing games in the dark*
> *And what they played was a masquerade*
> *And from behind the walls of doubt*
> *A voice was crying out*

The win at the Golden Globes for Best Original Song was just—*Oh, my God, this isn't real!* And not to jinx anything but that gave me hope whose name I dared not speak because the Oscars were up next.

But guess what else was nominated in the same category of Best Original Song—"Miss Celie's Blues." Crazy. I had to compete with myself (with Quincy Jones and Rod Temperton).

Decades later I'd watch contestants on *American Idol* having to wait to hear if they had won or lost, and I remembered sitting at the Oscars and getting to hear Gene Kelly, the legendary Hollywood actor and dancer, announce my name for "Say You, Say Me"—right before I turned to my mother, there with me, to tell her, "Hey, Mom, Lionel Richie won!"

And my dear mother said, "You better go up there before they change their mind."

I said, "You're right." When I got up there, I looked out at

Quincy and Spielberg. The one cloud over that Oscar ceremony was that *The Color Purple*, after eleven nominations, was robbed and went home without any awards. Whatever I said next, it remains a blur.

I LEARNED A new coping mechanism. It's called compartmentalization.

Here's what was happening all at once: Brenda and I were growing apart, outgrowing the *us* that had been our glue, but I didn't want to admit it. We had been together for fifteen years. We had gone to every pinnacle together—all the way to the Oscars. We never stopped loving each other, but along the way I discovered another me and I'm sure she discovered another her.

Then there was Nikki, my heart, whose well-being Brenda and I cared about totally. The song "Ballerina Girl" was a song I wrote for Nikki after watching her joy in a dance class. She was my joy, as she was Brenda's.

We went on vacation and Nikki and I went to Silly-ville nonstop. She'd pretend to almost tickle me—*Uh!*—and I'd scoot away. Then I'd come back—*Uh!*—and she'd dart off. Brenda laughed with us.

Compartmentalization allowed me to set aside the nagging concern that another shoe could drop at any time so I could stay focused on the present—and on the Business, the fuel keeping everything aloft.

After many delays in the summer of 1986 I delivered another hit-studded album, *Dancing on the Ceiling*, a #1 Pop album with six—count them: *six*—singles that kept me on the charts from November 1985 to March 1987. The album went on to sell four million copies.

In this whirlwind, I met the legendary Stanley Donen—who, I learned, had directed the 1951 classic *Royal Wedding* starring Fred Astaire in which he danced on the ceiling—and I convinced Donen to do my video!

After hearing me describe how, everywhere in the world, fans were finding ways to hang from the ceiling, he took that vision and transformed it into a film. In a snap, I became a dancer, doing all those eighties steps with a dance troupe on a set that was designed to turn upside down.

Donen invented shit never heard of and shot it in three days—the highest cost for a short-form music video to date. There were two main differences technically from the 1951 version—which Donen described as a turning box powered by an idling airplane engine. Because of the idling, the speed was inconsistent when the box turned, making the wall become the floor and then the ceiling the floor and so on. Also, in *Royal Wedding*, the camera was strapped to the camera operator who was turning at the same speed as the box and turned upside down while Fred Astaire stayed upright. Now, with our version, we could control the speed, and because we had a remote-control camera, it could defy gravity, even giving us a shot with right-side up dancers in the same frame as the rest of us who were dancing on the ceiling upside down.

The challenge for me was to remember to step left as I went from the floor to the wall to the ceiling, and not to let that trip me up. When I forgot to step left, I fell into the lamp and the sofa. Fred Astaire had three weeks to finesse his dance whereas I had three days. And by the time I was done, I was covered in bruises like I'd been in a prizefight.

Stanley Donen was a rock star. We went on to win the AMA for Best Pop/Rock Video.

The *Outrageous / Dancing on the Ceiling* world tours were off the chain. Wherever I went, there I was, in the USA and around the world—Australia, New Zealand, Japan, the UK, Germany, and back again to Canada and Madison Square Garden in New York City, in my second hometown.

And then there was Diane—who was in the "Dancing on the Ceiling" video. Otherwise, when I saw her, not often, we didn't have to talk about the Business. We enjoyed each other's company and conversation, which was mainly about her goals and future plans. That was refreshing to hear from someone who had never seen the world.

Compartmentalizing helped me forget that I was moving dangerously fast and that the altitude was too high. Still, I was trying to slow down.

I was trying.

THE LAW OF physics tells us that what goes up must come down.

Most of us understand the principle of gravity. I should have been better prepared. But I was floored at hearing the news given to me by Ken Kragen during a meeting he called.

"We Are the World" had changed Ken's life. His dream now was to teach at UCLA while continuing his activism.

The thought that he was leaving the management business—leaving me—was unbearable. Maybe, I suggested, the other focus could be a second calling, not full-time.

Ken Kragen—tall, lanky, the guy who once he got on an idea was a pit bull and was never going to get off it until he won—listened thoughtfully but his mind was made up.

"Ken, you know the *Dancing on the Ceiling* tour is taking over the planet! Why would we stop now?"

He reassured me his departure wouldn't be immediate. He was just giving me a heads-up.

When I vented about Ken's decision to leave management

to Joe Layton—the director who had helped me develop every show I had done since going solo—I was sure Joe would say, "Why would Ken do that?"

Instead, Joe said, "How dare you? How dare you assume everyone is meant to ride your rocket forever?"

Harsh.

Joe saw people who came into our lives as our important guides, as boosters to help us fly on our own. "One person gets you to this one part of your career and falls away, and another person to the next."

Made sense.

"Ken's not supposed to stay on your ride. He's doing his dream. Yours is for you."

He was right. I wasn't being abandoned. I was being empowered.

"Rather than 'Go to hell,'" said Joe, "what you should say to Ken Kragen is 'Thank you. Thank you so much for all that you've done for me and my career.'" And he was right.

I took the lesson to heart. When you part ways with a mentor who has poured their best into your dream, don't miss the chance to tell them how they forever changed your life and how profoundly grateful you are.

Cut to: 2013, at Ken Kragen's inaugural Music Industry 106 class, "Stardom Strategies for Musicians," where Quincy Jones and I showed up as guests. Ken, a stellar teacher, offered classes for years at the Herb Alpert School of Music at UCLA. What an awesome calling!

However, in the interim, I tried to shake off the anxiety and make inquiries about who would be best to take Ken's place. In that mental state, I received crushing news from Dad.

"No need for alarm," my father said on the phone, which immediately alarmed me. His health was deteriorating. A few years earlier, he had some general complaints, and I'd flown him to LA to have a full Beverly Hills checkup.

Only, I had to lure him out without him realizing that was my goal. Instead, I decided to announce that I was flying him and Mom out to attend a splashy event with me—a birthday party for none other than Diana Ross. When I got them settled after their trip, I realized that Dad's suitcase was empty—other than socks and underwear.

"Where are your clothes?"

"Your mother didn't pack them." To which my mother said she had put everything out on the bed. Classic L. B. Richie. He wanted new clothes. Did he say so? No, of course, not. He said he couldn't go to the party. Well, naturally, we went to the stores in Beverly Hills, and everywhere we walked in, my father got so excited by the elegant, tailored men's designer clothing. Then he'd see the price and say, "Oh, I could never have you pay that much," but he would lean into the salesperson and say, "Do you have this in a 44 Long?"

I'm telling you my dad was a ham sandwich. The best treat of all was getting to meet Richard Pryor at Diana's birthday party. Dad proceeded to describe the last Richard Pryor movie he had seen in vivid detail . . . to Richard Pryor.

In fine spirits, Dad agreed to go to the doctor for a checkup.

After running a battery of tests, the doctor called Dad and me into his office, and reviewed the findings. "Mr. Richie," he said, "you're suffering from too much salt, too much sugar, too much drinking, and too much smoking."

My father's comment back was, "Well, the only thing you left out was I can't touch his mother." There was a smile from the doc. Then Dad asked how much longer he would live if he cut out all those things. The doctor couldn't offer any guarantees. Dad said, "And there you go."

He managed to cut out smoking, but he was an army man, not about to change the drill much.

I had understood it to be more of a chronic condition, not life-threatening. But when he called this time, I was much more concerned.

I took a break from the tour, shifting some dates, and flew to Alabama directly. When I arrived in Tuskegee, where my parents had returned to live full-time, everything seemed normal.

Dad and I hung out downstairs, and he was just himself, cantankerous and silly, and I didn't want to believe we could lose him. Before I left, he asked to talk to me upstairs.

My mother, knowing my dad could be an antagonist, said, "Lyonel Sr., leave him alone, let him go, he wants to get back to the tour."

"No, Alberta, I want to ask him something."

We climbed the stairs. He sat. I sat. He said, "I'll get right to the point, son. I want to ask you one question. When does a Black man become a nigger?"

I was dumbfounded. "What are you talking about?"

"Just answer the question."

"I don't know, Dad. *When?*"

The answer he gave was, "When he leaves the womb."

That landed hard. Dad had more to say. I waited.

"I don't care how big you think you are," he went on. "You are famous because you're famous. But there are opposing forces out there that don't see you the way you see you."

I couldn't guess how much my father knew or what he knew.

"Now, I'm worried about you. You want everything, but you haven't been tested."

Well, I wouldn't say that . . . but I didn't argue.

"You have no idea what it means to lose because all you've done is win." He was genuinely worried. "I just want to make sure you understand that you should be careful because you haven't been tested yet."

What did he see that I didn't?

IN JUNE OF 1988 came the dropping of the other shoe.

What very few people knew was that Brenda and I were separated. I got a place at the beach, and I was hiding out there, trying to be alone, trying to decompress somehow, because it was killing everyone.

It's early in the morning when I drive into town, and I happen to stop to see Diane, who has an apartment in a house there. Shortly after I arrive, there is a knock at the door.

This is not a security-buzz-you-in place, not a gated residence, just an apartment that opens to the street. When the door opens, Brenda is standing there. There is a massive confrontation. Diane is in total shock and I'm trying to leave, to draw Brenda away.

It's the most awful screaming match of my life, and it's all in this small entryway. The question is—*How to stop it? How do you physically move a tragedy that is exploding in front of you?*

I believed that if I left, Brenda would leave. She did get in her car, at first. But once I was gone, she went back and resumed the argument. The neighbors called the police. Charges were brought and then dropped.

The story became the scandal of my century. It took on a life of its own. Thankfully, there was no social media.

Normally, I'd use my Southern upbringing to underplay the drama. Understatement is the watchword in the South. Like—

"What's going on Lionel?" *Everything's fine.*

"How's the family?" *Great.*

"What happened to your cousin?" *Oh, he's doing well.*

"But Lionel, he's in prison."

There's always a way to spin everything. Not this time.

The most painful part, the tragedy of our lives, was that Brenda was heartbroken. And I get it. Ladies and gentlemen, I get it.

You never know what you are going to do or feel until you're in the moment and it's in your face. None of us had been in this situation. This wasn't Alabama; this was a brand-spanking-new miniseries right here. And nobody was prepared. We all deserved a pass because we didn't know what the story was going to be. It was just raw and ugly and disastrous.

Prior to that morning, I recall there was a cloud of uncertainty as to whether I wanted to try to reconcile and not be separated. From then on, though, the way back was harder to find.

That's the saddest day in the life of a marriage. When you know you may love each other, still, and you have a history that you will always have, but it's over. And you know it.

MY FATHER WAS the first person to call when the news about my marriage hit Tuskegee.

"Well," he said, "are you out in the front yard, looking at people, and waving as they drive by, or are you hiding behind the sofa?"

And I said, "What does that mean, Dad?"

"Now you're being tested. Can you recover from this? If you can't recover from this, then you're not being a strong winner. Winners are only determined by the punches they can take, not how many punches they can throw."

We never want to get smacked upside the head by a lesson in

the middle of getting punched, but this was Lyonel Richie Sr., and I needed to hear his words about being tested.

His most important message came next. "What you have to do," he said, "is stand up, face what's in front of you and deal with it, with integrity, and move on." And that was exactly what I had to do. He spoke with a choke in his voice, a clue that he was fighting back tears, because he knew this was something he couldn't do for me. I had to do it for myself. Stand up and be a man.

He reminded me of his philosophy of the five Ds. In life, he said, these were the tests: divorce, disease, disaster, death, and disgrace.

I took all of this in, realizing a lot had to change. My father was dying, my marriage was ending, I needed risky throat surgery and was being told that I might not sing again. I needed time off to land for a minute and figure out where the hell I was. "A year" was the length of the break that I announced to my team and inner circle. It would soon become three years and then some.

A decade later, when I caught up with Skip Miller, Motown's longtime promotions man and one of my dearest friends, I said, "You know what, Skip, man, if I hadn't stopped, I would have had a nervous breakdown."

He said, "Lionel, you stopped because you had a nervous breakdown."

True. At age thirty-nine, I was forced to slow way down.

And in doing so, I saved my own life.

19

Blue Period

INSTEAD OF ANNOUNCING THAT I'D jumped ship at a time when I was famous as hell, I stepped away quietly. Nobody realized I was taking a time-out. Most of the public and even some friends thought I was still on that rocket charging across the sky.

But mentally, physically, emotionally, I had bailed. I saw Nikki frequently for brief visits—and I tried to just be Dad for her because that was our commitment, and our visits were joyful, no matter what.

I discovered something that I had tried to outrun for twenty years, another *D* word—depression.

Anxiety, I understood. I was no stranger to fear and doubt or to feeling broken. For twenty years I'd been trying to outrun my ADHD—which experts were finally talking about in this period. Apparently, it was common in high achievers. What was not talked about much was how a person with ADHD might react to suddenly slowing down.

I found a therapist, a first for me, and he was helpful. His insight was that I had been avoiding my feelings for too long. I had to stop compartmentalizing. The time had come to get face-to-face with myself—with my deepest, true feelings. All of them.

When I did move out, I was in my own place, but now Diane was in the picture.

Adding to the uncertainty, I found myself on shaky ground as far as a recording home. How ironic. Not only was my marital situation front-page news, but on the very same date, in the business section, there was other news: Berry Gordy had sold Motown.

Two years earlier, I'd gone to Berry and asked, "Let me buy the company."

I think my offer meant a lot to him, maybe by virtue of the fact that without him and Motown I wouldn't have been in a position to explore the possibility. After he gave me the tough love talk about going solo, I remember him doing something he almost never did in those years—and that was to show up at my solo debut arena show at Universal's amphitheater. He was grinning ear to ear when he came backstage to congratulate me after the show. Even more unheard of, about a year later, was that he surprised me by attending a dinner party celebrating my birthday.

Berry Gordy floored me that night when he stood to give a toast I will never forget. He kept it brief. "Up until now," Berry said, "I was the star of Motown. And then Lionel came along . . . and he's the star. And I'm very proud of him."

This was the father of Motown, showing the same paternal pride as my own dad would have.

Even so, when I tried to buy the company, Mr. Gordy turned me down.

Clearly, I wasn't a corporation that could guarantee the sustained growth of an institution like Motown, not just with cash to stay afloat but also to cultivate the careers of new talent.

Berry sold the record division for $61 million—a combined effort on the part of Boston Ventures and MCA. The deal did not include the much more valuable Jobete, his music publishing arm, which he later sold, in stages, for close to $320 million. The terms for the sale of the record company included the assurance that Motown would be headed up by a respected Black executive at MCA, Jheryl Busby. The Motown name would go on, later as part of Polygram, and Universal after that, and so on.

To me, the tragedy was that after the sale of Motown, it was never a label again. You can blame it on the nature of the corporate conglomerates, but the insult of life was later on—after Jheryl Busby was gone and most of the Black executives from the old guard got fired—when Motown was relegated to being the R&B department of Mercury Records.

My immediate concern was that when my hiatus was over, I could be homeless, label-wise.

Everyone tried to reassure me. *You'll be fine, take your time off, come back when you're ready.*

To show you how fast I'd been traveling and how many shows I'd been on for years, during all that time I took off, whenever awards season came around, people kept calling and saying, "I saw the American Music Awards. Congratulations. You won again." Or the Oscars, or the Grammys. No, I hadn't won anything. They were watching clips of previous wins. This saved me from saying, "I blacked out and left my body and don't know where I am, and I'm not writing or playing or connected to music. What's up with you?"

IN MY HAZE, I managed to reach out to a few father figures, not wanting to worry my dad. Much to my sorrow, my great friend and mentor Sammy Davis Jr. was also seriously ill with throat cancer. In our last communications, all I could do was to try to let him know how deeply grateful I was for his friendship and belief in me from the start. His funeral would be among the first of too many losses to come.

Sidney Poitier had befriended me early in my solo career. I admired him infinitely.

In the middle of my marital crisis, in need of some wisdom and guidance, I called Sidney, who had been through a divorce of his own with his first marriage.

I confided, "You know, Mr. P., I'm failing miserably at being as eloquent and as cosmopolitan as you. Tell me what I'm doing wrong."

He paused for a beat. And, then, with a hint of his Bahamian accent, he asked, "How old are you, Lionel?"

I told him that I had just turned forty.

He got very quiet before telling me, "Lionel, you're making the same mistakes I did at forty years old."

"How on earth did you manage to survive, Mr. P.?'"

Sidney Poitier gave me a very simple truth. He said, "You can't avoid the pain. You can't avoid the humiliation. You can't avoid the lesson." How did he survive? He laughed and admitted, "I went through it." That was it. "You just have to go through it."

I sighed.

"In fact, Lionel, you're doing it a lot better than I did."

"Really? You've got to be kidding."

"Oh yeah," he said.

I took him at his word, even if that wasn't the case. He made me feel a lot better.

Gregory Peck also gave me words of wisdom. In that very deep, authoritative, God-like Atticus Finch voice, he said, "Lionel, Lionel, listen to me. If this would have happened in Tuskegee, Alabama, it could have been grounds for suicide."

He was right.

But, he reminded me that this was Show Business. "You can't upstage the scandals of Hollywood, Lionel." Mr. Peck's point was, "A messy divorce is just another day in Hollywood."

With that counsel, he encouraged me to attend an upcoming event, what I recall was an American Film Institute gala at the Beverly Hilton. He was being honored, and he said, "It would mean a great deal if you would join us, as my guest."

Very much single at the time, I accepted, as long as he knew I'd come alone.

When in history had I ever gone anywhere alone?

Making my first public appearance in at least a year terrified me. But I was tired of the Blues of a marriage on the rocks, my father nearing the end of his life, and my depression.

The Beverly Hilton ballroom was full of the stars and studio heads and producers and agents there to honor Gregory Peck, and to raise money for AFI, for the preservation of great films and the education of future filmmakers.

I saw folks I knew who hadn't seen me in a while and had never seen me show up to any social event like this *alone*. Everyone seemed to be confused and/or amused.

What in the hell has happened to Lionel Richie? He doesn't like galas and sure as hell isn't here to pay $50,000. They came right out and asked, "What are you doing here? Where are you sitting?"

Perfect timing. Gregory Peck appeared at my side, and said, "Lionel, we're about to start. Come on down, we're down here," and he started off toward the front table to my spot next to him and Elizabeth Taylor.

A few friends were caught off guard as I went to join my good friend, the guest of honor—whom they had no idea I knew. And I truly enjoyed their aggravation when I turned back and said, "I'm sitting with him."

Mr. Peck, in accepting his award, talked about the power of entertainment.

"Making millions is not the whole ball game, fellas," he said. "Pride in workmanship is worth more, artistry is worth more. The human imagination is a priceless resource. The public is ready for the best you can give them. And just maybe you can make a buck and, at the same time, encourage, foster, and commission work of quality and originality."

Whether it was this night or during another evening when Mr. Peck was being honored, I have a vivid memory of witnessing him hold up an honorary award that was given to him to mark his Oscar win for Best Actor in 1963 for his performance in *To Kill A Mockingbird*. He said, "You know, every once in a while someone comes along and gives the performance of their lives, and did it so well that when it is time for you to do your line, he handed you the Oscar." This was how he brought up the veteran Black actor, Brock Peters, who played the role of the young man Atticus Finch defended in the movie. Mr. Peck explained, "The person who delivered the lines before me did such an amazing job, all the camera had to do was film my reaction. Tonight, I would like to give this Oscar to the guy who gave me my Oscar."

The gesture left such a mark on me, even if I don't recall all the details, that it changed how I saw fame.

What I realized that night at the Beverly Hilton was that being famous is not the end goal. Famous is easy. You can be famous tomorrow, get a hit record or have one movie, maybe two. Okay, you're famous.

This is a life—a career of hits and misses. Through it all you survive. This is a lifetime of elevating your community, of standing for something. I've never forgotten during the standing ovation for Gregory Peck, seeing real respect. Now *that* you don't get to see every day.

DURING VISITS TO see my dad in this time, I gained new insights about the five Ds. At first, I was sure he had exaggerated, as he could. Divorce, disease, disaster, death, and disgrace all sounded frickin' ominous, even taken one by one.

The thought that I was going to get tested by all of the Ds, all at once, was too much.

What I didn't realize yet was that in my survival kit, somewhere stashed away, was a secret defense mechanism that happens to also be a *D* word—defiance.

It had been hiding in plain sight for some years and I hadn't noticed. Sometimes it takes a Blue Period to discover undervalued assets. In my case, buried in all that people-pleasing, there was a part of me that was starting to no longer care whether you liked me or not.

I had heard it all—the overused *Lionel crossed over and can't get Black.* It got old. But so did questions from reporters who wanted to hear how I overcame poverty and struggle. They wanted headlines: *When were you selling drugs in Detroit?*

No, my years of struggle were when I took Latin at twelve years old in Tuskegee and sucked at it.

And what gang were you in? I was in the Alphas, the same fraternity as Dr. Martin Luther King Jr. and Thurgood Marshall.

We get it. So, your father was strict, and he beat you because you shot someone?

No, I got an ass-whuppin' because I came home late and talked back to him. *Fuck, what was I thinking?*

I'd learned over the years that my mother's wonderful line came in handy, "Sometimes—yes, your kids are supposed to know about you, but not everything about you."

The same was true when talking to the press. You don't have to say everything. You are not on trial.

As a recovering people pleaser, I learned something about the public. They don't own you. They don't have to know every invasive detail. And when I felt an interviewer was about to corral me, my defiance was what politicians know how to do—that is, no matter what question they ask, you answer with the answer you want them to have.

Okay, so Lionel, were you ever in the Communist party?

"Guys, I had trouble even being in the Cub Scouts. Who's got the next question?"

You get them to laugh, and you move on.

From the start of my career to the present day, frankly, I often felt the media wanted me to apologize for not having the right backstory. *I'm so sorry I did not grow up in the streets of Chicago, and I never sold drugs on the corners in New York City. I'm sorry I never was a lead singer in a Gospel choir.*

After "Endless Love" I stopped apologizing. My defiance came to me after the invitation to do a special hosted by Barbara Walters.

Well, Barbara and I were good friends, and this was summer 1986, and she pitched me her take: "We're coming to Bel Air. You're going to show off your house. And it's going to be called, 'Lionel Richie, Rags to Richie.'"

I paused and said, "No, I really want to show where I came from."

Barbara was eager to feature the luxurious mansion, in the days when the perception was that all I had to do was clear my throat and out came a hit. Did I not want to show the glamour?

"No, I want to have it in Tuskegee where I was raised." I convinced her that my parents and my grandmother would be available, and we could start on the university campus.

At the appointed hour, Barbara and her crew arrived.

During the tour of campus, a few photos were taken. As we headed out, through the gates, and started to cross the street, Barbara shared that her mother, then in her seventies, suffered from a bit of senility. "And I noticed that you want to hang a lot of this interview on your grandmother."

Before I could respond, we reached Grandma Foster's house.

Barbara seemed confused. "Now, what is this place?"

"This is where I was brought up."

"No, where's the house that you grew up in as a child . . . in the rural—"

I said, "I grew up on the university campus."

She looked disappointed.

Just then, Adelaide Foster, Grandma, came out on the front porch.

Barbara exclaimed, "Oh, who is that? This must be your lovely mother."

"No, this is my grandmother."

Grandma spoke. "Welcome, Mrs. Walters, to the house, I've heard a lot about you, and we're so excited to have you here."

Barbara stared in disbelief. I smiled, noting that Grandma did look youthful for ninety-three. Not to mention that she was a survivor of breast cancer, which she'd battled in her eighties.

And then my mother and father walked out onto the front porch with Deborah right behind them. Barbara asked, "Now who are these people?"

And I said, "Now that's my mom and dad and my sister."

Barbara Walters turned to me, amazed, and said, "Where did you get these people from—central casting?" She meant it as a humorous compliment that my family members were so impressive, but it came across as if we were just brought in as actors. Not that they could be my real family.

This was one of those tone-deaf comments that was meant to be funny. But this was kind of my point—because, sadly, for America, the world, and for much of the public, there is a central casting for Black Southern folks who look like they're not far from the plantation.

Something along these lines happened with the Pepsi commercial script—with a storyline that I was coming home to Alabama and had just driven from the airport to surprise Grandma outside while she was tending to her garden.

Before the shoot, I asked the wardrobe people that whatever they decided, "Please, first run it by the director and by me."

Somebody forgot. There was quite a moment when the wardrobe lady, who spoke slowly and carefully, said to my grandma, "Now Mrs. Foster, we have a pretty little pink flowered apron here for you, and a nice little scarf to go on your head." She made the mistake of leaning in, because she thought my grandmother couldn't hear.

Grandma didn't look at me. She simply turned to the lady and said, "I don't wear an apron in the garden, I wear a Pendleton jacket. I don't wear a rag on my head, I wear my straw hat. And I brought both with me."

The lady backed up and said, "Yes ma'am." And she walked away.

She had run into a buzz saw named Adelaide Foster. Whoever proposed an Aunt Jemima head rag never lived it down. Grandma was a highly educated Black woman—as in, *do not fuck with who I am and my history*—who grew up with Booker T. goddamn Washington and George Washington Carver.

This wasn't just about white people holding stereotypes of African Americans. Tuskegee was just unlike anywhere else I can name. Years later I invited Bob Johnson to my hometown to see the project I was developing with the university. Bob Johnson—the man who founded BET with his then-wife, Sheila, before selling it to Viacom for a stock deal worth three billion dollars—was a Southerner like me.

Unlike me, Bob had grown up poor, with a family that worked the fields. He may have assumed my childhood was not so different from his. Every time Bob and I got together, we talked about overcoming the struggle—like, "Yeah, we went from the country to the city, alright. We sure have come a long way."

When Bob flew to Tuskegee, I had the police meet him at the highway and escort him through town—the full fanfare. He was to pick me up at my grandmother's house, which I eventually owned, before we went to campus.

Bob strolled up to meet me on the porch and asked, "Now, what is this place right here?"

I said, "This is my house where I grew up." I told him its history.

Bob laughed and said, "Don't you ever talk to me again about struggle!"

Once I told him that it wasn't always like this and I had renovated it extensively, he understood its roots as the dream of a better day, not as the trappings of status. After that, he was even more enthralled with my upbringing.

The more time that went by, the clearer I saw how rich my life growing up really was, something I appreciated even more in my parents' last years.

IN THE FOG of this time—my Blue Period—I became aware of the connection between ADHD and depression. Where did that phrase "Blue Period" come from? Turns out it came from Pablo Picasso—who they say went through a period of four years when he was turning out moody paintings in dark blues and blue-greens. He also was said to have had traits associated with ADHD and was known to suffer from depression.

Picasso learned to channel his somber feelings into his art. He literally painted his Blues.

Sadly, my desire to get back to the studio wasn't there.

I tried meditation, but I kept getting distracted and couldn't let go. Memories I thought were gone flooded my brain.

I had never fully appreciated the gift of growing up in a home with parents at the dinner table every night until this period. It occurred to me that my daughter had seen me more often backstage than at any semblance of a dinner table. Whenever I could, I tried to schedule meals with Nikki. As often as possible, I also went to Tuskegee to sit at the table with Mom, Dad, Grandma, and Deborah.

Little had changed. Mom was serious because she understood what was likely to happen, from the point of view of medical science and health. But Dad refused to leave this world living his last days in tragedy. No matter what serious issue my mother raised, my dad had fifteen jokes ready to take the edge off.

Maybe it was all tragic, but his question was, "From who's perspective? Yours or mine?" From his perspective, it was what it was—material.

Tragedy or inspiration? My father could remember a time when he was growing up and his mother gave him second servings, only for him to find out she gave him her only serving.

In my state of denial, in the face of losing my father who was my best buddy, the greatest character of my life, the one person who promised me he would teach me to survive and did, I'd cling to memories. He took so much pleasure in getting to come along on parts of my ride. And he did the funniest things to make it clear to me he was enjoying it too.

I can't tell you how many times he would throw his American Express card on the table, and say, "What does that name say, son?" He'd egg me on. "Read the name off that card."

"Um, that says Lionel Richie." He never bothered to change the spelling. Then he'd pretend to run off with my identity, laughing, "See ya!" He never got tired of doing that. And he would tell me all the time, "The greatest thing I ever did was name you Junior."

When the governor declared Lionel Richie Day in the state of Alabama, they had banners up over the streets across Tuskegee, and nobody took more pleasure in it than my father.

"Get in the car, boy. I want you to see something." And he drove me around, pointing to *his* name up on banners for all to see. All he could say was, "Son, it's a fine day in the state of Alabama."

He was thrilled and I was for him, because he had a life of accomplishment and he got to witness his children coming into their own. Dad proposed we share who got to represent the name. He said, "I'll take the state of Alabama. You can have the rest of the country."

Whenever he came to different stops on the *All Night Long* tour, I made sure he and my mother had the best seats in the house. She urged him to sit in his seat and enjoy the show, but he had discovered the power of an all-access pass, and he was not about to sit in that seat and miss out on using the power.

Dad walked all over the building, backstage, out in the lobby, to the seats in the back, and occasionally he'd walk down front. You can do that with an all-access pass. He'd look up at me, and gesture to let me know that the sound sounded great in the back. He'd turn around, look at the audience, and then walk back up the aisle to check out the sound in another part of the arena.

At the end of the song, when the applause subsided, my usual comment was, "Ladies and gentlemen, you have noticed that man who came down the middle of the aisle to give me a signal that everything was okay at the back."

In Sydney, Australia, in 1987, when Elton John surprised me by coming onstage to join me.

With Quincy Jones, legendary producer, friend, and mentor, who I talked to daily at 3 a.m.

With my brother and true soul mate and dear friend Kenny Rogers in the studio in Nashville.

Among my most cherished memories—a life-changing afternoon spent with Nelson Mandela in South Africa.

Michael Jackson and Elizabeth Taylor—larger-than-life superstars whom I was blessed and thrilled to have as friends.

In 2012, singing "Three Times a Champion" at a tribute to Muhammad Ali.

Rehearsing in Modena, Italy, with Luciano Pavarotti in 1999 for Pavarotti and Friends.

Onstage in Houston in 1986.   With my heart and partner, Lisa.

At the piano in Montreal in 2023, while on tour with Earth, Wind & Fire.

Honors along the way (*clockwise from top left*): Picking up six awards at the American Music Awards, 1985; being inducted into the Rock & Roll Hall of Fame, 2022; receiving the Icon Award at the American Music Awards, 2022; and being recognized at the Kennedy Center Honors, 2017.

Performing at Glastonbury in June 2015.

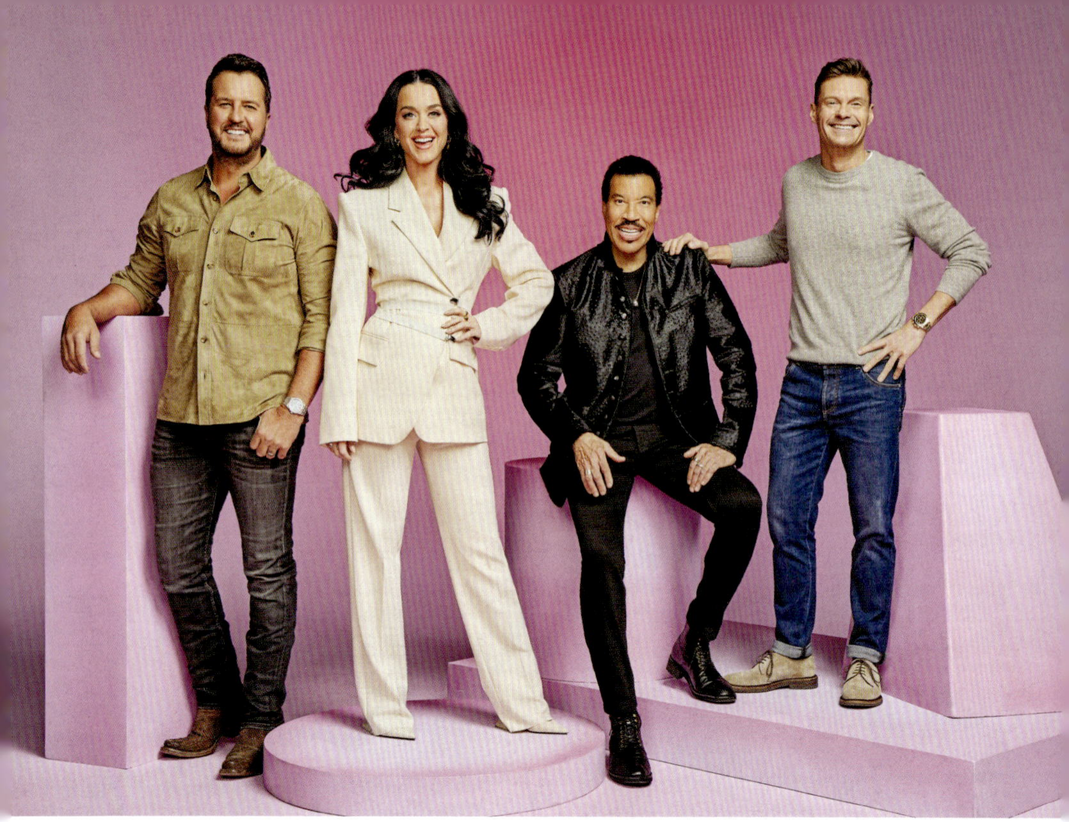

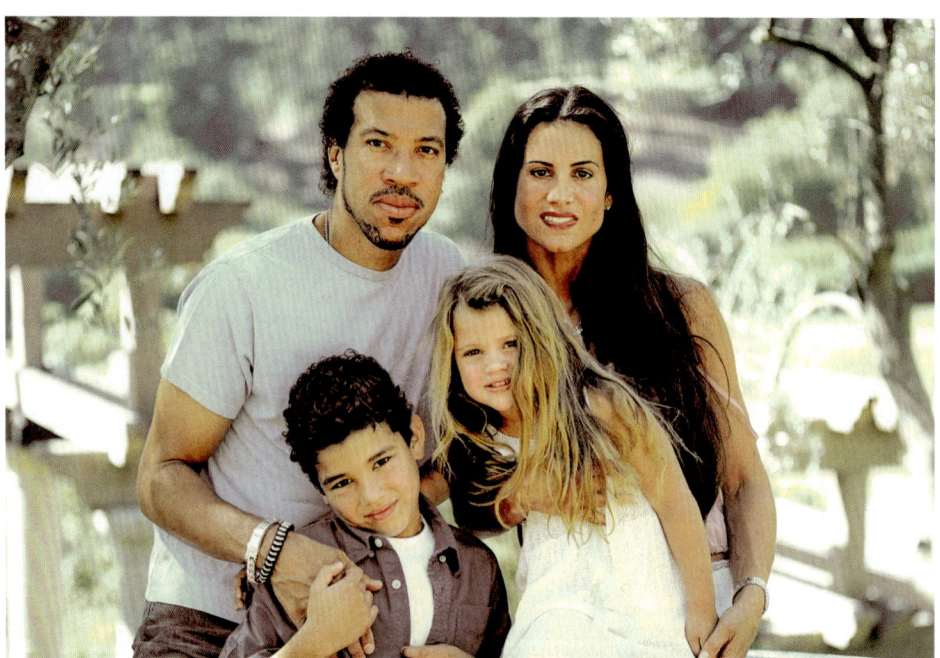

With my fellow *American Idol* judges Katy Perry and Luke Bryan, and host Ryan Seacrest. (Disney/Art Streiber. Copyright © 2024 Disney. All rights reserved.)

Family is everything. Here with Diane and the kids, Miles and Sofia.

Heads would nod. I'd hear some commentary—*Buzzz, buzzz.*
"That is my father."
Applause, applause.

I can still see my father turning around and nodding, savoring every minute.

"That's him. He suffers from an overdose of pride." A beat. "Now, if you happen to bump into him, would you please tell him how great his son is? He'll definitely appreciate that."

And the full audience would give him a standing O, as he walked victoriously all the way up the aisle, until he either disappeared from view or went back to sit down with my mother who was totally embarrassed.

Deborah and I made the decision to bring Dad and Mom out to Los Angeles during what turned out to be his last year of life. We hoped the warmer climate would be easier for him and that he might benefit from some of the medical treatments that were more accessible in California.

Though his body was in decline, he was mentally there, 100 percent. He saw my success and me having a family.

Whenever I went to sit with him, I'd tell him stories and thank him for passing that ability on down. We would talk about the journey he had taken.

It struck me one afternoon that he only seemed to have been on my ride but, no, I was on his all along—standing on his shoulders, on those of his fellow Army officers and the Tuskegee Airmen, and all who had set the bar high for me and my peers.

In one of our last conversations, he said, "From the start of my life, all the way through to your life, I've had one hell of a ride, son." He wouldn't have changed a thing.

My father died on October 31, 1990, a Wednesday. He and my mother had been married for forty-seven years. We all traveled to Tuskegee for the funeral. The services were conducted by the Reverend Vernon A. Jones and held at the Tuskegee University Chapel.

At anyone else's funeral, the congregation would have looked to Dad to tell a story that would have allowed us to laugh through our tears and have a spiritual catharsis.

There was no one who could fulfill that role at the service for Lyonel Brockman Richie Sr. When I spoke at the funeral, I talked about him and his life, and I had to add, "I realized something sitting here listening today, that from now on, I have to learn how to be original." It was true. Every mannerism, every joke, every way of trying to figure out how to make life work. When you spend your life imitating your dad and then he's gone, you face the challenge of learning to be original. That's how I ended, with—"This is going to be an interesting period."

I was completely heartbroken.

And I felt more lost than ever.

20

Wandering Stranger

GRIEF WILL ROB YOU OF your joy and your hope. It takes away your sense of time and place—and erases your story. Grief is also the great teacher of what matters most.

Over the course of the four years that followed my father's death, tests from the other Ds were kicking my ass. The divorce was torture. Had I been the best husband? Hell no. Was I the *worst?* No, of course not. I mean, this was the classic breakup scenario—one person feels wronged, and the other one feels guilty. I'd been a freakin' dumbass at times.

Divorce is a death all its own, however.

In the dissolution of everything you built together, the concept of what is meant by community ownership of intellectual property was new to me. The lawyers explained, "It's not that your wife has a right to half of the song, she has a right to half of the idea of the song."

In the royalty split, it's the same money, by the way, only in California law the question is, What is more important, the inspiration or the perspiration? In other words, Who's the real artist?

And the judge ruled, "If you didn't have the inspiration, you wouldn't have written in the first place."

Your honor, I object.

The example I offered was "Truly." The inspiration was Barbra Streisand. "Three Times a Lady" was inspired by my mom and dad, though I wanted Frank Sinatra to sing it. And when I was singing it, as a gentleman, I sang it to my wife, who had stuck by me for all those years.

My backward writing process was now on trial. I tried to explain how I didn't always write a love song because I was in love or a sad song because I was sad. The song I wrote was inspired by the story I found.

The hardest part was what the process did to my self-esteem. The years had taught me to take pride in my craft and value my gifts, which were my livelihood. The law didn't care about that. The opposing lawyers convinced the judge that there should be an assumption of inspiration provided by the spouse at the time. I'm sitting in a room, having lawyers carve up my creations. Might as well have put a stake through my heart. The thing that killed me most was that my whole identity came from being the songwriter, the creative person who thrived in the studio—my sandbox.

This only pushed me further toward divorcing the Music Business for good. As in, *I don't want to do this shit no more. I'm out of here.*

If I needed an excuse just to throw up my hands and be done with the madness, this part of the disentanglement of our lives was it.

We at last arrived at a place where it was time to sail on, for lack of a better song to sing. Money's money and my position was, *You want the money, you've got the money.*

Nobody was putting me out on the street, after all.

The divorce would not be finalized until 1993, after about three years of tearing ourselves apart. Was there still to be life after that death?

The one coping mechanism I found was looking for glimmers of light, moments where I could feel grateful that I was still breathing. And I was grateful that Diane was in my life, that we had waited.

We moved in together in a house on Oriole Drive in Beverly Hills that once had belonged to Tony Curtis. It was more of a bachelor pad, tucked away yet charming, more modest and less attention-getting than the big Bel Air mansion. In my Blue Period when I was ready to be done with the music industry altogether, I found relief in being with someone who wanted nothing to do with Show Business ever.

If I never went back to my career, that was fine with me. Or so I convinced myself.

The reality was that buried underneath the grief and the depression and the guilt was my dear old friend—*fear*. Three questions made me the most uncertain: 1) What was life going to be like after the death of my father? 2) How would everything else change after the divorce? And 3) How was I supposed to deal with the news that I might need a risky surgery to save my voice? Fear had me leaping to the worst-case scenario of: *You'll never sing again.*

I NEVER FORGOT Quincy Jones telling me about his lowest point, when he spotted the church sign that read, "Worry is a by-product of indecision."

I took that to mean as long as you decide on a course of action, everything will be fine.

No, there are actually good decisions and bad decisions. You just can't get stuck in fear. You have to focus on making better decisions—including the choices about your health.

Starting in the mid-eighties, I had begun to suffer the consequences of the overuse of my vocal cords. Like athletes, many artists end up injuring ourselves with constant performance. What was first diagnosed as a polyp was further complicated by a hemorrhage of one of my cords. To fix it, the little broken blood vessel needed cauterizing.

Simple enough. *Except* . . . the instrument of choice was a laser. At the time, surgical lasers were hot, which ran the risk of limiting the vibration of the vocal cord. My decision was to buy myself time. The problem was that I was singing incorrectly to avoid the broken blood vessel but wasn't addressing the causes of the hoarseness and vocal fatigue—which led me to go ahead with three different procedures. They were less risky but didn't help.

If nothing changed, I was told, maybe the fear of "You'll never sing again" wasn't irrational.

To make this even more depressing was the timing—as I sank to the depths of grief over losing my father and as my divorce neared its painful conclusion. If anyone questioned whether this could be labeled a nervous breakdown, I answered it when I found myself in Jamaica, alone. There I spent five days sitting in a hotel beach chair at the water's edge, oblivious to the tide sending waves up to my waist, and damn near passed out from drinking a daily bottle of Cristal by myself.

Ladies and gentlemen, this is what a nervous breakdown looks like. Each day at sunset, as the tide rolled in, the hotel staff would come out, pick me up in the chair, and retrieve my empty champagne bottle, now full of saltwater, to bring me back up to dry land—waking me before I drowned. Which, at that time, I felt might have been a good idea.

On each day, I noticed an older Jamaican man—a local, I assumed—who walked with a cane, as he made his way to his regular spot not far from me, but on the public side of the beach. On the last day, after sitting there not drinking my usual daily bottle, I brushed off the wet sand and started back up to the hotel when this gentleman approached me.

"Young man," he said, sounding like a mix of James Earl Jones and Morgan Freeman, and then added, "Lionel," to let me know he was a fan. He said, "You *must* survive . . ."

"Oh, yes . . . yes. . ." I didn't argue.

"You must survive because you are our beacon of hope." He smiled. "If you make it, we know we can make it. If you accomplish, we know we can accomplish."

For five days I'd been in Jamaica trying to get a message from God but, for some reason, had been unable to receive it. (Could the drinking have dulled the signal?) Yet here I was on the fifth day, and something broke through. It wasn't in the form I'd expected, but if I closed my eyes, the message "you must survive" was what I'd been waiting for.

Now what? This was late 1991, my three-year hiatus was up. How was I supposed to save my voice, finish the album I owed, secure new representation, and manage to get myself out of my Blue Period? I needed more clarity about how to pull off this wonderful message from God.

So, I decided to go home to Tuskegee to see Mom and Grandma. Sometimes help for a nervous breakdown can be found in some good old-fashioned Alabama grounding.

THE NIGHT I arrived, I stayed up late, pacing and talking to myself in the living room. Little did I suspect that I was being overheard.

My ninety-seven-year-old grandmother, spry as ever, appeared next to me, arms folded, catching me by surprise. She asked, "What on earth are you doing? Why are you talking to yourself?"

"Grandma, I'm lost," I admitted. "I . . . I'm trying to figure out my next move."

She asked an odd question. "Did you decide to attend college in Tuskegee to join the Commodores?"

I shrugged. "No."

"Did you call Kenny Rogers and tell him you had a song for him?"

"No."

"Was it your idea to do a duet with Diana Ross?"

I shook my head no.

Grandma's point was clear. "Why don't you get a good night's sleep? God has your next move."

Her message was like Quincy's church sign. Figuring out the future was above my pay grade. Time to turn the decision-making over to my higher power—no small leap of faith.

If it was God's will that I never sing again, that would be my answer.

Blessedly, as other events fell into place, other answers would follow. Over the next couple of years, I discovered that diet and stress were adding to my vocal problems.

Can you believe it? One of the culprits was something as simple as acid reflux and addressing it was the beginning of my recovery. You know how you eat ice cream and drink milk shakes when you have your tonsils out? Well, dairy can be a killer for acid reflux. So can hamburgers. Small changes in my diet did wonders. And next, glory, hallelujah, technology caught up to provide the real answer to the problem.

FLASH FORWARD: FIVE or so years later, out of the blue one day, I received a phone call from my superhero ENT, Dr. Madison Richardson, a leading voice specialist in Beverly Hills. He wasted no time before announcing, "I found the person who can fix the hemorrhage."

He had recently learned of a promising young surgeon, Dr. Steven Zeitels, a Harvard Medical School professor who practiced at Massachusetts General in Boston.

In addition to treating the most treacherous forms of cancer of the throat and larynx, Dr. Zeitels was known for his innovations in voice restoration surgery.

Dr. Zeitels agreed to see me right away. I learned he also had a passion for music—especially Rock. Like Dr. Madison Richardson, he understood not just the many stressors put on the vocal cords of leading artists but also the intricacies of what made singers' voices sound like us.

Dr. Zeitels began by reassuring me that up until this point, I'd been given the best of the options that were available.

"That's it?"

Dr. Zeitels laughed and said, "Actually, it's not . . ." He paused and looked directly at me. "You must be the luckiest guy in the world. Because what you've been waiting for was just invented." Instead of the risks of a hot laser, the new technology used a cool laser.

Man, he was right about me being lucky. Although, just before surgery I panicked. "Doc, you sure you know what the hell you're doing?!"

He assured me, "Lionel, it's going to be a piece of cake."

Sounded great, I thought, but on somebody else's throat. But after all my apprehension, he was right. It worked like a charm.

Great news! I had a clean vocal cord. Bad news? I had to learn to sing all over again.

And how do you do that? I began where one does . . . in the shower. The shift would involve going from having to think about hitting the note to not thinking about the note.

I talk about this all the time to young vocalists. Great singers don't think about the mechanics of singing, they just hit the notes, using their vocal instruments in connection to the story they're telling.

You can always tell when a singer is thinking or trying too hard. Likewise, you can tell when a singer goes to a state of complete abandonment, when we go—*Whoa, they're singing totally out of their head.*

The saga of almost never singing again gave me a life lesson that might be helpful when you feel lost, when you've been kicked down by the five Ds and need to get back up. Start first with what gives you joy, and focus on that. You can face all the disasters of life, but at some point you will turn the corner and know that you made it. That then becomes a healing moment, which is called gratitude.

When I started with, *Thank you, thank you God, thank you Universe*, that's when the weight finally began to lift.

IN AN ACT of defiance, in early 1992, I managed to birth three new songs—"Do It to Me," "My Destiny," and "Love, Oh Love." Once they were cleared by the army of divorce lawyers (what a shit show), I rushed them to the team at Motown. The A&R team decided to put together a greatest hits compilation album with the addition of these three previously unreleased singles.

I had not done a compilation album yet as a solo artist and questioned the timing.

My concern was the growing disregard for the craft of song-writing. Marketing was now king.

Truly artist-friendly executives were always a rare breed. Besides Berry Gordy, there was Herb Alpert, Mo Ostin, and Clive Davis—and a handful of others. But now you bring in people who specialize in selling products, mass shit. They don't know how to talk to creative people.

Label heads were constantly changing through conglomerate mergers and takeovers. One day I might be on Motown, owned by MCA, but the next day I was switching to PolyGram, which owned Mercury, and before long we would be under the Universal umbrella with Island and Def Jam and, oh, Motown. With every merger or acquisition, they'd get rid of the team that knew you as an artist or how to market your music. Everything was in flux. Pressure on profit-making was taking away the kind of support that creativity needs.

Artists digging into their souls were just expected to drop a baby on demand. Imagine walking up to a new mom who has just been through labor and she's going, "Oh my God, I birthed a miracle, look at this beautiful baby," and everybody's checking their watches and saying, "Hey, cool, when can you have another?"

No, guys, wait. Could you at least look at the baby?

The support went from "I love your album! I love your song!" to "Got any more content, and can you have it delivered in the third quarter?"

You're telling me "songs" are now called "content." *Note taken.*

After the release of the compilation album, *Back to Front*, in May 1992, the reception was eye-opening. In the US it went Platinum, reaching #7 R&B and #19 Pop—not bad at all, given that I'd been inactive for almost five years. The surprise was that it went to #1 in the UK (quadruple Platinum) and triple Platinum in France, as well #1 in Australia, New Zealand, and across Europe. When I later made my handful of engagements in smaller venues (my request) in the UK and in France, I was treated like visiting royalty.

People started asking, "Are you ready to come back full-time?" The answer was no.

"How much longer?"

I didn't know. I needed to be at peace with myself, and I wasn't. I had to agree with Diane that the Business would kill me. I saw what was happening to friends and to the Music Business. Everyone was speeding faster, but doing so without guidance, without control, with no way to slow down and find balance—even a place to land.

Common sense tells us that human beings are not designed to fly at top speed without returning to earth. For the time being, earth was where I chose to be. Until I found some form of balance, I wasn't getting back on that rocket.

FROM FAR OFF in the distance, I started to hear more song snippets. Diane and I had barely moved in together before she began to suspect that I was missing my old life in the game.

Me? No! The game has changed.

I was crazy about Diane. She was a fixed star in the night sky. And she was sensitive to my emotional trauma.

The rule was unspoken. Our biggest issue—and it was nonnegotiable—*no mention of anything having to do with the Business.* Why engage with the sincerely insincere Hollywood movers and shakers? Why give the time of day to the crooks and thieves who claimed to have your better interests, or indulge any talk of making deals, and who was hot and who was not?

We both agreed, "Stay away from all of it." None of it was good.

Once, though, I asked, "Do you know anything about this Business?"

"No." As a dancer she knew how it could be cutthroat.

"Do you care anything about this Business?" Meaning, *Could you enjoy aspects of the rewards?*

"No." She couldn't stand any of it.

Diane's conviction made me wonder if there was something wrong with my liking certain perks. "Maybe it wasn't all terrible," I'd say now and then. Diane was unconvinced.

Eventually, after turning down years of invitations, I decided we would go as a couple to an Oscar party, and she could experience the royal treatment of being a celebrity by walking the red carpet with me. She was very shy and didn't want the spotlight, but this was a chance to have her Cinderella story moment that I was sure she would love.

After avoiding the rah-rah, I wasn't sure how I'd feel, but the minute we arrived I thought, *Maybe I don't hate this.* Diane would surely feel the same rumble of exhilaration. In my experience, people are so adamant that they don't like something until they do it, and then they go—*Wow, that's like nothing else, I loved it.*

At the end of the red carpet, I turned to Diane for her reaction, and she glared at me and said, "I *never* want to do that again."

She knew she hated it before, and we now had confirmation, she still hated it.

Well, if Diane didn't want anything to do with the Business, I could choose the same.

Whatever she loved, I loved. How about antique shopping? Yes, let's go!

So here I am wandering among the goods at the LA Antique

Fair, trying to be Mr. Regular Guy. But some people recognize me and come over to ask, "What are *you* doing at the LA Fair? When are you gonna start being Lionel Richie again? When is your next album?"

I'm going—"No, I'm doing antique shopping now. I'm looking for antiques." They look dumbfounded. Can this be real? Mr. All Night Long, Mr. Hello himself, is standing in the middle of the antique fair saying *what?* If they ask about music, I say, "No, no, no, I'm not doing that anymore, thank you."

They looked at me like I was crazy.

And I was. I had lost my fucking mind.

Except . . . I started hearing the music. One day I was humming, and the next day I was singing in the mirror and then setting up my little keyboards and—*What?*—playing the saxophone. Before I knew it, I was writing again.

[|||·|||]

THE POETRY OF life never fails to amaze me.

What most threw me into a depression was the loss of my father. And what really brought that time of mourning to an end was being saved by the miracle of being a father.

Once, twice, three times a dad.

This was to be a team effort.

In early 1994, Nicole was twelve and a half years old, going on eighteen, and an undeniable charmer of the first degree. She never said, "Daddy, snap out of it, you've been sad for too long," but that's what I started to feel. Bit by bit, though, she egged me on, out of the rabbit hole of depression, just in time for me to realize, to my terror, that she was only a few years away from getting her driver's license!

That kind of woke me up—as had the reality that Diane and I were expecting a baby to be born in late May of 1994.

We were excited and nervous and everything you'd guess, but I didn't know how euphoric I'd feel with the arrival of a son. As soon as I held him in my arms the first time, I knew that this baby, my fellow Gemini, Miles Brockman Richie, had arrived not a moment too soon, as a reminder for me to start living fully again.

I became the classic doting father. Diane was just a beautiful, natural mother, and we were both in love with this baby together.

Nothing else mattered but, *Did he smile? Was it gas? Oh, he's laughing! Oh, he's making sounds! He's brilliant! He's handsome! He's an artist.* It was like one of those things where you're happy staring at this baby all day, going, *Miles, you are brand-new!*

We had bliss. And four years later, right behind Miles, came little Sofia, the sweetest, most precious angel. Nicole joined us as the proud, protective big sister, and I could have sworn that they were a conspiracy to help me, their dear daddy, grow up—using their superpowers of pure, unconditional love. The three of them were the lights of my life and they are to this day.

Period, the end.

Every day was an adventure, a fresh start. With Miles I could be a grown-up, a responsible parent, but a kid again too.

Everything good that my dad had taught me about survival, I was going to teach Miles, and I was going to do everything in my power not to pass on my fearfulness. How? Improv!

I started telling him stories before he could walk. We'd be driving somewhere, and I'd point out landmarks, talking about the Commodores and where we first stayed in LA. He was a baby in his car seat and had no idea what I was talking about, just like I had no idea when my dad used to begin every story with "Back in the War . . ." And then I'd tell Miles about all the changes in the Music Business, and I sounded so much like Lyonel Sr. "Let me tell you about that sonuvabitch."

Oh, yeah, among the new cast of characters out there were some double-crossers.

"Miles," I told him, "I love that you are not in the Business because you can never double-cross me."

My toddler kid would clap and laugh at that. And so would I.

LIFE WAS SWEET. Toward the end of 1995, when Miles was about one and a half years old, we went home to Tuskegee, and everyone was smitten: *Oh my God, Lionel, we love your baby, we love Diane, you all seem so happy!*

This was Grandma's last year of life, and that part of the trip wasn't easy. Adelaide Foster was 102 years old, much slower than she had ever been, but very much with it. Two years earlier, in January 1993, we had celebrated her one hundredth birthday—and the 160th birthday of Tuskegee—with six hundred invited guests. Mayor Johnny Ford declared January 23 "Adelaide Foster Day," and during the festivities Grandma sat and listened proudly as highlights of her remarkable life were described—from her graduation with a degree in music in 1912 from Fisk University in Nashville, to her journey as a music instructor on the Tuskegee campus, to her contribution playing piano for our veterans at their church services and as the organist at St. Andrew's Episcopal Church.

I had the pleasure of paying tribute to Grandma and acknowledging how much I would have benefited from learning to play piano had I not been so impatient to play the sax. Grandma nodded in agreement. I had occasion to repeat a recent exchange I had enjoyed with my grandmother when I told her, "Grandma, you are so wise. One day I want to be as wise as you."

"Yes," she answered. "Unfortunately, what comes with wisdom is age."

And that story brought down the house.

The celebration was joyful yet at times heartbreaking for me. Every time I looked over to see my father's reaction, he wasn't there.

When I took Diane and Miles to visit, that same heaviness was not there. The seasons of life had changed, and everything was colored by my excitement in showing off our son and showing him the world that raised me.

Before we returned to LA, a friend of the family, attorney Milton Carver Davis—fellow certified member of the Home-Boy Association—stopped by to say hello to my mother and grandmother and to see me, Diane, and the baby off.

I began introductions, saying, "This is my girlfriend, Diane Alexander. And this is our son, Miles Brockman Richie."

"Nice to meet you Diane Alexander, and good to meet your son, Miles Brockman," Milton said.

We talked for a little while with Milton telling more lies about us growing up, and then as Diane went to finish packing, Milton said he had a question. "Lionel," he asked, "did you ever hear your father call your mother his girlfriend?"

I looked at him and said, "No, but . . ."

"You weren't raised like that." Milton had just called me out on my Hollywood ways. He went on, getting me to see it as folks in Alabama might. As in: *You're famous, you've got a kid, that's the baby mama.* Like there was no commitment.

Milton's honesty painted a very clear picture in my mind about my responsibilities and creating family stability. He was right.

In my defense, Diane and I were already planning to be married. Of course, she was going to be Mrs. Richie—not Baby Mama or Dad's Girlfriend. A short time after our visit, in December 1995, we made it official—in a very intimate ceremony with only family members and a few of our closest friends. To mark the Christmas season, we decided to get married in New York City, which always had been magical for me, with the tree at Rockefeller Center, and the snow, and the lights and decorations up and down the avenues. A wonderful setting.

Diane was happy and that made me happy.

No longer lost, I felt found. No longer a wandering stranger, I found purpose every day.

Family was my anchor. And bit by bit, I discovered my authentic feelings again. With my children, my heart was across the room looking out. There's Nikki, and then there's Miles, and then here comes baby Sofia, a tiny angel, and I'm having the greatest time in the world.

Only . . . all of sudden, one day, guess what happens?

Here come some changes.

Change happens. Every day of our breathing, it does.

FOR YEARS AND years, I have referred to my remedy for handling all kinds of crises as a combination of medication and meditation. That's a joke, but not really.

Let me make a point here that if you have grappled with depression, loss, anxiety, or any of the Ds, *please* cut yourself some slack and, if needed, seek professional help or join a support group. Doing so is not an act of weakness. On the contrary, it's an act of self-love.

The gift was no longer being numb. How great it was just to feel and, yes, to feel good again. I'd wake up in the morning, eager to experience life.

"What are we going to do today?"

"How about the flea market?"

"Over on Fairfax? Oh, great!"

And then I'd put on my hat and sunglasses, and pretend no-body could recognize me. And we'd go, but then, somebody would say, "Oh my God, there's Lionel Richie." So, to avoid that, we were in the habit of going early, sneaking in, and then leaving fast.

With the kids, we could organize our day around what to do with these little crazy people—we had two of those bad boys now—plus the visits of their big sister, and that was time-consuming. In opening up again, I recognized that being busy was not the same as being productive. And, holy crap, not only did I like to write, but it's what I did.

Not for a minute was I tempted to admit out loud that maybe I liked the Business. I couldn't bear the thought of one more sincerely insincere person standing in front of me, "You're the best, you're the greatest, you're a superstar!"

Bullshit, bullshit.

Anything that came out of the record company was nau-seating.

Bullshit, bullshit.

Only, as I was coming back into my writing, I began to suspect that it wasn't so intolerable—for me. If I was really being honest, some of the bullshit was entertaining. Or chal-lenging. And it sparked my competitive drive, giving me the memory of the juice of winning. Oh my God, I wanted to feel that again.

To do so required developing a tolerance for the sincere in-sincerity. And, you know what? There was something about the madness of the crazy-ass Business that was calling to that kid in me formerly known as the escape artist.

Of course, I loved my family and our happy bubble. But that's the problem—the bubble can become confining. I didn't need to be zooming across the starlit sky at top speed. I just needed some new material to write about.

Where's the action?

The hitch was that if you want to be back in, you gotta do something that can be deadly—*you gotta hang.* Almost all the key players were new. We had new executives, new produc- ers, new musicians, new artists. If you didn't know them, good luck finding any action. If you wanted to know them, you had to hang, and that was not the best word for a family guy.

Let's try again.

Rrrrring! (That's the sound of an old-fashioned phone, back in the mid-nineties). The person calling me was Skip Miller, the great Motown promoter and friend, who wanted to run an opportunity by me.

Skip, by the way, knew everybody. The brother could have been a model or an actor, except for the fact that he loved record promotion. He knew the main players not just in mu- sic but in film and TV, including Denzel Washington. And that's why he was calling, to say he put my name up for a role in a movie called *The Preacher's Wife*—starring Denzel and Whitney Houston, directed by Penny Marshall.

I had known Whitney for years, along with her mother, one of our great Soul and Gospel singers, Cissy Houston, and her cousin, the spectacular, iconic Dionne Warwick. Those were a lot of superlatives for Whitney to live up to. But from the mo- ment she stepped into the limelight, in 1984, after being signed to Arista by Clive Davis at age nineteen, all she had to do was open her mouth and sing. Watch out world.

Skip told me the movie's basic premise—an angel is sent to help a preacher and his wife (Whitney) save their church and rekindle their marriage. In the process, the angel, played by Denzel, takes the wife to a Jazz club and through the help of the club owner helps her find her voice again.

"Denzel said to call Penny," Skip said, and she'd set up a reading. My assumption was that they wanted me for the part of the club owner, Britsloe Jacobs, and this was just a formality.

Fortunately, Skip didn't mention it was, in fact, an audition. Nobody told me that they were also seeing Luther Vandross and Herbie Hancock for the role. I might have slid out the side door had I known. Instead, with no fear, I just walked into Penny Marshall's office, enjoyed catching up with her, and then we got down to the reading.

To make sure I had the chops, I had memorized the lines and wisely hired an acting coach for a session. My coach gave me the best advice. She said, "Remember, they don't know who the character is until you bring it to them."

"Ready?" Penny said.

Going for it, I stood and became the character, adding a walk that wasn't mine. I leaned right toward Penny and asked, "How you doin', sweet thang?" My Britsloe was inspired by every club owner I'd ever met. Most of them had a kind of a raspy voice and were slick as hell.

Penny adlibbed back to me. I nodded and smiled, and said, "Good to see you. My name is Britsloe Jacobs," and I stuck out my hand. "So good to meet you."

Penny nodded with approval. Or so I guessed. Then she said, "Lionel, you do this very well, but you don't have much training as an actor, do you?"

"Well, yes, I do," I said, "I'm Black." She laughed and so did I. Yet, that's the truth for anyone who's had to learn to walk through doors that don't want to open, and try to make it look easy. It's called acting.

Soon after that, I was officially told I had the part. *Huh, so it was an audition, after all.*

We had a wonderful time shooting the scene. The set was a club, and me, Whitney, Denzel, Courtney Vance, and a bunch of other folks made work look like play. About five years later, I was asked who my favorite current singer was, and there was only one answer: "Whitney Houston, without a doubt."

I said it then and would today—that Whitney was an all-around entertainer, with a voice that was the best in the business. What I knew about her perfection I learned when we shot the scene of her singing "I Believe in You and Me" in the movie.

At the time, I said that Whitney was much bigger than most of us knew. She was effortless in her delivery and range. There was so much more to come, though I predicted, "Unfortunately, the music world will not appreciate her talents until, heaven forbid, she should pass."

I don't know if I had a premonition about losing Whitney too young. My comments would still hold, "Whitney's voice is a gift from God, she is music without end."

The best thing about doing the movie was that it reminded me that I was happiest with lots of irons in the fire. My ADHD needed it and, more and more, our lives required that. Who has the luxury to just do one thing? Better to hedge your bets. At one point, my kids got together and asked me what were the two major things I had liked about going to school. My answer was consistent, "Sandbox and recess." And if I had to add one that's more academic . . . gym.

That pretty much sums up my life.

I WENT BACK to the studio. And I loved being there. The deal with Diane was for me to focus on the creative part of music and not go on tours or do the Hollywood shuffle or leave town, with only a few exceptions, and I absolutely would not bring the Business home.

Per my contract with Mercury, in 1996, I delivered a labor of love of an album, *Louder Than Words*. Though it fell short of what it could have done (because of a changing array of executives), it was certified Gold and proved to my fans that I was alive and well—sounding in top shape vocally. I was happy to be evolving as an artist, and writing from such a deeply personal place, working not only with James Anthony Carmichael but with other producers like David Foster, as well as guys like Babyface and Jimmy Jam and Terry Lewis. Three of the songs on the album—"Don't Wanna Lose You," "Ordinary Girl," and "Still in Love"—were Top 10 R&B hits.

The next two albums on Mercury, *Time* (1998) and *Renaissance* (2000), were emotionally cathartic to write. And, again, they included songs that did well on the R&B charts.

At this point, tours boosted your standing on the charts, and they were the main way to make money. But there was no way I could sell that idea at home.

Technology—first Napster and then iPods and MP3 players—was changing the delivery system and process of monetizing recorded music forever. There was no longer an option for artists to make a living by releasing music without performing live.

Suddenly, we all began to question whether there would be a Business at all.

Around this same time, the Richie family had outgrown the bachelor pad on Oriole and I bought the big dream house that Diane and I could renovate together. While the remodeling took place, we rented a home in the flats of Beverly Hills.

That meant we needed the income stream to pay for all of it. At some point, I would have to be in the Business.

Diane didn't agree. Every time we discussed the reality, I understood her side and then I'd look over and see Sofia and see Miles, and then there was Nicole, eighteen years old, who was not just driving, but she and her best friend, Paris Hilton, were already trying to kill me.

This was even before the reality show *The Simple Life*—which was soon to be in the works. The premise was to do a reality show with a sitcom flavor. The inspiration was *Green Acres* with two likable but pampered young ladies from Beverly Hills having to function in small-town country living without their creature comforts.

Brenda and I, as ex-spouses, didn't talk a lot, but we remained committed to co-parenting, only, *Lawd, have mercy*, what hell awaited us as we tried to agree on the path of how best to raise a kid after *The Simple Life* made Paris and Nicole household names. We had no training for the daunting job of making sure our daughter would survive in Hollywood, California, as a star on a reality TV show.

It's hard to be a parent, let alone a divorced parent, whether you live in Birmingham, Alabama, or London, England. The only difference is that, in Hollywood, normal is anything that goes. We had years of train wrecks to anticipate.

THE PLOT THICKENS. For better or worse, I decide it's the ideal time—let's say when Miles is about four and Sofia is about one—to complicate my entire life.

The thought is, *Why not have a meeting in our living room with some managers because I'm thinking about getting back all the way into the Business?*

Did you hear that explosion?

I know I'm in trouble when Diane comes home, walks by the living room, and freezes. There is a full-on management meeting going on. The main advisor plotting the return of Lionel Richie to the global stage is Freddy DeMann—the

manager of Madonna and Michael Jackson and every superstar on the scene. We are not just walking in low. The plan
is for me to go flying right back at the highest altitude, full
speed ahead.

For as long as I live, I will never forget Diane's face as she
stood there. I went to her and she pulled me aside and asked,
"Lionel, who are all of these people in the living room?"

I told her their names and said something that came across
like total bullshit but let her know this was what was happening.

She listened and then turned to go down the hallway to our
bedroom.

I followed her to the door that she had closed behind her.
When I opened it, Diane was sobbing. To her, everything was
over that night.

*Maybe I don't hate the Business. Let me just do this. It doesn't
have to be the end.*

Whatever way you rationalize how it can hold together,
when you know it's broken, you know. The heaviness in the
house was overwhelming. If there had been a fight, it might
have been easier. Instead, it was sadness beyond words. She
knew what the next chapters were before I did. And, to her,
credit, she was the one who left me—which I found out about
on a flight back from London after one of the guys in the band
handed me a British newspaper that reported how we were
headed for divorce.

If it had been up to me, I would have forged on—with our
wonderful kids and everything—and just tried to make everyone happy, even if, in my heart of hearts, I was married to being
in the Music Business. She probably did us a favor by calling
the situation for what it was, though it was no less tragic. And
it was a painfully slow drip—death by a thousand cuts—for
the next four years until the end.

Sometimes I'd ask myself, *Did I ever hate the Business?* At one time I did. But was it because I loved Diane and was trying to please her, or because my father died, or because I just needed a time-out? All I know is that, it was true, I'd changed my mind.

I didn't want to have any regrets. Maybe that's selfish, but I don't think we live our lives in order to double-cross ourselves.

My discovery was that I could sink into another dark period, or I could wake one morning and realize, okay, if I didn't have this experience, who would I be?

When you fall in love, you don't start out trying to hurt somebody. I did not. Love deepens and evolves, and it becomes a story, an adventure, a movement, a change.

In the end, it became a tragedy, and it became a blessing. And when we moved on, a part of that love moved on with us, and another part remained.

Reinvention

(1999 to present)

"Let the music play on," would be my legacy.

—SKEET, A.K.A. LIONEL RICHIE

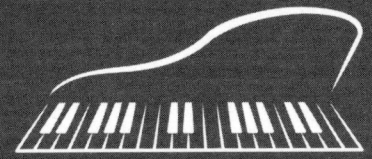

21

Citizen of the World

AT DIFFERENT TIMES IN MY life, I read a book or two.

Of course, that's an understatement.

But, I admit, for me to read a wordy, full-length book, it better hold my interest. There's my short attention span—which is not much longer than three minutes and forty-three seconds (the typical length of a recorded song) or about two pages worth of printed lyrics.

However, I've always been hungry for knowledge and the edge-of-your-seat, gripping stories you only find in great books. So, at some point, I decided that if I couldn't read all about it, I would go out into the world and discover as much as I could for myself—firsthand.

Guess what? Being in the music business was just my cover story.

Instead of being told about "those people," my mission would be to meet them in person and make up my own mind.

Hello!

That right there has been my passport.

At age fifty in the year 1999—and for the next dozen years—I reinvented myself in the mode of a modern-day explorer who so happened to be an entertainer. In the process, a new, most unlikely story began, as unlikely as what came before.

At some point in my travels, two books came highly recommended to me, and I read them both, start to finish. In many sittings. One of them was a self-help book called *The Road Less Traveled* by M. Scott Peck. The premise—and the first line—of the book is actually, "Life is difficult." Once you accept that truth, you are then able to transcend it.

This book helped me prepare more wisely for things I couldn't control. Because, after all, they were gonna happen anyway.

Self-reliance was the key. The world does not exist to be how you believe it must be for you. It just *is*. And to quote Richard Bach, "The original sin is to limit the *Is*. Don't."

That line was in his book, a novel, called, *Illusions: The Adventures of a Reluctant Messiah*. The story recalls the author's journey as a young man—in a setting that reminded me of the cornfields of Joliet, Illinois. Richard learns to fly a small plane after meeting up with an older character, a mechanic and self-described messiah, who teaches the secrets of how to defy the laws of gravity and reality. The people who pay for plane rides believe they're being saved from their earthly woes and beg Richard to stay longer, but all he wants to do is to go fly his plane. He doesn't want to be the savior; he wants us to be messiahs for ourselves, to remove the limitations on how far and how high we can fly.

And that, ladies and gentlemen, is called magic.

That was the theme of my life in my fifties. Not much about getting back in the airplane and learning to fly again was magical, trust me, but I tried never to take any of it for granted.

For most of the 1990s, I could count the times I performed publicly on my two hands. Then, in May 1999, before I had plans to tour again, I was on vacation in Jamaica with my family and had just climbed onto a Jet Ski—when my cell phone rang.

Buzzzzzz!!!

I'd already driven the Jet Ski a short distance from the shore. This could have been a disaster. *Except* . . . cell reception at the resort was terrible unless you got out on the water about two hundred feet.

"Hello?"

"Lionel! How are you? . . . *something something* . . ." as a man with a pronounced Italian accent asked me a question that I couldn't hear.

I zipped over to another spot and heard loud and clear that the person calling me was Luciano Pavarotti.

Did you hear that? I'm on a Jet Ski on a cell phone with bad reception with the legendary tenor, who is inviting me to perform in the upcoming benefit concert of Pavarotti and Friends, in Modena, Italy—his hometown. This is to be the sixth in a series of ten benefit concerts raising money for War Child, a nonprofit dedicated to helping orphans and children and refugees from war-torn places.

Mariah Carey is going to be there, as will B.B. King, Joe Cocker, Ricky Martin, Gloria Estefan, and others. This concert's focus is on kids and their families in Guatemala and Kosovo. Pavarotti says he would love if at the end of the concert I could lead everyone in singing "We Are the World."

"Absolutely."

He goes on, "In the concert I have all the artists sing a duet with me . . ."

I recall that the duets are of the artists' popular hits. "Yes, yes."

"And what I would like to sing with you is"—immediately I'm wondering if he'll choose "Easy" or "Hello," but instead of one of my better-known songs, Pavarotti continues—"a song that you write for me." He imagines something more classical to be performed together with the eighty-piece orchestra, a song that carries the emotional weight of the cause.

Lionel Richie has only one response: "Of course!" And then I get up off the floor—or off the side of the Jet Ski—after having a nervous breakdown.

This is so beyond next-level for a guy who can't read or write music, and now I'm going to compose a classical song to sing with Pavarotti as a duet. And I'm going to do it under a time crunch. One month.

For the next few days in Jamaica, I barely slept, and went straight to the Source, throwing myself into that creative cave on the Other Side, already filled with many voices calling out strands of melodies. Back at home, I took out a mirror, set it up near my keyboard, and hummed what I was hearing, then talked back to myself.

What do you think? Dah-da-dahhhhh—but where do I go next?

Sounds weird, I know, but there was no time to argue with the process.

Soon the melody took form. For Pavarotti I had to build to a peak in the music, as in the majestic "Nessun dorma" by Puccini. My song had to rise to that crescendo, that highest of impossible notes, and I almost had it. But at that peak, I needed a shift in the movement, where the two voices go apart and then back together. I also needed the lyrics tomorrow— because me and the cave dwellers had next to *nuth'n.*

I had to let go of the demand on myself to be the sole writer.

There was only one songwriting team, a husband and wife, who could deliver in this moment of need—Alan and Marilyn Bergman. I'm talking about the award-winning, brilliant duo, who, with Marvin Hamlisch, wrote "The Way We Were" for Barbra Streisand.

Alan and Marilyn composed the lyrics to my melody for the song "The Magic of Love":

> *And the winds are storming above*
> *Deep within the night we wonder*
> *If we've lost the magic of love*
> *But there's something inside us*
> *That looks to the sun*
> *We dream that this light will guide us*
> *With love for everyone . . .*
>
> *When the world is free of thunder*
> *And the skies are peaceful above*
> *Once again we'll know the wonder*
> *Of the magic power of love*
> *Oh, the magic of love*

Meanwhile, Walter Afanasieff—a powerhouse writer/producer who worked with everyone from Celine Dion to Mariah Carey—helped get me to the almighty crescendo changeup I'd been trying for. After arriving in Modena—two days before the concert—I had one day to present the song to Pavarotti and the next day to rehearse with him and the orchestra. He loved the song. Now came the shock that I'd written a melody with notes my voice couldn't hit.

Let me tell you about the magic of singing with Luciano Pavarotti. In his presence, you discover the voice that you never knew you had. When you are in harmony, hitting those notes becomes effortless.

I had no idea that our one rehearsal was all that we had before the concert the next day. And that concert would be recorded live for broadcast and for the record's release.

A voice of reason kicked in. Luciano Pavarotti knew what

he was doing—to give me time would have allowed me time to freeze up. The experience was a gift.

In 2003, I returned to Modena for the tenth and final Pavarotti and Friends concert, a benefit for the Iraqi people. Among the artists were Bono, Eric Clapton, Deep Purple, Queen, and Andrea Bocelli. Another amazing group.

Eric Clapton and I had crossed paths at different stages—both in the studio and socially—and as intense as he is, I always felt he understood me, picking up on my sense of humor, my Gemini personality. I'll never forget the time he made a toast in my honor, saying, "Here's to Lionel Richie, a great group of guys."

In Modena for this last concert, Pavarotti and I sang "The Magic of Love" again, this year with his verses translated into Italian.

The experience of both concerts gave me needed validation. This was also my version of taking the road less traveled, proving maybe I had some courage in me.

After a half century of living with self-doubt and fear, I had developed a new method for no longer being the kid afraid of his own shadow—thanks to lessons given to me by one of the original members of the Home-Boy Association, Howard Washington Kenney Jr.

REMEMBER THE REFRAIN from my parents and grandmother every time I tried to leave the house alone: "And who's going with you?" And you probably remember that all I had to do was mention Harold or Howard, and I was allowed to go.

Howard—whose family lived five doors up from us—had been my friend since preschool. He was the Home-Boy I confided in more than any other. Howard's mom was our Cub

Scout den mother. I was at the Kenneys' house practically every day.

Howard was perhaps the only friend who knew of my imaginary singing life as Sam Cooke. It was a secret, and as fellow Home-Boys, we were sworn to keep secrets to death. We must have been twelve or thirteen when a group of us went up to Deadman's Peak, as usual, and Howard confessed to me only that he thought about singing too.

He had a fantastic voice. And he wasn't shy like me. I knew Howard would be the one of us to make it big as a singer. I must have joked and said, "Okay, you try it out first and then if it works out I will too."

Cut to: Freshman year in college, and Howard put together a group called the Duponts, made up of four Tuskegee Institute students—himself, Tom Joyner, Killer Craig, and Shorty Miller.

Howard had the voice you'd die for, and the girls went crazy for him. He could have had his pick of any one of them. *Except* . . . Howard knew by this point that he was gay. Not a problem with me. But, man, I used to think if only I had his looks, I'd get all the girls.

There was a stretch when the Commodores went to Harlem and the Duponts came up to perform with us. We were their backing band during their sets, and they'd fill in for us vocally—because in those days Michael Gilbert was the only singer, and I was only doing my two or three songs. We almost merged, but the Duponts wound up having their own manager.

We went off on our separate journeys. Howard landed in Los Angeles, no longer a Dupont, when I was going solo, and came with me on the road—as my security blanket. If I ever said, "I can't do this" (whatever it was) or if he saw me being scared, he'd scream and holler: "What do you mean you 'can't'?! What do you mean you're scared?!"

"Why are you screaming at me, man?" I'd ask him.

"Because I'm mad at you!" Howard went on, "I'm screaming at you because I'm scared to death, and if I see you doing it, then I know I can do it!"

You see what he did there? He used my argument from childhood against me. He meant it. My victories became his.

When I went through the separation in my first marriage, Howard stayed in the guest room of my bachelor house. If I needed to escape somewhere, his first question before helping me book the trip was, "Warm weather or cold weather?" As my backup travel buddy, he'd tag along too.

Shortly before my dad's health began to fail, I became alarmed at how thin Howard had become. He had a hacking cough that really got my attention. "You gotta get that checked out, Howard," I urged him.

He said he would.

My hunch was it was serious. Cancer? Whatever it was, I didn't hold back from saying, "Why don't you go home and get checked out?" There were medical doctors in his family who would take care of him.

Howard wasn't big on that suggestion. If it got worse, he'd consider going home. He didn't call them either. Per the bylaws of our Home-Boy Association, which were for life, if he didn't want his parents to know something, I couldn't tell them. We keep secrets up to death.

Yet an intervention was in order.

Under the pretense of going to visit my family, I flew to Tuskegee but arranged a meeting with Howard's parents.

When I got to the Kenney household, his mom met me at the door. She hugged me and then I couldn't wait, I just blurted it out. "I just want you to know that Howard is sick . . ."

She nodded. "Yes, we know, Howard has AIDS. . . ." Nothing prepared me for that. I remember losing my balance.

This was the late 1980s and there was talk of the epidemic

as a death sentence. Yet very few reports told how fast people were dying.

When I went back to LA, devastated, I tried to keep Howard comfortable at the bachelor house, and to find help—*we can pay for it, money can fix it*—but to no avail.

Other than the time when we lost Kathy Faye LaPread, I had never been in close proximity to a friend my age whose death was in sight.

As helpless as I felt—as we all felt—I couldn't let Howard see me afraid. He was afraid, of course, and so the only offering I could make was to take this ride with him, and to allow for many heartfelt, difficult conversations. He was both a best friend and a Home-Boy for life. No one could tell me what the final days were going to be, and at a certain point, I had to go to Paris, but it was going to be a quick turnaround.

He said he was feeling good. "I'll see you as soon as you get back," he said.

Two nights later, I called from Paris to check in. Howard asked, "How was the show?" He sounded tired. I knew we'd see each other in a few days, so I signed off, not thinking that would be the last conversation.

Howard died the following night, before I could get back.

If I had my way, nobody would leave. I began the grown-up task of understanding that when you hurt so deeply it's because you love so deeply.

In the coming years, with the pileup of losses and changes, I realized that when the worst is happening, there is little time left over to be afraid. And honestly, we are here for such a short time, giving in to fear is a waste. That's when I started to do the exercise that Howard taught me: Let me go for the adventure and get past the fear, so somebody else can feel less fearful too.

And one day, when I was wishing that I could tell my friend what I had done, I looked up at the window of where I was living, alone, at the time, and right at the window, staring right into my face, was a hummingbird.

Oh! I have always loved hummingbirds. The first thing that popped into my head was, "Hi, Howard, nice to see you."

From that day on, until today, I've seen the hummingbird I know as Howard everywhere I've lived. I know it's not the same hummingbird but, now and then, a little poetic license is in order.

FOR MUCH OF the early 2000s, home was Europe.

Fate—operating through Barrie Marshall of the UK, who ran tours for Paul McCartney, Elton John, Sade, Cher, and Pink—flipped an opportunity back to me that had been given to Tina Turner in 1984. Barrie had been the one to ask for Tina to open on my earlier tour, and now, in 2000, he asked Tina about my opening the first leg of her *Twenty Four Seven* tour—which was four months in the US and Canada before moving to the UK.

The North American portion of the tour became the top grossing for the year—with $80.2 million in earnings. The reviews took me a bit by surprise—like the part in *The Cap Times* after the show in Madison, Wisconsin, the second stop on the tour:

Lionel Richie opened the show, on the comeback trail after years spent somewhere other than on the pop charts. He was welcomed back with open arms by a very enthusiastic audience as he performed an audience-friendly collection of his hits.

Richie looked and sounded so good that he may have spent the last decade in the cryogenic freezer next to

Walt Disney. He seemed unabashedly happy to be back on stage, as he got the crowd dancing with his up-tempo hits ("Dancing on the Ceiling," "All Night Long") and swaying with his ballads ("Hello," "Stuck on You"). Best of all, he resurrected some insanely funky old Commodores hits like "Brick House."

My first reaction was, "Comeback?" And I wasn't too sure about the reference to being on ice like Walt Disney. But thank God nobody was writing, "Lionel *who?*"

Most artists would say that when you go off-grid and then return, you are starting from the bottom. I never felt that way. Tina and I were just soulmates, willing to reinvent when necessary, homies for life.

I'm not saying it was a walk in the park—not with the con artists and rumor mongers who do not have your best interests at heart. I felt safe just venting to Tina Turner without fear of judgment.

"Tina! Did you see what they wrote about me?" The second divorce was not finalized, but it wouldn't have been so ugly if it weren't for the tabloids.

I'd read those papers and think, "Who are those cartoon people?"

Tina helped me lighten up. She told me much more about what she went through when she left Ike, and I understood that every time she danced on the stage, she was stomping on the embers of everything that she'd conquered.

The *Twenty Four Seven* tour was supposed to be her last. But she changed her mind and came back in 2008/2009 for her 50th Anniversary tour, at age sixty-nine. And then she was done. She made it to the point where she was clear. She got tired of the dance. She could have released an album called *Tired, Worn Out, and Sick of This Shit Dancer*. Tina had found her husband—who loved her beyond words—and then she fully retired in Zurich.

In 2021, when finally the Rock & Roll Hall of Fame invited her to be inducted on her own, without Ike, she said, "I can't make it." Tina Turner had lived one of the most iconic stories of all time—not just as a survivor but as a creative force of nature.

When the news came later that she passed away in the summer of 2023, I had just come home from an early screening of the documentary, then untitled, about the making of "We Are the World." I had just been looking at her on the big screen and listening to her sing her line, "We are all a part of God's great big family," and cracking up at an outtake of Tina, forty-five years old, sexy as ever, calling out at 3:30 in the morning for, "Fish burger, fish burger!" She was badass to the bone.

I was brokenhearted that she didn't live long enough to see herself in footage that had never been shown before. Then again, she made it to eighty-three.

The saddest fact was that I couldn't say the same about everyone I loved and knew well.

SOMETIMES WHEN THE cell phone buzzes it rattles my nerves. You suspect it's not good news. In July 2000, I had just left the second UK show of my own summer tour and was headed to Switzerland for the Montreux Jazz Festival when my sister called.

Deborah's voice shook as she described why she had brought Mom to the hospital in Montgomery and that she was admitted to the ICU with a serious mystery infection.

There was only one thing to do if she took a turn for the worse—call everyone and cancel the tour. When I explored the possibility of doing that, I didn't need to be reminded of what Barrie Marshall had said when he promised, "This is the tour that will bring you back to Europe."

Canceling would be a problem. But if this was the end of my mother's life, I would never forgive myself if I wasn't at her side.

I talked it over with Barrie, and agreed to stay on tour for the time being and closely monitor her health. At any point, if Mom's condition worsened, I'd cancel and be on the first plane home.

Deborah gave me constant updates. After a week, thank God, Mom improved. Another two weeks went by, with some progress. After two months, our mother was able to go home.

Those first weeks, though—in England, Switzerland, and Italy—were the best and worst of times. The tour was a smash everywhere, but it was painful from the moment I walked off-stage to the moment I walked back onto the stage the next night. Was it worth it? Absolutely, because these were the dates that solidified my touring status in Europe for the next decade.

In the meantime, Alberta Foster Richie defied all the original predictions, and I was able to go spend quality time with her. When I was hit by the finality of her death at the age of eighty-three in January 2001, I experienced a kind of shock that I had never felt—not when Dad died in 1990, not when Grandma passed away in 1996. Both of those losses were devastating. But in both cases, Mom was still with us, the anchor.

Unlike my dad, who outlived his outrage over my chosen profession only to become my biggest promoter, my mother's pride was quieter, more understated. Yet it was strong and constant. She was a force in her own way. Without her, I wouldn't have known how to structure a song. And even more important, Alberta Richie, the educator and principal who never gave up on me, was always right there in the front row of my journey. She never gave up on any young person, the example set so that I too could one day champion and teach other creative kids like me.

IN THE MID-2000S, in places where there were serious divides within the population, I kept hearing a particular phrase that went something like, "We don't agree on anything except for you."

That was flattering but I couldn't have explained what it was about me that prompted such a response. One of the first times I heard that phrase was at a UNESCO meeting where I'd been invited to perform and to speak about the power of music in bridging differences. In attendance were representatives from Middle Eastern countries, including Israel, Egypt, Jordan, and others. In the afternoon I was invited to a tea party, and I had to ask, "I know why you all are here, but what am I doing here?" The answer was that I was the only person who everyone could agree on.

Then it started to dawn on me that my songs were not written for one group of folks versus another. Maybe the message of "I know how you feel" was the bridge.

Then I heard more accounts from a *Nightline* reporter who had visited Iraq in the years after the American operations began there. He interviewed me before writing his piece, which described how people on the streets were talking about the war, democracy, and me:

> Grown Iraqi men get misty-eyed by the mere mention of his name. "I love Lionel Richie," they say. Iraqis who do not understand a word of English can sing an entire Lionel Richie song.

This was very humbling, although the piece pointed out that I was mostly famous to Americans at the time for being the father of Nicole Richie of *The Simple Life*. Nobody in the US understood how I could become an Iraqi icon. On the other hand, when the reporter mentioned to me that Nicole was not as famous in Iraq as I was, my response was, "I'll be sure to tell her that she needs to work harder."

One of the craziest stories I heard came from a commanding officer of American forces who were among the first to go into Baghdad in March 2003. They came up with the idea of showing goodwill by putting speakers on top of their Humvees and then rolling into Baghdad playing "Dancing on the Ceiling." But in the dark hours, as tanks rolled in playing that song, the American and allied troops realized—wait—they were being greeted by another song. From dusk until dawn, local Iraqi citizens blasted "All Night Long" even louder. I heard that side of the story from Iraqi leaders as well.

The American commander I met said it was an unplanned moment of Richie meeting Richie.

If my music was the one thing that could be agreed upon and was believed to belong to everyone, who was I to argue? It gets more interesting. When the US began its drawdown from Iraq, the aviation regiment designed a stencil of my face that was displayed on all kinds of gear and even on a CH-47 Chinook helicopter. To this day, whenever that same Chinook is used by the national guard and other units to deliver supplies for disaster-relief in the United States, my face is still on it.

How cool is that?

I'm not saying that becoming a citizen of the world was without some hair-raising moments.

In 2005, for instance, I was invited to attend and perform at the World Economic Forum in Jordan. Accompanied by a small group of crew members and musicians, I stepped off the plane and saw a few town cars waiting to drive us some distance to the hotel where we would stay and perform.

Picture this: Armed guards, not just at the airport but stationed along both sides of the road into the desert. There's not even a crack in the wall of uniformed guards as far as the eye can see.

I'm sitting up in the front passenger seat of the lead car to be able to see where we are going. The driver explains that the guards are there to prevent any attempts at setting roadside bombs.

Halfway to our destination, we reach a major checkpoint—a military tank on an embankment with a guard in combat gear on top of the tank. We stop. Not sure what's supposed to happen, I see there's a fellow in uniform—the commander—approaching us. He walks around to the driver, who lowers his window.

The commander stands there and says two words: "Your papers?"

The driver looks at me, and I turn around to the guys in back, part of our detail. "Anybody got any papers?"

Nobody has papers. He doesn't mean passports, he means something else. We call our other people in the two cars behind us. No papers. My nerves kick in. We're all freaked out.

The commander glares at the driver, then walks around to the front passenger window. It's tinted dark, and so he taps on the glass.

I lower the glass and look right at him.

He looks at me and leans closer. *Pause.* I take a breath.

And a whimsical look appears on the commander's face as he sings, "Hello. . . Is it me you're looking for?" Then he turns to all the guards around him at the checkpoint and he almost cries, "Lionel Richie . . . *aaaaaaahhhhh!*"

A chorus echoes him, "Lionel Richie???!!!!" followed by more crying out of *"Aaaaaaaahhhhh!"*

I don't know if this sound is a word or an expression, but it's being echoed by everyone.

The commander is overjoyed. "Welcome home," he says to me and invites me and the rest of my people to step out and take pictures with all the guards who come running.

What finally tells me we're safe is when the armed guard in the helmet on top of the tank climbs down to come get his picture taken. After fifteen minutes or so, the commander assembles a caravan of cars to escort us to the hotel.

Sometimes I miss going under the radar, but if ever there was a time to have a recognizable face, when I needed to look like Lionel Richie, that was it.

I LEARNED A lot about the qualities of leadership from observing Andrew Young, the Civil Rights activist, US ambassador to the UN, congressman, and mayor of Atlanta who brought seventy billion dollars of investment to the city and helped spark a movement of Black entrepreneurship. Not only a mentor but a dear friend, Ambassador Young set the example that if you want to inspire others to listen to you as a leader, you look for meaningful ways to enhance their lives.

I liked the concept but wondered if music could really do that.

An answer came to me one day in this era while I was at a resort in Sardinia, sitting by the pool overlooking the Mediterranean, on my way to play a private engagement.

In the harbor below us were several beautiful, large yachts, most of them bearing flags of their home countries. Many of the diplomatic delegations from different nations sailed here, lowered anchor, and would come by smaller boat, spend the day at the resort, and then return to sleep on the yachts at night.

As I was looking out, a gentleman approached, apologized for the interruption, but wanted to tell me something important. Before I could respond, his wife hurried over, with kids in tow.

Next thing I knew, he took out a little wallet with his wedding photos—"You see my wife and I, at our wedding? She came down the aisle to your song, 'Truly.'"

As I admired their wedding photos, a second man approached and said, "I don't want to interrupt but I had to tell you, my wife and I"—and he beckoned his wife over—"we love you." Now they took out their wedding photos, and she said, "Your song 'Truly' was playing when my father walked me down the aisle."

The first couple laughed and relayed that we had just been having the same conversation. Now the two families were admiring each other's wedding photos.

Everyone was delightful and thanked me so much for taking the time to speak to them.

Once they all walked away, the hotel manager hurried over and said, "Oh, my God, I've never seen that before in the history of this hotel."

"What are you talking about?"

He pointed to two of the yachts. One of them belonged to the first couple—from Lebanon, he believed—and was protected by heavy security. The second yacht was part of the Israeli delegation, also with a good deal of security.

Both families had been coming to this resort every summer for years. They had never spoken to each other. They would eat on different sides of the restaurant and their kids had nothing to do with one another. Now they were laughing and be-coming friends, sharing something in common.

Maybe music could do that. Yes, I was honored to be in-cluded in their life stories, to be welcomed as a member of their families. Even better was getting to be part of the connection the two families now found with each other. If that's what a love song could do, I was not about to quit my day job.

SOME DAYS AREN'T like other days.

A prime example took place in 2006 when I received a request from the State Department to be one of three international art-ists to take part in a peace concert in Libya on the twentieth anniversary of the US bombing of Libya. On that occasion Muammar Gaddafi's adopted infant daughter, Hanna, had been killed. The Peace Day had been named for her.

Now Gaddafi wanted to return to the world order with a concert. The request for me to perform in Tripoli had come from Gaddafi himself—through his daughter Aisha, a lawyer I had met before in London.

The relations between the US and Libya had been poison-ous for years. This was not an attempt to erase the pain of the bombing or the downing of the American flight long believed to have been caused by Libya. After mulling the pros and cons of going, I decided—why not go and get a sense of the reality on the ground for myself?

When I called Barrie Marshall to ask if he would be able to recommend someone who knew how to get me in and out of Libya alive, he didn't waste a moment. "I've got the perfect person."

Mark Hamilton, originally from Scotland, reminded me of James Bond. Mark had been on the security side of massive entertainment and sports events since the 1970s. His main job at the time was as Sir Paul McCartney's security director, but, luckily, he was available.

In planning, Mark did all the advance work, from arrival to departure—the intelligence gathering, tapping the right contacts at the State Department, the British Embassy. He explained that there were two main aspects of going into really foreign territory, where there were hidden risks: 1) assessing the potential of something going wrong, and 2) planning for how to get out safely and quickly.

As soon as we touched down—in an airfield frozen in time with aircraft and tanks strewn around, dating to the 1950s or so—I was met by Libyan security forces, all men in black. My apprehensions vanished as I exited the plane and was greeted as a son of Africa. The lead officer said, "Welcome home." They then proceeded with a ceremonial washing of my feet.

Everything ran smoothly, except for one huge oversight made by my manager at the time who had said, "Call me when you land"—which I found out was impossible as there was no cell service. Still not a reason for alarm but I was not naïve. You had to be aware. You could say the wrong thing and suddenly weapons would be drawn.

On the way to the Corinthia Hotel, the only place to stay, I was told by an American delegate from the planning committee that there had not been a visitor from our country since 1957.

At the hotel we were met by a manager who was surprised when I asked if it was possible to do some sightseeing the next day before the show. What I recall most—beyond the fact that Tripoli was only coming back to life after many long years of war—were the miles and miles of untouched, stunning white beaches, like Miami back in the day. We went to the gold market and took a tour of the mosques, and everywhere I went the people spoke to me in English, calling out to thank me for coming to perform for Hanna Peace Day.

When we left for the performance being held in Gaddafi's massive compound in the middle of Tripoli, Mark Hamilton gave me the layout in detail. The huge stage was positioned in the center, outdoors, surrounded by one thousand chairs, in front of the ruins of the house that had been bombed twenty years earlier.

The only answer Mark had been given as to whether I would be meeting Colonel Gaddafi was, "We don't know."

Mark mentioned an unusual-looking rock he found near the stage. As he bent to investigate, his escort sharply told him, "We need to move on." He realized the rock was a recording device. There were several of these rocks planted nearby.

"Good to know," I mumbled. In case I had any state secrets to share with anybody.

The compound itself was like a movie set for an outdoor concert under a starlit sky and a full moon. There were huge tents and palm trees spread out like painted scenery, and the occasional camel strolling by.

My only really uncomfortable moments came before the band and I went onstage, during the performance of Spanish opera singer José Carreras. Every time he finished a musical number I heard loud popping sounds over the otherwise polite applause. When I asked, I was informed that was gunfire—a customary form of audience approval.

In the Arab world, I knew well, there is a taboo against any man touching any woman in public, but when I was being introduced by Gaddafi's daughter Aisha, I walked onto the stage and she hugged me. And I hugged her back—as if we were in London meeting on the street.

There was a hush among the audience of various dignitaries, mostly male. Was this an international incident? No, it soon passed. I started the show with, "Hello, Libya!" and we began to play.

The night was spectacular. Before long, we got the party going and everyone started singing along, many coming up onto the stage with me and dancing as I sang. We could have been anywhere in the world.

At the final bow, I heard a chorus of "Thank you!" and "We love you."

Many of the people in Gaddafi's inner circle lived in these mansion-sized Bedouin tents some distance from the stage. My understanding was that no one ever knew which was the tent where Colonel Gaddafi stayed. Mark and I both thought at one point that we saw a figure standing next to the tent that was closest to us, though far enough away that we couldn't tell if it was him or not.

The clue was that Gaddafi was known to have female body-guards and we both saw a small team of women in military outfits near the figure we had spotted. If it was him, that would have made sense, that he had stepped outside to hear the music and have a look.

Once my show finished, we returned to the hotel. What I did not know, and what Mark Hamilton did not know, is that we both had quietly arranged our own plan Bs for getting out of the country fast, in case anything happened. My backup plan was to secretly pay the pilot of our private jet to stay posted close by in case we needed to leave earlier than scheduled.

This is where the plotlines got twisted. When we arrived at the airport, there was no plane. The pilot—who had been waiting for me to call on the cell phone if we needed him sooner—didn't know there was no cell service!

Mark Hamilton was cool as a cucumber. Not me. The sweat poured from me as I panicked. At the last minute, our jet appeared on the tarmac, the pilot waving madly, and we boarded the jet and flew back to London. My revelation was a new understanding of the wrongs of war based on religion.

If my travels taught me anything, it was that God has many names. He or She can be called God or the Almighty or the Universe or the Great Spirit. We call to Jesus Christ or Buddha or Allah or Jehovah—depending on where we grew up and what we were taught. None of those named, I am certain, would have us seek to destroy our fellow human beings.

Years passed before I had an occasion to run into Mark Hamilton—just as a friend and I were coming out of a hotel somewhere. He spotted me first, and as I turned to him, there was that James Bond smile.

I introduced Mark to my friend and said, "See this guy. He was the security wizard who we hired to get me out of trouble when I went to Libya."

My friend was impressed. "What happened?"

I joked, "Oh, he didn't have to do anything. He was just along for the occasion."

Mark grinned and then said, "Well, the guy with the fishing boat down in the harbor and ten grand in his pocket might beg to differ."

Seems that Mark had secured an escape route by boat to Italy or Cypress if we had encountered any real trouble. And that's when I realized that my plan—which almost backfired—didn't qualify me to work in secret intelligence. So much for that as an option.

AN ENGAGEMENT IN Egypt, when I was hired to perform at a private event for a thousand people in Cairo, gave me a chance to hire Mark again. In this instance, the main security issue was that the female guests rushed the stage, clapping and singing along, causing the male guests to become extremely upset.

Mark wound up having to calm the men down. He began, "It's okay, this is normal. It's just the excitement. This always happens."

The men were not calmed.

Mark tried again. "Everything is fine. Go back to your seats, your wives will come back." Finally, he said, "Lionel is quite shy in person. He means no disrespect."

That saved us from an international incident.

This trip to Cairo was not my first, however. In August 1999, when I was rarely on the road, I couldn't miss the chance to travel to Egypt for a show on a stage that was to be built in the desert for three thousand spectators—in front of the Pyramids of Giza. In front of the Great Sphinx to be precise.

Because it was excruciatingly hot during the day, we had to rehearse at 1 a.m. the night before. It was on that early morning, as I will never forget, that I saw the most incredible sight of a twelve-year-old boy walking along the side of the road, leading his camel with a rope in one hand and holding a bucket of water in his other hand. If I looked over his shoulder back toward Cairo and civilization, there was a completely modern sight—though the buildings seemed tarnished, in need of upkeep. But up ahead, in front of the kid and his camel, were the Pyramids and the Great Sphinx. These massive, ancient structures looked in better shape than Cairo, yet they had been there for thousands of years. They had stood the test of time. I remember having to stop what I was doing and just take in the two different worlds in one view.

When I returned on that brief trip eight or nine years later with Mark Hamilton, I was determined to go back and get a closer look at the Pyramids of Giza again.

Mark arranged for a car and we set off, only to be stopped on the way because of renovations at the time. We managed to get permission for me to walk up to the largest pyramid by myself.

I walked slowly up the sand, as close as I could get without encroaching on any of the structure, considered to be the oldest of the Seven Wonders of the World.

I have never, before or since, experienced that kind of silence. It was surround-no-sound. No wind, no birds, no movement anywhere, no voices inside of me, no melodies asking to be sung.

There was just the sound of my heartbeat and my own breathing.

22

Coming Home

BEING A LOVING, SUPPORTIVE DAD has always been central to my identity. But the truth is that I was away a lot, missing all kinds of special events in my kids' lives. That was the trade-off— having a relevant career and being a good provider or spending more time just being dad.

I will forever give it up to both of my exes for being strong, loving, and devoted moms. Nicole and Brenda were two peas in a pod from the start. Miles and Sofia adore Diane, as she adores them both.

The comedy part of my dad act is that every time I had them staying with me or if we had plans together, I put so much effort into being the grown-up leader, a father figure who would give them structure and boundaries—and all they would do is laugh. They treated me like a kid like them. Sometimes they'd call their moms, complaining that *Dad has no clue!*

Not true! But I have always felt a sense of guilt for not being home enough, especially when I was most needed.

Nicole once corrected me during an interview. "I wish you wouldn't say that," she said. "You were always there when I needed you."

In this era, my divorce with Diane was final, and I made the most of my time with Miles and Sofia, who were nine and five. They were the most curious, most interested two little humans. In their younger days, they really loved my stories, and for a while could hear them more than once. As time went on, of course, I'd hear, "Okay, Dad we know that story."

One day little Sofia, no bigger than a morsel, got a ring in her Cracker Jack box and said, "Here, Daddy, now you have this ring, and I can marry you."

"Absolutely."

"Don't lose it."

"Never!" I got a chain and wore that tiny ring on the chain for a while until I realized I needed to wear a ring from Miles and one from Nicole. Those are the three rings I continue to wear on a chain around my neck to this day.

If you want to know who I am, that's it in three rings.

I WROTE, I recorded, I toured. In 2006 and 2007, I was on the road for stretches of time—mostly overseas—promoting *Coming Home*. The album's "I Call It Love" was one of the biggest singles that charted for me in the US in a long time.

Though the plan was to travel less, there was no way to turn down an invitation to play two concerts in postapartheid South Africa and attend a summit meeting with Nelson Mandela.

Eighteen years earlier, the call that we'd been praying for had come—the announcement that Mandela was being released from prison after twenty-seven years. His crime, as a lawyer, had been to speak out and oppose the corrupt regime of apartheid. And then, in June 1990, we learned he was coming to the United States to rally support for the cause of freedom. I'd been asked to help out with a Los Angeles reception for Mandela—Madiba, our father, as he is known in South Africa. My assignment was to go with his wife, Winnie Mandela, to buy him clothing suitable for the major media coverage he would have and the many events planned for him.

Other celebrities and activists were contributing by paying for the plane and the hotel, and so forth, but the Richies were going to take care of a day of shopping at Neiman Marcus and Saks Fifth Avenue.

Winnie had never experienced anything like getting to walk into those department stores and go to the men's department to pick out power suits. We were careful to select them in two sizes, just to be sure. She ran from counter to counter, pointing to socks and button-down shirts and shoes and belts. Then she and Brenda went to pick out dresses and women's suits for her. Every time she made a selection, her eyes grew large as she'd ask, "Do you really think I can have this? Is it possible?"

It was just a joy to feel like I had a magic wand in my hand—also known as a credit card.

When I went to the reception that night, I did not expect to be able to receive an introduction to Mandela. It would be enough to stand in the back and hear him speak. The ballroom was overflowing with prominent folks from every walk of life—with lines of people waiting to meet him.

Winnie spotted me, and unbelievably, she took Nelson Mandela by the hand, weaving through the crowd—saying "Excuse me" and "I beg your pardon"—and brought him, the guest of honor, directly to where I was standing in the back.

"Nelson," she said to her husband, "it's Lionel Richie."

I was stunned. Unprepared. I shook his hand and stammered, "It's . . . it's . . . so good to meet you, sir. You are an inspiration."

No air was in the room. I was in awe of his composure and presence, his lack of bitterness and defeat, even after that many years in prison.

"Young man," Nelson Mandela said to me, "I want to thank you for your lyrics and your music. Your songs got me through many years while I was in prison."

I was at a loss, so I did something incorrect. I hugged him. And it was as if I was stepping into his aura—at once huge and also familiar. I felt that I was hugging my father, as if I had been hugging Mandela my whole life. And then I started to cry.

"I'm sorry," I apologized, and then hugged him more, leaning my head on his shoulder and weeping. It was a family member hug, as if he was comforting me. He was a father to all of us.

We remained friends throughout his time as President of South Africa, which lasted until 1999. And so in 2008, when I was invited to go to South Africa to meet with world leaders and him, as well as to perform there for the first time, I couldn't wait to see him again.

Days before my departure, my assistant buzzed me on the intercom. "Mr. Richie," he said, "I have Madonna on line one for you. And Nelson Mandela on line two."

How 'bout that for a life mantra? *Nelson Mandela on line two!*

"Tell Madonna I'll have to call her right back," I said, because she and I talked often since we shared the same manager. I went for line two.

"Madiba," I began, telling him how excited I was to come to the meeting.

"I understand you are supposed to come with the delegation to the economic investment meeting, but I don't want you to attend it." I was disappointed until he explained that he wanted to have time to spend just with me, without the larger group.

We met at the Nelson Mandela Museum and spent the most extraordinary part of a day as he showed me around, giving me an education in his journey and legacy, with breaks to sit and talk. I came away from our exchange with an awareness that Madiba understood the power of forgiveness. He could have carried the bitterness forever. He didn't allow it to deter him, to keep him from showing people a better future. With forgiveness he had been able to lead a country forward.

I can't help but wish that we could just take a page out of Madiba's lesson plan that he left us, to learn to see the world as it is, and to see the possibilities for what we can accomplish together.

WHEN GRANDMA DIED in 1996 at the age of 103, I assumed that the mystery identity of her father, my great-grandfather, was to remain unsolved forever. And then, in 2011, at a time in my life when I was thinking how meaningful it would be to my kids to know about their ancestors, I got a call from a producer of the TV show *Who Do You Think You Are?*, inviting me to appear in return for uncovering the missing pieces of my family puzzle. I couldn't say yes fast enough.

The story began in Nashville, Tennessee, with a diary belonging to a white plantation owner, Dr. Morgan Brown. In 1839, the eighty-year-old Dr. Brown wrote of the impending birth of a baby to Mariah—who, it was clear, belonged to him as a slave. My assumption is that Dr. Brown had fathered her child and that he truly loved Mariah. That baby was christened John Louis Brown. In Dr. Brown's will he stipulated that Mariah and John Louis be given their freedom upon his death. Mariah was to be given a portion of his land and property, while the child was to inherit money for his education.

There he was—John Louis Brown, Adelaide's father, my great-grandfather. When he married Volenderver in 1890, she was fifteen years old and he was fifty-one. Three years later Adelaide was born. Now, J. L. Brown had already lived a remarkable life, having risen to prominence as the head of a Black fraternal order, the Knights of Wise Men. The group promoted education, moral virtues, and civic engagement; members could buy life insurance—in the days when few if any white banking institutions would sell to African Americans.

Volenderver and J. L. Brown divorced when Adelaide was a toddler—which may explain why Grandma said so little about him. Perhaps she wasn't keeping him a secret. She might not have known him. She might not have known he had moved to Chattanooga during hard times.

First there was a smallpox epidemic that depleted his insurance company's coffers. Then there was a theft by an officer, and Jim Crow laws making it harder for Black fraternal orders.

J. L. Brown lived to age ninety-one. At the time of his death, in 1931, he was employed—get this—as a gardener and groundskeeper at Pleasant Gardens, Chattanooga's African American cemetery. When I saw his photograph, I saw his resemblance to me—same shape of our forehead and a similar expression in the eyes. Could there have been a connection, an inheritance, in the love for gardening and groundskeeping that has been my passion for the past thirty years of my life? The connection made sense to me.

When I visited my great-granddaddy's burial place—somewhere in the leaf-strewn "paupers" section of Pleasant Gardens—I grieved that there had been no one to help pay for a headstone, that he left this world without knowledge of what became of his daughter, or her children, or their children. Yet he was remembered in a Chattanooga directory of important members of the Black community—for encouraging young people to get an education, to strive for wisdom, freedom, and equal access to the American Dream.

After the show's taping, I rushed home to tell the kids of my discovery, and how it's never too late to learn your history. We are not lone travelers in a life disconnected from the ones who came before us. I wanted my children and grandchildren to know that the reality of our lives was thanks to our ancestors' dreams and prayers for us—and to remember and honor them, always.

INTO MY EARLY sixties, I faced a long-overdue truth. The Business was a youth-driven marketplace. Was I a cool cat with the latest pickup lines? No, and I had never been.

After several years of not being married, though, I accepted that maybe fame was a way to compensate for being shy. Instead of having to walk across the room to introduce myself, the room usually walks over to me.

And what is the opening line the girl says? "I love you."
What do I do?
While she's hugging on me, she says, "Have you met my husband?"

The husband goes, "She loves you."

Then she says, "And I'm going to give you a kiss."

And her husband goes, "Please, man, give her a kiss."

This has nothing to do with me, except that I just went from shy to . . . *Wait a minute, hold it, wait* . . . "Somebody come get your wife! Somebody come get your girlfriend!"

The bottom line is that from "Sweet Love" in 1975 on, for the next fifty years and counting, there's a question I never get asked: "What's your rap?" The songs do it.

They were the same songs that got me into rooms with world

leaders and behind enemy lines in the middle of conflicts. Not to mention the untold numbers of guys getting laid and even married on words I've been singing.

You are welcome.

This is to confess, artfully, that there were certainly love interests in my life in these years. Had I stopped being an incurable, hopeless romantic? No, there was no cure. That said, I did not see myself as ready to settle down yet, if ever. My track record was not the best.

But you know, it's hard to shake our younger selves. Probably the reason I survived that habit was my security/father figure, Bobby Adams, who started working for me when I went solo. Dad was so impressed with Bobby that he said, "I'm going to deputize you to take care of my son." For twenty years, Bobby had one phrase for keeping me out of trouble. He'd come up and tell me, "Say good night, Cap'n."

Career-wise, I still thought about a backup plan, as I once mentioned to Jay Cooper, my first lawyer after becoming a solo artist, who handled everything legally for "We Are the World." In all sincerity, I said, "I might need to go to law school if my career goes off the rails."

Jay said, "You could never be an attorney. You're too sensitive." Good thing he didn't say it was a little late to rethink my day job.

But everyone in music had to rethink their careers right then. Tower Records filed for bankruptcy in 2006. Seeing the sign come down on Sunset Boulevard was like being at a funeral. There was a time when you'd make thirty million dollars if you were the writer, arranger, producer, publisher, and artist selling mechanical units. Please, that's five checks before you leave the house. But no more.

The Business had become exhibit A for "Who moved my cheese?"

My saving grace was that I was battle-tested enough to know that it was never a question of *if* you're going to get robbed, but only *when* they would rob you. They love to cheer you on, they love to get you in trouble, and then they love to buy your estate for a dollar and a quarter.

Who do you trust?

I wasn't sure. When I started to feel like it was time to warm myself by the fires of the younger generation, many of the ones who had been inspiring us all were gone.

WE ARE NOT supposed to outlive our peers and loved ones who are younger. Our psyches feel betrayed. Even when there were warning signs.

I talked to Luther Vandross—*What a voice!*—about a collaboration not long before he died in 2005, at age fifty-four, from multiple health complications. Likewise, I kept meaning to co-write with George Michael, with his pure Pop voice and hit songwriting. His death at age fifty-three in 2016 from heart and liver disease was a shock.

In 2012, Whitney Houston, forty-eight, was found dead in a bathtub—an accidental drowning, complicated by heart disease and cocaine. Four years later came the incomprehensible news of Prince's death from what was called an accidental overdose of fentanyl, an opioid he may have thought was Vicodin. My mind went immediately to—*Why?* Why didn't we know? Was his need for privacy a deterrent to getting the right help?

Michael Jackson was the one who told me—when we were sitting there as kids—that we would be immune to all the things that can bring you crashing down.

In 2009, when I heard he died, I heard him talking to me and saw that twelve-year-old, the way he looked into the future and only saw his vision of being bigger than big, always certain that he was protected from the bad and terrible things that could go wrong.

Michael promised: "We're never going to let that happen to us, Lion-*nel*." It was by no accident that he called his home Neverland.

What happened? Pain.

There was the fire that happened on the set of his Pepsi commercial shoot, the pain of the issues with his nose and the surgeries, the pain of having too much success, the pain of not learning the lessons of adulthood because of a lost childhood. There was the pain of not being able to hang, as hard as he tried to have the regular life he never could have or understand. He couldn't put the pieces of a normal life together, and so he retreated to a life of fantasy and make-believe—a world he created and lived in.

There was also the pain of not being recognized as the king, because even if you named yourself the King of Pop, and took pictures of yourself with a crown, sitting on a throne, you were still Black—and you never would be [fill in the blank] enough, and Elvis, no matter what, was forever the king. I know that ate at Michael, though it didn't kill him. What killed him, I believe, came down to the medications and to loneliness. And his death was wrong and tragic and shocking.

The memorial service was at the then–Staples Center, televised for the millions and millions of fans around the world who could honor him as the greatest entertainer of our time, and let his family feel that love.

Among the speakers that day was one of my dearest friends, Smokey Robinson. We were often mistaken for one another—to the point that he signed his autographs, "Lionel Richie," and I signed mine, "Smokey Robinson."

Smokey recalled the day when Berry Gordy introduced the

Jackson 5 to some of the Motown family and how ten-year-old Michael sang "Who's Lovin' You" by Smokey Robinson. Smokey couldn't believe that a kid his age could have that much soul and that ability to *know* the pain of what that song was about.

Would we ever see his kind again? Never.

I did not envy Smokey having to stay composed, having to speak for us all. I didn't envy myself when it was time to get up and sing.

The last time I ever performed the song "Jesus Is Love" that I wrote as a Commodore was at the memorial service. It took everything in my power to keep my voice from cracking and to stop the tears from falling. Inside, I was shattered. Afterward, I made up my mind to stop going to funerals because I believe that, when you lose someone you love, you lose a part of yourself. I didn't need to show up to prove my love for that person. My goal was showing up for them in life.

If you want to catch a glimpse of who Michael Jackson was, watch the documentary *The Greatest Night in Pop*. Alone in the studio to test out his vocals when we weren't there, Michael goes to the mic and does several takes, in the purest most out-of-this-world voice conceivable. He's wearing his sunglasses and raises them at one point so he can see the face of the sound engineer, Humberto Gatica. There's a look in Michael's eyes that's only his—like he's looking at you and me and all of us, as if to say, yeah, he sees us, and we see him.

▐▌▌▐▌▌

"A COUNTRY ALBUM? Lionel, now what are you saying?"

There was a lot of static on the line with the latest executive on my contract that had me back at Mercury. I repeated my pitch.

There had been suggestions: Why not a tribute to the Gershwin catalog or Cole Porter?

My thought was, *Why don't I do a tribute to Lionel Richie's catalog?* I wasn't going to do Rap. Metal was not my thing. So why not pay tribute to my Southern roots and do a Country album? And sing duets with a multigenerational range of artists.

There's a whole argument I could have raised about the fact that Country has its roots in Black music—from the banjos to the fiddles and more. Instead, I talked about Tuskegee, Alabama—in *the* country. The musical blend of Country, R&B, and Gospel was a Tuskegee sweet tea.

"You know," the skeptical executive said, "this will ruin your career."

The magic words.

After I put out feelers, the response was *crazy*.

The album included duets with thirteen incredible Country stars—Blake Shelton ("You Are"), Jason Aldean ("Say You, Say Me"), Darius Rucker ("Stuck on You"), Little Big Town ("Deep River Woman"), Kenny Chesney ("My Love"), Rascal Flatts ("Dancing on the Ceiling"), Tim McGraw ("Sail On"), Shania Twain ("Endless Love"), Willie Nelson ("Easy"), Billy Currington ("Just for You"), Sugarland's Jennifer Nettles ("Hello"), my great friend forever Kenny Rogers ("Lady"), and Jimmy Buffett ("All Night Long").

These collaborations were among my most rewarding, creative experiences. Out of the chute, in the United States, *Tuskegee* debuted at #1 on the Country album chart and #2 Pop on the *Billboard* 200. The first week we saw sales of almost two hundred thousand copies—the best first week I'd seen since the 1980s. It went on to be certified Platinum.

Just when I landed in Europe for a tour, I got a call from yet another new record executive, asking when they could expect my next album.

Cussing under my breath, I said, "You know I did the Country album?"

The Business had imploded so much, there was no budget to support the album further—even when I mentioned one of the songs on it was a #1 hit in Europe. All they had to do was promote the singles in the US. But the personnel who were there when I recorded the album had been replaced.

When I was a young artist, I noticed that the more difficult artists got more attention. I chose not to take that route because I felt careers were built on relationships, not just on hit records. You can have everyone catering to your ego or choose to have allies. I went with the latter, sometimes to my detriment.

For a week or so, I was depressed. The Business was upside down, and the whole "Ta-da!" was missing, and at sixty-three, I didn't have a wise guide to tell me how to navigate the next chapters. Over the past dozen years, I'd been with various managers, some helpful, some not. The nagging issue was feeling like they really didn't know who I was.

"DO YOU KNOW who you are?"

Was there an echo around here? At my first meeting with a potential manager, Bruce Eskowitz, the COO of Red Light Management, formerly the CEO of Live Nation's North American Music, he must have asked that question a thousand times. Give or take.

Bruce—from Houston, Texas, and a graduate of the University of Texas at Austin—was a combination of easygoing and intense. I could see that he was not going to be messing around if he took me on.

Bruce had studied music theory, more than me, and had a vast working knowledge of media in general after a stint at

Clear Channel, as well as touring and concert promotion from his years helping build Live Nation into the powerhouse it became. He had been at Red Light for five years when we met. As COO, he oversaw all operations but was able to also be my personal manager.

Red Light was already the largest independent management company in the world—after starting with the Dave Matthews Band and growing to include Phish, Luke Bryan, Alicia Keys, Miley Cyrus, and two hundred or so other top artists.

Bruce noted, "You were inducted into the Songwriters Hall of Fame in 1994. Do you have the Johnny Mercer Award?"

"No."

"What about the Gershwin Prize for Popular Song from the Library of Congress?"

"Uh . . . no."

"Do you have the Kennedy Center Honor?"

"No, I don't."

"Do you have the Rock & Roll Hall of Fame?" I shook my head, and Bruce asked, "Why don't you have that? You should have that."

"It's not available."

"What do you mean 'it's not available'? Do you know who you are?"

By now, this riff was rhetorical, and these were the things that could and should be pursued. He asked about the hands and feet at Grauman's Theatre in Hollywood. Everything he asked about, Bruce would make happen. And then some.

He was still not sure. "Do you really know who you are?"

Sheepishly, I said, "You know, I think that I know who I am."

Bruce laughed. Well, he said, "One thing that's clear is you're probably the only artist right now who could have a #1 Country album, be invited to appear on the Country Music Awards, and be in line to get a BET Lifetime Achievement Award."

Now I had to laugh. *But were we being too ambitious?*

"Let me give you one word, Lionel," Bruce said. "It's *GOAT*. It stands for 'greatest of all time.' It means having a legacy. You're Lionel Richie."

I sat there digesting what he had just said. And who was I, Lionel Richie, to argue?

I MET SOMEONE. From Switzerland. Circa 2014.

You know that thing I told you before about how I didn't have to walk across the room because the room came to me? Well, it's true and it worked for me. Almost too well. And then I started to think, you know, I might be good at writing love songs, but I am not good at *it*.

Because I'm a disaster. Or, should I say, it's not easy to stand next to someone like me who has been operating from a place of having not gotten enough attention in my youth—as my friend Elton John likes to say.

How fortunate and surprising that I met someone, not in a social setting where the room came to me, but through a friend of hers—and mine—whom I'd just interviewed for a job as a French tutor for one of my kids. After the interview, I walked my friend to her car and met her friend—sitting in the back seat, after tagging along on her friend's interview. That was *it*. Thunder rolled. Lightning struck.

You understand that there was no intended introduction or setup. She was just the most breathtaking young woman on the planet who was waiting for the interview to be over.

By no means was I looking to meet someone. In the past, the first reaction was usually the male thing of, *She's hot, gorgeous, just killer.* And then there was the falling in love part that would let me go out and slay the dragon or get hit records. Old school.

That had been a pattern in my single years. Then I started remembering what my parents and the old folks used to say in Tuskegee: "You need to find a partner."

Okay, yeah, but I'm looking for hot.

Only, you know what, hot is hot. But you reach a certain place in life and start to think about someone who makes more sense—in terms of compatibility and all that entails. You want someone who shares your level of curiosity, who offers the excitement of the cerebral dance too. Can we have a conversation about the world outside of just us? You want someone who can tell you stories about their life that keep you spellbound, and vice versa. And in the case of Lisa Parigi, she's from Switzerland, has no bloody concept of Alabama, and didn't even know where Tuskegee was located.

The kicker though was that just about the first question she asked me was, "Well, what do you do for a living?"

So much for stepping on my opening line (which was usually just my name).

"I'm a songwriter." Instead of going into anything heavy because I saw no flash of recognition, I continued, "And I was in a group called the Commodores."

"Well, I've never heard of them." And, sweetly, she asked what kind of songs we did.

"I had songs called 'Easy' and 'Three Times a Lady.'"

"No, I've never heard those."

Clearly, I'd made a mistake in not trying to lead with my best shot. So I decided to go to the next level. I named off three or four of my solo number one hits. Lisa said no about three or four more times. And then I went into a panic and went straight to, "You know, 'All Night Long.'"

And she said, "Yes, I think I've heard that."

And then I went right into, "Okay, 'We Are the World,' right? I mean, come on?"

She said, "Oh, 'We Are the World.' Yes, I know 'We Are the World.'"

Hallelujah, thank God.

This was a relief but no *Eureka!* No *Oh my God, it's really you?*

Instead of being disappointed, I found the conversation amusing, and very refreshing.

And, of course, she's stunning, and hot, a model and a tech entrepreneur whose background is a mix of Swiss and Caribbean and Chinese, and she speaks four languages.

A few days after I asked her out, Lisa was on the phone with her mother, saying, "I met this guy, and you know, Mom, he's really funny but he claims he wrote 'We Are the World.'"

"Really?"

Lisa had watched the video released in the eighties, and she said, "He said he wrote and sang in it, and I checked and he's not in 'We Are the World.'"

"What's his name?"

"Lionel Richie."

Lisa's mom confirmed that my claims were true. Apparently, Lisa had skipped the beginning where I sing, "There comes a time . . ." After that, you don't see me anymore.

Eventually, Lisa kind of figured it out. But even when she heard about some of the stories behind the songs like "Hello" and "Endless Love," she still didn't know about "Ballerina Girl" or "Se La" or "Just to Be Close to You." I invited her to a concert, and Lisa came running back afterward to mention different songs and to ask, "You wrote that?"

She's still putting the pieces together, helping connect and assemble the stories of my life in getting to know where I've been and who I am. Lisa has always known who she is. She worked for Dell when we met and is a computer nut, understands online commerce, enough to develop a tech startup or two. And she has never had any ambition to be an actress or a singer. That means there's no competition with me, no asking, "When are you going to do my album?"

As a listener, though, Lisa understands the creative breakdown that can happen in my head, or the daily logistical collisions of the "you can't make this shit up" life that I live. She is all heart too—my heart.

As you know, I had baggage. And yet, I knew now what my parents meant about finding a partner. Hopefully, if you're lucky enough in this life, as I have been, you'll find somebody who, if you have baggage, will help you unpack it.

And hopefully, you'll find somebody who meets you and doesn't know who you are but who falls for you, because of you, and who, if you really, really are lucky, is open to sharing in the adventure.

23

The Gardener

Sunday Afternoon, June 28, 2015
Glastonbury Festival
Worthy Farm, Somerset, England

The beauty of playing Glastonbury's Pyramid Stage—and overcoming my nerves despite the shock of performing for an estimated overcapacity crowd of two hundred thousand folks—is that it brought me full circle.

As you are my witness, that is one hell of a flashback.

There's one part of how this all came together that I should also mention.

Two years earlier, in 2013, when I first went to Red Light, Bruce asked, "Have you ever thought about playing a festival?"

"My music doesn't work for festivals."

"Are you kidding, your music is perfect for festivals."

In October 2013 Bruce saw to it that I was booked at the Austin City Limits Festival, along with some killer bands, including the Cure, Depeche Mode, Kings of Leon, Muse, Wilco, Vampire Weekend, Arctic Monkeys, Kendrick Lamar, D'Angelo . . . to name a few.

Bruce knew I had many misgivings about whether I'd draw

much of a crowd with my songs. Going with my old standby of starting out at the piano and playing "Hello," I had my back to the audience as Bruce stood off to the side, seeing what I couldn't—that somehow a mob of forty thousand kids had gathered behind me and were singing the words with me. As soon as I sang, "Is it me you're looking for?" I looked over my shoulder and saw this massive crowd.

I smiled at Bruce and shrugged—*Who knew?* He nodded with a "Told ya so."

Was it a fluke? After all, Austin prides itself on being weird.

Apparently not, because the following summer, Bruce booked me at Bonnaroo in Manchester, Tennessee, the largest three-day camping music festival in North America—with acts like Kanye West, Elton John, Jack White, Frank Ocean, Lauryn Hill, Ice Cube, Cake, and Mastodon. *Why be coy,* I thought? Rather than changing up my music, I decided to lead with comedy by poking fun at myself for probably being more familiar to everybody's parents. I killed. The reviews were fantastic. At one point, when I was on one stage with Kanye playing nearby on a bigger stage, suddenly a horde of kids from his show left to join my audience.

We were rolling now, so Bruce ambitiously went after a slot at Glastonbury. He ran into resistance from Barrie Marshall, of all people, who knew and loved me, but who told Bruce, "Lionel doesn't do festivals." Bruce kept pushing. Eventually Barrie offered the Legends slot. The rest, ladies and gentlemen, is now history.

Being a Legend meant they had an area at the festival called "Shrinal Richie"—a shrine with historical artifacts of Yours Truly. Like a pop-up museum.

My running phrase for the day—*What the hell?*—came out again during the show when I looked down and saw that there were two rows of security staff doing rehearsed choreography to "Dancing on the Ceiling." Above them was an inflatable likeness of me—nude—with a hard-on.

That I had never seen . . . but I was impressed.

Within days of my appearance at Glastonbury, a compilation album of Lionel Richie and the Commodores, released twelve years earlier, went to #1 in the UK.

The footage from the festival was so fantastic, our people proposed doing a feature documentary, and that concert film was exhibited in movie theaters worldwide.

I remember leaving Glastonbury and thinking, *You know, I'm kind of getting the hang of this Lionel Richie gig. I might just keep it.*

At the same time, I talked to Lisa and to Bruce, and said, "Hey, why maintain a blistering pace? We could reinvent the rocket ship but make sure it moves more slowly. Southern style."

Bruce agreed, but he knew I didn't mean it.

Pretty soon he had me touring and playing larger and larger venues worldwide, as in my younger days. The following summer I was the closing act at Outside Lands in San Francisco, on a bill with Chance the Rapper, Radiohead, Lana Del Rey, Miguel, and J. Cole. Sixty thousand music fans in the Golden Gate Park singing "Easy" really sounds good.

That same year, I returned to Las Vegas—starting at Planet Hollywood where I would play regularly for three years and then moving over to a residency at the Encore Theater at the Wynn.

Every time I step onto the stage, it's a moment of coming full circle, taking me back to a time after my first divorce and my father's death, when Steve Wynn called to check in on me.

I realized at the time that often when you are at your lowest, you find out who your true friends are.

Genuinely concerned, Steve insisted on flying me to Vegas. To distract me, as soon as I arrived, he said, "I want to show you something," and we drove out to a spot that was all desert. Or at least that's what I saw.

Steve smiled and began to describe his vision for what he wanted to build there. He showed me where there would be fountains and beautiful grounds with pheasants running around, and then he said his resort would have a showroom like no other where there would be dancing all night long.

And I said, "Steve, I only see sand. How do you see all that?"

He had a simple answer: "I can't write music." Instead, as a visionary, he was creating his dreams, his music. And he was telling me to get back to mine.

The Wynn Encore showroom feels like I'm throwing a party for friends—where I can offer an intimate concert experience with more storytelling and comedy. Soon after landing there, I did a live album, my first on Capitol Records, and it soared to #1 on the *Billboard* charts.

And I was loving every minute of it. Maybe that's why, after nine years, I'm still there.

ONCE A STUDENT, always a student. I spent the first half of my career asking mentors the secrets to achieving success: "How did you overcome the obstacles and break in?" My studies shifted focus in the second half of my career. Now I was in search of secrets for keeping success: "How do you attain longevity and stay relevant?"

One of the best answers came from Yul Brynner, the

spectacular Broadway and film star best known for *The King and I*. Yul and I had never met in person until the summer of 1985, when he reprised his role as the King of Siam on Broadway and we met backstage between the matinee and evening shows, near the end of his run.

Gracious and regal, he stepped out of his dressing room to meet me, one arm bent with a hand on his hip, the other reaching out to me. He placed his hand on my shoulder. Very *King and I*–ish. "Lionel, thank you for making the time," he said, at full volume.

We made small talk, like old friends, until I popped the question, "What is the secret to your long-standing career?"

Yul thought for a beat. And then, as if he'd never told anyone before, recalled the day he went to the doctor and received the diagnosis of lung cancer. "And the doctor told me I had six months to live."

"Oh no! What happened?"

Yul Brynner told the doctor, "That's impossible." He repeated, "That's impossible, I'm committed to do a show for two and a half years." Seeing my concern, Yul smiled and said, "And next month those two and a half years will be over." In other words, he had defied every worst-case scenario by continuing to do great work that he loved. He passed away three months after his final curtain call.

In 1993, I was given a similar answer from the one and only George Burns—the cigar-smoking comedian who played the Almighty in *Oh, God*. He was ninety-seven years old and just wrapped a movie when I ran into him at the Polo Lounge. He greeted me with a, "Howya doin', kid?"

We chatted, and I joked, "I'm trying to figure out when to retire but you—ninety-seven, still going strong? What's the secret?"

He looked at me and said, "Stay booked, kid. Stay booked."

WHEN I BECAME friends with Miles Davis, one of the most influential yet elusive Jazz musicians in history, I realized his advice would have been, "Keep reinventing yourself, kid." One early morning at 5 a.m. I got a phone call from Miles.

Didn't he know that's when I crashed for the night? But I took the call. First thing he said was, "Can you play a gangster?" I said sure I could. "Yeah," he went on. "I'm doing a video, and I want you, Prince, and Michael Jackson to be in it and play gangsters."

I sat up. The concept broke every rule. "I'm in!" I said. "When do we shoot?"

He didn't know. Miles admitted, "I haven't written the song yet."

Miles was also in visionary mode as a painter. He called me up one weekend and invited me over the next day to his home in Malibu because, he said, "I have something I want to show you." When I arrived, he had his artwork spread out everywhere, including on the floor. It was all amazing—wild and moody and powerful, like his music. Miles kept steering me to pieces he was sure I'd love and told me to pick out what I wanted. Then I saw one on the wall I loved.

Miles said, "No, that's been with me a long time. It's a favorite and I don't want to sell." He showed me other options, which I liked, but I kept looking at the painting he didn't want to sell.

"Man, that's killer," I told him, "I really like it." He kept repeating how he couldn't part with it after so long. At one point, I had made a few selections, and he excused himself to go upstairs to the bathroom. Well, while he was gone, I went over and touched the painting, which you should never do, but I wanted to feel the texture. Would you believe—it was still wet!

Miles at that moment came down the stairs and had something new to say. "You really like that painting?" I nodded, and he said, "I could sell it to you for fifty thousand."

Jesus Christ. "Oh, man, I only have fifteen thousand on me," I said.

"Sold!" Miles said, and took it off the wall.

The lesson was clear—the best way to stay vital is not to lose your hustle. I had been hustled by one of the best.

The other secret to lasting success I'd hear from many peers is finding the means to serve a higher purpose. You never knew what those causes might be.

For example, during my many years performing in England, I had the honor of appearing at several charity events connected to the Prince's Trust—the initiative founded by then–Prince Charles to support at-risk youth and young working adults throughout the UK. In 2015, while performing at Alexandra Palace—a benefit for Jewish Care, a charity in England— Prince William was in attendance and I was able to tell the story of meeting his mum and how she had loved the song I was about to play, "Hello."

On that occasion, in the 1980s, I had brought leather jackets as gifts for the two princes, William and Harry—pretty cool, even if they were only four and two at the time. As we waited to meet the princess, we were instructed in every minute detail of the formalities steeped in tradition. The rules were ironclad. Under no circumstance were we to touch any of the members of the royal family until they first extend their hand.

No sooner had Princess Diana walked into the greeting area, but she looked at me, and before I could bow, she walked right up and hugged me.

Maybe, they didn't tell her the rules. The princess then said, "Have you met my husband?" Instead of saying the prince, he was Charles, her husband. They were like a normal married couple. We spoke like old friends, and that was when she told me that my song was her favorite.

Meeting her son so many years later brought back the shock of hearing the news of her death in Paris—when her limousine crashed in a tunnel after being chased by paparazzi. The tragedy was incomprehensible.

Prince William loved hearing the song, he said. What both of those sons went through after losing their mother, in front of the world, has always been heartbreaking. Maybe there are some people's lives that qualify as forever charmed, but I have yet to meet those people.

In 2019, Prince Charles asked me to serve as the first global ambassador for the work of the Prince's Trust—what became the King's Trust. Did it matter that I was serving in such a capacity and wasn't a citizen of the United Kingdom? Not that anyone mentioned to me.

I did joke with my team, during the planning stages for my participation in the 2023 coronation, that I should give myself my own title.

My kids—Nicole, Miles, and Sofia—told me not to be ridiculous.

Who gives himself a title? What would you call yourself?

Maybe, I suggested, I could be a lord. Or should I say *lawd*? As in, "Lawd Have Mercy."

WHEN BRUCE STARTED lining up the major awards he aimed to secure for me, I began hearing myself referred to as a songwriter's songwriter. Barry Gibb of the Bee Gees told me every song they wrote was measured against my writing. Maurice White of Earth, Wind & Fire talked about striving for the emotional truth of my songs.

Those comments mattered. Did I need to do the rounds of the honors and induction ceremony circuit? Then I recalled a conversation back in the eighties when I ran into Don Cornelius. He said, "You should come on *Soul Train*, it would mean a lot to the audience."

Politely, I said, "Thank you, Don, for the invitation, but with all the television I've been doing, I don't want to get overexposed."

Don replied with a plain fact: "Lionel, I just want to tell you something—you're Black, man. You can never get overexposed." The more visible my success, the better we'd represent how success for Black folks could look. I went on the show.

In accepting awards, I stick to a theme, usually starting with, "We are here tonight to celebrate the songs that people said would ruin my career."

In 2016, I was honored as Person of the Year for MusiCares, the Grammy's charity arm. It was the first time I had ever asked friends to show up and buy tables and, well, they did. We raised a record $7 million. In 2017, I received the Kennedy Center Honors Award. In 2022 I was overwhelmed to be honored with the Gershwin Prize from the Library of Congress—in front of many of the members of Congress!

I couldn't help wishing Mom, Dad, and Grandma had lived to witness that moment. In accepting, I told how my father goaded me about wasting time with "that old band," but then had claimed to Barbara Walters that he had stood by me and my choices every step of the way. "He lied through his teeth," I confessed on his behalf. I thought of a young man, a kid, who was hired by the medical team to keep an eye on my father when he was lapsing into a coma. The kid sat quietly the whole time I said goodbye to my dad, saying how much I loved him.

At this most bleak of moments, the kid said to me, "I want to let you know that you're very lucky." I looked at him in confusion. My father was in a coma. How could I be lucky? The kid explained, "I was just thinking, I wish I had a dad to love as much as you love your father."

Sometimes you can have a delayed reaction to your life. The tragedy of loss can reveal the blessing: I had a dad and a family and a community to love that much.

All that came to me at the Library of Congress. Later that same year, in one of the most raucous celebrations many of us had experienced in a while—with the lingering effects of the COVID pandemic—Lenny Kravitz, my dear friend, presented my award when I was inducted into the Rock & Roll Hall of Fame.

Nobody was more excited that night than Bruce Eskowitz— although my kids and Lisa were right behind him. Bruce quietly mentioned that there was a small group of artists who had received Kennedy Center Honors and the Gershwin Prize, and had been inducted into the Rock & Roll Hall of Fame. At this writing the group includes: *Elton John, Joni Mitchell, Smokey Robinson, Billy Joel, Willie Nelson, Paul McCartney, Stevie Wonder, Paul Simon,* and now *Lionel Richie*.

My feeling is, well, I guess this means I'm not such an underachiever after all.

GARDENING, I DISCOVERED, was not only a passion and an outlet, but it became a therapy for a grown-up Gemini with ADHD.

Do not call it a hobby. Whenever I'm in town, I spend full days and nights cultivating the grounds that surround my house. Many of the trees, plants, flowers, vines, and grasses have been brought in from places where I've performed or visited. I love color and the contrast of different types of plants, but more than anything I go for fragrance—limes, oranges, lemons. I love lavender and night-blooming jasmine. Desert flowers do well in the California heat. The beauty of bougainvillea can't be denied, and it grows like a weed in Los Angeles. Half the time I'm up on a ladder in my olive trees or out with shears trimming hedges. The kids call me Lionel Scissorhands.

After years of trying without success to meditate, I discovered that in the garden that's what I was doing. I just get out with a shovel and plant some seeds or pull some pesky weeds, and soon I'm off in a state of ease and relaxation.

I don't charge for my services, at least not yet. I usually show up once or twice a week at the homes of my kids, keeping things in good order. Nicole was asked by a neighbor, "Who is that man out in your yard trimming your hedges and humming to himself?"

"That's my dad," she admitted.

"Oh, so Lionel Richie is your gardener?"

Yep, that's me.

We had an incident one day when I was over cutting down some branches for Nicole and her husband, Joel Madden. My grandson Sparrow, young at the time, was watching me closely when a branch that I cut down fell and knocked down a nest of newborn birds.

"Mom, Mom!" Sparrow yelled to Nicole, "Pop-Pop is destroying the environment! And he is killing the animals."

Nicole and her friend Cameron Diaz came running and saw the baby birds were in distress and went rushing off to the vet.

I looked at Sparrow and said, "You're making me look bad, kid."

Thankfully, the little birds were okay.

There is an irony to me that my great-grandfather J. L. Brown sought peace as a groundskeeper. It's ironic too that Tuskegee's George Washington Carver, a friend of my grandmother, used to go for a walk among the flowers in the woods every morning. When asked where his ideas came from, he'd say, "I talk to the flowers."

Every day I now do the same—whether I'm out in the same Alabama woods where Carver used to walk or in my backyard in California, in my garden, in solitude where I speak to the flowers and listen to the breath of God.

The only hint I get about being older is that whenever I'm up a ladder trimming tree branches, someone has to say, "What are you doing up there?" Obviously, to them a man of my age should not be up on a ladder. Not amusing. They didn't used to say that.

I want you to picture the day in late 2017 that Lisa came running and found me outside, up the ladder leaning up against the trunk of an olive tree, lost in meditation.

"Bruce says to call him right away," Lisa says, holding up the phone, and waits for me to climb down.

Phone in hand, I hurry over to my hideout, which I call the Birdhouse.

"American Idol?"

The lowdown is in 2018 there's going to be a reboot for the show and the producers feel I would be an ideal judge. I laugh, thinking how it might seem I'm trying to follow my daughter into the reality show business.

Nah, I tell Bruce, I'm happier out back trimming the hedges.

Except . . . I don't totally say no.

Another call came in. The producers had a question. Turns out that Katy Perry, one of the judges already chosen, was who first suggested me. They now wanted to know if I could suggest a third judge, and I immediately thought of Luke Bryan.

Before I knew it, I was walking onto the set and having the absolute time of my life.

There is no way to explain the runaway success that took place for Katy, Luke, and me over the next seven seasons. We instantly had great chemistry. Part of the reassuring magic is the presence of host Ryan Seacrest.

Katy and Luke were always amazed that I can give a no that doesn't come across as a rejection. They joked that contestants would thank me after I rejected them.

The best moments are when I see my younger self walking into an audition and I either want to laugh or cry. The kid goes, "I don't know . . ." and I say, "I'm seventy-five years old and I still don't know." Because the journey is "I don't know. I'm not sure," until it becomes, "Maybe it's okay to be different, maybe it's okay to write ballads in the middle of Funk." And it's okay, as I say from my wiser self, when something scares you so much that you have to push yourself—that's when you're really growing.

I try to pass the torch of the wisdom that's been handed to me over the years. My dad had a great saying about how to combat fear. He would ask me, "Son, what is the similarity between a hero and a coward?" The answer he gave was that they are both scared to death, but one takes a step forward and one takes a step back.

We ask a lot of our contestants. We want them to know who they are and to use that to give us songs that are stories with beginnings, middles, and ends. And that takes a lot of living to learn. Whenever I hear, "I'm scared," that means something real is happening. I say, "Good, me too." And if you're not scared to death, you're not moving in the right direction.

Whether I'm on the TV show or I'm performing live, what I'm offering is simple. It's compassion. It's "I know how you feel" because I do too.

So often, I am speaking to my younger self, like the time I

listened to a kid who was auditioning tell us his tragedies: "You know, I grew up poor, and nobody liked me, and I was bullied at school, abused at home—" and I had to interrupt him.

The advice I gave to that talented kid was, "If you try to go back and scream at the past, you could trip over your future."

I put that note in my hat.

Sometimes it's also good to look back and discover or revisit lessons you may have forgotten. That's why history matters. Bruce came to me one day and proposed that we take advantage of never-before-seen footage and produce a documentary on the making of "We Are the World." I resisted, questioning whether there was an audience for what was such an impossible undertaking that nobody could believe we pulled it off.

That night was the ultimate in "you can't make this shit up." At some point in our conversations, someone said it was the greatest night in Pop (which became the title of the documentary). Bruce was convinced we should give it a shot, and I decided, well, if we pull it off, my kids won't have to hear me try to tell that story one more time.

"Pop-Pop, not again! We know that one!"

Bao Nguyen, the director, approached it as a thriller—an *Ocean's Eleven*–like heist movie with a job we had to do under a time constraint. When I saw the rough cut, I cried my eyes out, for many, many reasons. All those friends no longer with us—that killed me. I cried for gratitude to have been there and done that. And I cried because I discovered a young man who knew what he was doing, without second-guessing himself. I was that young man, the gardener of my own dreams. That's what the movie did for me—thirty-nine years later. It gave me "Zoom"—the reward of the foolish dreamer.

The reception for the documentary—at 1.3 billion minutes streamed in its first year, making it the most watched music documentary for the year 2024—has also restored my faith that empathy and compassion still matter.

That's one of the reasons I love what we do on *American Idol*, now with Carrie Underwood, who came on board in 2025 to replace Katy Perry.

Compassion is a practice. It's taking the time to thank the entire crew, to shake hands with security staff and janitorial services, and to take selfies too. It's why I break the rules and go hug the contestant who has just slayed me with the beauty and pain of a song written for a father recently passed. It's why I shed unapologetic man tears. Every time.

What are you gonna do? I'm an artist. I'm sensitive.

If someone asks for a hug and it's not an invasion of privacy, maybe it can help. Suge Knight, now incarcerated, blew me away with his introduction. He came right over and said, "Excuse me, Mr. Richie, can I get a hug?" I said yes. Why withhold a gesture that costs little to give? In the same keepsake area where I have a needlepoint pillow that George Washington Carver gave to Grandma, I have a book signed by Governor Wallace: "To my dear friend, Lionel Richie, from George C. Wallace." The staunch segregationist from the state of Alabama who, through music and growth, rethought some of his positions in time.

Compassion and empathy are underused instruments of peace.

Compassion is the ability to see ourselves in others, and hopefully, they can see themselves in us. Music is the elixir that helps make the connection.

Dave Chappelle always says, "I just want to hug you." Every time I see him. He says that I reassure him. "You're the most positive person I ever met." He says he wakes up in darkness.

I tell him, "I know how you feel." I wake up in the darkness too but find a way to turn on the light.

So I hug him. Dave makes me laugh uncontrollably, as he works out his existential doom.

What I'm saying to you, dear reader, is that whatever your point of view or platform, offer it with compassion—with love for your fellow human being. And for yourself.

YOU KNOW THE great irony of life for many of us is that we finally grow up, maybe as late bloomers, but then God gives us kids and grandkids.

They keep us on our toes. I'm so much like my dad, standing at the end of the driveway, talking about, "Hey, before I mow your lawn, did I ever tell you . . ." And then I'm trying to tell all the stories that they've already heard. They humor me sometimes, but usually they're off and running.

When I can't get the kids to hear the old stories, I go for the new ones, like telling them my latest with a project dear to my heart—Hello Park. In honor of Booker T. Washington and George Washington Carver, my parents and grandparents, I'm actually taking over a building next to the campus where I grew up and I'm calling it the Brick House. Students can gather there to discuss their dreams and look for ways to create that place called freedom for us all.

This, by the way, gets the attention. "Oh, sounds amazing!" But then, they gotta go.

Whenever we all gather—as I recently observed as I sat down for Thanksgiving with Lisa and our growing numbers—it is as close to a miracle as possible. We survived real disasters and close calls. I blink, and there is Nicole with her husband, Joel, and my two grandkids Sparrow and Kate (a.k.a. Harlow), and they are the most perfect family. Sparrow is the star athlete, in every sport, and Kate is the amazing gymnast and award-winning dancer of the family. And there is Sofia, the youngest of my three kids, with her husband, Elliot Grainge, and their little one, the enchanting Eloise. And in the middle is Miles Richie, my son, involved in the fashion business and passionate about important causes.

I'm thinking to myself, *Who are these people?* That's how proud I am of them.

The part that moves me the most is that they are proud of me. That is the secret to all success. Do great work, be a good person, strive to be the best version of you that there is.

All the other stuff—the awards, the accolades—they are important, but they are not the measure of who we are. In the end, there is nothing that can top making my family proud and knowing that friends and colleagues who were part of the journey share in the pride.

I'll leave you with where I began—with love. If I have learned anything about what really matters about what we do here on this planet, that's the only measure that counts. Life, we hope, is long. It can be tragic. It can be glorious. It is a song—with a beginning, a middle, and an end. The test of life comes at the end, when you take stock and know in your heart that you have loved deeply, purely, and truly.

Acknowledgments

With gratitude to everyone for your part in my journey so far, with special thanks to:

Lisa Parigi

Nicole Richie Madden, Joel Madden, Harlow Madden, Sparrow Madden

Miles Richie

Sofia Richie Grange, Elliot Grange, Eloise Grange

Deborah Richie

John Dixon

Brenda Harvey Richie

Diane Alexander Richie

Redlight Management

Bruce Eskowitz—Manager

Sarah Diebel—Day to Day Manager

Mim Eichler Rivas—Co-Author

Business Management:

Ron Nash—Business Manager

Brian Dentel—Associate Business Manager

Jessica Stout

Rosemarie Passerino

HarperOne/HarperCollins Publishers:

Judith Curr—President and Publisher, HarperOne

Elizabeth "Biz" Mitchell—Editor

Paul Olsewski—VP, Publicity

David Wienir—Associate General Counsel

Aly Mostel—Executive Director, Marketing

Anna Calame—Editorial Assistant

The Home-Boy Association:
  Harold "Cookie Man" Boone
  Milton Carver Davis
  John "Sonnyboy" Hines
  Tom "Fungus" Joyner
  Kenneth "Shorty" Miller
  William P. "Smitty" Smith
  Howard "Peahead" Kenney

CAA:
  Rob Light, Chris Dalston, Robert Norman
  Cait Hoyt, Allison McGregor, Khalil Roberts

Marshall Arts:
  Barrie Marshall, Jenny Marshall, Doris Dixon, Ben Martin

Dirk Vanoucek—Creative Director
Al Silfen—Photographer
Bernie Boyle—Tour Manager
Rome Reddick—Tour Management
Phay MacMahon—Production Manager
Jan Henke—Security
Dave Thomas—Stylist
Mateo Pieri—Assistant Stylist
Sunny Tor—Wardrobe Assistant

The Band:
  Chuckii Booker—Musical Director/Keyboard
  Ethan Farmer—Bass
  Dino Soldo—Horns and Keyboard
  Oscar Seaton Jr.—Drums
  Grecco Buratto—Guitar

Legal:
  Allen Grubman

Don Friedman

Grace Kim

Publicists:

Jeff Raymond, Lexi Klein

Stuart Dawbell, Pippa Evers, Maria Barham

The Commodores

William King

Ronald LaPread

Thomas McClary

Walter Orange

Milan Williams

Michael Gilbert

Additional thanks to:

Tuskegee University and the Community

My brothers of Alpha Phi Alpha Fraternity, Inc.

My *American Idol* Family

Suzanne de Passe

Tony Jones

James Anthony Carmichael

Bill Harvey

Bobby and Jamesetta Adams

Joseph Rouzan

Aaron Gutierrez

Mark Hamilton

Pattie Spaziani-O'Neal

Lionel Richie Fanclub

Live Nation

AEG

Global Tour Creatives

Merch Traffic

237 Global

Credits

Universal Music Publishing Group and Brenda Richie Publishing

Universal Music Publishing Group and Hal Leonard LLC/Warner Olive Music LLC (Universal Music Publishing/Alfred Music), Spirit Music Group, and Brenda Richie Publishing

Universal Music Publishing Group and Hal Leonard LLC/Spirit Music Group and Kobalt Music Group, Sony Music Publishing